The Morgan THREE-WHEELER
Gold Portfolio
1910-1952

Compiled by
R.M.Clarke

ISBN 1 87064 283X

BROOKLANDS BOOKS LTD.
P.O. BOX 146, COBHAM,
SURREY, KT11 1LG. UK

A -MOR3GP

ACKNOWLEDGEMENTS

The Morgan Three-Wheeler has played an important part in my life. My first car was a 1931 JAP powered Family model bought for £50 in 1952 which went on to inspire my first book — the Morgan Three-Wheeler Handbook — a few years later.

Researching this book has brought back many nostalgic moments, such as the time a valve snapped in the ohv Anzani twin propelling my then current pride a 1931 Super-Sports, stranding us in Worcestershire late one Sunday evening. Another time was when the Lancaster joystick which served as a steering wheel became severely detached whilst driving through London which caused my passenger's heart to beat a little faster.

This book is different to most in our series in that we did not have access to original copies of much of the early stories printed here. We have therefore had to cull them from different sources and apologise for the raggedness of reproduction of some of the pages.

On the plus side, we are very fortunate that in 1965 Bill Boddy wrote a splendid comprehensive history of the Morgan three-wheeler in Motor Sport. I strongly recommend that you move briskly on to page 5 and absorb his informed comment.

Our front cover photograph was kindly loaned to us by John Sheally who in 1980 crossed the US from coast-to-coast in his Matchless powered 1935 Super-Sports. The full story of his adventures can be found on page 150.

Our back cover illustrations are of 'Satan', a 1929 Blackburne engined Super-Sports Owned by Derek Evans. Derek and his late brother George befriended me in my early Morgan days and managed to keep GT 4032 on the road in spite of my mechanical shortcomings.

Our thanks also go to the group of international authors and publishers who once again have supported our reference series by allowing us to include their copyright road tests and other stories that first appeared in Autocar, The Automobile, Autosport, Car and Driver, Collector's Car, Cycle World, Fast Lane, Light Car, Modern Motor, Morgan Sports, Motor, Motor Cycle, Motor Cycling, Motor Sport, Practical Classics, Practical Motorist, Road & Track, Sports Car World, Thoroughbred & Classic Cars and Wheels.

R.M. Clarke

CONTENTS

Continued Overleaf

Brooklands Books

CONTENTS — CONTINUED

THE VINTAGE YEARS OF THE MORGAN 3-WHEELER

PROVING ITSELF.—H. F. S. Morgan setting off to establish a new Cyclecar Hour Record at Brooklands late in 1912, his single-seater Morgan averaging just under 60 m.p.h. On the extreme right, in top hat, Prebendary H. George Morgan, Vicar of Stoke Lacy, who was a strong advocate of his son's products, hopes that the Morgan will break the G.W.K.'s record.

[From time to time fairly superficial histories of the Morgan 3-wheeler have appeared in various journals, but to celebrate the demonstration race by members of The Morgan Three-Wheeler Club at the V.S.C.C. Oulton Park meeting on the 19th of this month, I thought something rather more detailed was merited. Peter Morgan, Managing Director of The Morgan Motor Company Ltd., very kindly delivered to me his late father's cutting-books, which greatly facilitated my task. What follows is dedicated to one of the most sporting economy cars of all time.—ED.]

H.F.S. MORGAN was born at Stoke Lacy Rectory, Hereford, in 1881, the son of the Rev. Prebendary H. George Morgan. He went to Stone House School, Broadstairs and Marlborough College and finished his education at The Crystal Palace Engineering College. He then served as an 18-year-old pupil under the Chief Engineer of the G.W.R. works at Swindon, graduating as a draughtsman, a post he held for about seven years. H.F.S. Morgan's first motoring experience, we are told, was on a hired 3½-h.p. Benz, which ran away down the hill between Bromyard and Hereford. He later owned an 8-h.p. De Dion Bouton-engined Eagle 3-wheeler and a 7-h.p. 2-cylinder Little Star, the latter a make not found in Doyle's.

Leaving the G.W.R. in 1906, H.F.S. opened a garage at Malvern Link and ran a 'bus service between there and Wells, and later between Malvern and Gloucester, using 15-seater 10-h.p. Wolseleys, as he had the Wolseley and Darracq district agency. His experimental work had included the design of a 3-wheeled tubular chassis and into this he installed a 7-h.p. vee-twin Peugeot engine intended for a motorcycle. Most of the machining was done in Malvern College Workshops by permission of the engineering master of Malvern and Repton and the vehicle was finished in 1909.

How it began.—It is significant that right from the start much of the construction was similar to that retained to the end of 3-wheeler production in 1950 and the i.f.s. of which is still found in similar form on the current Morgan sports models. The tubular ladder chassis had a central backbone tube and four tubes at the front acting as the engine bearers, the side tubes served in lieu of exhaust pipes for the vee-twin engine set across the frame, and independent front springing was provided by sliding-pillars and coil springs, a system which Lancia introduced for their Lambda after the war. Transmission consisted of a simple clutch, a propeller shaft running inside the tubular backbone of the chassis to a bevel-box, and chains-and-dogs giving choice of two speeds to the single rear wheel, which was sprung on ¼-elliptic springs attached to a channel-section mounting across the rear of the frame tubes. No reverse gear was required on a 3-wheeler

weighing under 7 cwt., and throttle control was by Bowden hand-lever on the steering wheel.

As the other classic pioneer of i.f.s., the Sizaire Naudin, which also used sliding pillars but with a transverse leaf spring, did not go into production until 1905 and the G.N. 4-wheeled cyclecar which also had dog-and-chain transmission, was not evolved until 1909 and did not have the engine set across its frame until 1912 (see MOTOR SPORT, August 1949), H.F.S. did his share of pioneering!

Favourable comment on his nippy little single-seater runabout decided Mr. Morgan to go into limited production. His father, the vicar, provided finance for some machine tools to be bought and the garage extended, and manufacture began in 1910. Patents were obtained on the i.f.s. system, etc., for which John Black (later Sir John Black of Standard's) did the drawings. Morgan took a stand at Olympia in 1910, showing single-seaters powered by 4-h.p. single-cylinder and 8-h.p. vee-twin J.A.P. engines. These original Morgan 3-wheelers were very crude, with side tiller steering, and the simplest of bodywork, but they performed well and offered better protection, at all events for the driver's legs and feet, than contemporary motorcycles.

The success of the Morgan tricar seemed assured when H.F.S. gained a gold medal in the M.C.C. London-Exeter-London Trial but a 2-seater was called for, which soon made its debut, powered by an 8-h.p. engine. The prototype was a very simple device, with no mudguards and side-by-side seating; it carried the same Reg. No., CJ 743, as the car H.F.S. drove in the 1911 A.C.U. Six Days Trial, although this had the now familiar open-fronted coal-scuttle bonnet, mudguards and lamps, and was steered by wheel instead of tiller.

One of the nicest aspects of the Morgan affair, incidentally, was the personal interest which H.F.S. Morgan took in competition driving. He was frequently to be found driving in trials, from one-day to strenuous six-day events, accompanied by his wife Ruth, daughter of the Rev. Archibald Day, Vicar of St. Matthias, Malvern Link, while in later years George Goodall, who joined the Company in 1925, competed with his son as passenger, just as Peter Morgan, who controls Morgan destiny today, drove 4-wheeler Morgans in competition from 1947 onwards, accompanied by his wife.

Orders for the Morgan 3-wheeler came in readily, some 30 being secured at its first Olympia showing, and supply failed to meet demand. As none of the big manufacturers wanted to help, H.F.S. bought more machine tools, extended his workshop still further, and in time for the great cyclecar boom of 1912, had formed a private company, The Morgan Motor Co., of which his father was Chairman and he was Managing Director.

All through the early days of the Company the Rev. George Morgan, Vicar of Stoke Lacy, was a staunch supporter of his son's endeavours, and an even more prolific writer of letters to the motor magazines than S.F. Edge had been in an earlier era.

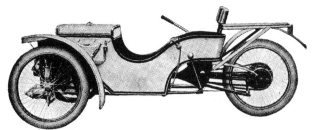

The original Morgan 3-wheeler of 1910, with tiller-steering and the minimum of bodywork.

Fighter ace, the late Capt. Albert Ball, V.C., D.S.O., M.C., *in his G.P. Morgan.*

The Pre-Vintage Days.—At that astonishing Olympia Motorcycle Show of 1912, when the first issue of Temple Press' new weekly, *The Cyclecar*, is said to have sold 100,000 copies, the Morgan 3-wheeler was well established. It was shown on Stand No. 18 as a still quite sketchy 2-seater, powered by an 8-h.p. vee-twin a/c. 85×85-mm. J.A.P. engine under the traditional bonnet, pulling high and low speeds of 4½ and 8 to 1. Steering was direct, the type size 26 in. × 2½ in., the bodywork, such as it was, being of wood and sheet steel, and the price being 85 gns. The weight was quoted as 3 cwt.

Excellent publicity had been secured when H.F.S. broke the cyclecar hour record at Brooklands late in 1912, covering 59 miles 1,120 yards in the 60 minutes in a narrow-track, high single-seater with a/c. o.h.v. vee-twin engine and fuel tank behind the leather-helmeted driver. The Vicar of Stoke Lacy, a tall figure in top hat and formal overcoat, was naturally present to encourage his son. The Morgan was responding to a G.W.K. challenge, this car's record being 56 m.p.h.

This was by no means the Morgan's only pre-1914 racing appearance. At Brooklands in 1913, A. W. Lambert drove a Morgan with 85×77.5 mm. (880 c.c.) engine into 3rd place in the First Side-Car and Cyclecar Race, lapping at 54.96 m.p.h. (E. B. Ware was still a Zenith rider), but already 3-wheelers were suffering from being neither sidecar nor cyclecar in the eyes of the authorities, not being allowed in subsequent B.A.R.C. Cyclecar handicap races that year. However, a 1914 Whitsun Light-Car and Cycle-car Handicap did include Ware's 76×82 mm. (744 c.c.) Morgan, which lapped at 48.92 m.p.h. and this driver's Morgan-J.A.P. (of 77×83 mm., 773 c.c.) finished second behind a Bugatti, lapping at 63.76 m.p.h. The Morgan family took part in numerous reliability trials at this time, H.F.S.'s sister Dorothy being a regular competitor, while in a Cyclecar Club Fuel Economy Contest in 1913 R. D. Oliver's 965 c.c. Morgan-J.A.P. won the 1,100 c.c. class with 69.4 m.p.g. in spite of its filler cap having been left off. It weighed 7 cwt. 60 lb. and used Shell petrol, and a B. & B. carburetter.

W. G. McMinnies, who was on the Editorial staff of *The Cyclecar*, owned a special single-seater Morgan called "The Jabberwick," with s.v. 8-h.p. J.A.P. engine having a cylindrical tank behind it, which scaled 350 lb. with road equipment, could be started from the seat on the side handle, and gave 50 m.p.g.

In the field of serious racing, too, the pre-war Morgans were notably successful. In the 1913 Cyclecar G.P. at Amiens, McMinnies' Morgan, with Frank Thomas who prepared it as passenger, although held up by a puncture and a broken truss-rod, was the first to complete the 163 miles, having averaged 41.9 m.p.h., but the officials said it was a sidecar and gave first place to a Bedelia. These G.P. Morgans had a chassis lengthened by 11 in., wooden bodies with seats several inches lower than standard, and steeply-raked steering columns. Those entered by Morgan and McMinnies had 90×77.5-mm. o.h.v. w/c. J.A.P. engines, Holder's a water-cooled Blumfield twin, and Ware's entry a water-cooled Precision engine. In fact, only McMinnies' winning car, H.F.S. and Rex Mundy started, the former breaking a piston, the latter a front wheel. The J.A.P.-engined model subsequently went into production, having a neat radiator with "water tower" filler of Napier type in its water-cooled form.

The war resulted in production gradually ceasing in favour of munitions, but not before Morgan had introduced a 4-seater model in 1915, developed from a remarkable long-wheelbase prototype obviously built to carry members of the enthusiastic Morgan family on a couple of simple, unprotected bench seats, their luggage piled above the back wheel.

Morgan prestige was enhanced during the war years because Capt. Albert Ball, V.C., D.S.O., M.C., the famous R.F.C. pilot, drove a water-cooled M.A.G.-engined model with disc wheels, and Lieut. Robinson, V.C., who shot down a German zeppelin, also drove a Morgan, with discs on its front wheels and an aeroplane mascot above its "water tower." Capt. Jack Woodhouse, M.C., another R.F.C. officer, had a G.P. model with pre-war long-stroke w/c. Precision engine and twin aero-screens, which Selfridge's offered for sale in 1917.

As the war neared its close, Malvern offered a 10-h.p. a/c. model with enormous, vision-restricting hood and the w/c. De Luxe model was improved by deleting the fan (formerly belt-driven from the fly-wheel), as a new full-width radiator was used, with the wedge-shaped oil and petrol tanks behind it to aid air flow, while the bonnet louvres were replaced by gauze-covered openings and the pedals were enlarged and rubber-covered. For some time an improved Ferodo-lined clutch had been fitted. A 3/4-seater version was still available, and Cass' Motor Mart offered a cloverleaf 3-seater Morgan for £155.

I must confess to being puzzled at a 1918 experiment, whereby a Morgan-J.A.P. was run with one w/c. and one a/c. cylinder! But there was no doubt about it, H. George Morgan, as he signed his published letters, was busily championing the simple cyclecar, even as a substitute for taxi fares. In 1917 *The Light Car & Cyclecar* tested a post-bellum model with 82×103.5-mm. (1,093 c.c.) M.A.G. engine, which gave a speed range of "from 7-42 m.p.h., and slightly over 60 m.p.g."

With the approach of the Armistice the Morgan models were announced as the Sporting Model, at £130 with a/c. M.A.G. engine, £135 in de luxe form (which meant with a door!), or £135 with w/c. J.A.P. engine, while the G.P. model was unchanged from pre-war days. Cars could only be supplied against Ministry of Munitions Priority Certificates and the w/c. M.A.G. engine was temporarily unobtainable. The de luxe Morgans had a new dash, with open cubbyhole.

1919.—The year 1919 opened with extensions to the Malvern Link factory, with a new body and finishing shop about half-a-mile from the original premises. Mr. Hales was the Works Manager, and about 50 post-war Morgans were nearing completion, although shortage of certain bought-out components, particularly tyres, was holding up production. The latest improvement was a hinged tail to provide access to the rear wheel, spring clips like those securing the bonnet normally holding it down.

About this time H.F.S. had an unfortunate mishap, falling into a lathe and having to suffer amputation of two fingers on his right hand. However, he drove CJ 743 in the 1919 M.C.C. London-Edinburgh trial, his car white with black mudguards, and gained a gold medal, in company with the Morgans driven by George Pettyt, Eric Williams and Lt. H. G. Bell. Indeed, Morgan 3-wheelers were winning so many awards in the resumed competitions that to list them all is quite impossible.

E. B. Ware, of J.A.P.'s, had a 4-seater Morgan and C. Perham of the Admiralty a streamlined 22 in.-wide single-seater with 90×85 mm. M.A.G. vee-twin engine, pulling speeds of 3½ and 6 to 1, and capable of an easy 65 m.p.h. It used an Amac carburetter with 36 jet. Lt. B. Alan Hill's w/c. Morgan-J.A.P., which weighed 8 cwt., 3 qr. 14 lb., normally gave 60 m.p.g. and averaged 50 m.p.g. for the entire Scottish Six Days' Trial, in which a puncture and a broken top-gear chain were its only misfortunes. Mrs. Hill went as passenger in this red G.P. Morgan, which gained a silver medal.

Inevitably prices rose, to £145 for the Sporting Model, £150 for the G.P. and a/c. De Luxe, £160 for the w/c. De Luxe. Disc wheels cost 75s. extra, but a special body colour was now 30s. extra instead of 50s.

In mid-1919 H.F.S. made fastest passenger-time with a stripped

M.A.G.-engined Morgan at Stile Kop hill-climb (56.8 sec.) and P. Houel's pre-war G.P. Morgan won the cyclecar class of the Circuit de l' Eure race at 34.5 m.p.h. for the 178¾ miles. H.F.S. gained a "gold" in the A.C.U. Six Days' Trial in his 980-c.c. 759 lb. Morgan, in organising which T. W. Loughborough of the A.C.U. had tried out the hills with a Morgan and a 3½ h.p. Sunbeam. On Oct. 16th, 1919 new works of 38,400 sq. ft. were opened at Pickersleigh Road, Malvern Link, but the machine shop, carpenters' shop and tinmens' shops remained in the old building near the Link station. This gave a total of over 50,000 sq. ft. and the aim was 40-50 cars a week.

Harry Martin had a special Morgan with o.h.v. J.A.P. a/c. engine and type-Z Claudel Hobson carburetter.

1920.—For 1920 a ball thrust in the clutch, longer bearings for the steering heads, and stronger bevels of different tooth formation were adopted. Awards continued to be won by Morgans in competition events of all kinds, and some 20 cars a week were being turned out in spite of a shortage of engines. Mr. Morgan owned a big Studebaker but still covered an appreciable mileage in Morgans and had patented a detachable rear wheel.

When racing was resumed at Brooklands Ware drove a single-seater Morgan-J.A.P. with a cut-down G.P. radiator and Hawkes a stripped 2-seater model built for the abandoned 1914 Cyclecar T.T., with an 82 × 104 mm. (1,098 c.c.) 8-valve M.A.G. engine and now known as the "Land Crab." Ware was the more reliable, lapping at 59½ m.p.h. to win the 3-wheeler B.M.C.R.C. race. It had an abbreviated tail, disc wheels, a big cut-away 4-spoke steering wheel, bracing tubes from the tops of the steering heads back to the cockpit and a hoop across the back-wheel to give the spindle rigidity.

Mr. Morgan now owned an Austin 20, which made light work of the 1 in 3 Old Wyche Cutting in Malvern carrying three passengers. Success after success was won by his 3-wheelers, such as H.B. Denley's "gold" in the Scottish Six Days, five "golds" in the Edinburgh, etc., and a couple of Morgans served officials well during the I.O.M. motorcycle T.T. races. Hawkes eventually beat Ware at Brooklands, but Ware won a later race at 69½ m.p.h., Hawkes' engine proving unreliable. H. George Morgan continued to bombard the Press with letters !

In the very tough A.C.U. Six Days' Trial the Morgans of H.F.S., S. Hall and F. James gained "golds"; respectively they drove 980 c.c. 756 lb., 1,000 c.c. 756 lb., and 1,100 c.c. 812 lb. cars. J.A.P.'s built Ware a special w/c. o.h.v. 90 × 85-mm. Morgan for the Cyclecar G.P. at Amiens but a piece blew out of one cylinder and it finished the course slowly on one "pot."

A private owner wrote to say his Morgan-J.A.P. won its class by 10 sec. from a G.N. in the Northants M.C. Speed Trials without any special tuning whatsoever, and a census on the North Road gave a count of seven Morgans, six G.N.s, three Rover 8s and two Tamplins amongst the light cars and cyclecars. *The Light Car & Cyclecar* then had the idea of a freak climb at Nailsworth Ladder; as in 1914 and in 1919, an 8-h.p. Morgan made a clean ascent, Hall's car getting up on an 11 to 1 bottom gear. The Morgan was now in production in France, taking fifth, sixth, ninth and tenth places in the Gaillon Hill-Climb. Advertisements proudly announced gold medals in the Scottish International and English Six Days' Trials of 1920.

THE SIMPLICITY OF GENIUS.—A diagrammatic picture of a vintage Morgan, showing the tubular chassis, the two tubes of which served as exhaust pipes for the motorcycle-type V-twin engine, strengthened by the central backbone within which ran a propeller shaft, with squared ends soldered and rivetted in, taking the drive from a cone clutch with exposed thrust-race to the bronze bevel-box soldered to a cross tube. Final drive was by 2-speed chain-and-dog transmission to the single rear wheel, and even in the late vintage period the gear-lever was just a piece of bent metal topped with a primitive wooden grip. The coil-spring i.f.s., with phosphor-bronze castings doing duty as steering pivots and suspension plungers, can be seen, mounted on transverse cross-tubes. An "X"-formation of tubular bracing at the front of the frame was extended to support the engine plates. There were contracting band brakes on the rear wheel. Steering for many years was direct—very direct !—and the starting handle was at the side. With some 30 b.h.p. to propel less than 7 cwt., the vintage Morgan was no sluggard, but jealous rivals said it combined the discomfort of a motorcycle with the cost of a car !

1921.—The 1921 Morgans shown at Olympia in 1920, when 30 a week were being built, had several important improvements. The new easily-detachable back wheel by means of a re-styled fork and chains of equal length was introduced, the high gear now being 18 × 33 (4½ to 1), against the former 14 × 25. Low gear remained at 8 to 1. The hand-brake now had a larger drum, 6½ in. in diameter, and the back wheel had a Leo Swain rim band to stop the cover creeping. Flat wooden guards over the chains protected them from mud off the tail and the back fork hinged on an improved, taper bearing. Bigger front-wheel taper hubs on ⅝ in. ball bearings, spun brass covers in two halves enclosing the springs to stop the upper crowns coming adrift from the upper cylinders, a guide and support for the starting handle, and a simplified clutch facilitating engine removal were other improvements, while a small flywheel pulley enabled a Lucas dynamo lighting set to be fitted (£25 extra). The dynamo clipped to the n/s. tube behind the engine and was driven by Whittle belt. The battery was under the seat, the switchboard on the left of the dash, over an oddments tray. The dash carried a clock.

A new model was the Aero, with V-air-deflector behind the radiator and streamlined tail. Prices were up to £228 for the De Luxe, the least-expensive being £206 for the a/c. Sporting Model with hood and screen but no lamps. H. F. Edwards of South Kensington offered a special streamlined model at £226 and Barkers Motors of Balham a detachable tail seating one adult or two children for £12 10s. in one flat coat of paint ready for the colour of the customer's car.

It was claimed that the entire 1921 output had been ordered in advance by Morgan's agents. Incidentally, while car tax was up to £1 per h.p., 3-wheelers paid £4 a year. Yet another variant of extra seating was the Pillionette, costing 18s 6d. and enabling a child to be carried on the tail of a Morgan, the invention of L. Marcus of Golders Green.

It is interesting that amongst Morgan drivers in the 1921 Paris-Nice Trial were Darmont and Sandford, both later to bring out their own versions of this 3-wheeler in France, while in England Eric Longden, who eventually brought out his own 4-wheeled cyclecar, raced a 988-c.c. Morgan.

In the A.C.U. Six Days' Trial this year H.F.S. Morgan's 983-c.c. Morgan which weighed 814 lb., Boddington's 1,090-c.c. 928-lb. model and Elce's similar Morgan which scaled 782 lb., all won "golds," H.F.S. doing 67 m.p.g., 44 m.p.h. and 2,596 m.p.g of oil in the various tests—it still carried Reg. No. CJ 743 !

In spite of the post-war slump the factory was working at full capacity, turning out "close on 120 machines per month," *vide* one Press cutting. In listing the competition successes scored in June alone the Company proudly coined the slogan "The Private Owner can win on a Morgan." Douglas Hawkes had evolved a very special racing single-seater, "Flying Spider," built at Malvern, which dispensed with the frame tubes, relying only on the backbone, had the 8-valve M.A.G. engine set far back in the extended chassis with its crankcase streamlined, and so slim a body that the driver could only just get into it after removing some side panels. The B.A.R.C. no longer allowed 3-wheelers to compete at its meetings, so the car was confined to mixed club days and B.M.C.R.C. races, and its hey-day was yet to come.

Although Ware's Morgan was supported by four French-built Morgans in the G.P. de Cyclecars at Le Mans it broke a push-rod and in the end only Stoffel finished, fifth and last. However,

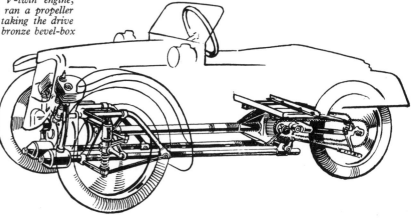

The 1918 Morgans

The De Luxe model.

The Sporting model.

The Grand Prix model.

Ware's 1,096-c.c. Morgan-J.A.P. held Class H2 records from 1 kilometre to 50 miles, its best speed being 86.04 m.p.h. over the kilometre, but in the J.C.C. 200-Mile Race his w/c Morgan-J.A.P. retired with clutch failure. But racing Morgans were certainly doing the knots!

Although the " Aero " Morgan had been briefly mentioned, it was not among the 1922 models, being built to special order, with ship's ventilators, snake horn, aero-screens and nickel fittings. The range comprised the] new Standard 2-seater at £150, with shortened wheelbase and no running-boards, the G.P. costing £180, the a/c and w/c De Luxe models, priced respectively at £175 and £186, and the Family jobs, costing £180 with a/c engine, £191 if water-cooled. Equipment included hood, screen, acetylene lamps, horn, tools and mats! And so the Morgan was able to hold its own with L.S.D., T.B., Castle Three, New Hudson, Reynolds Runabout, Economic, Scott Sociable and other 3-wheelers when it appeared on Stand 63 at the 1921 Motorcycle Show, which opened at Olympia in a London fog.

1922.—Morgans continued to be as active as ever in trials and speed events, H.F.S. setting the example to drivers like F. W. James, N. Norris, W. A. Carr, G. H. Goodall, W. H. Elce, H. Sawtell, S. Hall, F. W. Dame, A. G. Gripper, R. Whiffen, A. C. Maskell, H. Beart, S. McCarthy, H. Holmes, the disabled P. Garrard, and others too numerous to list, while Ware continued to race his trim Morgan-J.A.P. against the motorcycle combinations and Hawkes' single-seater " Flying Spider " won a Surbiton M.C. Brooklands' race at 73.56 m.p.h. H. Martin's 1,074-c.c. Morgan-Anzani also beat the sidecars in a B.M.C.R.C. race won at 70.58 m.p.h. Morgan advertisements in April proudly showed the A.C.U. " Stock Car " Trial team of six cars lined up outside the Worcester Road works. H.F.S. won the premier award and Norris the highest cyclecar award. The Rev. Prebendary Morgan went on letter-writing, defending his son's 3-wheelers, for instance, against the £100 4-wheeler, which, he remarked, " one meets more often in the correspondence column than elsewhere." An article headed " Will the 3-Wheeler Survive ? " spurred him to statistics. Taking " the outstanding events of the past 12 months—the English and Scottish Six Days, the three great M.C.C. trials and the A.C.U. 'Stock' Trial," the Rev. Morgan emphasised that the under-£200 4-wheelers, numbering about a dozen, had won two " golds,"

five " silvers," whereas the 3-wheelers, a mere half-dozen of them, took 23 gold and 12 silver medals, as well as six special certificates—and, he added magnanimously, " these include the awards (three " golds," one " silver ") obtained by the Castle Three and New Hudson, which should perhaps be excluded, as they cost over £200." His letter brought a rebuke from A. Frazer-Nash of G.N.

In mid-1922 *The Light Car & Cyclecar* tested a w/c Morgan-M.A:G. between Malvern and London, getting close on 60 m.p.g. from the still-stiff engine, at an average of 25 m.p.h. Eight gold medals were won in the London-Edinburgh and for the 1,100-c.c. class of the second J.C.C. 200-Mile Race at Brooklands Hawkes had a Morgan with 8-valve twin-carburetter a/c Anzani engine with a shaft-driven o.h. camshaft over each cylinder and a Best & Lloyd oil pump driven from the n/s camshaft. No bonnet was fitted and a flat tank was mounted on a fairly normal tail. Ware had a s.v. Morgan-J.A.P. with open-ended tail, Martin a push-rod o.h.v. Morgan-Anzani, all three having a hoop over the back wheel to give anchorage to a Hartford shock-absorber. Alas, all these retired, Hawkes' with a cracked cylinder, while Ware gave up the unequal struggle of trying to repair a leaking water jacket with tin-tacks!

An assortment consisting of H.F.S.'s 978-c.c. Morgan-J.A.P., S. Hall's 1,096-c.c. Morgan-M.A.G. and W. Carr's 1,090-c.c. Morgan-Anzani, normal 2-seaters, not G.P. models, came through the A.C.U. Six Days' Trial with flying colours and three gold medals. By October prices were down to £135, £155 and £160 respectively for the a/c Standard, De Luxe and Family models, and £160, £165 and £170 for the Grand Prix, De Luxe and Family versions with w/c engine, either 8-h.p. J.A.P. or 10-h.p. Blackburne. A w/c M.A.G. cost an extra £7, an o.h.v. w/c Anzani £5 extra. Someone in Wakefield put a lofty coupé body on a Morgan, not the first incidentally, two proprietary reverse-gear conversions were announced, and for 1923 prices were again lowered, the Standard costing only £128, the w/c G.P. £155.

A year which had opened with 3-wheeler owners in trouble with the Law unless they displayed car-size number-plates, ended with Hawkes taking several records with his 200-Mile Race Morgan-Anzani, the fastest the Class H2 f.s. kilometre, at 86.94 m.p.h. At Olympia, the Morgan Company showed eight cars and a stripped chassis on Stand 139, finished in green, white, dark mauve, dark red, yellow, grey and royal blue. The brakes on all models were now cable-operated. The star attraction, however, was an 8-h.p. o.h.v. Anzani-engined 200-Mile Race replica with Binks 2-jet carburetter, M.L. magneto, K.L.G. plugs and exhaust-heated induction pipe, the body being of polished aluminium, and radiator and tank nickel-plated. Priced at £200, it was called the Aero model in the Press but Morgan advertisements as yet made no reference to it.

1923.—By 1923 the conventional small car had already made life difficult for cyclecar manufacturers and many had expired. Now Sir (later Lord) Herbert Austin dropped that bombshell amongst them, the 4-cylinder, water-cooled, 3-speed, 4-wheel-braked Austin 7.

" Omega," writing in *The Auto*, strongly attacked the 3-wheeler, remarking that he would rather have a Rover 8, for example, " than the finest 3-wheeler Mr. Morgan's Company could produce, with all the " knobs " imaginable, and I feel now so bold as to predict that the number of people like me will steadily increase." This led to correspondence with H.F.S. and his father, although I cannot trace that this journalist, who had road-tested a G.N. in 1918/19, ever had his request for a trial run " in a representatively good Morgan " granted. Mr. Morgan was able to remark that " a 3-wheeler has never overturned at Brooklands " and that " the G.N., which Omega knew, is no longer with us," while he countered the suggestion of *The Auto*'s correspondent that he might " kick away the ladder which has served him so well " and make a 4-wheeler (an " Omega " prediction 13 years ahead of its time!) by commenting whimsically that " Some day, perhaps in the dim and distant future, it is possible that I (or perhaps my son, if he shall have taken my place) may duplicate the three wheels, and concentrate on a 6-wheeler ! "

Meanwhile, the Morgan 3-wheeler continued to amass awards in all the leading trials. The Austin 7, in tourer or Chummy form, cost £165, and Morgans £128 to £153 in a/c and £155 to £163 in w/c form. The provision of front brakes on the new Seven was countered by Morgan announcing at the end of March that Bowden-cable-operated internal-expanding hand-applied front brakes could be fitted to existing Morgans at a cost of £6.

A Standard-model £140 Morgan-J.A.P. fitted with these new f.w.b. scored one of its most convincing victories at this time.

A RACING MORGAN OF 1923.—E. B. Ware, of J.A.P.s, at the pits during the J.C.C. 200-Mile Race.

Driven by Ware, it won the Westall Cup for best performance in the searching J.C.C. General Efficiency Trial, a success Morgan was to repeat in 1924. In gaining maximum marks, 1,743.15 out of a possible 2,000, the Morgan achieved 56 m.p.g., lapped Brooklands at 55.71 m.p.h., averaged 13.4 m.p.h. up the Test Hill (fastest time), was best in the brake test, best on top-gear acceleration, and best in the s.s. acceleration test. It weighed 715 lb. unladen, the only lighter contestant being a 670-lb. Tamplin. This was a convincing performance, in a contest in which three G.N.s and Gordon England's 957-lb. Austin 7 (48 m.p.g., 47.4 m.p.h. lap speed, 6.2 sec. slower up the Test Hill) took part. The final placings put Ware 76.55 marks ahead of Frazer-Nash's G.N., Chinery's Gwynne third. At the time Ware was greeted by a car-icature in *The Light Car & Cyclecar* reading :—

> Did he once ride a tricycle,
> Cool as an icicle?
> Who knows? Perhaps.
> Were his legs much too slow for him?
> Not enough go for him?
> Who knows? Ask J.A.P.s!

The Morgan went on winning races as well, A. Horrocks, the Bolton agent, producing a nicely streamlined version, with curved nose behind the engine and the seats dropped below the prop-shaft tunnel, and Martin demonstrated his 1,074-c.c. Morgan-Anzani on the 503-yard Herne Hill Cycle Track (1 mile in 1 min. 30.2 sec.). The Stratford Wireless Co. fitted up a G.P. Morgan with an overhead aerial and twin Magnavox speakers in front of the engine, the valve panel being placed vulnerably outside by the driver, to receive 2LO, Norris' car with the new w/c. Blackburne o.h.v. engine did well at Kop and H. V. Hughes' s.v. racing-bodied Morgan cleaned up four firsts and a second at Southport.

Towards the end of 1923 Hawkes' Morgan-Anzani took the British Class H2 f.s. kilometre record to 92.17 m.p.h., the mile to 90.38 m.p.h., and secured s.s. and longer distance records as well, while Norris' Morgan-Blackburne cleaned-up the 1,100-c.c. Three-Wheeler Championship Race at a B.M.C.R.C. Brooklands' Meeting, at 86.77 m.p.h. This atoned for Norris' misfortune in the J.C.C. 200-Mile Race, when his car was destroyed by fire in London on the eve of the race. A normal w/c. Aero-Blackburne was substituted, but it retired with a broken valve rocker, but not before it had harried the Salmsons, lapping at 84 m.p.h. Ware's s.v. w/c. Morgan-J.A.P., after some laps with its steering tie-rod trailing after a hurried wheel change(!), managed 70 laps but was unplaced, and Hawkes' w/c. 8-valve o.h.c. Morgan-Anzani retired after 30 laps with a broken valve cotter. It had the radiator moved back 8 in. to accommodate twin carburetters, the fuel tank carried oil, and there was a 14-gallon petrol tank under the chassis.

To offset these " 200 " disappointments, at the end of the year Morgans held the Class J1 (750-c.c. single-seaters) f.s. kilometre record (Poiret on 668 c.c. in the Bois de Boulogne—77.92 m.p.h.), the 10-mile, 50-mile and one-hour honours in this class (Ware, at Brooklands, with J.A.P. engine, at 47.26 to 59.5 m.p.h.), the Class H1 1-mile to 5-mile records (for 1,100-c.c. single-seaters) by Hawkes' 1,078-c.c. Morgan-Anzani, at 76.85 to 89.5 m.p.h. (the fastest British records did not count as World's records), and the Class H2 (1,100-c.c. 2-seaters) 1-kilometre to 10-mile records, by Norris' Aero Morgan with Blackburne o.h.v. 1,095-c.c. engine, at 85.78 to 90.82 m.p.h.

The Motorcycle Show saw the price of the a/c. Standard model reduced to £110 (lighting £8 extra), while amongst the exhibits was a very exciting single-seater Morgan-Blackburne for which 75 m.p.h. was guaranteed. The Aero-model, which now had an external gear-lever, beside the brake-lever, was listed officially, at £150 with s.v. w/c. engine, although the Grand Prix Morgan was still available, at £145, or £135 in a/c. form By December a s.v. Aero was advertised at £148, an o.h.v. Aero at £160, the w/c. De Luxe was down to £140 and the w/c. G.P. cost £138. This Aero model, especially in later a/c. versions, was aptly named for, as C. E. Allen has observed, the cockpit was reminiscent of that of a radial-engined 'plane, " that merry twinkling of the rocker gear, the odd sparks which fly from the exposed exhaust ports at night, the odd spot of oil and grease thrown back onto the aero-screens, and on a bumpy road it's rather like taxi-ing over a grass aerodrome. . . . No wonder they called it the Aero model! "

H. F. S. Morgan driving in an early A.C.U. Six Days' Trial.

THE VINTAGE YEARS OF THE MORGAN 3-WHEELER

FIRST TO EXCEED "THE TON."—Harold Beart's Morgan-Blackburne which took records at Brooklands at over 100 m.p.h. during the 1925 season, and averaged 91.48 m.p.h. for an hour. The protruding pipes gave a mild boost effect to the carburetter air intake.

1924.—By 1924 the popular four-wheeler was very much established and the 3-wheeler was more than ever forced to base its appeal on sporting performance and low running and first costs. Morgan faced the light car opposition with five basic models, ranging from the a/c. 976-c.c. Popular (£110) to the 1,098-c.c. s.v. Aero (£148), a single-seater o.h.v. racing version of the latter being listed at £160.

The Aero was a truly sporting proposition, with petrol and oil fillers inline along the brief bonnet behind the tall radiator cap. The cockpit, protected by two adjustable aero-screens, was pretty stark. The dashboard had a central oil drip-feed, its exposed pipe running under the scuttle, a Lucas ammeter-cum-switch panel on the left, a speedometer on the right, Bowden levers clipped to the steering wheel, ship's-type ventilators on the scuttle, and a snake bulb-horn lying along the o/s. mudguard.

Normally, Morgans still had 700 × 80 tyres, a 6-ft. wheelbase (the Family model was a foot longer), two speeds of 4½ and 8 to 1, and the simple chassis was said to weigh 2¾ cwt. The chassis backbone ran above the floor and the brake-lever was clipped to it, exposed cables running forward to the front brakes, if fitted, and providing some degree of compensation. Ignition was by M.L. magneto and there was a choice of Amac or B. & B. carburetter. "Omega" of *The Auto* was still attacking the Morgan, stating at the time of the 1923 Show that he was puzzled "that sensible people, with babies, could ignore the appeal of the 4-wheeler against the 3-wheeler, price for price and running-cost for running-cost."

Certainly the £165 Austin 7 was now very firmly established, and well publicised by racing successes. (The Trojan 2-stroke cost £157 10s., the Rover 8 £160, an A.V. cyclecar £105, a Tamplin £120, the revised 4-cylinder G.N. £250, while amongst 3-wheelers the Bramham cost £145, a Scott-Sociable £135.) There were three vehicles costing less than £100, namely the belt-drive Bleriot-Whippet (£82 19s.), Gibbons (£65), Harper (£80 17s.), and L.A.D. (£60.) The Morgan was to outlive them all. . . .

The Light Car & Cyclecar published a survey of readers'

experiences—shades of *Which?*—to indicate the comparative cost of running a cyclecar versus a light car. From this it was estimated that running costs over 6,000 miles, including a J.C.C. subscription, would work out at £54 12s. 3d. in a Morgan, £68 15s. 5d. in a Rover 8, £65 18s. in a Jowett and £65 14s. in an Austin 7. (Petrol was 1s. 6½d. a gallon, oil 6s. 9d. per gallon, tax £4 on a 3-wheeler, £9 on the Rover.) The fuel and oil m.p.g. were : Morgan 50/1,540; Rover 43/740; Jowett 42/1,500; Austin 45/1,800. Repairs equalled 3s. a week, a comprehensive Lloyd's policy £8 5s.! A tiny point in Morgan's favour—Frank Spouse, who drove a T.B. 3-wheeler in trials, had been appointed sole Morgan Distributor for Scotland!

At the 1924 Scottish Show all the Morgans on view had w/c. Blackburne engines, the new o.h.v. version of which gave approx. 35 b.h.p. and was supplied to the Morgan Co. with the flywheel balanced with the engine. A funnel-like air-intake was used close up behind the radiator.

In the J.C.C. General Efficiency Trial E. B. Ware's s.v. De Luxe Morgan (ME 4835) again made the best performance, gaining 330 out of a possible 385 marks. A Gwynne 8 was second (321 points), G. N. Norris' w/c. o.h.v. Aero Morgan Blackburne with oversize tyres third (306 points). Ware recorded the best petrol consumption, speediest acceleration in top speed and won the brake test. Norris made best time on the "Brooklands' Test Hill, best acceleration "through the gears" (his two speeds!) and fastest lap of the Track. This time the actual figures were not published and there was some controversy as to the validity of the various tests and the manner in which they had been organised. *The Light Car & Cyclecar* was tactless enough to suggest that the little 269-c.c. tiller-steered Harper Runabout, a 3-wheeler with single front wheel, could have won. This brought long and involved correspondence from H. F. S. Morgan and the Rev. H. G. Morgan, from which I will refrain from quoting at this late date.

At Brooklands, Norris' Morgan-Blackburne won a 5-lap Passenger Handicap from scratch, at 87.22 m.p.h., during the B.M.C.R.C. Easter Meeting. H. F. S. and G. H. Goodall tied for fastest cyclecar time at Kop Hill (28.6 sec.), and H. F. S., driving a Standard model Morgan, made f.t.d. in the acceleration test in the Midland C.C. Economy Car Trial. But at the Neath & Dist. M.C. Margam Park Speed Trials, Parsons' Morgan repeatedly gave best to Sgonina's G.N. In Malay, an Anzani-Morgan made f.t.d. in the passenger class of the speed trials.

Although a busy manufacturer, H. F. S. continued to drive in a variety of events, but the J.C.C. took him to task for not supporting theirs. Harold Beart, the Croydon Morgan agent, had begun his Brooklands career, finishing a good second to Dunfee's Salmson in a J.C.C. race.

The Morgan was again prominent in the A.C.U. 1,000-Mile Stock Trial (it was barred from the R.A.C. Six Days), being the only competing machines to be driven North to the start, accompanied by an A.C.U. observer—the motorcycles all went by

A side view of H. Beart's 107 m.p.h. Morgan. It was developed from the car he raced during 1924.

The Morgans of 1924

The Standard model.

The Family model.

The Grand Prix model.

The De Luxe model.

The Aero model.

WELL-KNOWN MORGAN EXPONENTS.—E. B. Ware and his passenger Allchin, in their 1922 s.v. Morgan-J.A.P. They were both badly hurt in the accident depicted below.

Indeed, successes continued to come in from all quarters, so that my ambition to quote them all, with Reg. Nos. of the successful Morgans, is defeated by space restrictions. For the Hereford Speed Trials H. F. S. used a Morgan-Blackburne with new, enlarged front brakes, and covered the ½-mile, from a f.s. of 50 yards, at 70.2 m.p.h., beating Goodall's red Morgan and even Harvey's new racing Alvis. In Tcheco-Slovakia (contemporary spelling) Meyer's o.h.v. Aero won its class in the Kralon-Pole-Sobesice hill-climb. Beart won at Brooklands from a McEvoy-Anzani to which his Morgan-Blackburne gave 3 sec. start, at 84.7 m.p.h., but in another race had fuel-feed trouble, leaving N. A. Lowe's similar car to beat Baragwanath's P. & P. combination, although Spring's Norton and sidecar was the winner. At the Madresfield Speed Trials H. C. Lones won his class in a stripped o.h.v. Aero and Norris easily won a 50-Mile B.M.C.R.C. Handicap in which an Austin 7 was competing, after Beart had retired with plug trouble. In the Scottish Six Days' Trial, H. F. S. won a silver cup in his smart blue 8-h.p. Morgan-J.A.P., he and Mrs. Morgan attired in spotless white and the car still carrying Reg. No. CJ 743, Spouse, now Aero-Blackburne mounted, a silver medal, but Carr's Morgan-Blackburne De Luxe (NP 65) retired after hitting a wall on Tornapress. R. R. Jackson had made an appearance in sprints, in an Aero-Blackburne (NP 3394), Bullough was going well at Southport, R. T. Horton was driving

DISASTER.—Ware's o.h.v. Morgan-J.A.P. after its crash in the 1924 J.C.C. 200 Mile Race, which resulted in a ban on 3-wheelers racing with 4-wheelers at Brooklands.

train! This time H. F. S., accompanied by his wife in matronly dress, who helped polish the car before the start, drove a s.v. Aero-J.A.P. (NP 3871), Goodall a s.v. Aero-M.A.G., Carr a Standard-model Morgan-Blackburne (NP 4080). All three won gold medals. All used standard ratios of 10¾ and 5 to 1

In France the Darmont-Morgan was in active production at Courbevoie, and at speed trials in the Forest of Senart near Paris Dhome's French Morgan, Darmont's very slim single-seater 750-c.c. Darmont-Morgan and Pierpont's 750-c.c. 2-seater Morgan set new records over the f.s. kilometre, respectively at 97.23, 125.742 and 119.8 k.p.h.

a Morgan in trials. The Morgan Club was holding social runs, as it does today, eleven members rallying to the "Red Lion," Hatfield, for a run to Bedford, and a 500-c.c., using one twin Blackburne o.h.v. cylinder, ran in the French Cyclecar G.P. Someone had rigged up an Aero with streamline prow, disc wheels, searchlight and Motometer, etc.

Then, in the J.C.C. 200-Mile Race a most unfortunate blow befell Morgans and, indeed, the whole sporting 3-wheeler world. The Morgan had never been particularly fortunate in this long-distance Brooklands race. For 1924 three cars, outwardly like Aero models, but with the big (external) silencers now demanded by the Track authorities, were entered, the "works" cars with Blackburne engines, for Norris and Beart, Ware's naturally J.A.P.-powered. Although these 2-seater Morgans were reported as capable of lapping at around 90 m.p.h., they had much trouble in practice, Ware's engine blowing gaskets, the driving chains breaking, and one car having a narrow escape when a steering arm broke. In the race Ware's engine refused to pick-up, and when it did get going, a top-gear dog broke and had to be changed. Norris, however, was duelling with Zborowski's Salmson, which it passed, only to coast in, the top-gear chain having broken. Beart was delayed long at *his* pit while a flat rear tyre was changed, after which his engine resolutely refused to start.

Then it happened! Ware had got going again, lapping probably at over 85 m.p.h., but on his 33rd lap his rear wheel appeared to be wobbling. (Parry Thomas, having troubles of his own in the Marlborough-Thomas, had reported a smell of scorching rubber when he overtook Ware.) Two more laps, and the Morgan suddenly swerved as it was crackling across the Fork, hit the fence and spun round, flinging out the occupants before it overturned. Ware and his mechanic, Allchin, eventually recovered, but Ware died some years ago.

The race went on, the Salmsons victorious in spite of overheating. Beart, understandably, stopped to increase the clearance between the tail of his Morgan and the tyre! This accident caused the J.C.C. to ban 3-wheelers not only from the 1925 200-Mile Race (which incorporated artificial corners) but from their High Efficiency Trial (also over a "road" course) which replaced the General Efficiency Trial and which Morgan was naturally anxious to win for the third time in succession. The B.A.R.C. was firmly behind the ban.

Meanwhile, H. Beart beat Norris in the B.M.C.R.C. 3-wheeler Championship race, averaging 83.99 m.p.h. for three laps and later he broke Class H2 records in his o.h.v. Aero-Blackburne, at speeds of 96.33 m.p.h. for the f.s. kilometre to 89.88 m.p.h. for 10 miles.

Commercially, the year ended well for the Morgan Motor Co. Correspondence in *The Light Car & Cyclecar* from owners who purported to have been held up in their 40/50 Mercedes and 50-h.p. Daimlers "by those beastly 3-wheelers" resulted in a lively response in favour of the Morgan (could H. F. S. or his father have compiled both sides of the argument?), and for 1925 improvements were made and prices drastically reduced—in time for competition from the 4-cylinder D'Yrsan tricars, the chassis of which was very like that of the Morgan, but used a conventional gearbox with reverse gear. At the Motorcycle Show on Stand No. 53 a canary-yellow Grand Prix Morgan with spotlamp between its aero-screens attracted attention. Spiral-bevels running on double-row ball-bearings, a higher bonnet forming a straight-line to the scuttle, and the latest J.A.P. engines and bodywork improvements were adopted. 20 in. × 3½ in. Dunlop S.S. balloon tyres with flared front mudguards, and metallic-lustre paintwork were available on the Aero model, in which flexible exhaust pipes ran into external silencers, this arrangement costing £1 extra.

The Standard model now cost £95, or £105 with Lucas dynamo lighting set, the w/c. Grand Prix-J.A.P. with electric lighting £128, the De Luxe £120 or £130 in w/c. form, the Family £3 more than the De Luxe, and the Aero was priced at £135 with J.A.P., £140 with o.h.v. Anzani, and £147 with racing Blackburne engine. All the Aeros would exceed 70 m.p.h. and you could get a hood for them for £3. Front brakes cost £6, wheel discs £2 10s., hood covers 15s., a speedometer £4, special colours £2, and the oversize Dunlops £2 per wheel extra. The Standard model was supplied only in grey at normal cost, but, like the Family, had slightly raised body sides (as had the G.P.), the other models being in a choice of grey, red, blue, purple or green. Incidentally, the 1925 Austin 7 cost £155, the Carden £90.

By the end of 1924 Morgans held all the British Class H1 and

Morgan 3-wheelers lined-up for a race on Southport sands.

H2 records, the fastest being Beart's one-way f.s. mile, at 97.32 m.p.h. (mean = 94.21 m.p.h.), and the year closed with H. F. S. in the chair at the Morgan Club dinner at Ye Olde Cock Tavern, Fleet Street, which 70 people attended.

1925.—For some time controversy raged about the J.C.C. ban, but the Club remained adamant and it was not until four years hence, with the formation of the New Cyclecar Club, that 3-wheelers were to race against 4-wheelers at Brooklands, and only last month that the V.S.C.C. relented sufficiently to allow Morgans to race, on their own, at one of their meetings. . . .

This did not deter Morgan drivers from competing in any events open to them. Goodall, for instance, drove a Standard model (NP 636) *sans* bonnet, to take a "silver" in the Victory Cup Trial, in which H. F. S. gained a "gold" and Chippendale's Morgan overturned without damage in the brake test. And in the last of the public road speed trials, Goodall's Morgan "Jim" won its class at Hereford, being 1.4 sec. faster than Taylor's Brescia Bugatti, the fastest 4-wheeler, and in those near Tavistock on the same day, H. Dobbs' Morgan Blackburne beat Grogan's Frazer Nash.

As ever, the "Land's End" attracted Morgan exponents, Maskell running a stripped Aero (XR 11), the trilby-hatted Marshall a Standard (CJ 5649), a dozen Morgans winning between them four "golds," three "silvers" and a "bronze." The rest retired, as did a lone D'Yrsan. In the 1925 A.C.U. Stock Trial Carr drove a s.v. w/c. Standard (AB 9602), Goodall a w/c. Aero-Anzani (AB 16); both taking gold medals.

About this time experiences of readers and professional testers began to be published. Gordon Oxenham wrote of his 1925 w/c. Grand Prix-J.A.P., which would do 60 m.p.h. when the engine was clean, 56 when it was "full of carbon and pulling a load of 20-stone." It gave 60 m.p.g., climbed Brockley Hill at about 35 m.p.h., Kop Hill at 20-25 m.p.h. *The Light Car & Cyclecar* reported on the latest Aero-Blackburne (XX 8647), which weighed 7 cwt. 1 qtr. 21 lb. and developed over 40 b.h.p. at 4,500 r.p.m. This gave an easy 70 m.p.h. "on reasonably smooth roads. The tester decided that "the anticipation of a skid (on tramlines) was more terrifying than its reality" but that "getting away in low gear on a greasy road tends to throw the rear of the car sideways until the back wheel can obtain sufficient grip to drive the machine." The hood was criticised for cutting off all visibility to sides and rear and making hand-signalling impossible, the fabric-lined cone clutch was fierce until treated with engine oil, and overall fuel consumption was about 45 m.p.g., while roughly 2,000 m.p.g. of oil was obtained, at about 20 drips per minute from the Best & Lloyd drip-feed. (The handbook recommended 30, but owners used anything from 15 to 90 d.p.m.) The direct steering was disliked and it was thought that a simple form of reduction gear would be a distinct advantage. (From driving my 1927 Family Model I couldn't agree more, but it was many years before the Morgan Co. relented and fitted a reduction box, or a reverse gear!) As tested, the Morgan cost £167.

Up at Southport, Bullough in what I suspect was the ex-Hughes Morgan, A. Moss (Stirling's dad?), Ron Horton (in OM 4000) and S. Keary were successfully mixing it with the G.N.s, which tended to be superior. Morgans were out in force in the "Edinburgh," even to Hall's 1912 model (CB 88) bought for £12 a few days beforehand. It did not gain an award, but neither did H. F. S. However, the other Morgans collected six "golds" and two "silvers." In the International Six Days' Trial Carr's lone Morgan (NP 15, with spare wheel carried in a well in the n/s. running-board), teamed with an Ariel and a Humber motor-

Beart and Norris about to contest the Cyclecar Championship at a 1924 B.M.C.R.C. Meeting—Beart gained an unexpected victory at 83.9 m.p.h.

cycle, won the B.M.C.R.C. Championship, and 13 Morgans took part in the Morgan Club's own trial, in the Hatfield area, for two cups presented by H. F. S. (where are they now?)—why doesn't the present Morgan 3-Wheeler Club repeat it? *The Motor Cycle*, commenting on Carr's performance in the Six Days', remarked that he lost one time mark only and climbed all the hills splendidly, adding " His passenger deserves special praise."

Meanwhile, Harold Beart had evolved a very special racing Morgan at his Croydon works. The frame was strengthened and each rear spring had seven graduated leaves, a single Hartford shock-absorber being mounted over the rear wheel on a bracket above the bevel box and a stirrup secured to the fork-ends. At the front cast-steel sliding axles replaced the normal bronze ones, so that forward-projecting brackets could take Hartford shock-absorbers anchored at the bottom to steel brackets, and swivelling with the wheels. The axles slid on hardened and ground Ubas-steel pins screwed-in and grease-gun lubricated. Spring-loaded ball-joints on the track-rod, and a Ford epicyclic reduction gear on the top of the steering column, further improved control. A 4-to-1 ratio was achieved, with a forged-steel drop-arm slightly longer than standard.

The rear wheel was brakeless, the foot-brake having been dispensed with, and was shod with a 27 × 4.20 Dunlop. The front tyres were 26 × 3.75 Dunlops, on wellbase rims.

This Beart Morgan had ratios of 5.95 and 3.33 to 1, a magneto button on the top of the external gear-lever facilitating gear-changing without the need to slip the clutch or ease the throttle. A spring-loaded selector mechanism prevented the dogs coming out of mesh. Chains and bevels were oiled, *via* a drip-feed and copper pipes, from a pressure-fed tank. The engine was a 1924 w/c. o.h.v. 85 × 96.8 mm. (1,096 c.c.) Blackburne with racing cams, c.r. increased by machining the heads, a B. & B. " mouse-trap " carburetter controlled by a foot accelerator, and M.L. magneto. A bowl behind the air intake, fed by two projecting pipes, maintained atmosphere pressure to the carburetter irres-

pective of speed. Fuel was carried in a tank under the frame, supplemented when required by a tank in the body, giving a combined capacity of approx. 14-gallons. The large oil tank fed two drip-feeds, adjustable by the riding mechanic, and the radiator was special. No attempt was made to reduce weight but the body, which cowled-in the engine, weighed only 43 lb.

This fascinating Morgan could do over 60 m.p.h. in low speed, and 100 m.p.h. in top at about 4,300 r.p.m. on the tachometer, which was driven from the bevel-box countershaft. Yet in a season's Track work, it averaged 24 to 25 m.p.g. Beart brought it out in July at Brooklands and set Class H2 records for 5 miles and 10 miles and the equivalent kilometre records, the 5-kilometre record being at fractionally over 100 m.p.h., *the first time a 3-wheeler had been timed at this speed, officially or unofficially.* A *one-way* kilometre was clocked at 104.63 m.p.h. and the f.s. 5-mile record fell at 99.67 m.p.h. In August Beart took the f.s. kilometre and mile records at 103.37 and 102.65 m.p.h., respectively, and the following month captured the 50-kilometre, 100-kilometre and one-hour records, his speed for the hour being 91.48 m.p.h. In October Robin Jackson filled in, as it were, with the s.s. kilometre and mile records in his Morgan-Blackburne, at 64.04 and 71.03 m.p.h., respectively. Beart also raced Horton for the B.M.C.R.C. Cyclecar Championship, starting slowly but winning by six yards, at 83 m.p.h.

" Shacklepin," who wrote " Cyclecar Comments " in *The Light Car & Cyclecar*, bought an Aero-Blackburne in April and, giving his experiences after 7,000 miles, complained of clutch slip oil running down the tappet rods, and an inadequate dynamo output, but generally praised the car, which had been fitted with Bentley & Draper shock-absorbers to the back wheel. Morgans met 4-wheeled cars again in the M.C.C. High-Speed Trial at Brooklands and, required to average one m.p.h. more than a 1½-litre car to get a " gold," nine Morgans started and eight won gold medals.

The only alterations for 1926 were better bodywork on some of the touring models, the De Luxe model having 1-in. higher body sides and, in company with the Family model, a better hood and 2-pane screen. The latest 1,086-c.c. J.A.P. engine with big valves was available for the Aero and the new Blackburne engine had stronger valve gear with the cups in the top of the push-rods instead of in the rockers. All models now had dynamo lighting sets, and an electric horn was fitted to all except the 980-c.c. Standard model. Front brakes, now only £4 extra, were by no means universal. The 1926 prices were £115 for the a/c. De Luxe, or £125 in w/c. form, £123 for the w/c. Grand Prix-Anzani, the Family costing £116 with a/c., £126 with w/c. J.A.P. engine. The Aero cost £130 with s.v. w/c. J.A.P., £135 with Blackburne and £142 with Anzani engine. The Standard still sold for £95. Thus the Morgan challenged the Austin 7, now down to £149, while interest in 3-wheelers was by no means waning, for the famous Malvern make was joined at the 1925 Motorcycle Show, where it occupied Stand No. 32, by the flat-twin w/c. Coventry-Victor and the Omega-J.A.P.

(To be continued)

THE VINTAGE YEARS OF THE MORGAN 3-WHEELER

ONE-LUNGER.—*The Morgan was given engines of various sizes for racing, including small vee-twins and single-cylinder power units. This is Eric Fernihough's 500-c.c. Morgan-J.A.P. of 1926, described in* MOTOR SPORT *of that year.*

1926.—Enthusiasm for Morgan was unabated, in spite of one unkind cartoon which depicted a Grand Prix Morgan and two kids in a pram, the caption reading " The Two-Seater They Talk About Before Marriage—And The One They Get!" One Aero owner made a replica of his car to a scale of ¾ in.=1 ft. and set it up on the Morgan's radiator cap, and in the serious sphere of speed events R. T. Horton was racing at Southport sands where Bullough's Morgan was in winning form while R. R. Jackson and Eric Fernihough, in the Inter-Varsity Hill Climb, gained first and second places in the unlimited sidecar class. Fernihough, later to become one of the World's fastest motorcyclists, then still an undergraduate at Cambridge, had built a single-cylinder Morgan Special (*see* MOTOR SPORT, August 1926), using a 1925 494-c.c. a/c. push-rod o.h.v. J.A.P. engine which ran up to 5,700 r.p.m. With this he was very successful. At Brooklands on March 31st he covered five miles (f.s.) at 73.12 m.p.h., five km. (f.s.) at 73.37 m.p.h., ten miles (s.s.) at 69.65 m.p.h. and ten km. (s.s.) at 70.37 m.p.h., passing Pratts spirit through the Amac carburetter and using Castrol oil and Avon tyres. These were new Class I records, and in June Fernihough was out again, clocking 71.81 m.p.h. for a f.s. km., 71.91 m.p.h. for a f.s. mile. On the last day of August, taking his *fiancée*, Miss Butler, as passenger, he went after long-distance records in the half-litre Morgan. He set up new records from 100 km. to 6 hours, at speeds around 57/59 m.p.h., although for the six hours the average had dropped to 49.51 m.p.h. Best speed was 59.7 m.p.h. for 100 miles. But unfortunately the rear tyre burst and the driver and his girl passenger who had been sharing two-hour spells at the wheel, were thrown out as the Morgan overturned, but were not badly hurt.

This was the age when record breaking paid well in respect of bonus money, so the very next day G. E. Tottey, the New Imperial rider who still turns up at B.M.C.R.C. Brooklands Re-Unions, took out a 490-c.c. Omega-J.A.P. 3-wheeler and raised Fernihough's 50-mile, one-hour and 100-km. records, respectively to 60.09, 60.52 and 60.52 m.p.h. However, Fernihough put a 599-c.c. J.A.P. engine in the Morgan, and covered 50 km. at 62.29 m.p.h., 50 miles at 62.61 m.p.h., 100 km. at 62.72 m.p.h. and averaged 62.69 m.p.h. for the hour, new Class I records. (J. J. Hall, with the 1,100-c.c. Omega-J.A.P., took Class K records for three hours (58.84 m.p.h.), four hours (58.64 m.p.h.), five hours (57.9 m.p.h.), six hours (57.34 m.p.h.), seven hours (56.59 m.p.h.), 200 miles (59.14 m.p.h.) and 500 km. (57.88 m.p.h.)—happy days !)

In trials, naturally, Morgans went on scoring successes, and it was estimated that since 1920 they had won 27 gold, 14 silver and nine bronze medals in the " Land's End " alone. H. Beart & Co. of London Road, Kingston were fitting steering reduction gears and foot throttle controls to Morgans, the Aero owned by " Shacklepin " of *The Light Car & Cyclecar* being amongst them, and Jackson and Booth of Congleton sold a proprietary reverse gear. (At least one policeman was obviously unaware that 3-wheelers were not compelled to have a reverse gear, incidentally!) In the Scottish Six Days' Trial the 1,096-c.c. Morgans of Spouse and Watson gained silver medals but H.F.S. and Carr retired, the former with leaky water joints, the latter damaging his chassis on Loch Losgoinn. In the strenuous International Six Days Trial Goodall (NP 636), Horton (CJ 6343) and Carr (NP 65), using w/c. Aero-J.A.P.s with the new 10-h.p. o.h.v. engine, did magnificently, all winning " golds " and the Team Prize in their class. Their total loss of marks was only 20, whereas the sole surviving team of sidecars lost 310 marks.

Performances like this were excellent publicity and in the face of fierce competition from 4-cylinder small cars the Morgan remained extremely popular, Homac's advertising that they could not give delivery in under 14 days. The *Motor Cycle & Cycle Trader* reported that the 10.4-h.p. w/c. o.h.v. Blackburne-Aero would do 10-30 m.p.h. in 5.2 sec. on the 4.6 to 1 top speed, or in 2.8 on the 7.9 to 1 low speed, had a top speed of 72 m.p.h., and would stop in 34 yards from 40 m.p.h. using only the foot brake, in 26 yards if hand and foot brakes were both applied (this apparently with front brakes). Alternative ratios of 5 to 1 and 10 to 1 were spoken of, the tyres were 700 × 85, the petrol tank held three gallons.

Up to October 1926 a 349-c.c. Villard 3-wheeler held the km. and mile f.s. 3-wheeler records in Class H (up to 750 c.c.,) at 55.49 and 55.12 m.p.h. respectively. Class I (up to 500 c.c.) records were shared by Jackson (498-c.c. Morgan-Blackburne), Fernihough/Miss Butler (494-c.c. Morgan-J.A.P.) and Tottey (494-c.c. Omega-J.A.P.), Fernihough holding the majority, the fastest being Jackson's f.s. km. at 72.44 m.p.h., Class J (up to 750 c.c.) was Tottey's preserve, with a 730-c.c. Omega-J.A.P., but Sandford's 747-c.c. Sandford had the s.s. km. and mile records and the fastest was the Omega's f.s. km. at 78.29 m.p.h. Class K (up to 1,100 c.c.) was almost a Morgan monopoly, by Beart's 1,096-c.c. Blackburne and 1,097-c.c. J.A.P., except for the s.s. km. and mile records held by Jackson's Blackburne and the 200-mile and 3-hour records held by Hall's 1,097-c.c. Omega-J.A.P., fastest being the f.s. km. at 103.37 m.p.h. Passengers were carried in all classes.

At Olympia in 1926, with Morgan showing a dozen cars and a chassis on Stand No. 53, Omega and Coventry-Victor continued to exhibit and were joined by the single-cylinder £65 H.P. For 1927 the Morgan was grease-gun lubricated, 7-in. front brakes were standardised on the De Luxe, Family and Aero models, and the bevel-box was redesigned to allow a larger ball-bearing behind the pinion, while the rear fork and bearings, countershaft, dogs and rear axle were strengthened, and there was ample clearance for the largest rear tyres. The Standard model, now with double screen, electric horn and celluloid-covered steering wheel, cost £89. More commodious bodies figured on the De Luxe, Family and Aero models, and 4-in. Dunlops were standard. Prices were, respectively, a/c. £110, w/c. £120; a/c. £111, w/c. £121; w/c. Aero

£127, racing with 10/40 w/c. engine £140. An electric starter cost £10 extra. A Super Aero with V-mudguards and one-piece body, delivery taking two months or more, was offered at £145 with J.A.P. or Blackburne engine and a newcomer was the Family Aero, evoked by A. C. Maskell who drove one in the "Land's End," costing £142. Mottled aluminium dashboards were standardised.

Finally, as the year drew to a close the Morgan Club dinner saw 125 people at the Hotel Cecil and on Christmas Eve the Company announced that in the M.C.C. Brooklands High Speed Trial standard Aero Morgans had covered 67.8, 64.4, 61.9 and 60.7 miles in the hour, driven respectively by C. J. Turner, A. C. Maskell, R. T. Horton and J. L. Goddard.

1927.—Early in the year the Colmore Cup Trial proved a typical "mud-plug" and won Horton's Morgan a "gold," H.S.F. (in AB 16) and Chippendale "silvers," Goodall a bronze medal; D. S. Peacey drove a 498-c.c. H.P., and three Omegas competed. It was estimated that since 1913 Morgans had taken 18 gold and eight silver medals and the Evans Cup on three occasions in the Colmore and, since 1920, 15 gold, 11 silver and the Team Prize in the Victory Trial.

R. R. Jackson put a 60 × 88 mm. (496 c.c.) V-twin Blackburne engine similar to that which Wal Handley used in the 1926 Senior T.T. into a Morgan, running it at the C.U.A.C. Speed Trials at Hatley Park, and captured the 50-km. Class I record from Fernihough, at Brooklands, at 64.52 m.p.h., using Castrol oil, B.P. petrol and Dunlop tyres.

A wordy duel was fought out in the correspondence pages of The Light Car & Cyclecar between R. Siran and H. Beart. It centred round a supercharged S.C.A.P.-engined D'Yrsan which was said to have averaged 110 m.p.h. for two laps of Montlhéry Track and the latter's challenge. Although Beart agreed to put his Morgan-Blackburne against the s/c D'Yrsan over ten miles, or against a non-supercharged D'Yrsan over 50 miles at Montlhéry, the match never materialised, fizzling out as such proposals often do.

"Shacklepin" reported favourably on the latest o.h.v. 85.7 × 95 mm. (1,096 c.c.) 8.45-h.p. J.A.P. engine which had been fitted to his 1925 Aero (XX 8647) the previous August, which would pull down to 10 m.p.h. in top, or open up to 40 in low, 70 m.p.h. in top speed, giving over 50 m.p.g. from a B. & B. carburetter set for economy, or 45 in town work. A Mr. Russell of Harrington Gardens, S.W.7 was prepared to supply a fabric coupé body, called the Newt, on an Aero chassis for under £200 complete, claiming a weight increase of only about 5 lb., and drove one in the "Land's End," in which 16 Morgans competed (six "golds," three "silvers," four "bronze," the coupé taking one of the latter). F. H. Hambling of Kilburn foretold the future by offering a 3-speed gearbox, with ratios of 15.2, 7.66 and 4.4 to 1 and single chain, for £12, his demmo. car being a G.P. Anzani. In the "Welsh 24" H. Gallie's Morgan (BN 8706) won the cup for best passenger-vehicle performance and in the A.C.U. Six Days" F. James' Aero Morgan took a "gold" but Carr, in Aero-J.A.P. UY 761, failed a hill and had tyre trouble. In the "Edinburgh" 14 Morgans between them netted 11 "golds" and three "silvers," Vidler and Macaskie driving Aero models RK 6401 and MK 2448.

By the summer of 1927 there was a considerable crusade for a revival of races in which 3-wheelers could compete on level terms with conventional cars and various pleas for the safety of the tri-cycles were advanced, including a statement by J. J. Hall that he had driven 1,600 miles round Brooklands without mishap. Mr. Williams of Metro Motors offered temporary headquarters for the organisation of such a race, which was to take form in 1928. Meanwhile, a Scottish Morgan Club was formed, with a five-bob subscription. At Arpajon, Dhome driving a Darmont-Morgan covered a mile at 90.41 m.p.h., a Sandford the km. at 97.95 m.p.h., the mile at 97.28 m.p.h., and Dhome's 500-c.c. Darmont-Morgan the f.s. km. at 71.57 m.p.h.

The clamour for a Club to foster racing of 3-wheelers and cars on a level basis grew and the Morgan Club was re-formed as the New Cyclecar Club, with Prof. A. M. Low in the Chair and the racing committee consisting of H. Beart, J. J. Hall, E. B. Ware, Capt. A. Frazer-Nash and G. E. Tottey. The scare caused by Ware's 1924 accident was at last being overcome! Unfortunately, at this most inopportune time, J. J. Hall and Vic Derrington who was his passenger, were badly hurt when their 750-c.c. Morgan, during a record attempt at Brooklands, burst its Palmer back tyre on the Railway Straight. But this did not damp the new club's enthusiasm, Beart sagely observing that a standard Amilcar or Austin 7 might be safer in a 200-mile Grand Prix, owing to the fact that they would not be able to attain anything like the speed!

Before the accident Hall set new Class K records from one and two hours and 100 miles, his best speed 67.71 m.p.h. for the hour, the Morgan using R.O.P. petrol and Sternol oil. At Southport, where S. Brownhill's Morgan ran with a specially-lowered frame, the back wheel protruding through the top of the tail, Horton beat the fastest sidecar by over 5 m.p.h., covering the f.s. km. at 93.21 m.p.h. The perennial topic of tyre wear disclosed that well over 10,000 miles was possible on the original tyres. A typical journey was that accomplished by a 1927 s.v. w/c. De Luxe Morgan-J.A.P. (KM 8790), from Chatham to Liverpool in pouring rain, nearly 250 miles in 9¼ hours including stops, this owner using 26 in. × 3½ in. Dunlop s.s. cords which had punctured once in 7,000 miles, the front tyres hardly worn, the rear one just beginning to lose its tread.

"Focus" of The Light Car & Cyclecar used an o.h.v. Aero-J.A.P. (CJ 743) to cover the Scottish Six Days' Trial. It had an electric starter, front brakes, 27 in. × 4 in. balloon front tyres, a gear-driven dynamo, improved bevel-box, new type silencers and a pneumatic seat squab. Edinburgh was reached from London on the first day, and only Amulree and Kenmore put the Morgan onto the 10 to 1 bottom speed, for it could climb Fish Hill, Broadway, in top. Over the entire 1,800 miles, only two gallons of oil were used, and petrol thirst averaged 53 m.p.g. "Focus" got 30 in low, but found 65 m.p.h. in top speed enough, as prop-shaft whip came in thereafter, and he thought the steering heavy, the driver's left foot cramped, the clutch pedal travel too long, a rear shock-absorber and a handbrake ratchet desirable. But this "exhilarating and health-giving" vehicle, costing £140, proved entirely troublefree.

Not to be outdone, "Friar John" of the same journal took a holiday tour in a Family model (UY 761). Going out of London on the then-new-and-uncompleted Barnet By-Pass, the Morgan made mid-Lincolnshire, 135 miles, on the first day. In all, about 800 miles were covered, without need for a single adjustment, and the steering, geared about 2 to 1, was judged a great improvement. For 1928 prices were again reduced, the Standard model, supplied only in dark red; the De Luxe to £100, or £110 in w/c. J.A.P. form, the Family model to £102, or £112 with w/c. J.A.P. engine, the Aero to £119 a/c, £132 with 10/40 o.h.v. h.c. tuned J.A.P. engine, while the new Special Super Sports with this engine was priced at £155.

1928.—Although the roads were taking on a sophisticated air, with new by-passes and petrol pumps, etc., and small saloons were becoming the vogue, the Morgan continued to hold its own, especially amongst the sports light cars, the new Super Sports model with rounded tail, enveloping a rear-end crudely exposed on the Aero model, cycle-type front mudguards, low-level exhaust pipes, but retaining aeroscreens, being a match for contemporary Salmsons, Amilcars and Ulster Austins—even at a time when a 1922 G.N. in good condition could be bought for £4. Three-wheelers, in fact, continued to be much in evidence, Hawkes taking records at Montlhéry with a 490-c.c. M.E.B., the 10-mile record being lifted to 74.6 m.p.h. while H. F. S. continued to be very active, driving a Family model to Geneva and back and taking an Aero through the Scottish Six Days' Trial.

The main excitement, however, was the Brooklands Meeting organised by the New Cyclecar Club in August. Throwing caution to the winds, as it were, a "Grand Prix" course was devised with a sandbank S-bend in the Finishing Straight and another where the cars turned into the Railway Straight. To swell the entries, which totalled 74, 4-wheelers were admitted and the only accident befell an Austin 7, which overturned!

Several wide-track Super Sports Morgans, still sometimes called Super-Aeros, ran, and competition came from Vidler's racing flat-twin 746-c.c. Coventry-Victor. R. R. Jackson drove his old lowered 546-c.c. vee-twin Morgan-Blackburne, Horton his very fast Morgan with Beart's old Blackburne engine and pedal-applied Bowden wire-and-rod front brakes, all with Brooklands "cans" and fish-tails.

The first all-3-wheeler race, a 3-lap handicap, was won by Jackson, at 67.85 m.p.h., Horton second, Lones third. In another 3-lap handicap a T.T. Riley was no match for the Morgans, Horton's winning by over ¼-of-a-mile, at 92.4 m.p.h., from Maskell's and Lones' Morgans. Horton then won a 5-lap handicap, at 94.5 m.p.h., by ½-a-mile, from Jackson and Lones. He was lapping at 98 m.p.h. and must have reached the "ton" down the Railway Straight. The big race, however, was the Cyclecar G.P., over 20 laps of the special course, in three classes. Gardner's s/c. Salmson retired after three laps with a broken petrol pipe, Horton after five, with oil on the brakes. Maskell's Morgan broke its gear lever, being confined to top, and Lones won by a lap from Wilkinson's Riley and Smythe's Amilcar, the Coventry-Victor being fourth. Lones stopped once for water, as he was using a small radiator. His 1,096-c.c. Morgan-J.A.P. averaged 54.1 m.p.h. and used a B. & B. carburetter, ML magneto, Lissen plugs, Coventry chains, John Bull and Dunlop tyres, Newton and Hartford shock-absorbers, B.P. aviation petrol and Shell oil.

At the opposite extreme, a 1924 Family model (DC 4363) towed a collapsible caravan through the Lake District at an average speed of 20 m.p.h. And in the Scottish Six Days' Trial F. H. James drove the only Morgan (W 157) and won a silver medal.

Late in the season Jackson was out on Brooklands with his 498-c.c. Morgan, setting I Class records from 50 km. to one hour, the latter at 71.4 m.p.h. For 1929 the long-awaited geared steering, which had been an extra in 1928, was standardised, bevel-box and rear hub bearings were fitted with oil-retaining felt washers, heavier ball-bearings were used behind the bevel pinion, a greaseproof cover was fitted over the clutch, the sliding axles were provided with grease-containing cavities and anti-wobble steering pins were fitted to all models. The gear-driven dynamo, provided in 1928, was improved by using skew gears and a stronger dynamo bracket. The battery was placed in the tail of the Aero, which had a better hood. The other models were strengthened and improved in appearance and the sidescreens and battery were housed behind the squab on the De Luxe model. The a/c. 980-c.c. s.v. J.A.P. engine was standard on the non-sporting models, giving 55 m.p.h. in the 4.5 to 1 top speed, low speed being 8 to 1. The front brakes were operated by a central lever. Whereas the De Luxe model measured 9 ft. 6 in. × 4 ft. 10 in., and now cost £92, the wide track of the Super Sports gave it overall dimensions of 9 ft. 8 in. × 5 ft. 3 in. It had the w/c. 1,096-c.c. o.h.v. J.A.P. engine and could do 80 m.p.h. in the 4 to 1 top speed. The price was reduced to £150. Least expensive was the Standard model, at £86.

1929.—Perhaps the 4-wheelers were closing in, but still the Morgan exerted itself. H. F. S. (in AB 16) led a team in the Scottish Six Days', Wilton in CE 423, Reid in GO 7253 and Harris in ML 1142, all o.h.v. Aero-J.A.P.s, two with flared front wings, two with cycle-type, which won two " golds " and two " silvers," H. F. S. missing a Silver Cup because of a sooted plug.

Lones won a B.M.C.R.C. Private Owners' Handicap race at 81.7 m.p.h. and in the " Edinburgh " ten Morgans started and nine took gold medals, including Maskell's Family model, which carried four adults through the trial. The new Cyclecar Club again held its Brooklands Meeting, on August 31st. The first race was won by Sidney Allard's Morgan, at 73.37 m.p.h., from a couple of Austins. Seven well-known Morgan exponents contested the 3-lap 3-wheeler Handicap, Rhodes winning easily, at 87.9 m.p.h., from Lones, after Horton had retired, Maskell third. Horton's 496-c.c. Morgan won a mixed 3-lap Handicap, which included a Riley 9 saloon which lapped at over 69 m.p.h. and blown Amilcar, Salmson, Austin and Ratier cars, at 71.15 m.p.h., from Lones' 996-c.c. Morgan-J.A.P. and Gardner's Salmson. In spite of many retirements, Morgan honours were upheld in the 5-lap Handicap, which Rhodes' 1,096-c.c. Blackburne-engined car won at 89.74 m.p.h. by half a lap, in spite of a rehandicap. Austins unsuccessfully pursued him.

The 20-lap Cyclecar G.P. over the " road " course attracted 21 starters and some drama, Clayton's Amilcar and Maskell's Morgan both retiring after minor incidents at the artificial bends.

FASTEST 3-WHEELER EXPONENT of them all, Gwenda Stewart in her 115-m.p.h. Morgan at Montlhéry Track. Douglas Hawkes, who prepared the car, is standing behind it.

WORKS DRIVER.—C. T. Jay, the then-Stores Manager at Malvern, and his passenger, C. Curtis, who was Morgan's Chief Tester (not carried during the race), with the 730-c.c. Morgan-J.A.P. in which Jay won the 1929 Cyclecar G.P. at Brooklands at 64.7 m.p.h.

C. Jay, from the Morgan works, in Goodall's a/c. 730-c.c. Morgan-J.A.P., carrying ballast in lieu of an acrobatic passenger, won by nearly two laps from Gardner's scratch Amilcar Six, the Morgan averaging 64.7 m.p.h. Jay was duly presented with the *Light Car & Cyclecar* Cup by H. F. S. Morgan. An Austin 7 was third. The winner used an Amal carburetter, ML magneto, Discol fuel, Castrol oil and Dunlop tyres.

At another B.M.C.R.C. meeting Lones' single-cylinder 498-c.c. Morgan-J.A.P. won a 5-lap All-Comers Passenger Handicap at 77.81 m.p.h. At the end of the year prices were somewhat changed, the Standard and Family models to £87 10s., the Super Sports to £145, the Aero still being available at £110.

The outstanding Morgan occurrence of the year was undoubtedly Gwenda Stewart's record attacks at Montlhéry. Douglas Hawkes prepared for her an a/c. 998-c.c. Super Sports-J.A.P., with which she took the 5-km. and 5-mile records, at over 103 m.p.h. Later she put the hour record to 95 m.p.h. Hawkes then tuned the Morgan, raising the c.r. to 7¼ to 1, putting in a high gear that enabled the engine to run at 4,500 r.p.m. when lapping at over 103 m.p.h., and fitting 4.20 × 27 track Dunlop tyres. The stripped Morgan then set the hour record to 101.5 m.p.h., the first time any 3-wheeler had covered over 100 miles in the hour, for the motorcycle record stood at 89.4 m.p.h., while the 1,100-c.c. car hour record was only 1.74 m.p.h. quicker, by a blown 4-cylinder 2-stroke Cozette. The Morgan, running on large carburetters and undiluted alcohol fuel, averaged 15 m.p.g. The front tyres were worn at the sides and very little rubber was left on the back tyre.

This was only a beginning, for after smaller carburetters had been substituted, using a small quantity of benzole in the fuel, the c.r. lowered, and road-racing Dunlops of the same size fitted, four days later Gwenda Stewart successfully broke long-distance records, from 7 to 12 hours, at speeds varying from 66.39 to 67.46 m.p.h. The Morgan now gave 36 m.p.g. and the tyres were scarcely worn. Hawkes also installed a 730-c.c. J.A.P. engine in the Morgan, to enable Mrs. Stewart to set new Class J records for five to eight hours and 500 miles, at speeds of 70.57 to 71.09 m.p.h., breaking some of their own M.E.B.-J.A.P. records, the Morgan faster than in its 998-c.c. form.

Lones had been busy at Brooklands with his 346-c.c. Morgan-J.A.P., taking Class records from 5 km. to two hours, at speeds of 56.75 to 70.47 m.p.h. and then Mrs. Stewart excelled herself at Montlhéry. Hawkes provided 498-c.c. J.A.P. and 346-c.c. J.A.P. engines for further successful record attacks, so that during the year she broke 71 records with the Morgan, the fastest her Class K 5-mile at 106.3 m.p.h., the 350 engine doing 74.07 m.p.h. for 5 km., the 500 a speed of 77.24 m.p.h. for an hour and the 750 doing 85.2 m.p.h. for an hour.

1930.—The year opened with further activity at Montlhéry by the irrepressible Hawkes/Stewart *equipe* and the Morgan. With S. C. H. Davis as co-driver, Gwenda set new figures for records from 1,500 km. to 24 hours, the Morgan actually stopping after 21 hours, for which period it averaged 64.85 m.p.h. inclusive of depot stops. And for 12 hours it averaged 72.72 m.p.h. A broken piston stopped the car, but Hawkes had a spare engine ready. Subsequently Mrs. Stewart drove the Morgan over shorter distances, being timed at 113.52 m.p.h., the highest speed officially achieved by a vintage-type 3-wheeler. She also averaged 110.69 m.p.h. over five miles. I believe she was actually timed in a speed trial at 117 m.p.h.

Nineteen-thirty was the last year of the 2-speed Morgan, because in 1931 a new layout with 3-speed gearbox and final drive by a single chain superseded the famous 2-speeder transmission used from 1909 to 1930. However, the 2-speeders were still listed, to vanish finally in 1933, except for the £80 976-c.c. Family model. The M-type chassis had been introduced early in 1930, with underslung rear suspension and a knock-out rear spindle. An internal-expanding foot-brake was arranged inside the low-gear sprocket and the bevel-box was redesigned with two forged-steel wheel-supporting beams, arranged co-axially with the counter-shaft, and as the box was bolted to a flange on the end of the prop.-shaft it was easily removable, the smaller bevel-wheel shaft being mounted on ball-bearings and coupled to the end of the prop.-shaft. The wheelbase was shortened by some 3 in., and the shorter prop.-shaft was less prone to whip. The 2 to 1 geared steering was popular, although some owners thought a 3 to 1 reduction would be better. The twin aero-screens of the Aero model were replaced by a two-panel vee-screen and the racing J.A.P. engine was given enclosed valve gear.

" Sartor " of *The Motor Cycle* wrote very enthusiastically of his 1,098-c.c. o.h.v. Aero-J.A.P. (WE 6000), which was faster on a regular 53-mile journey than a motorcycle, by some nine minutes, " hardly touching the brakes and cornering a good deal more slowly."

The B.S.A. f.w.d. 3-wheeler began to compete in trials alongside the Morgans, but still the latter took most of the awards, such as 11 gold medals and two " silvers " in the " Land's End " and " golds " by Goodall, Walker, Cannon, Moss, Senior, and R. D. Smith in the " Edinburgh," in which event Welch and H. T. Smith gained silver medals.

And afterwards. . . . The Morgan in its new 3-speed form continued to flourish, but its vintage years were over. Morgans were allowed to compete with 4-wheelers in the L.C.C. Relay Race, in which the Morgan team was always a great sight, the cars crackling round at the top of the bankings, throttles held wide open by rubber bands, leaving the drivers both hands with which to steer! They never won this ingenious race, being heavily handicapped, but in 1933 the Morgan team of Rhodes, Laird and Lones finished second, at 89.01 m.p.h., the same drivers repeating this performance, and making the fastest speed, at 90.91 m.p.h., in 1934. For racing the wide-track front axle tubes were now in general use.

For a simple vehicle the keynote of which was utility, the Morgan 3-wheeler gained a quite fantastic number of successes in sporting events. Indeed, its sponsors, of whom the Rev. Morgan died in 1937 and H. F. S., at the age of 77, in 1959, purposely introduced the sports G.P., Aero and Super Sports models and encouraged competition activities, in which many of the works

THE EX-HORTON/JACKSON *Morgan as it appeared at this year's Brooklands Re-Union. The body can be described as the transitional Super Sports type, coming between the Aero and later sports bodies with spare wheel on the tail.*

personnel, from H. F. S. and G. H. Goodall downwards, participated.

In 1935 the 4-cylinder Morgan 3-wheeler, with Ford Eight (and, later, Ford Ten) engine, appeared and the first 4-wheeler, the Morgan 4/4, arrived in 1936. The 990-c.c. Matchless vee-twin engine was fitted to the Super Sports Morgan 3-wheeler, however, the last batch of these models being shipped to Australia after the war, and after 1934 all the vee-twin Morgans had these engines, in a/c. and w/c., s.v. and o.h.v. versions. The Family model had been endowed with a dummy radiator grille in 1933 and the spare wheel was mounted on the tail of the sports body. All chassis except the Super Sports were lowered 1½ in. by means of cranked front cross-tubes and detachable bolt-on wheels were standardised. For 1935 the barrel-body with spare wheel on the end was adopted for the F-model Super Sports. Peter Morgan joined the Company in 1947 and the F4 and F Super Ford-engined 3-wheelers were discontinued in 1950. The sporting tradition of the Morgan was carried on by the Plus Four 4-wheeler, introduced that year and still prominent in today's racing and other competition events. And the Morgan 3-Wheeler Club, with 1,200 members, keeps alive the great 3-wheeler tradition. These articles give but an outline of Morgan history. It is to be hoped that one day, perhaps, the knowledgeable Robin Richmond, aided by Lindop and Birks, may be persuaded to write a book about the famous 3-wheeler.

—W. B.

LATER MORGAN COMPETITION EFFORTS.—*On the left, C. A. Rhodes at a 1934 B.M.C.R.C. Cup Day at Brooklands, when he dead-heated with Muir's Norton. On the right, Henry Laird finishing second in a race at Donington Park at Easter, 1937, his Morgan averaging 58.37 m.p.h. over this road circuit.*

THOUGHTS AND OPINIONS

Side Wings for a Morgan Screen.

I enclose a photo. and sketch of a pair of side wings I fitted to the screen of my Morgan. This entirely does away with back draught. The alteration is made as follows:—Take two pieces of flat iron, 18 ins. by ¾ in. by ¼ in., heat and bend them as shown in the sketch. The longer part must be at the same angle as the front screen, with the shorter part in a straight line with the screen support, which is screwed to the body of the car. Drill a ⅜ in. hole a distance of 13 ins. down which should be the position at which the iron is bent, and then below this, a distance of 3¾ ins. in my case, drill and countersink a hole for the screw, as explained as follows: Take off the wing nut of the screen, withdraw the screw in the support just below, slip the piece of iron upon the set-screw, from which you take the wing nut; replace the wing nut and use a longer screw for the one which goes into the body, with the addition of a rubber washer in between the ironwork and the body of the car. Before fixing, drill the holes for the hinges, which are riveted to the irons by tinmen's rivets, and the screens are then attached. I made the frame of the screens out of oak, ¾ in. wide by ⅝ in. thick, and instead of making picture-frame joints, I morticed the four corners. The glass was set in putty, to keep out the wet and to avoid vibration. The two small pieces of wood were fixed to the irons by means of small brass clips fitted over the irons at the back and screwed through into the wood. The whole can be taken away by removing the wing nut and withdrawing the one screw.   COMFORT.

High Wycombe.

* * For the foregoing interesting suggestion we have awarded
* the sender a prize at his choice.—ED.

Side wings fitted to the screen of a Morgan.
(See letter from "Comfort.")

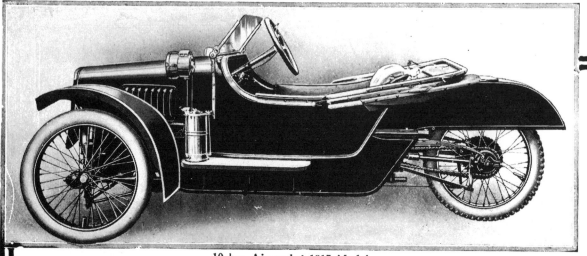

First Show Appearance –
OLYMPIA, LONDON, 1910

MORGAN RUNABOUT, No. 250.

4 h.p. Model : 85.5 × 85 mm. ; m.o.i.v. ; Bosch magneto ; J.A.P. carburetter, h.b.c. ; Dunlop tyres ; shaft and chain transmission.

Morgan and Co., Malvern.—A three-wheeled runabout which should on no account be missed by visitors to the show is the Morgan in the annexe. It is very lightly constructed throughout, and some very clever notions have been adopted in its design. It is low and rakish looking ; so low, in fact, that it might with its present sized wheels prove unsuitable for use in districts where the roads are very rough. The motive power is derived from a 4 h.p. J.A.P. engine situated in front of the machine where it receives a maximum cooling draught. It is placed transversely in the frame, and a self-contained metal to

A novel low-built runabout named the Morgan.

The engine and bevel driven magneto of the Morgan Runabout. The system of springing will be noted.

metal clutch with ball thrust bearings is fitted immediately behind the engine. This is operated by a push pedal on the foot boards. The drive is continued from a square joint in the clutch through a tube, to a bevel wheel on the countershaft. The latter runs on large size ball bearings, and at its extremities chain wheels of different sizes are fitted, one driving to either side of the rear wheel. Thus a different ratio of gearing is obtained by engaging one or other of the chain wheels by means of a pair of dog clutches sliding on the countershaft. The springing is of special design. The front axle has spiral springs above and below, the principle being somewhat suggestive of the Sizaire-Naudin car. The rear wheel is hinged at the back end

of the gear box, and its rise and fall is controlled by short laminated springs. Tiller steering is adopted. The rider's position is half reclining, and long footboards at a comfortable angle command attention. There are two brakes operating on the rear wheel. This runabout may be obtained with a single or twin-cylinder engine. Two models are being shown, one of 4 h.p. and one of double that power. In each case a long pipe is fitted to the silencer conducting the gases away to the rear of the machine. The control is by a throttle lever, and variable advance for the magneto. Two side levers control the brake and gear change respectively. Splayed mudguards complete the equipment of a very cleverly designed runabout for a single rider.

Details of the rear wheel springing of the Morgan runabout. The laminated springs are relieved of side stresses by the tubular radius rods. The change speed, brake and control levers will also be noticed.

1911: H. F. S. Morgan at the tiller, with his brother-in-law W. Copeland, in the prototype two-seater. The tiller steering was replaced later in the year by a steering wheel. Manufacture of the Morgan three-wheeler began that year, a Patent being granted—the Patent drawings being produced by a young draughtsman by the name of John Black; later he was to become Sir John Black of the Standard Car Company, which was to provide Standard Vanguard and Triumph TR engines for the later four-wheeled cars for the 18 years up to 1968.

.1919: The right-hand of these two Morgans was a special M.A.G.-engined single-seater built for a Mr. C. Perham of the Admiralty. With Amac carburettor, bore and stroke of 90 by 85 mm, and an R.A.C. horsepower rating of 10, the car was, the description in Motor Cycle stated, easily capable of 65 mph. The body width was only 22 in; two forward gears were fitted (the normal two-chain Morgan transmission of the day) with ratios of 3.5 and 6 to 1. The description of the car ended by stating "We are asked to state that the Morgan Motor Co. built the machine to Mr. Perham's special order, and that they are not prepared to supply duplicates until the termination of the next war!" The left hand of the two cars appears to be a standard Grand Prix model.

The following letter appeared in an issue of Motor Cycle in 1919, throwing an interesting side-light on the widely held view that all Morgan three-wheelers of the day had only two forward speeds (and no reverse).

THE FOUR-SPEED MORGAN.

Sir.—Some doubts have been expressed as to whether the four-speed Morgan, which, driven by a private owner, won all the premier awards in the M.C. and A.C. trial (" the greatest trial of the year "), was a standard type.

There is no question about it. The four speed model has been included in our catalogues, and, although through stress of work at the present time we are compelled to confine ourselves as far as possible to the manufacture of the simpler models, it will certainly appear again in our catalogues and advertisements. There are a considerable number of these machines on the road—probably more than the number of standard machines of some other makers.

For ordinary purposes we consider two speeds amply sufficient, but some of our riders require more, and we have endeavoured to meet their requirements by a simple device which duplicates the gears.

MORGAN MOTOR CO., LTD.

INTO BATTLE 1912-1926

2nd April, 1912.
THE FIRST CYCLE-CAR RACE.

A.C.U. Trial, August 1912: Mr. and Mrs. H. F. S. Morgan, in the "Morgan Runabout", as it was then termed. Above: Starting the ascent of Byber's Hill which, despite accounting for 24 failures and being one of the most difficult tests, was climbed by the Morgan. Below: On the second bend of Porlock. The Morgan was awarded a special cup for the best passenger climb of this West Country hill.

A motley collection of "trikes", of which only the Morgan survived as a make, gets away from the starting grid at Brooklands in the first cycle-car race, held at the British Motor Cycle Racing Club's first monthly meeting in March 1912. Harry Martin's Morgan Runabout (Above) was the winner.

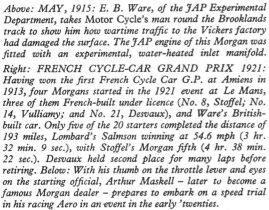

Above: MAY, 1915: E. B. Ware, of the JAP Experimental Department, takes Motor Cycle's man round the Brooklands track to show him how wartime traffic to the Vickers factory had damaged the surface. The JAP engine of this Morgan was fitted with an experimental, water-heated inlet manifold.

Right: FRENCH CYCLE-CAR GRAND PRIX 1921: Having won the first French Cycle Car G.P. at Amiens in 1913, four Morgans started in the 1921 event at Le Mans, three of them French-built under licence (No. 8, Stoffel; No. 14, Vulliamy; and No. 21, Desvaux), and Ware's British-built car. Only five of the 20 starters completed the distance of 193 miles, Lombard's Salmson winning at 54.6 mph (3 hr. 32 min. 9 sec.), with Stoffel's Morgan fifth (4 hr. 38 min. 22 sec.). Desvaux held second place for many laps before retiring. Below: With his thumb on the throttle lever and eyes on the starting official, Arthur Maskell – later to become a famous Morgan dealer – prepares to embark on a speed trial in his racing Aero in an event in the early 'twenties.

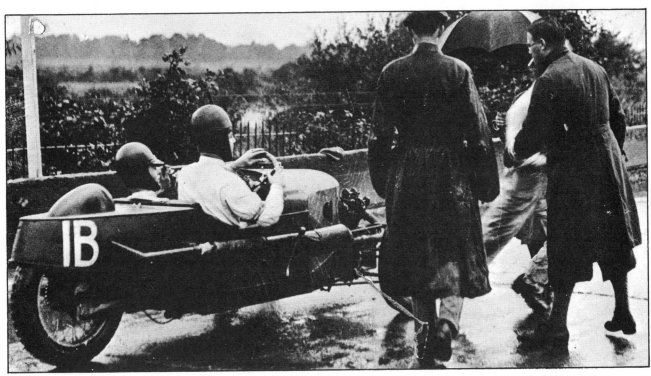

INTO BATTLE

Right: *1926: George Goodall's J.A.P.-engined Aero takes part in the Speed Test at Brooklands, following the International Six Days' Trial.*

Right: *1922—Morgan country: A very standard looking De Luxe 2-seater, driven by George Goodall, climbs Gambles Lane in the North-West London Club's London-Gloucester-London Trial.*

Below: *1925: Competitors take to the bank to pass a vast steam tractor and its attendant heavy load, in the A.C.U. Stock Machine Trial, headed by George Goodall's Aero.*

Morgan Runabout SWEEPS THE BOARD AT BROOKLANDS!

LIGHT CAR AND CYCLE CAR CUP

J.A.P. CUP

MOBILOIL CUP

MASKELL CUP

FIRST IN EVERY RACE
at the
NEW CYCLE CAR CLUB MEETING
(Aug. 31st.)

NOVICE HANDICAP - MORGAN 1st Won at 73·37 m.p.h.
3 WHEELER H'CAP - MORGAN 1st Won at 87·99 m.p.h.
   Also 2nd and 3rd.

3 LAP RACE - - MORGAN 1st Won at 71·15 m.p.h.
   Also 2nd.

5 LAP RACE - - MORGAN 1st Won at 89·74 m.p.h.
GRAND PRIX RACE - 50 MILES - MORGAN FIRST

HOUR RECORD BROKEN
at 101½ m.p.h.

Mrs. Stewart on the Montlhéry Track broke the Hour Record at 101½ m.p.h. driving a Super Sports Morgan.

MODELS FROM .. £87-10   **TAX ALL MODELS £4**

Write for Illustrated List—free.

MORGAN MOTOR CO. LTD.
Malvern Link, Worcs

Care and Maintenance of the Morgan

Some Notes on How to Obtain the Best Results.

By W. A. CARR.

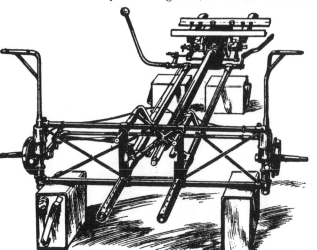

FOR some time I could not understand why Mr. H. F. S. Morgan appeared to be so apathetic to the appeals for such things as reverse gears and detachable wheels, and it was not until, as the result of trial work, I acquired close intimacy with the various working parts of the Morgan that I appreciated the wisdom of his policy. Owing to its simplicity, the average owner can tackle any maintenance work apart, perhaps, from dismantling the bevel gears and driving shaft. My object in this summary on the care of a Morgan is to endeavour to assist in some small way those who, like myself, want the best possible results from their machines.

Keeping the Engine in Tune.

Regarding the power unit, which is a proprietary article, the question of tuning would require too much space to go fully into the subject, and I cannot do better than refer those interested to the manufacturers' instruction booklets.

As expert engine tuning is not within everyone's capabilities, I would suggest that if such points as the valve clearances, the fit of valve stems in their guides, the induction pipe joints, and the compression, are in order, then the engine can safely be relied on to deliver the horses.

As regards carburation, I have found that very little improvement can be effected by altering the makers' setting. Careful attention to the feed and the float chamber is desirable, and in this respect it is surprising the amount of foreign matter which will be found to accumulate.

Fortunately, magnetos are now so reliable that one is apt to forget how essential they are, and even the little excitement one used sometimes to have when the fibre bush of the contact breaker seized up seems to have vanished. An occasional cleaning of the slip ring, and examination of the high-tension cables and brushes are generally all that is needed.

It is a good plan to see if the machine runs freely in neutral by testing it on a hard, flat surface and observing whether there is any undue stiffness of movement. If stiffness is noticeable, the adjustment of the brake bands and driving chains should receive attention; the latter adjustment should, of course, never be attempted when the back wheel is jacked up.

Front Wheel Wobble.

The driving wheel runs on two robust ball races, and, as these are well packed with grease, not much trouble will arise in this quarter if the nuts on the axles are kept dead tight. Any wear in the front wheel bearings can be taken up in the hubs.

Sliding axles do not last for ever, and excessive wear, together with any looseness in the tie rods and steering arms, will probably set up front wheel wobble. This can be eliminated by compensating for wear in the steering system, and employing washers of friction material between the tie rods and wheel arms.

Driving chains are usually patient sufferers, and in the majority of cases they are either coated with thick grease, to which mud and dust adhere, or they are entirely forgotten, with disastrous results. Their lives can be considerably lengthened if, after removal and scrubbing with a wire brush in a paraffin bath, they are allowed to soak in hot graphite grease. Before replacing the chains, allow the superfluous grease to drain off. Badly worn or stretched chains will have a tendency to ride the sprocket teeth, and may cause considerable damage. Chains may be tested for wear by laying them out straight on the ground and then alternately pulling and pushing on their ends.

Morgan chassis lay-out.

Care and Maintenance of the Morgan.

It is not wise to run the tyres to destruction if one wishes to avoid the unpleasant delays which are bound to occur. The removal of rust from the inside of the wheel rims will amply repay one's trouble. If standard tyres are used, then from the point of view of comfort it is not advisable to run them board hard, as they then convey shocks which are not appreciated by either the human or the mechanical frame; if, on the other hand, they are run too soft, there is the possibility of the tyres rolling off the rims. Generally, the best compromise results from the use of the maker's recommended pressures. The question of punctures brings one to that of roadside repairs, and even if it is necessary to remove the back wheel the job should present no difficulties. As an essential to this operation, I would advocate a jack which, when placed under the bevel box, is capable of lifting the car sufficiently high to enable the back wheel to be easily removed after the brake bands and chains have been uncoupled. This tool will remove a lot of the difficulties which are associated with the operation of repairing a rear wheel puncture.

The possession of a kit of serviceable spanners is very

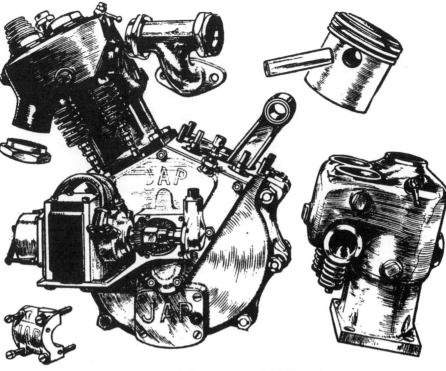

The twin–cylinder water–cooled J.A.P. engine.

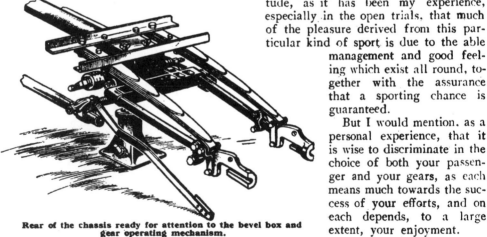

Rear of the chassis ready for attention to the bevel box and gear operating mechanism.

desirable, and with the exception of the one big adjustable, I much prefer the spanners to be of the flat type. Apart from the flat set spanners being easy to carry, they do not round off the corners of the nuts. If a flat box holding the spanners is placed in the bottom of the car, it forms a useful footrest for the passenger.

When the owner contemplates either touring or trial work, careful and systematic attention to the details I have mentioned will considerably add to the pleasure and success of the undertaking, and obviate the necessity for carrying a small host of spares.

On the subject of trials, there is no reason for Morgan owners to avoid the big events on account of their magnitude, as it has been my experience, especially in the open trials, that much of the pleasure derived from this particular kind of sport is due to the able management and good feeling which exist all round, together with the assurance that a sporting chance is guaranteed.

But I would mention, as a personal experience, that it is wise to discriminate in the choice of both your passenger and your gears, as each means much towards the success of your efforts, and on each depends, to a large extent, your enjoyment.

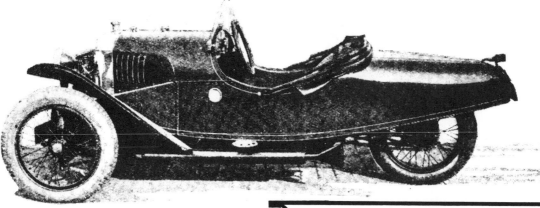

Two Thousand Miles with a Speedy Three = wheeler — the 1,100 c.c. "Aero" Morgan.

By "UBIQUE."

W HEN first I announced my intention of purchasing a three-wheeler I was the recipient of much good-natured chaff. Motor cycling friends began to speculate (aloud) upon my increasing   and to make unkind remarks about th   eed of a third wheel to keep me up in greasy weather.

In spite of this, I persisted, and when a racy dark blue "Aero" Morgan was at last revealed to their eyes these friends began to wonder if, after all, there was not something to be said in favour of my third wheel. It was not a family model, as they had pretended to expect, for excellent as these true utility machines are, I wanted something with rather more sporting lines, and, above all, a vehicle that would give me speed and acceleration comparable with that of a sports motor cycle. In this I have not been disappointed, and, as a matter of fact, my latest acquisition is faster than the majority of two-wheelers which I have possessed.

Luck was with me, for the manufacturers had managed to spare me a super-sports 1,100 c.c. overhead-valve J.A.P. engine with polished ports, high compression, and high-lift valves, and in its test stages the machine lapped Brooklands at well over the seventy mark.

A Perfect Little Lady.

I was not accustomed to three-wheelers and had been crammed with horrible tales relating to the ease with which they were upset. Therefore, for some hundreds of miles during the running-in period, I treated *Mabel* (the heroine of this story) with the utmost respect. Fortunately, she proved to be a perfect little lady, and would behave as such in traffic or at modest road speeds. A snatchless twelve miles an hour on top gear (4.5 to 1) is a simple task for the big engine, and from this speed *Mabel* will shoot away without any fuss or pinking; indeed, if the clutch be kept in proper order and used with discretion, the Morgan is, to all intents and purposes, a one-gear machine.

"An Aero" in Action

Now, about this clutch, which first of all gave me some worry. It has a fabric-faced conical driving surface, and if it is allowed to get dry it becomes most unpleasantly fierce. On the outside of the flywheel is a nipple through which grease can be injected on to the clutch surface, though only if the clutch pedal is depressed at the time. As this involved the calling-in of a helper, who was not always available, I shaped a piece of wood so that it could be wedged between the pedal and the front of the seat to fix the clutch in the "out" position for the duration of the greasing period. This system worked well, but the grease smelt horribly when the clutch was slipped, and the effect of each application did not last long. I therefore consulted the manufacturers, who supplied a far more simple and effective hint. All that is required is a force-feed oil gun with which to inject a good healthy dose of engine oil into the clutch. The oil is retained by the flywheel back-plate and the clutch will remain delightfully smooth in action for long periods. So much for the clutch; now let us get back to the road.

I very soon found that these tales of upsets were either founded on some myth or on the sins of some type of three-wheeler other than the modern Morgan Aero model. I daresay that it *is* possible to turn one over; but I have seen more than one four-wheeled car upside down. It may even be possible that an Aero will turn over more easily than a car. I don't know; I have never tried. But this I do know—if only a reasonable amount of care is exercised the Aero can be cornered at really high speeds without so much as a wheel lifting an inch. If the rear brake is jammed on when traversing greasy tram lines the machine will skid; so will a motor cycle, so will a car. But the cure is simple: use the front brakes, which are excellent. Here I would solemnly advise purchasers of Aero Morgans to make a habit of using the front wheel brakes; the lever is conveniently placed, the habit is easily acquired, and there is far less liability to skid the machine. These brakes will just stop the bus on a gradient of 1 in 7, and the foot brake will lock the rear wheel if applied with sufficient force. At a fairly

"... this most exciting three - wheeler."

The "Aero" Morgan toying with the gradient of Sunrising.

early stage in *Mabel's* career, my son, who is at the age when speed counts most, expressed a desire to travel fast. He came for a run with me, and even *his* speed lust was temporarily satisfied. I will not attempt to state the figure registered by the speedometer needle, which was still curving pleasantly round the dial when road conditions entailed deceleration, but one of the charms of the Morgan Aero is that it feels even faster than it is. This is brought about by the seating position, which is so low that it is possible to touch the ground by holding one's hand over the side of the body; the result is that speeds over the sixty mark provide a delightful sensation of record-breaking velocity; and 60 m.p.h. is child's play to *Mabel's* engine, and can be attained amazingly quickly.

Mabel on "Edge."

On that same run I thought it would be interesting to see how the machine behaved on a gradient, so as Edge Hill was handy we turned in that direction. We reached the hill, opened out, the result was astounding—Edge, with its 1 in 7 gradient, simply disappeared. The matter of changing down never entered my mind, which was only occupied with slowing down sufficiently to take the bends in safety. Having taken the last bend at a modest touring speed, I opened throttle rather further, but not fully, and *Mabel* accelerated rapidly on the last and steepest slope, the speedometer registering 38 m.p.h., and still

An "Aero" in Action.—
rising. I have never had cause to try the machine on freak hills, but I am convinced that nothing would stop her provided that wheel grip is obtainable; I have yet to be brought to the low gear by gradient alone.

When *Mabel* was delivered she managed to pick up a nail from the road, with the result that the rear tyre was flat next morning. As it happened, I had an idle Saturday afternoon, and this gave me the opportunity of tackling the job in a leisurely fashion. An inspection of the tread did not reveal the cause of the puncture, so I decided to remove the wheel just to see how it was done. A jack under the front end of the rear fork raised the wheel in a jiffy, and the rear brake band was disconnected from its operating lever and the anchor pin removed. All was then plane-sailing, and the wheel was removed in a few minutes without the necessity for disconnecting either chain. As straight-sided tyres are fitted to my machine the tube was easily removed and repaired. Then started the job of wheel replacement. The chains were slipped on to the sprockets and the pair of rather long arms which I possess enabled me to lift the wheel into its forks from above, but when next I tackle the job I rather fancy that it will be easier to sit down and lift from below.

The cockpit of " Ubique's " Morgan.

Attention to the Chains.

Being a careless person, I gave no attention to the chains other than an occasional dose of oil from the outside. This probably accounts for the fact that at the end of 2,000 miles the high-gear chain showed a considerable extension from the normal, owing to wear in the rivets Both chains have the same number of links, so they may be interchanged, and wear, therefore, equalised; if it becomes necessary to fit a new chain it is desirable, though not essential, to replace both, otherwise it may prove difficult to keep them in approximately correct adjustment.

During the 2,000 miles I have covered with *Mabel* our only involuntary road stops have been due to sooted plugs; it took me some time to realise that the engine runs so coolly that racing type plugs are unnecessary and that the oil supply can be cut down to a rate of only about fifteen drops per minute, which seems ridiculously inadequate for such a big engine. Plug trouble has now vanished, yet the engine is lubricated quite satisfactorily.

Starting has always been an easy matter, even in cold weather, but in winter the carburetter is apt to freeze up, causing poor and uneconomical slow running and sometimes a rather disconcerting freezing-open of the throttle valve. A shield between the cylinders, fixed to the nuts which secure the rocker covers, has overcome the trouble in *Mabel's* case, and is well worth the slight expense entailed.

I don't grudge a little time spent on tappet adjustment. The correct clearance is a rather tight "two thou.," all round, and if this is maintained the engine will tick over nicely and hold its tune well.

When this super-sports engine was first fitted to the Aero model (I believe I have the first) it was in the nature of experiment, and the balance was not quite perfect. The effect of this was to bring about an unpleasant vibratory period between 50 and 60 m.p.h. The fault was corrected on later engines, but though the manufacturers offered to rectify matters in my engine I put up with things as they were for a long time; it is only recently that *Mabel* returned to her home for re-balancing. The result has been satisfactory, though there is still a vibration period between the figures mentioned: it resembles propeller-shaft whirl.

Endless Power in Reserve.

In normal circumstances I do not drive very fast, but it is pleasant to be able to maintain or even to exceed a good round touring speed on any hill with a reasonable surface, and the sensation of endless power in reserve has a charm which must be experienced before it can be realised

I have owned more than one modern sports motor cycle, but I have no hesitation in claiming that the all-round performance of the Aero Morgan compares favourably with that of the majority of two-wheelers. *Mabel* has, then, the performance of a good motor cycle with—well, no, not quite—the comfort of a car; though the wheels are independently sprung a three-tracker is bound to get some of the bumps which could be avoided with two tracks.

As regards comfort, I have fitted B. & D. shock absorbers to the rear forks with most satisfactory results, and more recently Newton dampers have been added to the front springing. These have made a wonderful difference to the comfort and road-holding.

I have never regretted my choice of machine. The joy of a high power-weight ratio and the instant surge of power when the throttle is opened, even when one is travelling at 45 or 50 m.p.h., provide a fascination which never fails.

Cyclecar Comments

BY SHACKLEPIN

LAST week I dealt fully with the universal joints and track-rod pins of the Morgan steering. We can now turn our attention to the methods of checking play in the front wheels and sliding axles.

Jack up each front wheel in turn, and, holding the wheels at the top, pull and push sideways. A little movement here may be ignored, but if the amount seems at all excessive, attention is called for at some point in the locality. Having made certain that it is not the wheel bearings themselves which are in need of adjustment, see to it that the front spindle is not loose in the sliding axle. The special tongued or "star" washer—the three tongues of which should embrace the flats of the nut holding the spindle in the sliding axle—serves the very useful purpose of keeping this nut tight, but if it should have been left off, or if the tongues are not doing their job, the nut will almost certainly work loose in time, and this may lead to unpleasant results.

* * *

Having passed this point, the remaining possible source of trouble lies in the phosphor-bronze sliding axles themselves being worn. These are renewable at a cost of 10s. each, and while the job is in hand it is as well to fit new sliding-axle tubes, which are quite cheap. I have known cases where sliding axles have been bored out for a short distance each end and steel bushes inserted, with fairly satisfactory results, in spite of the fact that, in theory, steel running on steel is not to be recommended.

* * *

The top ends of the sliding axles seldom wear quite so rapidly as at the bottom, and if the axle tube is a fairly good fit here, there will be no need to bush the sliding portion at the top.

In order to remove a sliding axle, raise the front wheel from the ground with the jack (or a box), preferably under one of the middle lugs on the lower chassis cross-tube,

just behind the crankcase bottom. Disconnect the front-brake cable, if any, remove the front-spindle nut and, with a hide-faced or lead hammer, give the threaded end of the spindle a few heavy blows, when, complete with the front wheel, it should leave the sliding axle. Slack off, but do not remove, both nuts holding the chassis tie-rod, remove the wing, then the split-pin and nut at the bottom of the wing stay, when the latter may be withdrawn. Now, by lightly pressing the lower chassis tube downwards the sliding axle may be removed complete with its tube and springs.

* * *

As these springs usually have a tendency to fly in undesired directions it is a good tip to secure the bottom one to the sliding axle with a piece of stout wire passed through one of the coils and up to the hole where the wheel spindle normally fits. If the sliding axle is then pulled away bottom first the top spring will have no tendency to fly.

Reassembly calls for no special instruction, being merely a reversal of the foregoing proceedings in the main, but it will be found that wrestling to get the complete sliding axle back into position between the upper and lower chassis cross-tubes is made easier if the bottom end is put in first, making sure the sliding axle tube is properly located in the recess in the chassis lug.

* * *

Broadly speaking, there are only two types of geared steering found on Morgans. First, there is the maker's set, which gives a reduction of 2 to 1 between the steering and road wheels. The reduction gearbox is located a foot or so below the steering wheel, and beyond occasional greasing—a grease-gun nipple is fitted—calls for little attention. Any undue backlash in the gears may be felt on the steering wheel, and if it is desired to take this up all that is necessary is to remove the three $\frac{3}{16}$-in. hexagon-headed setscrews

which hold the upper portion of the steering column to the box.

This upper portion may then be turned by hand when, as the driving and driven wheels are eccentrically mounted in relation to one another, the teeth may be more deeply engaged. As a rough guide, it is safe to turn round the column by hand until it feels somewhat stiff. It is impossible absolutely to take up all steering-wheel play where geared steering is fitted, and in any event a little backlash in the steering box will not be responsible for wobble at the road wheels.

* * *

No difficulty will be experienced in starting the three setscrews in their threads, as there will be found a number of suitable holes drilled round the flange of the steering-column boss, and it is always possible to find three of these registering with the three threaded holes in the reduction box itself.

This system of steering, it may here be pointed out, gives either a "high" or "low" steering-wheel position. That is to say, the column does not run into the centre of the steering-box cover but meets it at one end. Therefore, assuming the wheel is now in the high position and it is desired to lower it, all that is necessary is to remove the four bolts which hold on the cover, and replace it with the erstwhile top edge, now at the bottom of the reduction box. In doing this job it is not necessary to undo any other fittings.

* * *

The other form of reduced steering, which, incidentally, is not fitted by the manufacturers of the Morgan, is usually an adaptation from a well-known American car. The ratio between the steering and road wheels is 4 to 1, and, owing to the comparatively large amount of travel which the steering wheel has to pass through with this gearing, it is almost essential to have a foot accelerator fitted, because the Bowden wires of the normal controls are apt to be "wound up."

THE 10-40 H.P. AERO MORGAN

Impressions of the Latest Model With the "M" Type Chassis Over a Distance of 1,000 Miles —Fine Performance A Prominent Characteristic

AT A GLANCE.

ENGINE: *Two-cylinder V; bore, 85.7 mm.; stroke, 95 mm. (1,096 c.c.); Treasury rating, 10 h.p.; tax £4; mechanical lubrication with sight-feed; magneto ignition; motorcycle-type carburetter.*

TRANSMISSION: *Cone clutch, 2-speeds forward (countershaft) (ratios 4.5 and 8 to 1), right-hand control, enclosed propeller shaft to bevel box, final transmission by ¾-in. pitch interchangeable chains.*

SUSPENSION: *Front, independent vertical helical springs; rear, underslung quarter-elliptics; wire wheels; 27-in. × 4-in. tyres.*

DIMENSIONS: *Overall length, 10 ft. 3 ins.; overall width, 4 ft. 9 ins.*

PRICE: *£128 10s.*

MANUFACTURERS: *Morgan Motor Co., Ltd., Pickersleigh Road, Malvern Link, Worcester.*

THERE is and always has been something altogether delightful about a Morgan which defies definition, and when one sets out to put on paper impressions gained during a road test of 1,000 odd miles, difficulties arise immediately. There is, in the opinion of the writer, no independent standard with which the performance can be compared; a Morgan is a Morgan, and it can be compared with nothing else but another Morgan.

The model tested was an Aero with a racing o.h.v. J.A.P. engine fitted in the latest "M"-type chassis. For the benefit of those not acquainted with the new chassis it should be pointed out that the rear suspension is now underslung and a knock-out spindle allows for easy removal of the back wheel. The foot brake is of the internal-expanding type arranged inside the low-gear sprocket and operated by a flexible cable from the pedal. A further improvement is the re-designed bevel box with its two forged-steel wheel-supporting beams arranged co-axially with the countershaft.

With the new design it is possible to remove the whole of the rear mechanism, for the bevel box is now bolted to a flange at the end of the propeller shaft tube—the smaller bevel wheel shaft being mounted on ball bearings and coupled to the end of the propeller shaft. This improvement means that the wheelbase is shortened by some three inches, although the body dimensions remain unchanged. Furthermore, the propeller shaft is also shortened, and any tendency to whip at speed is minimized. In other respects the chassis is unaltered. Geared steering with a ratio of 2-1 has, of course, been a feature for some time now.

The racing J.A.P. engine is of improved design,

the valve gear having been altered considerably. The rockers and push-rods are totally enclosed, neat aluminium boxes being mounted on standards screwed into the cylinder heads. The rockers run on roller bearings and the rocker boxes have quickly detachable covers to facilitate tappet adjustment. Another engine modification is the simplification of the oil pump which is now much easier to dismantle.

As regards bodywork, the Aero body, with its squat bonnet, streamlined tail and flared wings, remains unchanged except that a very neat and efficient two-panel V-screen replaces the aeroplane-type adjustable shields used formerly.

So much for the refinements. As to performance— it is perhaps easier to say that it is typically "Morgan." Readers who have themselves driven these cyclecars will understand what is meant; those who have never sampled a Morgan have missed an interesting and instructive experience quite apart from the fun and thrills which only motoring in something "live" can give.

The Aero is built essentially for the sportsman. Family men, potterers and the really genuine he-speed-coveters are catered for with suitable Morgan models, but the Aero appeals to that vast crowd of young, moderately well-off people who have become tired of motorcycles and yet require a vehicle with that comforting feeling of a big reserve of power which only motorcycles, very high-priced sports cars and three-wheeled cyclecars can give.

The most noticeable characteristic of the new Morgan —after the driver has recovered from the shock of the tremendous acceleration available—is the greatly improved stability and springing. There was a time when the charges of top-heaviness and a tendency to over-turn on corners were levelled against these three-wheelers. In the early days there was perhaps some small justification, for the first Morgans were much higher and narrower of track. Driver and passenger used to sit over the bevel box and, furthermore, high-pressure tyres did not make things any steadier.

During the past few years, however, the chassis has been lowered, the track widened, and the seating accommodation re-arranged; these alterations, together with the fitting of low-pressure tyres, have made the Morgan one of the steadiest high-speed vehicles on the roads.

The ease and safety with which fast cornering can be indulged in has to be experienced to be believed, whilst the machine's stability at speed over bad roads is almost uncanny.

Really shock-free suspension is not expected of a sports car, and Morgan springing is certainly not what is usual on a touring car, but nevertheless the new chassis reveals a great improvement and quite long journeys can be accomplished at high average speeds without either driver or passenger suffering any more fatigue than is natural when concentration and a constant alertness are necessary.

Ample Leg-room.

The pneumatic cushions and a well-padded squab are most comfortable, and there is ample leg-room for tall people—in fact, a driver of 5 ft. 9 ins. found it advantageous to put an extra cushion behind his back to enable him to reach the brake and clutch pedals more easily.

The V-screen gave quite adequate protection, whilst the hood can be very quickly erected and forms a good roof with plenty of head-room. No sidescreens are supplied, but it was found that little rain blew in.

The 2-1 geared steering, whilst being a little on the heavy side at slow speeds, was just right for the job when travelling fast. It would be interesting to try, however, a 3-1 reduction in order to learn if the high-speed-handling qualities would be marred by a ratio which would give greater ease of manoeuvrability in traffic and at low speeds.

The adoption of such a ratio would, of course, necessitate the use of an accelerator pedal—a fitting, incidentally, which it is thought would really be more useful and greatly appreciated. With the lever controls now used it was found somewhat confusing when the wheels were on full lock and the location of the levers changed either to top or bottom dead centre of the steering wheel. Furthermore, a foot accelerator would enable drivers to make much neater gear changes.

Another small point which would also help towards quicker and more accurate changes would be the arrangement of the gear lever in a central position.

These are, however, the only criticisms which need be made. In other respects the Morgan tested was in every way a wonderfully pleasant vehicle, and it says much for its appeal that not only was it used on every possible occasion—even on wet days, when a saloon car was available—but also that the number of interested and sometimes sceptical acquaintances who openly " cadged " for joy rides was most surprising.

Sceptics Convinced.

The sceptics were without exception convinced when the capabilities of the machine had been demonstrated to them. Few enthusiastic motorists can find it in their hearts to withhold praise for a machine which merits it, and if ever a 10 h.p. 1,100 c.c. two-seater car possessed a meritorious performance it is the Morgan. The manner in which the model whisked its way up hills, always with an ample reserve of power for sudden acceleration, was most impressive, whilst suitable " straights " on which the throttle could be opened wide were few and far between.

On the other hand, from a vital pulsing "75" the J.A.P. can be throttled down to a sedate, sweet-running tick-over, the 8-1 bottom gear ratio being ideal for traffic. The slow-running capabilities are most creditable—few fast engines will revolve as slowly and steadily as a well-balanced " twin." The foot-brake was sufficiently powerful at moderate speeds to bring about good retardation, and at high speeds the front-wheel brakes could be relied upon.

The equipment includes the customary electric control panel—with ammeter—horn switch, oil sight-feed, a magnetic speedometer on the stippled aluminium facia-board and coco-nut mats on the floorboards. The six-volt electrical system incorporates a dynamo positively driven from the countershaft, three lamps, and a battery which is stored in a locker behind the seat squab. The chassis of the model tested is black, and the body dark red cellulose with white lines—a most attractive vehicle.

FOR SPEED WITH ECONOMY.

Externally, the 1930 Aero Morgan differs little from its immediate predecessors, an improved screen and hood being the only important alteration. The model tested had the latest "M" type chassis which represents a considerable advance.

The 980 c.c. Family Model Morgan-J.A.P.

The 980 c.c. Family Morgan.

THE Family Model Morgan, the subject of this article, can be regarded as being a large sidecar outfit as far as tax and upkeep costs are concerned, but in other respects as a vehicle which provides many of the comforts of a car—at a price well below the critical £100 mark. It climbs hills, fully loaded, like any big-twin sports sidecar, has a very little higher petrol and oil consumption, and is simplicity itself.

As far as driving is concerned, a car owner might find it a little more difficult to manage than would a motor cycle owner, who would take to it at once and be quite at home after a few miles' running. The difficulties for the car man would be, of course, the absence of an accelerator pedal and the comparatively high gear of the steering.

On the machine tested the power unit, a 980 c.c. side-valve J.A.P. twin, pulled so very well that the gear lever was rarely moved from top position, a trait due to the fairly high power-weight ratio. Only when the speed had dropped below 8 m.p.h. did the engine give signs of distress as the throttle lever was opened in this gear; even that figure might have been improved upon if the mixture had not been on the weak side. The weakness was obvious, for the air lever was never opened beyond the half-way position at any time, and for continuous slow running it was found best to keep

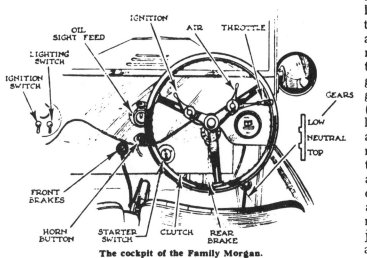

The cockpit of the Family Morgan.

it closed, or very nearly closed.

On normal hills, even when the Morgan was overloaded, it was only necessary to open the throttle a little wider than usual to romp up with a pleasant surge of power. Newnham Hill, near Daventry, with a maximum gradient of 1 in 6 was, with the help of some considerable initial momentum, and to the accompaniment of tail movements on the very loose surface, taken in top gear with the driver alone on board; normally, however, in the interests of steadiness, low gear would have been engaged. Stoneleigh Hill (1 in 9½) was a ridiculously easy climb with almost a full load, the machine accelerating all the way from the corner, and having to be throttled down over the pot-holes at the summit. The maximum speed proved to be just over 50 m.p.h., and a comfortable cruising speed on moderately good roads was 40 m.p.h., though this could be increased to 45 m.p.h., if road conditions permitted, without overtaxing the unit. Only after a great deal of low gear work was there any unpleasant smell in the driving compartment, and then it was noticed only when the Morgan was stationary.

Petrol consumption appeared to be in the region of 38 to 42 m.p.g.

Once the driver has accustomed himself to it, the Family Morgan could be held on the road with ease, and the only trouble on really bad surfaces was a tendency for the steering to be a little uncertain at speed, owing to tail movements. No wheel wobble was experienced at any speed, and even when driving all-out there was no need at all to be nervously on the alert or to grip the wheel tightly. The rather high gear for the steering increases the safety factor by making it more difficult to corner violently, and it certainly increases the machine's manœuvrability in traffic immensely. It is not exactly advisable to open wide out in low gear when the rear wheel is in a tramline, but even on the worst of tramlines and stone setts there is little danger of a skid if the driver makes certain of having his rear wheel out of the lines when there is any likelihood of his having to stop quickly. On normal wet roads there is no difference to be felt on corners unless they are taken too fast, when the rear wheel will move gently a few inches out of its correct path—a mild "tail-wag."

The driver soon accustoms himself to a certain hardness in the springing, and to the fact that three tracks "collect" more bumps than do two.

SPECIFICATION.
ENGINE: 85.5 × 85 mm. (980 c.c.) vee-twin side-valve J.A.P.
TRANSMISSION: By shaft, bevels, and ¼ × ⅜in. final chains.
LUBRICATION: By mechanical pump and sight feed.
GEAR BOX: Morgan two-speed. Ratios: 5 and 10 to 1.
CARBURETTER: Amal two-lever.
BRAKES: Front, internal expanding, 7in. diameter; rear, external contracting, 6½in. diameter,
TYRES: 27 × 4in.
WEIGHT (unladen): 7 cwt.
PRICE (with lighting, starter, speedometer, and side screens): £97 10s.
MAKERS: The Morgan Motor Co., Ltd., Malvern Link, Worcester.

weak the owner complains bitterly, and if they are too powerful he may get into trouble through over-eager application. The expert can be given powerful brakes, because he knows how to use them, but the novice must be catered for. Those on the Family Morgan were adequate and no more,-though the front ones could have had more bite with perfect safety. After the first hundred and fifty miles it was found necessary to attend to the brake on the rear wheel, as the pedal reached the floorboard before it was properly in action, but when correctly adjusted it could just be made to lock the wheel. On a gradient of 1 in 9, in neutral, it would pull the machine up in due course, but those on the front wheels just failed to do this; used together they could be quite smooth and powerful.

There is plenty of body room, and, unless grown-ups are put in the children's quarters, there is nothing cramped about it. Some little ingenuity is required for a big driver to get into his seat, but once there everything is beautifully placed, particularly the wheel; and the pedals do not make the ankles or legs ache.

The electric starter, a standard

Overlooking Stonleigh, Warwickshire.

Gear-changing with the plain dogs was, of course, perfectly simple, and when the situation was awkward there was no real need to have the throttle open when changing down. The clutch was on the harsh side; at first it tended to be either in or out, but later it became smoother and probably could, with the help of a little grease, be made quite progressive.

The question of brakes is a ticklish one. If they are

extra, proved to be an inestimable boon at all times.

Having praised and criticised where necessary, and treating the Family Morgan as a vehicle pure and simple, it is rather a surprise to remember its price. It is simplicity itself, is easy to handle, and provides a standard of comfort almost on a par with that of the small four-wheeler—with a far better performance on hills under full load.

Three Wheels v. Four. JULY 31st, 1930.

THE Light Car Club's meeting at Brooklands, held last Saturday, had a special interest in that it afforded one of the opportunities—all too rare in these days—for three and four-wheelers to match themselves together.

The result was instructive In the second race the winner, S. H. Allard on a super-sports Morgan, averaged exactly the same speed as the Brooklands Riley which carried off the following event, though this race was of five laps, as against the three of that won by Allard.

In general the Morgans, which were the sole runners in the three-wheeler classes, were undeniably fast, but, with the exception of H. C. Lones's machine, seemed to find the longer distances too much of a strain. Horton, Jackson, and Jay all had trouble of various kinds, while in the three-wheeler handicap there were only two finishers.

R. T. Horton (Morgan) leads another Morgan driver round the " Chronograph Villa" turn in a heat of the Grand Prix.

In the Grand Prix itself Lones's Morgan scored a well-merited win. The three-wheelers cornered safely and quite fast, the only bad driving on the bends being due to drivers of four-wheeled cars, some of whom found their brakes insufficient for the task. Those who had predicted failure for the three-wheelers were confounded. In spite of the handicap of two gears, as against the three and four of the cars, they were noticeably impressive in acceleration.

MORGANS EVEN CHEAPER TO BUY
Complete List of 1931 Prices and Models

THE main alterations for 1931 in the Morgan range concern the prices, for these have, in all cases, been considerably reduced and the cheapest model is now only £85. A few detail alterations have been effected in the cars themselves, mostly with regard to the Family model. This type now has a long bonnet, which eliminates the scuttle, the bonnet itself being hinged just below the windscreen.

The screen itself is sloped to a slighter angle and the sides of the bodywork are flush, having no visible screws or projections. Additional struts now support the dash, whilst two bonnet supports are secured to the bonnet sides to hold it upright when it is raised for reaching the petrol filler cap or making inspections of the engine. Cycle-type close-up fixed mudguards are now used on several types, the Family model being included, and the M chassis, which was introduced last year, is now fitted with both Aero and Family bodywork.

A glimpse under the bonnet of the new family model showing, amongst other things, the stiffening strut which is now employed.

The B chassis is retained unaltered and a two-seater standard body can be obtained on it, with an air-cooled J.A.P. engine at £85 or with a water-cooled engine at £90. For £10 extra an electric starter, side screens and speedo-

CATERING FOR DIFFERENT TASTES. (Above) The Aero model for 1931 and (below) the latest example of the family model—which is rapidly gaining in popularity.

meter may be obtained. The Aero bodywork is also available on the B chassis and this model is also unaltered, but the price is reduced to £105 with a sidevalve J.A.P. or o.h.v. Anzani engine, or £119 with the 10-40 h.p. o.h.v. J.A.P. The Family de luxe on the M chassis, with an air-cooled engine, is priced at £90, or with a water-cooled unit at £95.

With the 10-40 o.h.v. J.A.P. the price is £110, and £10 extra is asked for an electric starter, side screens and speedometer. The two-seater is also listed at the same figures.

On the M chassis the Aero model now has a vee screen and cycle-type mudguards; the prices are £110 with the side-valve J.A.P. or o.h.v. Anzani, or £124 with the 10-40 o.h.v. J.A.P. These figures include a speedometer and hood, whilst £8 extra is asked for the Lucas electric starter.

With the exception of the fitting of a vee screen no alterations have been made to the super-sports model, but the price has been reduced by £5 to £145.

Lea-Francis.

Although a new two-litre six-cylinder Lea-Francis is to be produced for the 1931 season the popular and well-known range of 12-40 h.p. four-cylinder models

is to be continued as well. Except for details the cars are substantially the same as during the past year; prices, too, have not been altered save in one instance—the sportsman's coupé, which now costs £425 instead of £420.

All bright parts on the whole range of cars are now chromium-plated and the windscreens on all models are of Triplex glass. The recently introduced Francis saloon has been furbished-up somewhat, furniture hide upholstery being included without extra charge. Rear fuel tanks are now to be found on every model, the feed to the carburetter being effected by means of Grav-vac suction-type tanks.

Another minor modification to the two-seater, fixed and drop-head coupés and the fabric saloon is the incorporation of the "Francis" type of faciaboard fitting, this component now being carried by pressings from the dash, so that it is completely insulated from the body.

The complete list of 1931 prices is as follows :—12-40 h.p. four-cylinder models : "Francis" saloon (1931 improved equipment and finish), £375 ; two-seater, £325 ; four-seater, £325 ; De Luxe four-seater, £335 ; coupé (fixed head), one spare wheel, £395 ; coupé (drop-head), one spare wheel, £395 ; fabric saloon, one spare wheel, £395 ; Sportsman's coupé, with one spare wheel, £425. 1½-litre supercharged models : two-seater, £495 ; four-seater, £495 ; Sportsman's coupé, £525 ; saloon, £595.

Bianchi.

The 10-30 h.p. Bianchi will remain substantially unchanged for 1931, although a number of small improvements have been effected. These include the fitting of a petrol gauge on the dash and a tell-tale light for the coil ignition, whilst the external appearance of the cars has been improved by a slightly taller and more imposing radiator. In addition, 28-in. by 5.25-in. wellbase tyres will be standardized. The actual prices are not yet available.

COMPETITORS in the Motor Cycling Club's classic 24-hour trials—the London-Exeter, the London-Land's End and the London-Edinburgh—if they are fortunate enough to qualify for a gold medal in the three events in one season, can compound their three gold medals and instead receive a "Triple Award." This, naturally, is a coveted trophy amongst members of the club.

How I should value such an award, the writer thought at the time of the last Show, if it could be captured on the three classes of vehicle, a solo motorcycle in the London-Exeter, a three-wheeler in the London-Land's End, and a four-wheeler in the London-Edinburgh.

Stage 1 happily was successful, but stage 2 at the time of writing is still in doubt. Whatever award may result from it, however, and no matter what stage 3 may bring forth, this year's London-Land's End trial will never be forgotten.

As the illustrations show, No. 117's chosen mount for the three-wheeler attempt was one of the very latest Morgan Super-sports models, a romantic racy low-built little beauty in battleship grey and scarlet. The dearest of the Morgan models, it costs, with full equipment, including an electric starter, £153. The refinement of an electric starter—which works extremely well, by the way—puts £8 on to the price of the cyclecar.

New Mechanical Features.

When the model was first taken over its various new features were viewed with great approval. Notable amongst them, of course, is the detachable rear portion of the frame, which is exceedingly robust, convenient and accessible. It provides easy chain adjustment, a much-improved method of supporting the back wheel, a silent adjustable bevel drive, a two-piece propeller shaft entirely free from whip and very easy access to the dog clutches and other parts needing lubrication. Further, it ensures definitely that the chain tension is always constant and unaffected by the action of the springs.

We made our way 45 miles to Virginia Water, the starting point of this year's London-Land's End trial, in torrents of rain, but in the best of spirits. The little machine behaved perfectly on the greasy roads, giving no anxiety concerning skidding and the great nobbly tyre on the back wheel paying no heed to tramlines. The hood was kept down as it restricted headroom and visibility, but the useful screen and the tall scuttle kept out almost all the rain whilst the car was under way.

With Virginia Water dropping astern, the powerful headlights throwing a splendid beam and the lusty

o.h.v. engine taking us over the ground at about 45 m.p.h. on quarter throttle, the world seemed indeed a very pleasant place. Inside all was snug. The rain had almost stopped and the driver's vision was not interrupted by the wet screen because, although it gives excellent protection, his line of vision is over the top of it.

The light of an electric torch showed that the dashboard drip-feed lubricator was taking care of the engine's needs, that the dynamo was charging with one amp. to spare over and above the requirements of the headlamps and that our maps and route cards were safely stowed beside the passenger's seat. Behind

the squab, sharing the space occupied somewhat extravagantly by the powerful starter battery, were two bulky haversacks, spare gauntlets and a heap of paraphernalia, whilst under the seats in two roomy compartments was a lavish tool kit and space for plenty more.

These under-the-seat toolboxes, incidentally, could be abolished and the seat lowered two or three inches if one wished. With the standard arrangement, however, the seats are so low that if the driver drops his arm over the side his finger-tips are on the road!

With this wonderfully low build the twists and turns on the way to Taunton were thoroughly enjoyed. The Morgan round any bend or curve was definitely faster than most four-wheelers, with no rolling at all and with the most admirable feeling of stability and security.

On the Hills.

It was not until the strenuous part of the trial began, however, that the cyclecar started really to unfold its charms. Grabhurst's gradient it devoured on a whiff of gas. On the two-mile pull up Dunkery Beacon, which set nearly all the cars boiling as they toiled their way up, it chafed at the 30 m.p.h. limit which was set and probably, if pressed, could have averaged 45 m.p.h. over the whole section.

Wellshead hair-pin was rounded with a triumphant swirl and a pound or two of its surface flung into the air as the back wheel bit the road and hurtled the little machine over the summit. Really it is a wonderful sensation to have some 40 b.h.p. at call and nothing to restrain it save $7\frac{1}{2}$ cwt. of rigid little motorcar!

Down Countisbury we trickled, not bothering to change down as the rear brake alone was more than sufficient for the 1 in $4\frac{1}{2}$ descent without the aid of the powerful f.w.b.

Lynmouth proved to be a repetition of Wellshead—just a matter of not turning on too much throttle in case the spectators should be alarmed. On Beggars' Roost, however, no such qualms for the onlookers' peace of mind was felt. The starting signal was given at the bottom, the clutch was let in and the throttle gradually opened until it reached its limit. With a bound, it seemed, this once-dreaded terror of the West was flattened and the f.w.b. hand lever was being grasped to check the speed for the right-hand turn on to the main road at the summit. Beggars' Roost to a super-sports Morgan is no more of an obstacle than is a mole hill to a greyhound.

There is no finer way to test the power, brakes and stamina of a car than to run it in the London to Land's End Trial. The photographs depict the ascents of (left to right): Ruses Mill, Hustyn, Beggars' Roost, and Bluehills Mine. A "broadside" of the car, showing its very low build and workmanlike lines, is given below.

They are splendid miles those 60-odd which the M.C.C. selects to include between Beggars' Roost and Launceston. The little Devon lanes wind and twist in all directions, dipping steeply, rising sharply, and giving a good car every opportunity to show the best that is in it. They left the writer's passenger a disillusioned man. He had started the run with the belief that three-wheelers are not stable—and arrived at Launceston declaring that with their £4 tax if everyone appreciated their advantages the Road Fund would be ruined!

And so to Ruses Mill and its preface of car parks, refreshment booths and what not, all pointing to a large crowd turned out to see a shambles. But again "fast" went down in the reporters' notebooks. And so it was on Hustyn, which brought 97 four-wheelers to a standstill. We trickled through the water-splash at the foot, turned on the gas and disappeared over the summit.

On Bluehills Mine No. 117 was not so clever. A disgraceful error of judgment concerning the amount of lock available involved rounding the bend in "wall of death" fashion with the off-side front wheel high up on the rocky wall which flanks the outside of the hair-pin. The little car was tilted to a perilous angle, but its wonderfully low centre of gravity saved the situation. The back wheel bit deep into the loose stony surface and flung us over the top in the by then familiar all-conquering manner.

Soon the End was reached and No. 117, with its numbers removed, was pottering back along the road to Penzance fit and ready for the 320-mile return journey, which it comfortably laughed aside in 7½ hours' running time on the following day.

For the whole run 53 m.p.g. of petrol was averaged and about 1,500 m.p.g. of oil. The toolbox was touched but once—to look at a plug at the foot of Countisbury, in case the long descent should have oiled it.

With the Land's End run behind us and before returning it to its owner, the Morgan was put through its paces and found to have a top gear (5 to 1) maximum speed of 76 m.p.h. with two up on a good road, and a bottom gear (10 to 1) maximum of rather more than 40 m.p.h.

With higher gears, which are very easily obtained, of course, by merely changing the sprockets, about 55 m.p.h. in bottom gear and over 80 m.p.h. in top gear would be obtainable. The 5 to 1 top gear, however, appeared to suit the car very well and gave a comfortable cruising speed in the neighbourhood of 60 m.p.h., with excellent slow pulling and first-rate acceleration even from a speed so low as 10 m.p.h.

We now come to criticism. Starting with the engine, it has a wonderful power output, magnificent acceleration and very good slow running. It is on the rough side, however, and there is more vibration than there should be.

The brakes are very good, but would be improved if the ratchet of the hand lever were more positive in its action. The springing and steering are both beyond reproach, but the steering column, probably because the reduction gearbox had been over-filled, was rather addicted to dripping grease into the driver's lap. The electrical equipment was very well behaved and the starter proved itself always capable of dealing with the lusty engine. The non-trip speedometer, however, was very erratic in its readings.

It is, perhaps, unfair to continue in this strain. One cannot expect a £153 machine which can hold its own and give a trouncing to most of the fastest cars on the road to be perfect in all its details.

An Enthusiast Modifies His Morgan

ALTHOUGH the super-sports Morgan is essentially a two-seater, it is possible, by the exercise of skill and ingenuity, to provide a third seat for a small passenger. A modification of this kind has been carried out very successfully by Mr. A. Norman Thompson, 52, Leander Road, Brixton Hill, London, S.W.2, who is an enthusiastic and energetic private owner.

The extra seat is arranged above the bevel box, a cockpit being formed by cutting away part of the top of the hinged tail. Ample legroom is provided by cutting an inverted U-shaped opening in the front seat squab.

By re-fitting the hood farther back the extra seat is fully protected, whilst to make up the length an extension piece is fitted to the front of the hood and arranged to clip over the top of the windscreen or to fold back, thus providing a form of opening roof which should be very useful in showery weather.

Neat aluminium valve covers and a badge bar figure amongst the special fittings on this Morgan.

Several mechanical alterations have also been made to the Morgan—which is a 1929 model—by its owner. A new rear brake of the internal expanding type is fitted. It consists of a drum machined from the solid and providing a braking surface of 8 ins. by 1¼ ins. The drum is secured to the low gear sprocket and is fitted with cast aluminium shoes faced with Ferodo.

A special re-arrangement of the control rods ensures a perfectly even braking force regardless of the vertical movement of the rear wheel on bad roads.

The need for periodically greasing the clutch has been overcome by Mr. Thompson by fitting an extension pipe to the crankcase breather so that oily vapour is blown into the clutch mechanism.

Another alteration in connection with the engine—a J.A.P.—concerns valve stem lubrication. Metal cups have been machined up to fit over the valve springs and under the bottom spring pads. The third, or inner, springs are discarded and thick felt washers are fitted over the valve stems and made a good push fit inside the inner springs. Oil is fed into the cups once a week, and Mr. Thompson finds that the stems remain effectively lubricated.

In the accompanying photograph can be seen the special aluminium valve covers which have been fitted, together with a neat cross-bar upon which the A.A. badge is mounted.

With regard to general running, Mr. Thompson says that his maximum timed speed has been 78 m.p.h. but that he has no difficulty in averaging 32 m.p.h. on a long journey without ever exceeding 45 m.p.h. Petrol consumption works out at 43 m.p.g. using a 175 jet and with the needle set in the second notch, not the third as is usually recommended.

It will be seen from the foregoing that Mr. Thompson is a skilled mechanic who makes his car his hobby—a sure method of obtaining a really satisfactory performance.

THE SPIRIT OF THE BIG RACING CAR!

NEW WORLD'S RECORDS

set up by Mrs. G. M. Stewart and Mr. W. D. Hawkes on the Montlhery Track, August 6th:—

5 Kilos at 113·52 m.p.h. = 182·704 k.p.h.
5 Miles „ 107·51 „ = 173·026 „
10 Kilos (from standing start) at 102·72 m.p.h. = 165·319 k.p.h.
10 Miles at 102·81 m.p.h. = 165·456 k.p.h.

And at Arpajon on August 24th:—

FLYING KILO

at **115·6** m.p.h.

FLYING MILE

at **114·8** m.p.h.

(Subject to confirmation).

The MORGAN RUNABOUT Super-Sports Model at £150 is built to provide the exhilarating speed and power desired by the sportsman. It embodies a wealth of experience acquired at that great racing centre, Brooklands, and in important road events all over the world. The special O.H.V. engine will attain speeds up to 80 m.p.h. and can be tuned to considerably exceed this speed. Tax is only £4, and running and maintenance charges are proportionately low, giving total figures equivalent to those of the motorcycle and sidecar. The new MORGAN List giving particulars of all 1930 models may be had post free—write TO-DAY for a copy.

The Morgan Runabout

MORGAN MOTOR CO., LTD.,
MALVERN LINK, WORCESTERSHIRE

Morgans with Three Speeds

Famous Three=wheeler's Break with Tradition : Three = speed and Reverse Gears, with Single Driving Chain: Two=speed Models Retained: Cylinder Angle Changed: Dry=sump Lubrication

The fitting of the three-speed and reverse gear has involved no very drastic alteration to the sturdy chassis.

TO state that the Morgan Motor Co. have designed a new chassis for 1932 would be quite unfair to the amazingly simple design which has characterised this most successful three-wheeler from its earliest days. The essential features of the three-tube construction are unchanged, but so far as engine and transmission are concerned the design has been brought so much up to date that it is difficult to regard the machine as a whole as anything but new. Those who know and love the old two-speed Morgans will still be able to obtain this type unaltered from the 1931 design, at very modest

The 1932 three-speed o.h.v. super-sports model.

prices, but the main range for the future will include a three-speed and reverse gear box with a single driving chain, and a redesigned engine which is available in all the usual types.

The biggest change lies in the transmission. Except that the layshaft is mounted directly above the mainshaft, the new three-speed box is of conventional design.

Running in deep-groove ball bearings throughout, the mainshaft is very well supported, for, in addition to the spigot bush, which is surrounded by the front main bearing, there are two other bearings, one at the tail of the gear box and one behind the David Brown worm gear. The deep-groove bearings take both thrust and radial loads, and the excellent support for the shafts makes the box extremely silent in action.

Two long bronze floating bushes surround the fixed layshaft, and lie between it and a continuous sleeve carrying the four layshaft pinions. Here, again, the rigidity of the construction encourages silence, and holes drilled from the bottom of the teeth to the centre of the sleeve

ensure adequate lubrication through the pumping action of the gear wheels. The reverse intermediate pinion is mounted on a separate stationary shaft.

Providing a reduction of just over 2 to 1, the worm wheel is mounted above the worm, and is housed in a circular aluminium casting formed in one with the gear box. The wheel is bolted to the cross-shaft and is carried on a deep-groove bearing on the near side and a roller bearing on the drive side. The ball race takes both thrust and radial loads, and both bearings have large grease-proof packings on their outer faces. Each of these journals is carried in a circular bronze end-plate, the outer periphery of the bosses being used as bearings for the radius rods. Since these radius-rod bearings are 3⅜in. in diameter, they should last almost indefinitely, but, should wear take place after a very considerable mileage, the bronze end-plates are easily detachable and renewable.

On the near side is a fabric wheel for the dynamo drive, the dynamo itself being mounted on a casting rigidly bolted to the side of the gear box. On the off-side the front sprocket for the final drive is mounted on parallel splines so that it may be removed with ease if a change of ratio is desired.

Keyed into the front end of the gear box driving shaft is a forward extension shaft carrying at its foremost end a four-jaw dog drive, and immediately behind the dog is a ball race which is housed in the propeller-shaft tube. This extension serves the double purpose of providing a

further support for the first motion gear shaft, and also of shortening the propeller shaft, and thus avoiding whirl.

There is no change in the rear portion of the frame, except that the twin radius rods are bolted rigidly together with a solid forging mounted immediately behind the worm box. It will be remembered that the system of mounting the radius rods concentrically with the cross-shaft centre was introduced last year, and this system, which maintains unvarying chain centres under varying spring loads, is retained, as is the drop-out rear spindle and the large internal-expanding rear brake.

Since there are two sliding members on the main gear shaft, one for first and reverse, and one for second and top, a gate change is required, and this has been arranged in an extraordinarily neat and practical manner. The selector rods are attached to flat strip-steel members which lie parallel with the propeller-shaft enclosing tube. At their forward end they pass through a light sheet steel bracket clamped to the tube itself, and between the two flat steel members is a third, fixed to the supporting plate.

The change-speed lever is pivoted above this bracket and has a downwardly pro-

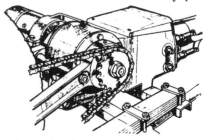

The new gear box with worm drive to the cross shaft. The dynamo is bolted to the side of the box. Note the section of the chain stay.

jecting lever of the same width as the strips. Sufficient rocking motion is provided at the lever pivot to enable the drop arm to engage with slots in either of the flat striking rods; this scheme provides a gate of the normal car type in a very compact way.

On the side of the tube opposite to the gear lever is clamped the hand-brake lever, which is of sensible length and is now provided with a spring-controlled ratchet.

In the forward end of the chassis there are no outstanding alterations except that the mudguards are now carried entirely on the chassis, having a rigid supporting bar at their rearmost extremities joining them to the lower frame tubes. It will be realised that the underslung worm arrangement permits of a slight drop in the rear end of the propeller-shaft enclosing tube, thus providing more room in the seating compartment.

Considerable changes have been made in the special J.A.P. engines employed. Though they embody all well-known J.A.P. features, the cylinder angle has been altered from 50° to 60°. Dry-sump lubrication by Pilgrim pump is incorporated, and there are two separate camshafts, through one of which the starting handle is connected to the crankshaft, while the other is employed to drive the combined distributor and make-and-break for the Lucas coil ignition system which is now standardised.

The crank case of this unit will be the same for all the new models, as also will be the capacity of 1,096 c.c., but either side- or overhead-valve engines will be available, with water or air cooling. In the case of the air-cooled side-valve engines, the cylinder heads will be detachable above the valve seats as in modern car practice.

It is stated that the change of cylinder angle has enabled a vast improvement in balance to be attained, and that the tick-over and starting with coil ignition have been greatly improved. Incidentally, full electric starting is standardised on all new models.

The new chassis will be available in the following forms :—

	£
Family model, air-cooled side-valve engine ..	95
Family model, water-cooled side-valve engine	100
Aero model, water-cooled side-valve engine ..	115
Aero model, " 10-40 " water-cooled o.h.v. engine	125
Sports Family model, water-cooled side-valve engine	120
Sports Family model, " 10-40 " water-cooled o.h.v. engine	130
Super-sports model, specially tuned o.h.v. engine ..	145

All the foregoing models have Lucas electric starting and lighting. a speedo-meter, and screen-wiper. The Family model will also be available in two-seater form at the same prices. In this case the rear seats are replaced by a luggage locker, while the top of the tail provides ample space for further luggage accommodation.

Prices for the two-speed models, which remain unaltered in construction, are : Family model (air-cooled side-valve engine), £75; Family model (water-cooled side-valve engine), £80; Aero model (water-cooled side-valve engine), £95; Aero model (10-40 h.p. water-cooled overhead-valve engine), £110.

As already mentioned, the chassis which has been described is common throughout the new range, but in the case of the super-sports model the overall height of the chassis is decreased by dropping the axles and rear springing.

The new Morgans are a model of straightforward engineering practice, and it would be difficult to devise a more simple and practical chassis than that which is illustrated in these pages.

1935 Super Sports

1935 SUPER SPORTS—in wartime guise. The beautifully finished 50-deg vee-twin, water-cooled, o.h.v. Matchless engine, with its 990c.c. and compression ratio of 6 to 1 gave a maximum speed in the seventies, coupled with surprising smoothness and flexibility. For several years this particular car gave much pleasure to the editor of this book . . . for a price, new, of £130-odd and a Road Fund Tax of £4.

MORGAN MODIFIED FOR DIRT-TRACKS

"The Blower" Gives Details of a Four-wheeled "Morgan" built by an Australian Cinder-track Expert for Use in This Country

Two views showing the neat appearance of the four-wheeled "Morgan." The car is considerably crab tracked and has remarkable stability.

LAST week, in a quiet corner of Bayswater, I made the acquaintance of what is probably a unique vehicle—a four-wheeled Morgan—and, as can be gathered from the illustrations on this page, the strange machine is by no means repellent, but has, indeed, all the attributes of a first-rate little sports car. The machine is the work of an Australian visitor, Mr. T. N. Sulman, who has brought to the task of building the car a profound knowledge of racing with four-wheelers on the cinder tracks "Down Under." Talking of dirt-track racing, Mr. Sulman spoke airily of entering bends at 80 m.p.h. in a Salmson and of resultant skids!

Mr. Sulman's idea in building the Morgan four-wheeler is to race the machine on dirt tracks in this country, and preliminary trials at Wembley have shown that the lap times of the car are within a very few seconds of leading dirt-track riders' match times!

Remarkable Steadiness.

A short run in the little vehicle was most interesting, the only disappointment being that my numerous inches forbade my fitting the somewhat confined space in the driving seat.

The stability of the Morgan was outstanding, and dry tarmac corners could be slid at remarkable speeds without the least sense of the car's lifting. The two Morgan driving chains allowed for ratios of 6 and 7.6, on which gears the acceleration of the car was little short of phenomenal, and, I should think, ideally suitable for work on a dirt track.

The original body of the 1926 Aero Morgan has been retained, and although it has a somewhat "cocked-up" appearance at the rear, suggests that exceptionally nice body lines could be developed on the four-wheeled chassis.

The original machine had been fitted with geared steering, using a Ford reduction box, and front-wheel brakes were fitted. In the reconstructed car the

rear wheel and forks were removed and a G.N. back axle, complete with radius rods, substituted. In order to take the extra strains imposed by this layout, the rear cross-members have been strengthened by stays to the tubular chassis members, and the rear springs are secured to the ends of the cross-members instead of close to the bevel box, as in the standard Morgan.

The radius rods work on bushes at the end of a rod fitted through the bevel box in place of the rear-fork swivel pin. The rod is bolted to special plates fitted to the extreme ends of the cross-members. In order to fit the narrower chassis of the Morgan the spring pads of the G.N. axle have been moved closer to the centre, with distance pieces inserted between the hubs and the brake drums, and between the hubs and the axle bearings. The whole of the back-axle assembly can be taken out and the original single wheel and forks replaced without any structural alterations.

Apart from the back axle, the only alteration to the car has been the fitting of an accelerator pedal, which has the effect of giving a very rapid opening and closing action, as rapid acceleration and deceleration are essential in racing on small dirt tracks—and the fitting of an outside gear lever.

There are four sprockets on the back axle, which can be arranged to give the following choice of ratios, in conjunction with the two bevel-box sprockets:—3.5, 5-1, 5.3 and 6 on the high-gear chain, and on the low chain, 6, 7.6 and 9-1.

A 7-inch Crab-track.

The car is considerably crab-tracked. The front track is 4 ft. and the rear 3 ft. 5 ins.; the wheelbase measures 6 ft. 9 ins.

Mr. Sulman explained that there were many features of the Morgan which, in conjunction with his own modifications tended to make the machine ideal for dirt-track work. He was particularly struck with the ease of altering gear

ratios in the G.N. back axle, the low centre of gravity of the whole job, its wide track and short wheelbase, and that the lusty big-twin J.A.P. engine will pull a car out of a skid without losing r.p.m.

At the moment Mr. Sulman's appearance in public at the wheel of this interesting little car is delayed through negotiations concerning insurance matters, but he hopes soon to be able to give a demonstration on British tracks. Any track managers or others interested in the car (Mr. Sulman would like to get in touch with any concern interested in marketing the reconstructed Morgan as a four-wheeled sports car) should communicate with him at Mansfield House, 24b, Clifton Gardens, London, W.9; telephone, Abercorn 2391. THE BLOWER.

T.T. Broadcast.

The concluding hour of the R.A.C. T.T.—which will be run on the Ards Circuit, Belfast, on August 22nd—will be broadcast from Daventry and other stations relaying the National programme.

A.A. Going Ahead.

The total membership of the A.A. is now 437,091, an increase of 18,038 since last year. These figures were disclosed at the annual meeting which was held in London last week when it was also made public that during the past 12 months the A.A. patrols had cost some £600,000, and had covered over 27,000,000 miles.

Saloons in the Ascendant.

Of the 15,487 new cars which came on to the roads during the month of May this year, 14,288 were saloons. Last year, in May, 17,645 new cars were bought, and of these 15,517 were saloons. Cars taxed at £8 easily dominated May sales, 4,011 new 8 h.p. cars coming on to the roads.

THREE-WHEELERS FOR 1932

A Review of the Morgan and Coventry-Victor Exhibits at the Motorcycle Show Next Week. The 1932 B.S.A. Range

ON Monday next, the Motor Cycle and Cycle Show opens at Olympia, and it is there, of course, that the three-wheelers are to be found in their latest form. This year, however, only the Morgan and Coventry-Victor concerns will be showing, the B.S.A. cyclecar being a notable absentee.

It is already well known that the Morgan Motor Co., Ltd., has introduced a three-speed and reverse chassis for 1932. This was described in some detail in our issue of October 9th.

The general layout of the chassis follows closely upon the usual Morgan practice; that is to say, the framework is of tubular construction, the "backbone" of the vehicle consisting of a heavy tube through which the propeller shaft passes from the clutch to the gearbox.

In the normal two-speed model a bevel and pinion within the box provide the necessary right-angle drive, and two chains convey the power from the bevel shaft to the rear wheel, either chain drive being engaged by means of dog clutches.

On the three-speed chassis the gearbox is mounted in place of the normal bevel box, whilst behind it, and in the same casting, is housed the worm drive. The worm wheel shaft carries a sprocket on one side, over which a chain runs to another sprocket on the rear wheel, whilst on the opposite side is a helical toothed gear wheel for driving the dynamo.

Direct-drive on Top.

Second, third and reverse gears are engaged by sliding the wheels into mesh in the usual manner, whilst direct top-gear drive is obtained by means of a dog clutch. The gearbox, in fact, follows current practice throughout. There are two gear selectors, connected by strip-steel rods to a lever mounted on the central frame tube, adjacent to the brake lever.

The steel worm meshes with a phosphor-bronze worm wheel, and a reduction of two to one is provided. The thrust of the worm is taken by a large ball race, whilst the worm wheel on the cross-shaft is carried in a ball race on the near side and in a roller bearing on the off side.

The dynamo is carried in a special cradle bolted to the side of the gearbox, and the driving pinion is of special material to ensure silent working and long life, without the need for lubrication. The rear forks are of girder section arranged to pivot about the worm-shaft housing, thus ensuring that the chain tension remains constant, irrespective of rear-wheel movement on bumpy roads. Underslung quarter-elliptic springs are used, and the rear wheel is carried on large ball journal bearings, provision for chain adjustment being made by means of slotted fork-ends and thrust-screws.

On the new Morgans a three-speed and reverse gearbox is fitted and the final drive is by single chain. Note the robust dynamo bracket.

The standard gear ratios provided are—4.85, 8 and 13.1 to 1 on the Family model, whilst on the two-seater models the ratios are 4.58, 7.5 and 12.4. It will be appreciated that with a single chain drive an alteration of the overall gear ratios can be made quite simply by substituting another size of driving sprocket.

The J.A.P. engines, which have been standardized for 1932, are produced especially for the Morgan Co. They have cylinders set at an angle of 60 degrees to one another, and the capacity is 1,096 c.c. (85.7 mm. bore and 95 mm. stroke). These dimensions are the same on all types of engine; that is to say, air or water-cooled, side valve or overhead valve.

No alterations have been made to the valve timing gear, which is still of the two-cam type, in accordance with normal J.A.P. practice. The engines are arranged for direct handle starting, a large boss being formed on the timing-case cover to take a detachable handle, which engages with the timing gear, thus providing a two-to-one turning effort. Another modification is the use of Lucas coil ignition, the distributor being mounted on the timing case and controlled through the medium of a Bowden cable from the steering column.

The engines are lubricated on the dry-sump principle by means of a duplex Pilgrim pump. One half of the pump draws oil from a one-gallon tank mounted in the scuttle and feeds it to the engine, whilst the other half of the pump draws the oil from the sump and returns it to the tank.

As usual, the Morgan Motor Co., Ltd., is offering a wide range of body types for 1932. The cheapest model is the Family, which, with an air-cooled, side-valve engine is priced at £75, or at £80 with a water-cooled engine. The Aero model, with water-cooled, side-valve engine, costs £95, whilst for £110 a 10-40 h.p. water-cooled o.h.v. engine can be obtained in the same chassis.

Three-speed Models.

The two models just mentioned have the standard type of Morgan two-speed chain drive; a three-speed Family model is available with an air-cooled, side-valve engine at £95, or water-cooled at £100.

An intriguing model is the sports Family, in which a special chassis 4 ins. longer than the standard sports model is used. With a water-cooled, side-valve engine it costs £120, or £130 with a 10-40 h.p. o.h.v. engine. The Aero model is available as a three-speeder at £115 with a water-cooled, side-valve engine, and at £125 with a 10-40 h.p. o.h.v. water-cooled engine.

Finally, there is the very popular super-sports model, which is now manufactured only as a three-speeder, and which is priced at £145. The modifications include a chassis 2½ ins. lower than standard, special

front axles, shock absorbers in front, and a high-compression, specially tuned o.h.v. 10-40 h.p. engine.

On all three-speed chassis Lucas electric lighting and starting sets are standardized, whilst the equipment also includes hood, speedometer and screen wiper. Starters are not fitted as standard on the two-speed models.

At the Motor Cycle and Cycle Show the Morgan Motor Co., Ltd., will occupy Stand 51 on the ground floor.

Since the first Coventry-Victor Midget was road-tested and described in *The Light Car and Cyclecar* last August, certain changes have been effected in its appearance. These are due chiefly to a new design of dummy radiator and to considerable improvements in the body. The radiator shell has slightly inclined sides and a centre rib, the general effect being attractive.

As for the body, the seat is both wider and lower, while the squab is deeper, the line of the tail having been altered to conform with this change. The result is a better body, both in appearance and in comfort.

The chassis of the f.w.d. B.S.A. The front brake is on the off side of the differential housing and the starter motor can be plainly seen.

It will be recalled that the Midget is obtainable for £75 with either an o.h.v. 600 c.c. engine or a side-valve unit of 688 c.c. Both engines are, of course, of the horizontally opposed type, in which the Coventry-Victor concern has specialized for some 20 years.

On September 18th we described the full four-seater "Family" model which had been added to the Coventry-Victor range. This model is, of course, still available, but it can now be obtained either with a 750 c.c. engine or with a new engine of nearly 1,000 c.c. capacity. In each case the price remains at £105, complete with hood, side curtains, and full electrical equipment.

Both engines have water-cooled and side-valve cylinders, horizontally opposed. Large plain bearings are used, the lubrication being effected under pressure. An attractive feature of the new design is that the valve,

The latest version of the Coventry-Victor Midget has a new and attractive radiator. The complete car sells for £75.

The 1932 edition of the Super Sports Morgan—one of the most handsome three-wheelers on the road. The chassis is lower than ever and now, of course, has a three-speed and reverse gearbox.

stems and tappets are completely enclosed by a quickly detachable cast-aluminium cover, which fits against abutments formed on the cylinder and the crankcase.

A single-plate clutch conveys the drive to the bevel box through a propeller shaft carried in fabric universal joints. The bevel shaft is fitted with two sprockets engaged by dog clutches and driving the rear wheel by means of heavy roller chains.

The reverse gear is mounted on the outside of the bevel box; it is engaged by meshing a pinion with a pair of bevel pinions on the bevel shaft, the drive being taken through the low-gear chain.

It will be recalled that the chassis frame is carried right back and completely surrounds the rear wheel, which is, however, readily detachable and can be lifted up through the floor of the rear compartment of the body.

Quarter-elliptic springs are anchored on each side to the rearmost part of the frame, and their forward ends bear on lugs on the fork which carries the rear wheel. The fork is pivoted to the main frame on each side so that its bearings are widely spaced and also coincide with the axis of the chain sprockets. In this way, chain tension is not affected by spring deflections.

A Super-sports Model.

The new large engine can also be obtained in the super-sports two-seater. With a three-speed gearbox and equipped with electric lighting and starting, hood, screen and side curtains, this model costs £115. For £120 a similar car can be obtained with an o.h.v. engine of the same capacity.

Eight models will be on view on the Coventry-Victor stand, which is No. 41. In addition, an example of the new three-speed chassis is to be shown in polished form. The finished cars exhibited will be a Family de luxe, a full four-seater, a sportsman's coupé, a sports model, a super-sports model, and a 5-cwt. commercial van. There will also be two examples of the air-cooled Midget.

The B.S.A. three-wheeler is gaining rapidly in popularity. It is, of course, the only front-wheel-drive machine of its type, the engine, gearbox, differential, and so on, being mounted as a single unit.

The engine is an air-cooled Vee twin, with push-rod-operated overhead valves, and is rated at 9 h.p. The three-speed and reverse gearbox is mounted forward of the engine, the drive being conveyed from it to a worm-driven differential from which side shafts carried in universal joints are connected to the front wheels.

Suspension Details.

Front suspension is by means of two pairs of super-imposed quarter-elliptic springs, whilst at the rear is a single girder fork hinged on a bracket bolted to the end of the frame members. A single quarter-elliptic spring is used at the rear; it is housed within a large tube forming part of the frame. The inner end of the spring works in a felt-lined steel slipper, to which it is attached by means of a Silentbloc bearing, which, of course, requires no lubrication. The wheels are detachable and interchangeable.

Brakes are provided on all three wheels, or, to be more accurate, there is a single brake drum at the front mounted outside the differential casing and taking effect on both front wheels. This and the rear-wheel brake are connected to the pedal, whilst the hand lever operates the rear brake only.

There is a good choice of body types on the B.S.A. chassis, the latest addition being the special sports-type priced at £115. There is also another sports model at £105, and a Family model, providing accommodation for two adults and two children, at the same price.

The latest Ministry of Transport returns show that three-wheelers are increasing considerably in popularity, no fewer than 239 machines having been sold in September, as against 75 for the same month last year.

In view of the improvements which have been incorporated in the 1932 models, it is safe to prophesy a still greater popularity for these fast and economical vehicles.

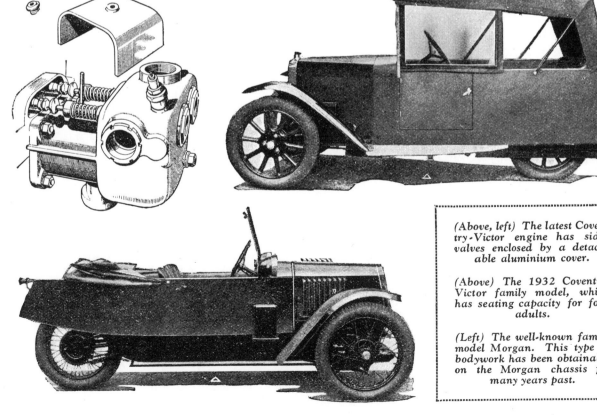

(Above, left) The latest Coventry-Victor engine has side-valves enclosed by a detachable aluminium cover.

(Above) The 1932 Coventry-Victor family model, which has seating capacity for four adults.

(Left) The well-known family model Morgan. This type of bodywork has been obtainable on the Morgan chassis for many years past.

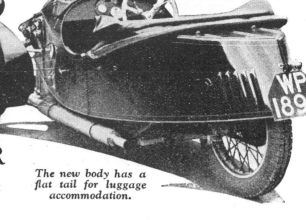

The new body has a flat tail for luggage accommodation.

Get to Know
THE LATEST SPORTS TWO-SEATER MORGAN

First Road Test of a New Fast Touring Type

AT the Show great interest was displayed in the latest Morgan chassis, incorporating a three-speed and reverse gearbox. For various reasons it has not been possible to carry out a road test until the present, and since the time of the Show other changes have been made.

The body of the model tested is of an entirely new type, to be known as the Sports Two-seater, and it is understood that this will replace the Aero model. In appearance, so far as the forward part is concerned, it resembles the Aero, but the tail is more reminiscent of the two-seater de luxe. A single door is fitted on the near side, but two doors are available to order, if they are required. In the same way, there is to be a choice of a vee-type windscreen, similar to that fitted on the machine illustrated, or a flat screen, more akin to that of the two-seater de luxe. This last variation naturally calls for different types of hood.

At the front of the machine two changes were noticed. The induction pipe of the 60-degree engine is now water-jacketed so as to improve the carburation. This jacket takes the form of a rectangular cast aluminium box, which is quite neat and which serves also to shield the body of the carburetter from the direct blast of cold air.

The other front alteration referred to is in the mounting of the headlamps. An additional tubular stay rises from the front axle framework to the mudwing, which is thus supported very rigidly. From the top of this tube a short bracket projects inwards and carries the headlamp.

Less obvious is the provision of an extra take-off spring for the rear brake. This spring is mounted on the cam lever and is, of course, auxiliary to the other springs which operate directly upon the shoes inside the drum. It serves to ensure that the shoes do not at any time drag and thus absorb power.

Inside the new gearbox there are one or two changes which, although they may appear to be of a minor nature, are, nevertheless, important in that they prevent oil leakage. Instead of the old type of felt packing, a special shaped leather washer is now employed. This has an L section so that part of it fits round the shaft like a bearing, and is held firmly against the shaft by means of a coil spring which surrounds it. In consequence, all leakage of the lubricant has been eliminated.

Washers of this type are now used on the propeller shaft where it enters the box, and on both ends of the cross-shaft which carries the worm wheel. A similar washer is also used on the brake side of the rear-wheel hub.

The model tested was fitted with a 10-40 h.p. o.h.v. water-cooled engine and is priced at £125. A similar car with a side-valve engine is to be marketed at £115 complete. Both engines, of course, are of the new 60-degree type introduced last year and have two-cam timing gear. The bore is 85.7 mm. and the stroke 95 mm., giving a cubic capacity of 1,096 c.c.

It will be remembered that the new three-speed gearbox follows conventional car practice, the indirect gears being engaged by sliding them into mesh and dogs being used for the direct drive. Behind the gearbox proper is an aluminium housing for the steel worm and its phosphor-bronze wheel mounted on a cross-shaft above. A single chain drives the rear wheel from the off side, and a helical-toothed pinion drives the dynamo on the other side.

Thanks to the chain drive it is, of course, a simple matter to raise or lower the complete range of gear ratios by changing the cross-shaft sprocket. An 18-tooth sprocket is standard and this provides ratios of 4.58, 7.5 and 12.4 to 1 forward, with a reverse gear of 16½ to 1.

Although not of the Super Sports type the engine of the model tested ran best on one of the various anti-knock spirits. In point of fact, National Benzole mixture was used during most of our test, and on this the Morgan behaved splendidly. Quite one of the most remarkable features of its performance is the excellent pulling in top gear at low speeds. To obtain the full benefit in this direction it is, of course, desirable to make proper use of the ignition lever, and the air lever should not be neglected.

Very much the same applies with regard to accelera-

tion. Given reasonable driving skill, it is doubtful whether the same standard of performance in this respect is obtainable on four wheels at anything less than three times the price of the Morgan.

With reference to the following figures, it must be borne in mind that the engine was not thoroughly run-in. Therefore a certain improvement might be expected later. Probably because of the 60-degree angle between the cylinders, the engine ran remarkably smoothly at low speeds. At about 45 m.p.h., however, considerable vibration was noticeable, and this was magnified by the drumming of something behind the dash. At higher speeds this unpleasantness disappeared.

With so new an engine—our test extended for a bare 300 miles—it was undesirable to leave the throttle fully open for long. In consequence, it is likely that the absolute maximum speed was not reached. Nevertheless, 65 m.p.h. was attained quite comfortably.

A Useful "Second."

The middle ratio is very well chosen, for really steep hills can be ascended at some 40 m.p.h. or more. The change from top to second is a particularly easy one. Taking all these things into consideration it is not surprising that the Morgan is capable of putting up some very respectable cross-country averages.

With regard to bottom gear, which, despite its comparatively high ratio of 12.4 to 1, is of the "dreadnought" variety, there was one defect on the particular model which we tested. Owing, probably, to some small fault in the gate mechanism, the change from second to first was accompanied by some uncertainty. On more than one occasion, in fact, the middle ratio remained engaged when the lever was moved through the gate. Fortunately, no harm was done.

While criticizing, reference must also be made to the position of the contact breaker. This is a matter which is admittedly unlikely to cause trouble in the ordinary way, but for those who ford an occasional stream additional waterproofing is desirable.

Although this particular car has the narrow track it looks as low and sleek as the Super Sports model. The close-up wings give very good protection and the front of the hood fits tightly to the screen.

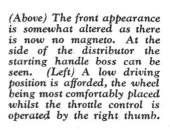

(Above) The front appearance is somewhat altered as there is now no magneto. At the side of the distributor the starting handle boss can be seen. (Left) A low driving position is afforded, the wheel being most comfortably placed whilst the throttle control is operated by the right thumb.

Reverting to the transmission system, it was a great advantage to be able to reverse when manœuvring the Morgan in a restricted space. Even so small and handy a machine is all the better for being able to proceed backwards as well as forwards in such circumstances. Another factor which undoubtedly assisted very much on such an occasion was an experimental clutch of a new type which is being tested out. Of this for the present nothing more need be said. If, and when, it becomes available to the public, it will be fully described in *The Light Car and Cyclecar.*

Before leaving the mechanical side of the model, it must be said that the engine was invariably easy to start. From cold it is desirable to flood the carburetter and to operate the exhaust lifter before pressing the starter button. When the engine is warm the starter is capable of turning it over, even if the exhaust lifter is neglected, but it is, of course, a help

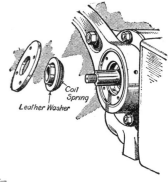

A spring-controlled leather washer is now used to prevent leakage of oil from the end of the mainshaft of the gearbox.

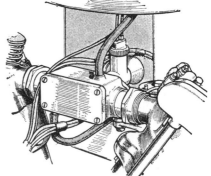

The induction pipe is provided with a water heated jacket which is connected to the radiator.

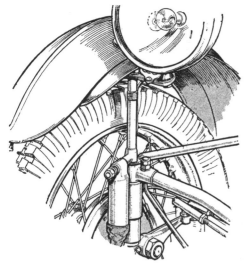

A substantial tubular support for the front mudguards cuts out all tendency to dither and forms a rigid headlamp bracket.

to the battery to lift the valves always. In any case the ignition should be retarded and the air lever brought back.

When taking over the vehicle at the works we were informed that the Amal carburetter needle was set rather high and that it should be lowered when the engine was run-in. Although this was not done, the consumption of fuel averaged about 55 m.p.g. in ordinary use.

Turning to matters affecting the body, access to the seats might possibly be a little easier if the door opening were carried farther forward. Once inside, however, there is plenty of room and reasonable comfort. Behind the seat squab is a space in which one large or two medium-sized suitcases can be carried.

For regular all-weather use it is probable that the flat screen, which is optional, would be somewhat better than the vee-type with the hood which accompanies it. Apart from the fact that the latter interfered with the action of the windscreen wiper, however, it was satisfactory, except in city streets, where it was found to restrict the driver's view of traffic emerging from side turnings.

On the open road or in country lanes the Morgan is a delight to handle. Its steering is accurate and, although not unduly heavy, it gives the driver the impression that he is driving a really big car. On rough roads the control is undoubtedly improved by the excellence of the suspension. Pot-holes and even railway crossings are scarcely felt by the occupants, and it is doubtful whether any light four-wheeled car gives one a more comfortable ride.

Above all, however, we must emphasize that the 1932 Morgan, although more ambitious in its specification, has lost none of its charm. It is still the nimble sporty little car that has enjoyed the enthusiasm of the keenest types of owner for a matter of 20 years.

Shelsley Walsh Regulations

AS was mentioned in this journal last week, the regulations for the Open Hill-climb at Shelsley on June 25th are available on application to Mr. Leslie Wilson, hon. secretary of the Midland Automobile Club, 415, Stratford Road, Birmingham. Entries close on June 16th.

The regulations are not being distributed broadcast, so we give herewith a summary of their contents.

There will be seven classes—subdivided into "racing" and "sports"—as follow:—850 c.c., 1,100 c.c., 1,500 c.c., 2 litres, 3 litres, 5 litres and over 5 litres.

In addition to class awards there are eight special prizes: the Shelsley International Championship Cup and £105 for fastest climb of the day, the British Championship Cup and £25 for best time by a British sports car, the T.T. Cup for best performance by a car raced in any international event in 1931-32, the Open Cup for the best aggregate of two

runs, the Garvagh Challenge Cup for the best over-1½-litre sports model, the C.P. Type Challenge Cup for the fastest 1½-litre car, the Ladies Cup and the Fray Team Challenge Cup.

There is a separate entry fee for those making a bid for these trophies. In the ordinary classes the trade entry fee is £5 and non-trade £2, but there is no entry fee if entered for the Shelsley Championship Cup.

An inclusive fee of 10 guineas (trade) or 8 guineas (non-trade) entitles competitors to enter a car for all appropriate cups.

Practice runs will be allowed—in the car entered—on the day before the event. Three-wheelers are barred.

In the normal course of events each car will be allowed two climbs where it has clocked under 60 secs. (65 secs. for the "850s") on the first run.

MANY MORGAN MODIFICATIONS FOR NEXT SEASON

A Single-plate Clutch and Entirely New Bodies on the Three-speed Chassis. Magna Wheels

A NEW MODEL. —— *The Sports two-seater, which has a new design of two-door body whilst the tail is shaped to carry the spare wheel. The price, in o.h.v. form, is £120.*

A NOTABLE feature of the Morgan programme for 1933 is that, although the old two-speed chassis will be available to special order, only the three-speed model will be catalogued. It will be supplied with four different types of body, the Super Sports, the Sports two-seater, the Sports Family, and the Family model.

Several changes are to be noted in the chassis itself. Foremost amongst them is the use of a dry single-plate clutch instead of the cone clutch which has figured in the Morgan specification for just 21 years. The clutch pedal operates three toggle levers through the agency of a carbon bush which requires no lubrication.

The levers withdraw a metal plate which normally is forced by six helical springs against a light disc which carries two friction rings, one on each side.

Chassis Alterations.

The forward end of the chassis is improved, in that the wing stays have been increased considerably in size. They are tubular and continue right through the bearing for the sliding axle, which now has rather less camber. The connection from the steering box to the off-side front wheel is also modified, and as a result of these various changes it is understood that the steering is very much lighter than in the past.

In recent years two separate chassis frames have been used, one for the Super Sports and the other for standard models. There is now only one type, however, and this is half an inch higher at the front than was the 1932 Super Sports. The other 1933 models are consequently much lower than their predecessors.

In appearance the new Morgans differ very considerably from the earlier types, not only because of the new body designs, but also because they have Dunlop Magna detachable wheels. The hubs have been redesigned, of course, to suit the Magna wheels, and a spare is carried on the tail.

To change the rear wheel it must first be removed from the forks, exactly as in previous models. The hub can then be separated from the wheel and attached to the spare. The tyre size is 26 ins. by 4.00 ins.

Other chassis details which should be mentioned include the adoption of a new type of ignition distributor which is said to be completely waterproof. In the gearbox there is a different type of oil-retaining seal, and the dynamo is driven by a compressed fabric gear wheel instead of a fibre wheel.

So far as the Super Sports model is concerned, there are very few alterations to the bodywork. It is, however, rather wider at the front, so that there is more foot room. A stainless-steel radiator shell is used, and the chromium-plated exhaust pipes are carried back along the body waistline, the silencers being behind the seats. A spare wheel is carried on top of the tail.

At the other extreme is the Family model, which has been entirely re-designed so as to improve both comfort and appearance. Undoubtedly the bonnet lines are much better, and the tail is also a great improvement. Behind the rear panel is mounted the spare wheel, and the panel itself can be detached so as to gain access to the rear wheel. In the bonnet there is a small sliding door, so that the petrol filler-cap can be reached without lifting the bonnet.

The New Sports Models.

Between the two models just described are the Sports two-seater and the Sports Family. The former of these may be best described as having the front end of the Super Sports and a tail very like that of the Family model. Instead of the rear seats there is ample space for luggage and a fairly wide door is now provided on both sides. Except for the fact that it has rear seats and therefore less luggage accommodation, the Sports Family model is exactly like the Sports two-seater.

As already mentioned, the two-speed chassis will be available if specially ordered, but only with an air-cooled engine and Family body, its price with hood, screen and electric light being £80.

The prices for the 1933 models are as follow :—Super-sports, £135 ; Sports two-seater, side-valve, £110 ; Sports two-seater, o.h.v., £120 ; Sports Family, side-valve, £115 ; Sports Family, o.h.v., £125 ; Family model, air-cooled, £98 ; Family model, water-cooled, £103.

A RILEY DEVELOPMENT

Salerni Transmission Adopted

IN introducing the new 14 h.p. Edinburgh saloon on Tuesday last to a gathering of pressmen, Mr. Victor Riley, chairman and managing director of Riley (Coventry), Ltd., stated that all 1933 Rileys would shortly be available with fluid clutch and pre-selection transmission built under Salerni patents. The fitting is an optional extra on the 9 h.p. and 12 h.p. cars, and costs £30 in the case of the former and £50 on the six-cylinder models.

THE LATEST FAMILY MODEL. —— *A new design of dummy radiator has been adopted for the Family models. Note the adoption of Magna wheels.*

A "FOUR-WHEELED MORGAN"
An Interesting and Novel Conversion

The Allard Special has distinctly imposing lines, and, although still in somewhat of an experimental form, has a workmanlike appearance.

AFTER two years of experiment and really hard work a cyclecar enthusiast—Mr. S. H. Allard, of Keswick Road, Putney—has brought to fruition a pet idea which he has had in mind for years. It is what can best be described as a "four-wheeled Morgan."

By that we mean that various parts of a Morgan are utilized, such as engine, radiator, front suspension and portions of bodywork, but the rest of the car has been built from components of many makes.

The result, as can be seen from the pictures on this page, is a distinctly pleasing car, which, incidentally, is capable of a very fine performance, and holds the road like the proverbial leech.

The chassis frame consists of two straight channel-section members, cross-braced at four points. This frame is carried well below the wheel centres.

At the front end there are cross-members as on the Morgan, and between the extremities of these are carried the axle pins and helical springs; these are controlled by Newton hydraulic shock absorbers.

The rear suspension is by means of eight transverse quarter-elliptic springs after the manner of the f.w.d. B.S.A., and a large Hartford friction shock absorber controls each set of four. It will be seen that all wheels are independently sprung, and this makes the car ride most comfortably over very rough surfaces.

A pronounced crab track is used, the front being 4 ft. 8 ins. and the rear 3 ft.

10 ins. The wheelbase is 7 ft. 6 ins. and the overall height, to the top of the small glass screens, is only 3 ft. 7 ins. In spite of its low build and squat appearance the car has a ground clearance of 5 ins.

The engine is an 8-50 h.p. o.h.v. water-cooled J.A.P., and is, in fact, the actual unit which Mr. Allard used on his Morgan which from time to time has done very well at Brooklands. It is a highly tuned unit and has very good powers of acceleration.

An additional flywheel is mounted just behind the crankcase, and from this a short shaft takes the drive to a Moss four-speed-and-reverse gearbox. The "clutch housing" of this is bolted directly to a square steel plate, which forms additional strengthening for the frame.

Behind the gearbox the propeller shaft is guarded by a tubular casing

(Right) The "cockpit." The ingenious form of remote gear control can be seen, also the large array of instruments. Mounted also on the facia board is the hand pressure pump for the fuel supply.

where it passes between the driver and passenger. The shaft has Hardy disc joints at each end. The rear drive is very interesting and reflects great credit on Mr. Allard and those who have helped him to build this car.

The spiral-bevel housing is mounted direct on to the chassis, and from it run two short shafts, in which are incorporated Austin Seven mechanical universal joints. On each side of the casing there are two external-contracting brakes which were taken from a Chrysler. The front wheels have Morgan brakes and the pedal operates on all four wheels. The brake lever acts on the front wheels only. The rest of the controls are quite normal and the gearbox has a clever type of remote control.

The bodywork has attractive lines, but is, of course, at the moment still very much in experimental form. The tail is taken from an Aero Morgan, and in it is carried a large battery.

Starting, incidentally, is carried out by a Lucas dynamotor taken from a Morris car. This is connected to the clutch shaft by an inverted-tooth silent chain with positive lubrication. The space under the bonnet is used for the fuel and oil tanks, and the facia-board is a mass of instruments.

The car is a very fine effort and readers will have a chance of seeing it perform in the London-Exeter Trial which starts to-night.

For Workshops or Garages.

A very well-designed stationary petrol engine of about 3 h.p. and known as the Coborn, has been introduced by Kryn and Lahy (1928), Ltd., Letchworth, Herts.

The engine is of the air-cooled, single cylinder type; it has a balanced crankshaft, running on taper roller bearings, detachable cylinder head and barrel,

(Left) This view shows the transverse quarter elliptic rear springing and the way in which the battery is carried in the tail. Note also the twin exhaust outlets.

and side valves. A vaned flywheel working within a metal cowl ensures an adequate flow of air for cylinder cooling purposes, and it is claimed to be impossible to overheat the engine.

The mixture is supplied by a vertical car-type Solex carburetter which is coupled to a governor. Ignition is by an impulse-starter magneto. The power unit is entirely self-contained and a reduction gear of 2.54 to 1 can be fitted if desired. With the gear the Coborn engine costs £19 7s. 6d., or without it £17 15s.

Power to Spare
—and Speed too
with the
MORGAN
SPORTS
TWO-SEATER

A Speedy and Comfortable Three-wheeler Which Provides Plenty of Room for Luggage

SINCE the Morgan Sports two-seater was first introduced about a year ago, it has been improved in several respects. For example, two reasonably wide doors now make entrance and exit an easy matter and, on the model tested, a flat windscreen and a folding hood ensure an adequate range of vision, even when the hood is up.

On the mechanical side the new plate clutch is a great advance on its predecessor, and a new design of ignition distributor makes for greater reliability in that it is waterproof.

Morgans are now fitted with spare wheels and on the sports two-seater the tail is specially shaped to accommodate this desirable fitting.

The body combines distinctly attractive lines with sufficient room for two people and their luggage; the legroom is generous. The seat itself is upholstered with Dunlop Latex cushions and is 34 ins. wide, the measurement from back to front being 17 ins. and the squab height 20 ins.; behind the latter is a locker in which two suitcases can be carried.

All the wheels are detachable and interchangeable and have large Magna hubs. These certainly give an appearance of solidity to the machine and the position of the spare wheel on the sloping end of the tail is also attractive. At the front the appearance is very similar to that of the famous Aero Morgan.

Acceleration Figures.

With its overhead-valve 10-40 h.p. J.A.P. engine, the sports two-seater has a high power-weight ratio and its acceleration is naturally good. Although it can be throttled down to about 10 m.p.h. on top gear, a lower ratio would normally be used to accelerate from so low a speed. Tests were therefore made from a steady 15 m.p.h., and it was found that 30 m.p.h. was reached in 5¼ secs., while an additional 8 secs. sufficed to raise the speed to 50 m.p.h.

It must be stated that the car in question was not thoroughly run-in at the time of our test. Even so, it could exceed 65 m.p.h., and there is little doubt that after it has covered a greater mileage it will be capable of 70 m.p.h. or perhaps 75 m.p.h.; presumably there will also be an improvement in acceleration. The second-gear speed of the car, as tested, was about 45 m.p.h.

When driven as hard as is permissible with a fairly new engine, the petrol consumption worked out at about 40 m.p.g. At a more gentle gait this figure rose to about 50 m.p.g. Oil consumption in the ordinary way is at

the rate of one gallon per 1,000 miles; this quantity also represents the capacity of the oil tank. The petrol tank carries four gallons.

As on previous Morgans, the rear brake is coupled to the pedal, while the two front brakes are connected to the lever, which is centrally placed. Consequently, in order to obtain maximum braking effect, it is necessary to use both controls. This is, in fact, to be recommended for general use, particularly if the road surface is at all slippery. From 30 m.p.h. the Morgan was stopped comfortably in 34 ft.

It is almost unnecessary to state that the sports two-seater is an excellent hill-climber; convincing testimony to this is supplied by the record of the Morgan in reliability trials. More ordinary gradients, such as those which are freely encountered in normal use, can generally be climbed in top gear. "Weatheroak," in Worcestershire, has an average gradient of 1 in 8, with a maximum of possibly 1 in 5. It was approached at 35 m.p.h. and at the top the speedometer showed 32 m.p.h., the whole ascent having been made in top gear.

Since the three-speed gearbox was introduced 12

months ago its control has been improved, and it is now both easy and certain. The new clutch is, of course, delightful, and its smooth take-up is a great advantage in traffic. Despite its unorthodox design the suspension system is remarkably good, and appears to be equally satisfactory on good main roads or on neglected by-ways.

The 1933 chassis, it will be remembered, is distinctly lower than that of all previous Morgans, except the Super Sports, and this alteration results in somewhat better road-holding. Moreover, the steering layout has been improved, and the car is remarkably controllable at all speeds and even on the roughest surfaces.

The electrical equipment is of Lucas manufacture and the headlamps gave a satisfactory beam which enabled quite high cruising speeds to be indulged in after dark. They are provided with pilot bulbs so that they can be used as side lamps.

The car had, of course, an electric starter, which was capable of turning the engine over when warm. On a cold morning, however, it was advisable to turn the engine through a few revolutions with the starting handle, which now fits into a boss on the timing case.

From what has been written it will be realized that the sports two-seater Morgan is a very satisfactory vehicle for general use. Naturally, it is especially attractive for "sporting purposes." Not only is it exceptionally lively, but it has an almost tank-like ability to cross quite rough country.

Given reasonable skill in driving it will propel itself over the "stickiest" course in a way which is very satisfying, and, once one has indulged in this pastime, all but the prematurely aged will seek for fresh fields to conquer.

Not the least attractive feature of the Morgan sports two-seater is that its high performance is coupled with very low running costs; 50 m.p.g. and a £4 tax spell cheap motoring.

AT A GLANCE.

ENGINE : *o.h.v. Vee twin; 85.7 mm. by 95 mm. = 1,096 c.c.; tax £4. Thermo-siphon cooling; coil ignition; Amal carburetter.*

TRANSMISSION : *Single dry-plate clutch; enclosed propeller shaft with centre steady bearing; three-speed and reverse gearbox; ratios, 4.58, 7.5 and 12.4 to 1; worm drive to cross shaft and single roller chain to rear wheel.*

GENERAL : *Wheelbase, 7 ft.; track, 4 ft.; overall length, 10 ft. 10 ins.; width, 4 ft. 9 ins.; tyres, 26 in. by 4 in.*

PRICE : *£120, as tested; (£110 with s.v. engine).*

THE MORGAN MOTOR CO., LTD., Malvern Link, Worcs.

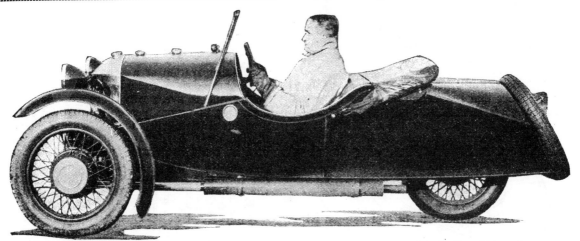

On the sports two-seater a large cylindrical silencer runs along on each side of the body. As can be seen from this photograph the addition of a spare wheel in no way detracts from the sporting appearance of the car.

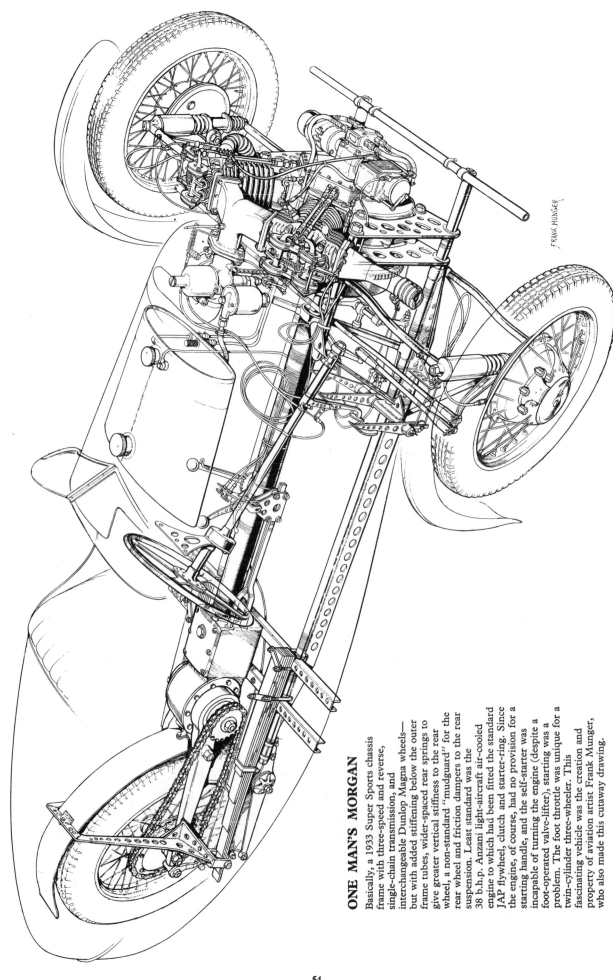

ONE MAN'S MORGAN

Basically, a 1933 Super Sports chassis frame with three-speed and reverse, single-chain transmission, and interchangeable Dunlop Magna wheels—but with added stiffening below the outer frame tubes, wider-spaced rear springs to give greater vertical stiffness to the rear wheel, a non-standard "mudguard" for the rear wheel and friction dampers to the rear suspension. Least standard was the 38 b.h.p. Anzani light-aircraft air-cooled engine to which had been fitted the standard JAP flywheel, clutch and starter-ring. Since the engine, of course, had no provision for a starting handle, and the self-starter was incapable of turning the engine (despite a foot-operated valve-lifter), starting was a problem. The foot throttle was unique for a twin-cylinder three-wheeler. This fascinating vehicle was the creation and property of aviation artist Frank Munger, who also made this cutaway drawing.

FRANK MUNGER.

54

A MORGAN-MATCHLESS

New Model Listed at £110

A FEW days ago we were able to make a short run in a new Morgan model, fitted with a water-cooled 990 c.c. V-twin side-valve Matchless engine, produced by the well-known motorcycle concern.

Set at an angle of 50 degrees, the cylinders are fitted with detachable heads. The valves are enclosed. The new Lo-Ex alloy is used for the pistons, and a compression ratio of 5.4 to 1 is employed. The ignition is by coil.

The two-seater sports chassis follows conventional Morgan lines; features are the detachable and interchangeable wheels, brakes on all wheels, a three-speed-and-reverse gearbox, and electric starting and lighting.

The Matchless engine will pull smoothly in top gear at 15 m.p.h., and a smooth start can be made from rest on second gear, provided that the clutch is used carefully.

The maximum speed (by speedometer) appeared to be in the region of 68 m.p.h. —easily attained on a short stretch of

This new sports model Morgan is fitted with a 990 c.c. Matchless water-cooled engine which is characterized by a smooth power-output at low r.p.m.

road; on second a speed of 45 m.p.h. could be reached without undue fuss; 22 m.p.h. seemed to be the maximum in bottom gear.

A speed of 60 m.p.h. could be reached from rest in 18¾ secs., which could be reduced to 17 secs. by accelerating from a start in second gear. From 40 m.p.h. to 65 m.p.h. the time taken was 12 secs.

The Morgan handled very easily and pleasantly, but with that innate "sporting feel" that all Morgans have. It is listed at £110.

Brooklands Loud Speakers.

A Philips 600-w. Public Address system has now been installed at Brooklands, and will be in operation tomorrow, May 6. There are 16 loud speakers, each with a ¼-mile range.

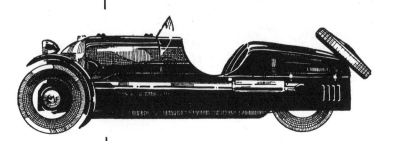

A MORGAN CLIMB *of* SCREW HILL?

A Promising Week-end Idea—Enthusiast's Specially Built Machine—Where Running Costs Count

By H. Sagar

NOW, you Morgan fans! I have had a letter from Mr. G. H. Goodall in which he expresses approval of my scheme for climbing Screw Hill, so it is up to you to rally round—in a double sense. Mr. Goodall thinks it would be a good idea for Morgan owners to rally somewhere in the vicinity, presumably before the so-called summer is over, so if you are at all interested, please write direct to the Morgan Motor Co., Ltd., Pickersleigh Road, Malvern Link. Action speaks louder than words, so do not spend a month endeavouring to

An interesting special three-wheeler powered by a K.M.A. racing engine. Its speed is in the neighbourhood of 90 m.p.h.

make up your minds, and then expect Mr. Goodall still to be interested.

It seems quite possible that Walna Scar, too, will be the scene of three-wheeler activities before long. A gentleman who knows quite a bit about handling three wheels is very interested in the idea and has definitely promised me that he will have a try "one of these fine days."

*　　*　　*

IF you have studied recent advertisements you will have noticed that the J.M.B. has been cleaned up considerably since the original experimental model appeared. This car, it will be remembered, is fitted with a 500 c.c. side-valve J.A.P. engine and other motorcycle components and will, I hope, attract many people who are still content with a sidecar although they could afford something better.

How many of you realize that there are now nine companies who have faith in three-wheelers? Although supplied purely for commercial purposes, the Fleet, James, Stevens and Croft cars are becoming increasingly popular, as is,

of course, the Raleigh—obtainable in a variety of forms for business use. To this list must be added Morgan and B.S.A., Coventry-Victor, who pin their faith to flat twins, and the J.M.B.

*　　*　　*

I HAD a letter from an enthusiast in Kensington recently, giving me details of a three-wheeler which has been built for him by Messrs. Taylor and Matterson. It employs Morgan clutch, bevel box, forks and transmission, but relies for its motive power upon a K.M.A. special racing engine, which gives it a speed of from 85-90 m.p.h. in standard trim. Its owner informs me that he is anxious to try it on the track, so it may be appearing at Brooklands.

How many enthusiasts are there who build their own machines? It would be interesting to compare idealists' varying opinions on the subect of the "ideal" three-wheeler, so if you have a home-built car, put your modesty on one side and let me know about it. There is, or was, a gentleman in the South country who converted a model T Ford into a three-wheeler. Whilst such conversions must be exceptional, I wonder if anyone else has found it possible to turn a four-wheeled car into a practical three-wheeler?

*　　*　　*

IT is always easy to do someone else's job—in theory, but I do think manufacturers are slow to make the most of their advantages. Take commercial three-wheelers as an example. You will find them advertised regularly in the

trade papers—in a fashion. One usually finds a sketch of the model, accompanied by the cold announcement that the tax is £4, the machine will do 50-60 m.p.g., and may be driven by a lad of 16. A photo would be a great deal better than a sketch, I am certain.

Now I have tried to persuade a business acquaintance to invest in a three-wheeler, as I am sure that it would effect a saving in his transport charges. I told him about the tax, which impressed him, and I believe I even conquered his long-standing objection to three-wheelers on the ground that they were unsafe; but when it came to the petrol consumption, he frankly regarded me as a liar.

If there is one business man of this kind, then there are others, and although I may not be a brilliant spokesman, I feel sure that three-wheeler sales in this sphere would benefit considerably were the A.-C.U., as the responsible body, to stage a demonstration on the lines of that arranged to show the capabilities of the 15s. tax motorcycle. The certificate issued at the conclusion of the test would give full details of performance, and potential customers would be able to see for themselves just what the running costs were.

It seems almost too good to be true, but a little bird which flew North recently informed me that we may see another four-cylinder three-wheeler making its bow next year. I am sure I am not alone in hoping that it may be so.

(Letters on topical matters addressed to Mr. Sagar, care of The Editor, will be forwarded immediately.)

A COMMERCIAL THREE-WHEELER. ——— *One of a number of Fleet box-vans used by the L.M.S. Railway Company for their goods and parcels delivery services.*

MORGAN MODELS FOR 1934

Several Important Detail Refinements

(Above) The new o.h.v. Matchless engine which is available on the sports two-seater. (Left) A view of the 1934 Family model showing the improved tail.

NO changes in the basic Morgan models are made for 1934, but there are various detail alterations. The Family model is now listed only with a water-cooled engine, and a new air-cooled o.h.v. engine is available for the sports two-seater. In addition, there are various detail improvements.

On the Family model there is a new radiator of larger capacity. The header tank has a sloping front so as to deflect air downwards through the film block. At the other end of this model it is to be noticed that the tail is now very similar to that of the Sports two-seater, being rounded instead of having a square section as in 1933.

All 1934 Morgans have an oil filter placed on the side of the tank and connected to the return pipe. Consequently the oil scavenged from the sump is forced through a felt cylinder before it reaches the oil tank again. Another improvement to be found on all models is a Borg and Beck plate in the clutch. This plate, of course, has a flexible centre which cushions the transmission by smoothing out the engine torque.

No changes have been made to the mechanism of the three-speed-and-reverse gearbox, except that a better oil sealing washer is now fitted where the shafts leave the box. This is a composite device consisting of an L-section leather washer contracted on to the shaft by a coil spring surrounding it. The casting of the box itself is now appreciably wider at the back so that it holds more oil.

As before, the lighting dynamo is driven from the gearbox cross-shaft, but a change has been made to the gear-wheels employed for this purpose. Straight teeth are now used to remove any end thrust and the larger wheel is made of a compressed fabric material of improved quality. The steel pinion on which most of the wear used to occur is now case-hardened.

As already indicated, the sports two-seater is now available with an air-cooled o.h.v. engine as well as with a side valve or o.h.v. water-cooled unit. The new engine is of Matchless manufacture and its lower half is similar to that of the water-cooled Matchless side-valve unit, but a separate lead is taken

1934 MORGAN PRICES.	
Family model, s.v., water-cooled ...	£105
Sports Family, s.-v., water-cooled ...	£115
Sports Family, o.h.v., water-cooled	£125
Sports 2-seater, s.-v., water-cooled	£110
Sports 2-seater, o.h.v., air-cooled	£115
Sports 2-seater, o.h.v., water-cooled	£120
Super-sports, o.h.v., water-cooled	£135

Morgan Motor Co., Ltd., Malvern Link, Worcs.

(Above) How the header tank of the radiator on the Family model is shaped to deflect air on to the film. (Right) The Borg and Beck flexible plate now used in the clutch.

(Below) The latest super sports model which sells for £135.

from the oil pump to lubricate the overhead rockers.

These are enclosed in a box on each cylinder head and a short pipe is taken from the rocker box to the inlet valve guide for its lubrication. Each pushrod is enclosed in a telescopic tube which can be raised to reach the adjustment on the tappet. Generous finning characterizes the cylinders and the heads, and the whole unit has a distinctly businesslike appearance.

Most of our readers are familiar with the general specification of the Morgan, but for the benefit of those who are not the following brief details may be added. All models have a Vee-twin engine which drives through a plate clutch and short propeller shaft to a three-speed-and-reverse gearbox, whence the final drive is by a chain to the rear wheel. The front wheels are independently sprung by means of helical springs, whilst the rear wheel is carried in a stout fork, the suspension being quarter-elliptic. The brakes operate on all wheels and are of the internal-expanding type. The latest models will be on view at the Motorcycle Exhibition at Olympia (November 25).

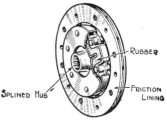

RUBBER
SPLINED HUB
FRICTION LINING

57

Over
ALPINE COLS
with a
MORGAN "SUPER

*Two Members of the
Fair Sex Prove that
the Continent Holds no
Terrors for a Modern
Three-wheeler*

(Above) The old fortress of Eze seen through the olives on the Grand Corniche. (Left) The harbour, Lake Iseo, taken from the Hotel Leon d'Oro.

LAST summer I was given an opportunity to put one of the new Morgan Super Sports models through its paces in the Alps, and having, in days gone by, driven many thousands of miles ·as an enthusiastic owner of earlier Morgans, I was much intrigued to sample the new vintage. Having heard that there were still in existence a few Italian lakes not totally surrounded by hotels and villas, we decided to risk the roads and have a look. So in the early summer we set off, myself and another girl, with a small quantity of compressed luggage.

We had mapped out a round tour; starting off easily with the marvellous motoring conditions of the Savoy Alps and Esterels, we would follow the Mediterranean to Italy, over the frontier at Sospel and from the Italian lakes north again over the real Cols of the Swiss Alps.

We crossed to Boulogne in perfect weather. The Morgan had done some 3,000 miles when we started and, running easily at 45 to 50 m.p.h., we made Soissons that night.

From there we followed the well-known road through Troyes—typically French and full of atmosphere, with its old buildings, winding cobbled streets

and still, dark canal—and on through Dijon to Tournus, where I have a pet hotel. As one walks out on to the crooked vine-covered balcony above the old courtyard one begins, for the first time, to feel again the atmosphere of the South!

Next morning a short run brought us to the foothills of the Alps. A rough calculation when we stopped for petrol in Grenoble showed that the big J.A.P. was doing about 50 to the gallon, which was satisfactory enough, but even so one could have done with a rather larger tank on the Continent, with Esso pumps so few and far between.

The Morgan, of course, revelled in the Col de la Croix-Haute: dropping into second on the corners, one accelerated some 30 yds. or so, then up into top again.

From Tournus, our next stop was Aix-en-Provence, and the following morning saw us swooping along the Grande Corniche—just under two-and-a-half days from Boulogne without undue haste.

After a few days by the Mediterranean, fresh oil and adjustment of the tappets saw the Morgan ready for the road again. Leaving Mentone, we climbed over the Col de Castillon to Sospel, whence more Cols followed and then the Italian Frontier, where there was a considerable military display and many formalities (including the careful sealing up of our aged Kodak in case we should be tempted to photograph any of "il Duce's" private frontier views!).

Shortly after this we had our first visitation of trouble, and it was of a rather nerve-wracking nature. The road was becoming distinctly "Alpine," the surface more loose and dusty, the hairpins sharper and steeper. The

fine panorama of Mentone Harbour and Cap Martin as seen from the Boulevard de Garavan.

By Lilian Fraser

Italian sun and the white road made the glare very trying as one climbed up, with a last final burst of really superb hairpins, to the entrance of the Col di Tenda Tunnel 4,331 ft. up at the summit of the pass.

Switching on the lights, we plunged into the blackness. For the first few yards my impression was that of impenetrable darkness and water—water dripping, water running down the jagged walls and rushing streams on either side, into which the narrow road dropped sheer. At this point the Morgan began to wag her tail with considerable violence, her single driving wheel waltzing wildly in about 2 ins. of greasy mud. I had just got back into the straight and narrow way by throttling down to the last ounce in top, when suddenly there was a fierce smell of burning and the whole of my lights blacked out. It was too dark even to attempt repairs and turning was also out of the question.

I will draw a veil, with a shaking hand, over the 3 kilos. which remained of that tunnel! There are faint lights that glow at intervals to guide one's direction— that is all.

Mobbed by Enthusiasts.

At Turin we filled up with petrol and the car was absolutely mobbed by Italians of all ages, shapes and sizes. (The inevitable question arises, why, if these Latin races are such super-enthusiastic sporting motorists, do they drive nothing but saloons like little black match-boxes bobbing along the roads?)

After Turin came our blissful introduction to the Autostrade (thinking bitterly the while of our own by-pass roads, converted into long dangerous streets by the new houses that line them). For 100 miles, driving at 52 m.p.h., we put up an average of 48 m.p.h. in the most perfect safety imaginable.

That night we stayed in Como—very fashionable, yet cheaper than I expected. Next day we found Lake Iseo, deep and still among the mountains; the old villages, clustering among the olives, gave contrast to the busy shores of Como, whilst, instead of smart steamers, the primitive sailing boats drifting lazily with their great striped sails, like Viking galleys, crept round the headlands of the tree-clad islands.

In the village of Iseo we stayed some weeks, spending much of the time rowing and swimming. The Hotel Leon d'Oro provided more than adequate comfort for the modest charge of 16 lire a day! Below the vine-covered terrace glittered the green shadows of the lake, whilst under our window our boat rippled softly at its

moorings. The days drifted by and so, at last, we disinterred the Morgan and swung her head for the Swiss Frontier.

A long drive through the heat brought us to the Customs at Castasegna, where we arrived with every inch of our car and clothing coated thickly in dust, even our hair and eyelashes being powdered snow-white! Thereafter began the long sheer climb up to Maloja at 6,000 ft. After about 5,000 ft. the engine began to lose power slightly owing to the more rarefied air, but there was more than enough power in hand to compete with this, and a higher middle-gear ratio would, in fact, have been an advantage.

The cool air blowing off the snow-covered peaks was almost unbelievable after the heat and dust of Italy as we drove up the long line of lakes in the Engadine Valley. Stopping to wash off a little of the dust in the icy brown waters of Silvaplanasee, we pushed on to Silvaplana for the night.

Nearly 8,000 ft. Up.

Leaving the valley at about 2 p.m. the following day, and setting our features in stern lines, we resolutely commenced our highest climb, up among the snow of the Julier Pass to the summit, nearly 8,000 ft. above sea level. At this point the effect of the height on the carburation became so noticeable that I seriously regretted not having brought some smaller jets in my tool kit. However, the big Hispanos and Isottas coming over from St. Moritz appeared to be feeling it also, for we slipped by them easily, the wide-tracked Morgan cornering beautifully.

Staying the night at a little village near Zurich, we reached Basle early next morning and crossed over into France. On through Alsace and the Vosges, we spent the next night in Rheims, to leave again at 7 a.m., bumping out over its cobbled streets, past the war-scarred buildings, on to N.44 to make the best time we could to catch the 2 p.m. boat from Calais.

At St. Quentin we made a really devastating mistake. Instead of the usual N.35 to Amiens, we decided to take the more direct road via Arras. For some miles the road was perfect; then suddenly the asphalt ended abruptly and we crashed down on to some 40 miles of soul-shattering cobbles of almost inconceivable antiquity! We were now in the late war zone, passing quite close to Vimy Ridge. The war must have passed many times over that road—I shall not do so again!

After averaging a steady 10 m.p.h. for most of the morning, our chances for the boat seemed very slender. However, striking civilized roads again soon after St. Omer, I got down to it and made the Morgan travel as she never had before. As we tore down the dead straight N.43, a sudden clatter and exultant roar denoted the violent departure of silencer number one! Having wasted some valuable minutes picking up the red-hot " bits," I then pushed the speedometer up to 65, whereupon silencer number two promptly followed suit!

At the end of its long trek the engine proved more than equal to the prolonged burst of speed, and ten minutes before the boat sailed we made our positively thunderous entrance into the streets of Calais!

THE ONE AND ONLY MORGAN

Minor Changes for Coming Season

FINE RANGE OF THREE-WHEELED LIGHT CARS

Two views of the striking bodywork which will characterize the Morgan Super Sports model for the coming season.

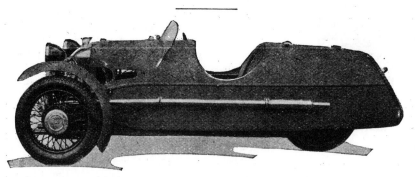

"NO change" is an almost accurate description of the 1935 Morgan programme. Were it not for the four-cylinder model and the super sports the phrase would be entirely correct, and even on these two there is very little alteration.

It is true that since the 1934 models were first described a year ago, there has been a change in the ignition system of all the twin-cylinder Morgans, but that change was made many months ago. It affects the contact breaker of the coil-ignition system. By a rearrangement of the high tension

leads and a new shape of distributor, this component has been made entirely waterproof.

Apart from that the Family model, the Sports two-seater and the Sports Family Morgan remain quite unaltered. Newest of all the Morgans is the four-cylindered machine, which made its first public appearance at the 1933 Motorcycle Show. Having lived with it for the best part of a year the good people at Malvern have decided that with just a little bit on here and the slightest bit off there, it would be even more handsome. And it is.

What it all amounts to is that the shape of the tail has been changed. Instead of sloping away as it did on

the 1934 Four, the tail retains a more circular section right to the end. The back panel or tail-end is recessed, and in this space the spare wheel fits. The result is a very appreciable improvement in the general appearance of the car.

This model, it may be recalled, has a four-cylinder engine with side-by-side valves and an aluminium alloy cylinder head. Its transmission system includes a single-plate clutch, a three-speed-and-reverse gearbox with worm drive to a cross-shaft from which a single chain drives the rear wheel. In this it resembles the twin-cylinder Morgans.

In many other respects it differs from them. For instance, it has a wheelbase longer by a foot, and the chassis frame is different, for the side members are Z-section pressings. Steering and front suspension are basically the same although the detail work is not. Further, all three brakes are connected to the pedal and the hand controls the rear brake only.

The Super Sports Model

As previously indicated, the only other changes for 1935 are to be found in the Super Sports. To prevent any possibility of the driver's or passenger's arm being scorched, the exhaust pipes are carried at a lower level along each side. This naturally makes a slight difference to the appearance.

Much more is to be noticed at the tail of the Super Sports. This is now barrel-shaped, something like the tail already described for the four-cylindered car. Moreover, the spare wheel fits into the end of the tail instead of sitting on top of it.

To finish the job off neatly, a polished aluminium disc covers the wheel except for the tyre and the edge of the rim. This disc carries the number-plate and the rear lamp. On top of the tail the space previously occupied by the wheel is now taken up by a simple luggage grid consisting of three aluminium strips mounted on wood bearers.

This model has an o.h.v. twin-cylinder engine, and there is the choice of either air cooling or water cooling. In both cases the unit is a Matchless, and the o.h. valves are operated by rockers and push rods, all enclosed and lubricated effectively.

Engines of the same make and design are used in some of the other Morgans, but those fitted to the Super Sports models are specially tuned. The Family model is an exception, for it has a water-cooled side-valve engine, and that unit is also available in the Sports two-seater.

Apart from the valve position, all these vee-twin engines are of similar design. They have a dry sump lubrication system with a separate oil tank which incorporates an oil filter.

These cars will not be on view at the Motor Show, but they will appear at the Motorcycle Show, which opens at Olympia on November 5.

1935 MORGAN PRICES

Family Model, water cooled, s.v.	£105
Sports Family, water cooled, s.v.	£115
Sports Family, water cooled, o.h.v.	£125
Sports two-seater, water cooled, s.v.	£110
Sports Two-seater, air cooled, o.h.v.	£115
Sports Two-seater, water cooled, o.h.v.	£120
Super Sports, air cooled, o.h.v.	£127 10s.
Super Sports, water cooled, o.h.v.	£137 10s.
Four-cylinder Model ..	£120

IN BRIEF

TWO-CYLINDER MODELS

ENGINE : Twin-cylinder, s.v. or o.h.v.; 85.5 mm. by 85.5 mm. = 990 c.c.; tax, £4; coil ignition.

TRANSMISSION : Single dry plate clutch with flexible centre ; enclosed propeller shaft ; three-speed gearbox ; ratios, 4.85, 8 and 13.1 to 1; reverse, 17.5 to 1. Worm-driven cross-shaft and roller chain to rear wheel.

DIMENSIONS : Wheelbase, 7 ft. 3 ins. (Sports Family model, 7 ft. 7 ins.); track, 4 ft. 2 ins. ; overall lengths, 10 ft. 4 ins. (Super Sports), 10 ft. 6 ins. (Family and Sports Two-seater), 10 ft. 10 ins. (Sports Family) ; width, 4 ft. 11 ins.

FOUR-CYLINDER MODEL

ENGINE : Four-cylinder, side valve; 56.6 mm. by 92.5 mm. = 933 c.c. Tax, £4; coil ignition.

TRANSMISSION : As above.

DIMENSIONS : Wheelbase, 8 ft. 3 ins.; track, 4 ft. 2 ins. ; overall length, 11 ft. 6 ins. ; overall width, 4 ft. 11 ins.

THE MORGAN MOTOR CO., LTD.,
MALVERN LINK, WORCS.

IT'S A FACT !

There is a real "sixty-mile" car,★ a stream-lined vision of colour and chromium—with powerful 10/40 h.p. engines (robust and mechanically simple), three-speed and reverse, having all the comforts of the modern Sports Car—finger-light steering, smooth action single plate clutch, powerful brakes—quick interchangeable wheels (with spare fitted as standard) ....and offering all these refinements for only £4 tax per annum!

★ "a real sixty - mile car" may not seem a big claim in view of modern road speeds (a Morgan holds the record speed of 115·66 m.p.h.)—but taken as an average you can be sure of, "sixty" is still a high figure for present road conditions.

CUT OUT THIS AD. AND POST BACK TO US for YOUR COPY OF THE NEW CATALOGUE THE MORGAN MOTOR CO., Ltd. Malvern Link WORC.

Morgan Features.

3-speed and reverse—single chain—redesigned engines—Lucas Electric Lighting and Starting—Cooper-Stewart Speedometer—Screen Wiper. Detachable Wheels and Spare Wheel fitted to all Models—Dunlop Tyres Standard.

IT'S A FACT....
Yes, of course, the only car it could be . . . . .

morgan super SPORTS
The Classic Three Wheel Car

PRICE

£135

COMPLETE

Morgan

YOU ARE INTERESTED, WRITE YOUR NAME AND ADDRESS ACROSS THIS AD. AND POST BACK TO US

A Jolly "foursome," . . . .
The Morgan Foursome. . . . . . .
Morgan Family. . . . .
The threewheel Fourseater—The small car with the extra room. . . . .
The most economical car you can ever run. . . . .
Four pound tax — low insurance — with three speeds and reverse—. .
10 horse engines — built on the strongest, simplest chassis — by the oldest Firm with the finest record.

AN ADVERTISEMENT OF THE MORGAN MOTOR CO. LTD., MALVERN LINK . WORC.

£95
WATER-COOLED ENGINE £100

Morgan
FEATURES
3-SPEED & REVERSE
SINGLE CHAIN
REDESIGNED
ENGINES
LUCAS ELECTRIC
LIGHTING
ELECTRIC STARTER
SPEEDOMETER
SCREEN WIPER
DUNLOP TYRES
STANDARD

THREE-WHEELERS for 1935

The Motorcycle Show, at which Three-wheeled Light Cars will be Exhibited, opens at Olympia on Monday. Here is a Review of Next Season's Prospects, together with Details of the Latest Models

By
— Triangle —

I HAVE just been looking through the latest Ministry of Transport figures regarding the number of three-wheelers registered for the first time. On the eve of the Motorcycle Show they make heartening reading. For the period from March to August, inclusive, the number of new models sold represents an increase over the corresponding period last year of no less than 18.9 per cent.

The increase, incidentally, has been very consistent and only one month (July) shows a fall compared with last year—and the fall in that case is a matter of three cars only.

Perhaps it savours a little of the I-told-you-so-attitude, but, in view of these figures, I cannot resist quoting what I said in January this year :—

"At the present time prospects in the three-wheeler world are brighter than they have been for many years. I know that in the past popularity in this type of car has ebbed and flowed . . . but I hardly think this is likely to happen in the future.

"The present appeal of the three-wheeler is too wide for that. Its attraction rests not on one feature, but on many, and in the fine range of models now available these different features are emphasized in varying degrees."

Still the Lowest Tax.

Exactly the same holds good to-day. True, conditions have been altered slightly by the grossly unfair exclusion of three-wheelers from the tax reductions that will apply to both motorcycles and four-wheelers next January, and the advantages which have previously been enjoyed by three-wheeler owners in paying £4 as against the minimum car rate of £6, will be much less marked. Even so, the minimum tax on four-wheelers will still be 10s. higher, and no car is made at the moment to benefit by this minimum rate.

I believe, moreover, that if the taxation rate on baby cars and three-wheelers were the same, there would still be a good market for the latter. The Road Fund licence, after all, represents but one part of the cost of motoring. If you go into the other items, you will find that three-wheelers score all along the line.

Petrol consumption naturally varies with different models, but, if you compare three-wheelers and four-wheelers of equal performance—and that, after all, is the only fair way—you will always find that the three-wheeler shows up at least 25 per cent. better. Repairs also are generally less costly, and in many districts the same applies to garaging.

Even in the matter of initial cost, the three-wheeler scores ; although the more expensive models in some cases cost more than the cheapest four-wheelers, you will find that once again the three-wheeler has it on a performance basis.

Enough, however, of generalities. Let us get down to a detailed review of the new season's models. In most cases there has been comparatively little change and this is doubtless due to the increase in sales this year, which shows that the models now being supplied are very largely what the public wants ; in the circumstances it would be foolish to make radical changes.

* * *

First, alphabetically, comes the B.S.A. Two main types are made and they differ in that in one case a two-cylinder, air-cooled, overhead-valve engine of 85 mm. and 90 mm. bore and stroke (1,021 c.c.) is used, whilst in the other, a four-cylinder, side-valve, water-cooled unit is employed : the bore and stroke in this case are 60 mm. and 95mm. (1,075 c.c.). Otherwise the two chassis types are practically identical.

In each case front-wheel drive is employed, the power being taken from the engine by a plate clutch, thence through a three-speed-and-reverse gearbox to a worm drive and differential, the whole of this mechanism being in unit with the engine ; the final stage of the transmission consists of short shafts with flexible couplings which drive the front wheels.

On the two-cylinder chassis there is the Standard model at £100, the De Luxe at £108, the Family at £110, and the Special Model at £115. On the four-cylinder chassis two body types are available : the Standard model at £125 and the De Luxe edition at £128.

For 1935 no material chassis alterations have been made, but small coachwork improvements have been incorporated and the four-cylinder de luxe has what is virtually a new body. It is of more sporting appearance with cutaway door tops, and instead of a detachable hood an ingenious folding type, incorporating telescopic joints and arranged to disappear into the tail behind the seat, is used.

Another alteration which applies to both the four-cylinder models is the adoption of a new radiator front, which is slatted and slightly bowed.

With the sole exception of the special twin-cylinder model, examples of the entire B.S.A. range will be found on the maker's stand at Olympia (No. 30), and, in addition, a plated example of the four-cylinder chassis is to be exhibited.

Coventry-Victor models for 1935 show very little change, although the programme has been simplified by concentration on two models, the Luxury Sports at £120, and the Family model at £99 15s.

The Family four-seater is entirely unchanged. Apart from coachwork, it differs from the Luxury model in that it has a side-valve engine of 750 c.c. (78 mm. by 78 mm.). The engine

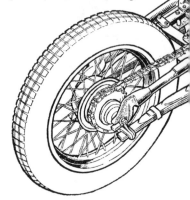

fitted to the Luxury model, on the other hand, has now been increased to 980 c.c. (78 mm. by 85 mm.).

In both cases the power unit used is a horizontally opposed, water-cooled, two-cylinder job and, in each case, side-by-side valves are employed. It is possible, however, to obtain an o.h.v. engine at an extra cost of £10. The engine is built up in unit with a single dry-plate clutch and three-speed and reverse gearbox, from which a propeller shaft conveys the power to a bevel box just in front of the rear wheel ; from this point the final drive is by a single roller chain.

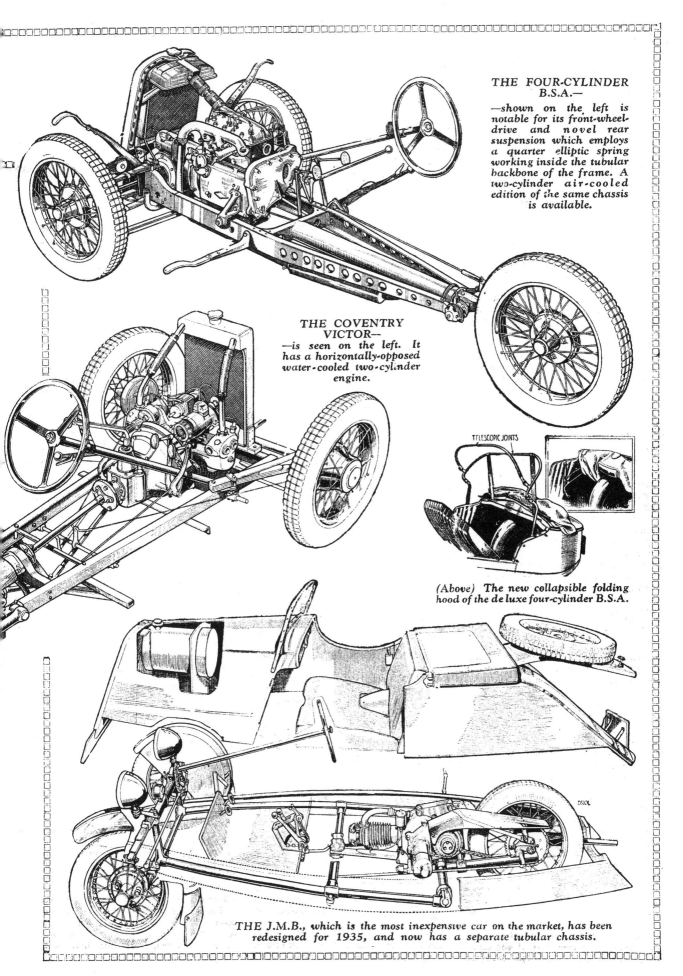

THE FOUR-CYLINDER B.S.A.—

—shown on the left is notable for its front-wheel-drive and novel rear suspension which employs a quarter elliptic spring working inside the tubular backbone of the frame. A two-cylinder air-cooled edition of the same chassis is available.

THE COVENTRY VICTOR—

—is seen on the left. It has a horizontally-opposed water-cooled two-cylinder engine.

TELESCOPIC JOINTS

(Above) The new collapsible folding hood of the de luxe four-cylinder B.S.A.

THE J.M.B., which is the most inexpensive car on the market, has been redesigned for 1935, and now has a separate tubular chassis.

At the front, a conventional axle and quarter elliptic springs are used, whilst the same type of springing is employed at the rear, but the wheel is carried in a massive tubular fork.

This year, the Coventry-Victor will not be shown at Olympia.

Next on the list comes the most inexpensive make on the market, the J.M.B., and here striking alterations in design have been made for the coming season. The same general layout and inherent simplicity have been retained, but, whereas a body-cum-chassis was originally used, the latest types now have a pukka tubular chassis.

Novel Engine Mounting.

The general arrangement is clearly shown in one of the accompanying sketches, and perhaps the most interesting feature of the whole design is the manner in which the engine and rear-wheel unit is mounted. As can be seen, the single-cylinder engine is placed horizontally and it is built up in unit with a multi-disc clutch and three-speed and reverse gearbox; this unit is mounted on a special sub-frame, which also carries the rear wheel and is pivoted on a pair of large-diameter oilless bushes to the rear cross-member.

Thus, the engine and rear wheel move as one unit so that deflections of the latter over road irregularities do not affect the tension of the chain used for the final drive. The rear suspension, by the way, is by means of a single quarter-elliptic spring bolted to the engine sub-frame and sliding in a special bearing on the centre cross-member.

The front part of the chassis is interesting in that no front axle is employed. Each wheel is supported on a pair of quarter-elliptic springs bolted to tubular uprights on the chassis and pivoted to extensions of the steering heads. The steering itself is of the chain and sprocket type, and independent drag links control each wheel, there being no actual track rod.

Improvements of the J.M.B. are not confined to mechanical details, as the coachwork has been very greatly improved, not only in appearance, but in comfort and convenience as well.

There are now three models; the two-

three-seater Gazelle, is fitted with a single-cylinder, air-cooled, side-valve J.A.P. engine of 497 c.c. (85.7 mm. by 85 mm.) with a power output of 14 b.h.p. at 4,500 r.p.m., and the price of the car is £75 12s. The two-seater Sports Mustang also has a single-cylinder engine of the same dimensions, but it is of the overhead-valve type and develops 21 b.h.p. at 4,200 r.p.m. This model, which costs £91 7s., is designed to appeal to the motorist who wishes to keep running costs low, but at the same time enjoy a more sporting performance than is provided by the Gazelle.

Both models, incidentally, have detachable wheels and a spare is supplied as standard on the Mustang; an extra charge is made for a spare on the Gazelle model.

Examples of each type will be on view at the J.M.B. stand (No. 132), and, in addition, the makers intend to

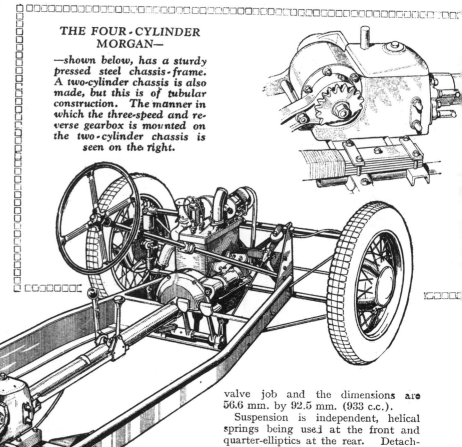

THE FOUR-CYLINDER MORGAN—

—shown below, has a sturdy pressed steel chassis-frame. A two-cylinder chassis is also made, but this is of tubular construction. The manner in which the three-speed and reverse gearbox is mounted on the two-cylinder chassis is seen on the right.

show an entirely new saloon model and an example of the side-valve chassis.

The new saloon body is mounted on the standard Gazelle chassis and is a striking two-door affair modelled on air-flow lines. It is nominally a two-seater, but the large luggage space behind the seats provides room for two

children. Steel panelling, cellulosed ivory white, is used up to the waistline, and the head is of polished black fabric. A sunshine roof is fitted. The price has not yet been fixed, but it will be well under £100.

Next there comes the Morgan, which might very well be described as the father of modern three-wheelers, as it has, of course, been on the market since pre-war days. Last year, it will be recalled, the familiar two-cylinder model was supplemented by a four-cylinder edition in an entirely new chassis, Both types are continued for 1935 and, except for coachwork alterations on the four-cylinder model and on the Supersports two-cylinder model, no changes have been made.

Dealing first with the four-cylinder type, this, as is well known, has a modified edition of the 8 h.p. Ford power unit. From the back of the clutch a propeller shaft takes the drive to a combined three-speed and reverse gearbox and worm-driven cross-shaft, whence the drive is conveyed to the rear wheel by means of a single roller chain. The engine, of course, is a side-valve job and the dimensions are 56.6 mm. by 92.5 mm. (933 c.c.).

Suspension is independent, helical springs being used at the front and quarter-elliptics at the rear. Detachable wheels are fitted and a spare is supplied.

So far as the coachwork is concerned the body remains substantially the same as last year, except for a rather important alteration in the shape of the tail. Instead of sloping away as it did last year, it now retains a more circular section to the end, which is recessed to take the spare wheel. The net result is very neat and businesslike. Two examples of the four-cylinder model are to be shown at Olympia, a cooled) £110, (o.h.v. air-cooled) £115, (o.h.v. water-cooled) £120; Super-sports (o.h.v. air-cooled) £127 10s., (o.h.v. water-cooled) £137 10s.

Practically all these models will be represented on the Morgan stand (No. 34), although in one or two cases the full range of engines will not be shown on certain of the body styles. In all, the makers will be staging a display of 10 models, a particularly interesting one being a special black-and-chromium Super-sports o.h.v. model at £150.

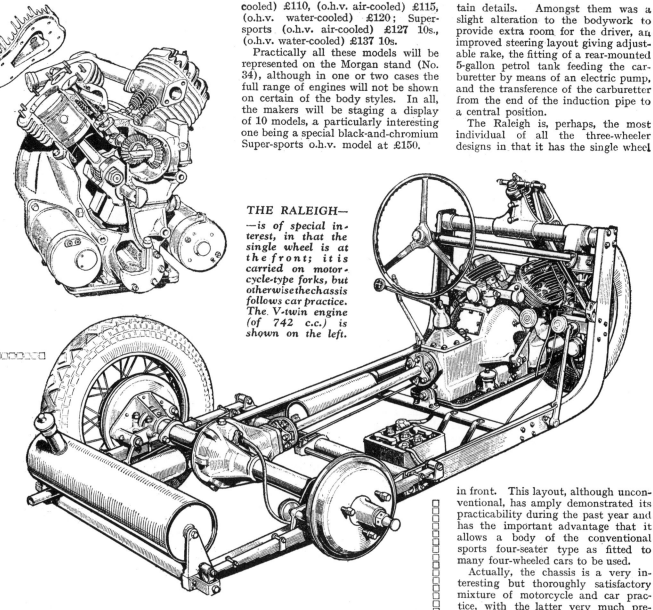

THE RALEIGH—
—*is of special interest, in that the single wheel is at the front; it is carried on motor-cycle-type forks, but otherwise the chassis follows car practice. The V-twin engine (of 742 c.c.) is shown on the left.*

tain details. Amongst them was a slight alteration to the bodywork to provide extra room for the driver, an improved steering layout giving adjustable rake, the fitting of a rear-mounted 5-gallon petrol tank feeding the carburetter by means of an electric pump, and the transference of the carburetter from the end of the induction pipe to a central position.

The Raleigh is, perhaps, the most individual of all the three-wheeler designs in that it has the single wheel in front. This layout, although unconventional, has amply demonstrated its practicability during the past year and has the important advantage that it allows a body of the conventional sports four-seater type as fitted to many four-wheeled cars to be used.

Actually, the chassis is a very interesting but thoroughly satisfactory mixture of motorcycle and car practice, with the latter very much predominating. The front wheel is carried on spring forks very similar to those used for motorcycles, except that, in the Raleigh, they are of very massive pressed-steel construction and are controlled, not by handlebars, of course, but by a proper steering reduction box and wheel.

The engine, too, is suggestive of motorcycle practice in so far as it is of the vee-twin type and is air-cooled, but there the similarity ends and, for the rest, the Raleigh chassis might well be that of a very up-to-date four-wheeler.

The engine, for example, is built up in unit with a single dry-plate clutch and three-speed and reverse gearbox, whence the drive is conveyed by an open propeller shaft to a spiral-bevel rear axle. The chassis frame itself has channel-section side-members, and is underslung at the rear.

The Raleigh exhibits at the Motorcycle Show will be found on Stand 29 and, in addition to an attractive example of the standard Safety Seven four-seater, a chassis will be on view.

blue and cream car at £120, and a duo-blue model at £123 10s.

The two-cylinder chassis differs considerably in that it is of tubular construction as opposed to the channel-section frame of the "four," but the general arrangement of the transmission is similar. The dimensions are, however, smaller, the wheelbase being 7 ft. 3 ins. (Sports Family model 7 ft. 7 ins.) compared with the 8 ft. 3 ins. of the four-cylinder job. The track in both cases is 4 ft. 2 ins.

The range of coachwork on the two-cylinder models is a wide one and includes a Family type, a Sports Family model, a Sports two-seater, and a Super-sports two-seater. Various engines are available on the different types.

Here are the actual models and prices :—Family (s.v. water-cooled) £105; Sports Family (s.v. water-cooled) £115, (o.h.v. watercooled) £125; Sports two-seater (s.v. water-

All these two-cylinder models, as we have indicated, are substantially the same as last year with the exception of the Super-sports, in which the tail is barrel-shaped and recessed to take the spare wheel after the manner of the "four." Another slight detail improvement concerns the exhaust pipes, which are now carried along the outside of the body at a slightly lower level so that there is no chance of the driver's or passengers' arms being scorched.

Finally, there is the Raleigh, which has proved so satisfactory that it is to remain entirely unchanged for 1935, except in the matter of its price, which has been reduced from £105 to £99 15s.

It is worth while mentioning, however, that at the beginning of the present year the original design, which made its first appearance at the 1933 Motorcycle Show, was modified in cer-

ACROSS FOUR FRONTIERS

in a

MORGAN

Only Seven Clear Days on the "other side" . . . but read how Ernest S. Turner made the most of them

In Rhineland—a halt beside the quaint "wine ship" on wheels at Rudesheim.

IT stretched away before us from Boulogne—Route Nationale No. 1. Our three-year-old Morgan, specially soft-tyred for pavé, and with a slightly self-conscious "G.B." plaque a-glitter, began to reel off the kilometres, and seemed quite content to travel "on the wrong side."

Except that we were to touch Paris, and were talking airily about the Rhine, our plans for the next seven days were no more fixed than those of Ethelred the Unready. Certainly we did not expect to shed perforated portions of our carnet in Luxembourg and Belgium, as well as in France and Germany.

Route Nationale No. 1, we found, was built and banked—and used—for rapid travel, and there was a fine fascination in speeding down those mile-long stretches with their high "naves" of arching trees, trunks white-blazed at every crossing.

Near Abbeville we had a welcome chance to further the Entente Cordiale when we found a young motorist who had run out of petrol (they do that in France, too), and thereby raised himself no higher in the eyes of his feminine cargo. Very gratefully he accepted a lift to and from the nearest petrol station. He was the first of dozens who wanted to know our maximum speed and petrol consumption. "Cent kilometres par heure," was easy enough, and certainly sounded impressive, but working out kilometres to the litre was a job for a senior wrangler!

Beauvais showed us the R101 Memorial, a great block of blinding white stone, so situated on the main road that scores of English motorists must pass it. By this time Paris was becoming within measurable distance. There was, of course, to be no "funking" its traffic, and we made quite a triumphal entry past Le Bourget and through the Porte St. Denis.

Next day the fun began. Versailles-bound, we had to cross the city in the rush hour, and soon knew all about it. Bells "exploding" like alarm clocks . . . red-flashing beacons . . . white admonitory batons . . . "Sans Interdit" everywhere . . . pedestrian crossings which had to be observed . . . endless bluff from taxis. . . . We prided ourselves we were getting on very well; but we failed to touch wood. In the Boulevard des Capucines our traffic line was suddenly halted, and we were struck in the rear by the following car. The culprit was apologetic, and gave us his name and address and that of his insurance company, while three agents stood round to see justice done. The garage mechanic who rough-straightened the damage was so touched by the sight that he refused to charge—even though this was Paris!

Next day saw us heading eastwards in terrific heat to the Saar. Through Chalons, near where a huge road sign cried "Danger De Mort," and where the interior of the cathedral was as cool as midnight, we passed to Verdun, unusually full of soldiers. By this time, huge drops

High aloft—the Morgan being loaded on to the Southern Railway cargo steamer at Boulogne.

of rain had begun to fall, and the baked roads were steaming like a swamp. Over the horizon the sky seemed like an enormous black bruise (" the menace of Hitler," said my passenger). Then came the deluge, à la G. K. Chesterton :

" The cataract of the cliff of heaven fell blinding from the brink,
As if it would wash the stars away as suds go down the sink.
The seven heavens came roaring down for the throats of hell to drink. . . ."

We stopped, perforce, for we could not see, and before we could go on had to free the carburetter of water, for the first time on record.

In darkness we drove to Metz, which on a Sunday night was in rather comic contrast to Paris the night before. However, one jazz band at least was playing, the leader bearing an English name, which is apparently more conducive to success.

Next day in the Saar notices became bilingual and then wholly German, and the marques of Citroën and Peugeot gave way to those of Opel and Hanomag. In Swastika-saturated Saarbrucken we received our first Nazi salute from two Brownshirts in an expensive roadster.

In the Land of Nazis.

Then Germany—and what a marvellously friendly people ! They showed embarrassing interest in the Morgan, and had we been born shy our faces would have been a chronic crimson. Indeed, when we stopped for petrol at Kaiserslautern the garage proprietor refused at first to serve us, but led us proudly to a shed which housed a single-cylinder three-wheeler he had made himself seven years ago. This enthusiast in a provincial German town knew the prices of Morgans and all about them.

Every other German car was flying the Swastika from little chromium masts on the wings or radiator, and the Nazi emblem also filled that space on the rear window sacred in Britain to diving girls or Mickey Mouse. Every village had its Adolf Hitlerstrasse, and Hitler postcards in the shops took pride of place over " local views."

By way of Mannheim, where a wrecked car was set prominently on a dais—safety propaganda—and Mainz, with its big aircraft shell standing in the centre of the town—political propaganda—we reached Frankfurt, famous for beer, sausages and its quaint mediæval houses. Thence back to Wiesbaden, and to the Rhine gorge at Rudesheim, with its picturesque " wine ship " on wheels, and across the ferry to Bingen, and so downstream—an indescribably fine drive between the terraced banks, crowned at every bend with wonderful castles. One of these, Burg Rheinstein, we visited— a treasure-house of Rhenish history. From the highest turret, where there hangs a metal fire bucket once used for signalling to ships below, there is an eagle's view of the broad, barge-burdened river. Slowly we went on, past the Lorelei Rock of Legend, to Coblenz, opposite the frowning fortress of Ehrenbreitstein, one of many places where Byron tried to work off his special brand of monomania. A night in an excellent hotel in Coblenz cost us 4s. 6d. each, using tourist marks.

Second only in natural glory to the Rhine was the Moselle Valley, up which we travelled next day. Cherry pickers were busy, and we had to negotiate their ladders, planted often in the centre of the highway, not always with a red flag attached. From the river, copper-torsoed canoeists saluted or waved to us perpetually, figures of superb health.

No Roads for Loitering.

When the signposts began to point to the Nurburg Ring we crossed into Luxembourg, to which we owe an apology. For we sped clean across the delightful little Duchy without spending a coin, so tempting were the roads, loitering only in the picturesquely built capital.

That evening found us in Belgium with no Belgian money, but a café keeper cheerfully accepted French francs and German cigars. Down through the wooded Ardennes we wound, and soon afterwards crossed into France again, into an area of war cemeteries. Our last night was spent at Le Touquet, a worthy finishing place and only a brief " hop " from Boulogne.

The Morgan had run as efficiently as ever it did in its previous shuttle-like career between Scotland and England ; and with a consumption figure in the forties we did not suffer seriously from the cost of petrol—roughly 3s. a gallon. Our deposit, by the way, was a humble " fiver."

Don't go three-wheeling abroad, however, if you hate to attract attention !

(Right) Under the Nazi flag— the Morgan looks a little incongruous in the village of Dielich, Germany, not far from the Luxembourg frontier.

(Left) Crossing the Franco-Belgian frontier near Maubeuge. Four countries were visited in a week.

£4-TAX CARS

Three-wheeled Models for the Coming Season

The Coventry-Victor Luxury model, which sells for £120, with a 980 c.c. side-valve engine. An o.h.v. engine can be fitted for £10 extra.

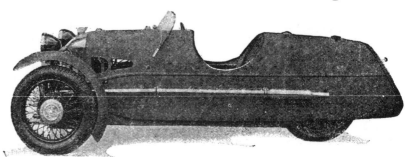

The Morgan Super Sports, which now has an improved body with spare wheel recessed into the tail; prices from £127 10s.

Extensively improved for 1935—the J.M.B. Gazelle model. Its price is £75 12s., without spare wheel. A photograph of the new J.M.B. saloon appears on page 755.

A review by our contributor Triangle of the 1935 programmes of all makes of three-wheelers in the British market will be found on pages 772-775. Details are included of the models which will be on view at the Motorcycle Show opening at Olympia on Monday.

(Right) Unchanged for 1935, but lower in price—the Raleigh, which now sells for £99 15s.

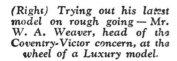

(Above) The new radiator, which is one of the 1935 improvements in the four-cylinder B.S.A. The price in standard form is £125.

(Right) Trying out his latest model on rough going — Mr. W. A. Weaver, head of the Coventry-Victor concern, at the wheel of a Luxury model.

The MORGAN FAMILY MODEL

(Left) Snapped head on and showing two noteworthy features —independent front suspension and a twin-cylinder engine.

Comfort and Performance on a £4 Tax and a 44 m.p.g. Petrol Consumption

---

IN BRIEF.

ENGINE: Twin cylinder, side valve, 85.5 mm. by 85.5 mm. = 990 c.c.; tax £4; power output 28 b.h.p. at 3,500 r.p.m.

TRANSMISSION: Single dry-plate clutch, three-speed gearbox. Ratios, 4.85, 8, and 13.1 to 1; reverse, 17.5 to 1. Final drive by enclosed propeller shaft, worm and single roller chain.

GENERAL: Cable-operated brakes; independent helical springs front and quarter elliptics rear; four-gallon petrol tank and one-gallon oil tank.

DIMENSIONS: Wheelbase, 7 ft. 3 ins.; track, 4 ft. 2 ins.; overall length, 10 ft. 6 ins.; overall width, 4 ft. 11 ins.

PERFORMANCE: Flying ¼-mile (mean speed), 56.3 m.p.h.; fastest speed over ¼ mile, 57 m.p.h. Standing ¼ mile, 26¼ secs. Petrol consumption, 44 m.p.g.

PRICE: £95.

MORGAN MOTOR CO., LTD.,
MALVERN LINK, WORCESTER.

PROBABLY there are still people who imagine that a three-wheeler is simply a two seater reduced to its bare essentials. If so, they are out of date. There was a time when this was true or very nearly so, but that time has gone. Many modern three-wheelers have all the features of a four-wheeler, except that the tax and other running costs are lower.

Of these a good example is the "Family" model Morgan, which has also the attraction of low first cost, particularly since the recent announcement that its price is now only £95. No reasonable person would expect for this figure the luxurious upholstery and equipment of a car costing three or four times as much, but the Morgan will not disappoint those who want normal comfort with adequate weather protection and equipment which is up to the modern standards of economical motoring.

This Morgan is able to carry two adults and two children in comfort. Even if the children be nearly full grown they can still find room in the back compartment of the latest "Family" Morgan. In the front there is ample space for the elders of the family and the seat position is adjustable.

Those who regularly follow our road tests will, perhaps, prefer definite figures. Here they are:—Width across front seat, 39 ins.; width across rear seat, 34 ins.; distance from rear squab to back of front squab, 21 ins. (maximum), 19 ins. (minimum); knee room between front edge of rear seat and back of front seat, 8½ ins. (maximum), 6½ ins. (minimum); depth (back to front) of cushions, 15½ ins. (front), 15 ins. (rear); height of rear seat from floor, 11 ins.; foot space in rear (back to front), 15½ ins.

The seats and the inside of the body are trimmed in good leatherette and the hood is of stout black twill. It is not of the detachable variety but folds away neatly at the back where it is enclosed by a hood envelope of similar material,

Safety glass is of course used for the single panel sloping windscreen. The side curtains are of thick celluloid mounted in metal frames which have hinged portions to allow of easy signalling and good ventilation. There are two doors and the rear seats are easily reached by tilting the other seats forward.

Equipment includes an electric horn and an electric screen wiper. These are auxiliaries of the Lucas 6-volt

lever is particularly easy to use because the movements through the gate are quite small.

As is to be expected with two large side-valve cylinders under the bonnet, the top-gear performance is good. Only rarely on main roads is it necessary to change down for a hill. The car is lively, and, especially in second gear, its acceleration is very much above the usual.

This quality is, in our opinion, of far greater importance than mere maximum speed. Only infrequently do the roads and the traffic in this country permit of high speeds, and it is, therefore, particularly necessary that a vehicle should be able to accelerate and decelerate rapidly if it is to put up a good performance on a journey.

No Sluggard.

Nevertheless, the Morgan is no sluggard. Against the stop-watch over a measured quarter-mile it is capable of a speed of 57 m.p.h. In circumstances which would normally be taken by an owner-driver as perfectly fair, its speedometer goes very comfortably over the " 60 " mark.

Another aspect of performance which is of more importance to many people is the petrol consumption. The carburetter found to be most suitable for the Vee-twin engine is an Amal of motorcycle type. This, of course, has an air lever in addition to the throttle control.

Although the Morgan can be driven quite well if the air lever is simply moved to the fully open position as soon as the engine is warm, rather better results are obtained if it is manipulated to suit the conditions of the moment. If that be done, the consumption is at the rate of 44 m.p.g., even when high average speeds are maintained. At lower speeds, no doubt, a still better figure would be registered.

In short, the Family model Morgan provides, at the minimum of expense, comfortable motoring for four at speeds which are distinctly above the average for a small car. It can be handled in just the same way as other vehicles and the fact that it has only three wheels can be ignored except for its favourable effect on the owner's bank balance.

lighting and starting set. The starter, incidentally, is sufficiently powerful to crank the engine unaided; in fact no exhaust valve lifter or other compression-releasing device is fitted.

So far as the driving of it is concerned there are only three points of difference between the Morgan and the average four-wheeled car. First, it has a hand-controlled throttle ; secondly, its steering-gear ratio is high, so that corners can be turned with very little movement of the steering wheel. (This is an undoubted advantage, especially when, as on so light a vehicle as this, it is not accompanied by heaviness or the need for much effort when manœuvring slowly.) Thirdly, the brakes are not interconnected. As the foot operates the rear shoes and the hand works the front ones, it is best to use the hand normally and to bring the pedal in as a reinforcement when really heavy braking is required. The habit is soon acquired, and it may be worth mentioning that it is a common practice amongst racing and trials drivers of all cars to use the hand brake chiefly.

Gear changing is carried out in the conventional way. The clutch is, as a matter of fact, very similar to that used on many other cars, and it has a Borg and Beck flexible centre which makes it very smooth in operation. The central gear lever, with a gate, controls the three-speed-and-reverse gearbox. When one is used to it, the

"Morgan-Adaptability"

The saying of it is not a Police test for "one-over-the-eight" but is very significant of the way the MORGAN fits *everybody's* needs.

- **Adaptable Expense ....**

  Purchase price low—easy terms to suit all pockets. Low tax (only £4). Inexpensive Insurance—ridiculously cheap running costs and maintenance.

- **Adaptable Speed ....**

  Wuffling along slowly and silently for the benefit of nervous aunts, or swifting silently at the sixties to thrill fair passengers in the "twenties."

- **Adaptable Range ....**

  Full Four-seater Family Tourers ... Comfy Two-seater speedsters ...... Hot-spot, keenly tuned Sports Models—aeros of the road in speed and acceleration.

All the comfort, speed and silence of the four wheel car at a fraction of the expense.

PROOF? .... Willingly ! ! Write your name and address across this advert, post in an unsealed envelope (½d. stamp) and a demonstration will be arranged, without obligation.

THE MORGAN MOTOR COMPANY LTD., MALVERN LINK, WORC.

Splendid Morgan news FOR THE FAMILY MAN

Sports Family with water cooled S.V. engine **£115**

★ **And the Sportsmen .....**
See the beauty of line and engine design of the Morgan Sports Models ... we leave you to form your own opinions, either at the Show or from our Catalogue, which will be sent on request.

Two Morgan Models for your choice, with yet further improved appearance and performance. Each a full four-seater vehicle, with all the speed, comfort, safety and weather protection of a four-wheel car, but at lower cost, lower tax, lower insurance, and lower upkeep. New stream-lined tail—spare wheel, interchangeable with driving or front wheels—improved gearbox design—and improved engine cooling.

See the Two Morgan Family Models at

OLYMPIA STAND No. 54

Opposite Addison Road Entrance

MORGAN MOTOR COMPANY, Ltd.,
MALVERN LINK ——————WORC.

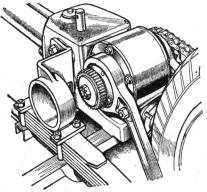

The gearbox and rear-wheel drive of the Morgan.

G ETTING the best from the Morgan three-wheeler does not call for specialised knowledge. Right from the early days of 1910 this pioneer three-wheeler has been of simple construction, and the present models, with their detachable and interchangeable wheels, three-speeds-and-reverse gearbox, single-chain drive, etc., make maintenance easier than ever.

Lubrication

One of the first essentials to good motoring is to pay strict attention to lubrication, and to use only those lubricants known to be specially suitable—follow the makers' instructions. Do not spend a fortune on polishes and begrudge an odd shilling on a pint of oil. Three parts attention to lubrication and mechanical adjustment, and one part to outward appearance is the ideal combination, but neglect neither. The reader is referred to the chassis plan which gives a clear indication which parts should receive attention. Figures in the circles represent periods at which attention is required in 100's of miles, i.e., 5 denotes 500 miles, 10 denotes 1,000 miles, etc. In addition, every 1,000 miles apply the grease gun to the nipple on the steering box, and every 500 miles apply a graphited grease to the dynamo drive. Periodically go round the Morgan with the oil can, applying a few drops to all brake and engine controls, door hinges, etc., to prevent wear and provide protection against exposure.

Keeping the Engine in Tune

Tuning the engine does not necessarily mean carrying out intricate alterations and adjustments that create phenomenal maximum speeds, but rather keeping everything in a proper state of adjustment so that the engine runs efficiently under all conditions. Maximum engine efficiency is dependent on correct tuning of the various associate components (carburetter, ignition system, etc.) so that they operate in perfect harmony. A dirty engine cannot give its maximum

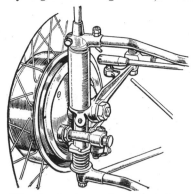

This sketch shows the helical front-wheel suspension and steering arm.

power output, so it is important to decarbonise at least every 4–5,000 miles. During this process do not forget the piston rings and valves. Remove all carbon deposit from the former and see they are free in their grooves and lightly grind-in the valves with grinding paste, being sure that they seat nicely. Worn valve guides are responsible for erratic running, and should be renewed. Check the valve springs for strength, and when replacing cylinder heads do not forget the extra tightening of the bolts after the engine has been warmed up. See that all water passages are clear, and allow sufficient water circulation. Tappet clearances should come in for frequent

inlet tappets should have .004 in., and exhaust .006 in. clearance. Clearance in the case of the overhead-valve engine should be the nearest approach to nil, obtainable with the engine cold. The end caps on the valve stems should be just free to be rotated by the fingers while no perceptible up-and-down movement of the rockers is possible. Regular attention to sparking plugs will help towards maximum efficiency, and the spark gaps should be kept to .018 in.

The Carburetter

Carburation plays an important part in the behaviour of the engine, and should receive occasional attention. It is advisable to remove the carburetter now and again and clean out carefully. Heavy, "thumpy" running can result from too rich a mixture, and this usually indicates the need for lowering the needle in the throttle valve. Where strict economy is desired, adjustment sometimes results in too weak a mixture, which makes starting difficult, and the engine has a tendency to fire back through the carburetter. In such cases the needle should be raised a notch. Needle positions are counted from the top of the needle, the top groove being No. 1. The normal setting of the needle is in notch No. 3.

The ignition should be

attention. Excessive clearances promote valve-gear noises, and in no way improve the running. In the case of the side-valve engine

kept in correct adjustment, as nothing has so pronounced an effect on the running of the engine as incorrect adjustment. The distributor should be kept clean, also the contact-breaker points. Do not file the contact-breaker points; they should be dressed smooth with an oil stone if they become worn, pitted or burned, and should be set to .018 in.

Brakes

With the engine in good tune the Morgan

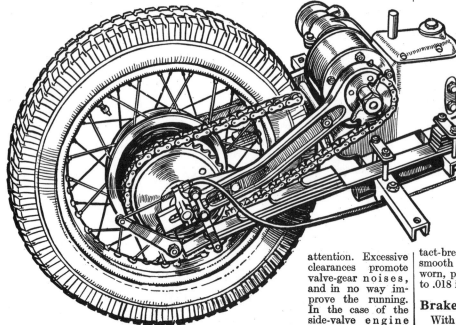

Morgan Three-Wheeler

owner-driver. Special refer-
vehicle, but the information
be of assistance to owners
models.

three-wheeler possesses considerable acceleration and speed, and it is imperative that
all brakes should be
in efficient working
order. See that
these are adjusted

any time the engine be taken out of the
chassis, damp the splined end of the transmission shaft with an oily rag—avoid
excessive oiling with the oil can.

Steering

The Morgan steering should be steady at
all speeds. Any tendency to pull to one side
can be traced to uneven tyre pressures.
The front wheels should be inflated to 19,
and the rear to 25 lb. per sq. in. Occasionally check the front-wheel track. It is
easily believed that having had this
attended to no further attention is necessary, but in the course of everyday motoring

rim is ⅛ in. narrower in the front than at
the back of the wheels. The track rod (the
adjustable ends of which allow the wheels
to be tracked) has a tapered pin at both
ends, which act as dampers. If too freely
oiled these are inclined to lose their
damping properties, and wheel wobble is
likely, so instead of applying oil with the
oil can, remove them at intervals and damp
with an oily rag, just sufficient to prevent
rusting and stiffness in the steering.

Gearbox and Rear Forks

The rear end of the vehicle calls for little
attention, except lubrication and brake
adjustment, as before mentioned. The gearbox requires no adjustment or other attention beyond "topping up" to the level
indicated on the dip stick. Keep the tie
bar holding the rear-fork arms together tight at all times, so that no side
movement can occur, and also the
rear-wheel spindle nut. The single
driving chain must be kept at the

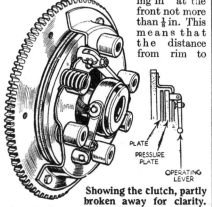

This illustration of the complete
Morgan chassis shows practically all of
the principal mechanical features.

periodically in the usual way, and ensure that
cables are free in their outer casings.
Brake efficiency can be impaired by cables
rusting, and interfering with ease in operation. Remove the cables occasionally, clean
and well oil, and if in correct adjustment
the brakes will be found to be powerful and
efficient at all speeds. After adjusting, it
is sometimes found that the brakes do not
pull the machine up as quickly as might be
desired. The cause may be traced to the
linings, on to which may have found its way
a smear of grease from the hubs. Constant
application of the brakes generates heat
and allows grease to escape past the felt
retainers. Remove the wheels in such cases,
and swill with petrol, or burn off the lubricant from the linings.

Clutch

Do not apply oil to the plate clutch. The
only points that need a spot of oil are the
toggles indicated in the chart. Should at

the front wheels receive quite a lot of
severe shocks sufficient to upset alignment.
Wheels are correctly tracked when "toeing in" at the
front not more
than ⅛ in. This
means that
the distance
from rim to

PLATE

PRESSURE
PLATE

OPERATING
LEVER

**Showing the clutch, partly
broken away for clarity.
Inset is shown a section through the plates.**

correct tension
—1 in. up and
down movement
in the bottom
run is sufficient.
Adjust with the machine standing on the
level. Lubricate as already directed, and
occasionally remove and immerse in
warm oil to ensure ample lubrication of the
rollers and rivets. Never allow the dynamo
gears to develop excessive backlash; keep
them well meshed, and maintain a constant
charging rate.

Electrical Equipment

Night driving calls for reliability from
the lighting equipment. In the summer
months one is inclined to neglect this very
important part of the machine, and finds
that when wanted the lamps do not give
the illumination necessary. Examine them
occasionally during the day-time and make
sure that bright and dim filaments are
sound, and the dimming gear in order. The
battery should receive periodical attention.
(Continued overleaf)

UPKEEP OF THE MORGAN THREE-WHEELER.
(*Continued from previous page*)

At least once a month the vent plugs should be removed, and the acid level checked.

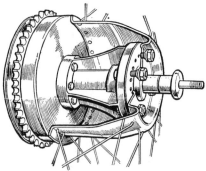

A view of the rear-wheel hub partly broken away.

This should be kept level with the separators and only distilled water added when "topping up." The battery should never be left in a discharged condition, and connections should be tight, and smeared with vaseline. The dynamo should require little attention, and only very occasionally should it be necessary to examine the brushes and commutator. See that the brushes press firmly on to the commutator, and that the spring arms securing them move freely on their pivots. Range of visibility depends on the correctness or otherwise of the alignment and focusing of the lamps, not to mention the comfort of other road users. Alignment and focusing is best carried out at night with the car on a straight level road. Metal polish should not be used on the reflectors.

In conclusion, a word to the driver—be modest in your driving. Nothing is achieved by accelerating violently from a stand-still beyond obtaining an expensive smell of burning rubber. Rear tyres have a short life when this method is followed, and unnecessary stress is placed on the engine and transmission generally. Your collosal acceleration used at the right time will get you out of a tight corner. Likewise your brakes, if properly adjusted and efficient, will keep you out of trouble, but avoid getting into a tight corner by applying them in good time.

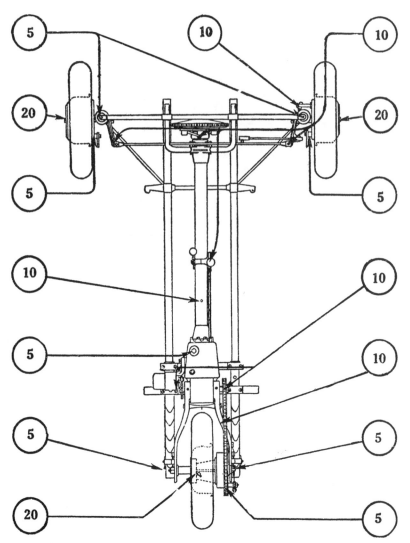

The lubrication points on the Morgan. These are referred to in the text, and the various points are, reading clockwise from the top left-hand corner: sliding axles; speedometer gearbox; steering ball joints, clutch toggle arms and gear lever; front hubs; front brake cams; fork pivots; chain; spring shackles; rear brake cam; rear hub; spring shackles; gearbox; transmission central bearing; front brake cams; front hubs.

ON THREE WHEELS

By Triangle

FOR 1936 the four-cylinder Morgan shown here will sell at the reduced price of £115 10s., and there will be an additional four-cylinder model in the shape of a super-sports two-seater at £120 15s.

I WONDER how many of my readers are regarding the end of this month with rather dismal anticipation as the end of their motoring for the year. The plan of laying up machines for the winter on September 30 is nothing like so common as it once was, but there are still quite a few who do it.

Personally, I am all against the idea —at any rate so far as the last quarter of the year is concerned. For one thing, the Indian summer that we often get in October offers ideal motoring conditions, and for another, I hate to find myself with no form of transport at Christmas. Shopping can be the very devil if you have to rely on trams and buses, to say nothing of the awful business of getting to and from the various festivities that happen round about the end of December.

I believe, too, that winter motoring holds attractions of its own that are every bit as enjoyable as the summer can yield. In this I may differ from the views of the majority, but that, I always like to think, is because the majority are not so clever as I am in making the most of the cold shorter days.

However, it is early yet to think of winter days, so I will not continue that argument. All the same, I do advise anyone who is thinking of laying up his machine to reconsider the idea very seriously. If laying-up is a necessity for some period of the year, make it the January-March quarter. That is the time when the weather is at its worst and the three months concerned should give even those with quite elaborate plans for overhauling, ample time for whatever they have to do.

* * *

MY forecast last month that no startling changes were likely to be seen in three-wheelers for 1936 seems to be coming true. Already the Coventry Victor concern has announced the continuance of its luxury models with small improvements, and now comes the news that the Morgan range for 1936 remains the same with, however, the addition of a new super-sports four-cylinder model.

All About Morgans for 1936—Is Laying-up Worth While?— Useful Hints

The existing four-cylinder chassis will, I gather, be used and the body will be similar to that of the corresponding two-cylinder model. Exact details are not yet available for publication, but the price has already been fixed at £120 15s.

In addition I am able to pass on the welcome news that, with the exception of the side-valve, water-cooled Family model, prices of the remainder of the range have been substantially reduced. Here is the full list with last year's figures given in brackets for comparison:—

Two-cylinder two-seaters: Sports model with s.v. water-cooled engine £101 17s. (£110), with o.h.v. air-cooled engine £107 2s. (£115), with o.h.v. water-cooled engine £115 10s. (£120). Super sports model with o.h.v. air-cooled engine £126 (£127 10s.), with o.h.v. water-cooled engine £136 10s. (£137 10s.).

Two-cylinder four-seaters: Family model with s.v. water-cooled engine £96 12s. (£95). Sports Family model with s.v. water-cooled engine £110 5s. (£115), with o.h.v. air-cooled engine £115 10s. (£120), with o.h.v. water-cooled engine £120 15s. (£125).

In addition, of course, there is the existing four-cylinder model which now costs £115 10s. (£120), and the new super sports four-cylinder model at £120 15s.

At these reduced figures I should say that Morgan prospects for 1936 look very bright indeed.

* * *

AN owner of an o.h.v. J.A.P.-engined Morgan sends me a useful tip, which seems worth passing on. In this engine, the ball joints between the tops of the push rods and the rockers rely for lubrication on oil mist blown up from the timing chest, but he noticed that, on his engine, these joints seemed absolutely dry. Puzzled, he tried running the engine on a fast tick-over with the rocker box covers removed, just to see what was actually happening.

To his surprise, several large lumps of hard grease were blown out of the push-rod tubes—and since then no further trouble with dry ball joints has occurred. The assumption is that the grease had at some time exuded from the rocker bearings and found its way down the tubes; as the tops of the push rods are thicker than the stems, it had been unable to return and had effectively screened the joints from oil mist.

* * *

HOW can fitting a new contact breaker spring cause pinking?—was a poser set me by a four-cylinder B.S.A. owner the other day. Apparently he had broken the spring, fitted a new one, carefully adjusted the gap, and then found to his amazement that the engine showed a pronounced tendency to pink.

The problem is not so difficult as it sounds. It all depends on the adjustment of the gap and its effect on the ignition timing. If the gap is very wide the points will open much earlier and the ignition will be correspondingly advanced. A small gap, on the other hand, will retard the ignition.

Obviously, in the case in question, the gap, before the spring was replaced, was too small and the ignition had been permanently retarded. Possibly the small gap had been brought about by wear on the fibre heel-piece that bears on the cam and had been reduced gradually, so that its effect was not noticed. At the same time carbon was forming in the head—also without its effect being noticed owing to the slow and progressive retarding of the ignition.

So soon as the ignition timing was advanced to its correct point, however, the effect of the carbon accumulation immediately became apparent by pronounced pinking.

Simple!

THE MORGAN THREE-WHEELER

How to Top Overhaul Both the Two and Four-cylinder Engines Forms the Main Subject of this Instalment

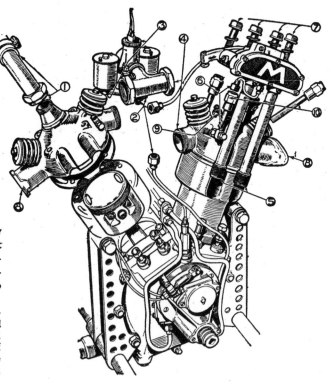

A specially prepared cut-away drawing of the o.h.v. Matchless engine with the parts numbered in order of removal for decarbonizing. The numbers show:—(1) water outlet joints, (2) petrol and oil pipe unions, (3) carburetter, (4) induction pipe unions, (5) push rod tubes—raise telescopic lower portion, (6) inlet valve oil supply union, (7) rocker-box head nuts, (8) exhaust pipe joints, (9) sparking plug, (10) cylinder-head nuts.

THE subject of lubrication was explored very fully in the first article of this series which appeared last week. Attention can now be turned to engine maintenance and adjustments, with particular reference to decarbonizing and valve grinding, before passing on to matters concerning the chassis.

So far as decarbonizing the twin-cylinder engines is concerned, the general procedure in the case of J.A.P. and Matchless types is very similar, and if the job is described in detail in connection with the Matchless, owners of J.A.P. models should have no difficulty in allowing for the slight differences in design when dealing with their own engines.

With water-cooled engines the first job obviously is to drain the radiator and disconnect the water joints from the cylinder heads by undoing the union nuts connecting the outlet pipes at the heads. With overhead-valve engines the next job is to disconnect the oil pipes both at the unions on the tops of the rocker boxes and at the T junction between the cylinders. The petrol pipe must also be disconnected from the carburetter.

Then slack off the two union nuts holding the induction pipe to the cylinders. This will permit the carburetter to be lifted out of the way, and although it can be laid on one side, still attached to the control wires, it is much better to unscrew the knurled ring at the top of the instrument so that the slides can be withdrawn and the carburetter itself put in some safer place.

The next job is to detach the rocker boxes, but it must be remembered that the small oil pipes carrying lubricant to the inlet-valve stems connect the boxes to the heads, and these must be disconnected at the cylinder-head end. It is also wise to push up the telescopic lower ends of the push-rod tubes. It is then possible to withdraw the rocker boxes complete with the tubes after the four bolts holding each rocker box to its head have been removed.

Before the cylinder heads are taken off, the two exhaust

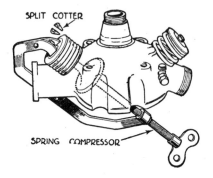

Valve removal on the o.h.v. twin-cylinder engines is best carried out with the aid of a spring compressor of the type shown.

pipes must be detached at their flanges, whilst it is a good plan also partially to unscrew the sparking plugs which, if tight, may prove troublesome to remove once the heads have been detached. The heads themselves are held in position by means of four bolts, the heads of which, incidentally, are tapped to receive the rocker-box bolts. Should the cylinder heads stick, a few taps underneath the protruding inlet and exhaust ports with a block of wood will free the joints.

The heads should be placed on the bench and the valves removed with some suitable valve-spring compressor such as the Terry, illustrated in one of the accompanying sketches. With the spring compressed with this tool it is a simple matter to take out the split-cone cotters and collars which hold the springs in place. The heads and piston crowns should be scraped free of carbon, whilst it is also a wise plan to clean out the exhaust and inlet ports as thoroughly as possible.

For grinding-in the valves a special tool will be needed, as the heads are not provided with either screwdriver slots or dowel-pin holes. One can either use a suction cone as in the case of the four-cylinder engines or a T-shaped tool with a socket to take the end of the valve stem and a grub screw to lock it in place. In this case, of course, pressure on the valve seat is obtained by pulling the tool while partially rotating it.

Reassembly of the engine is merely a repetition of dismantling, the only points worth mentioning being the need for taking care that the oil pipes are reassembled on the correct unions and the desirability of tightening the cylinder head (and rocker-box bolts) half a turn at a time, in the correct sequence. The best plan is to tighten the two diagonally opposite first and then the other two, and so on.

When all is reassembled, the valves must, of course, be checked for tappet clearance and the engine run for some distance, when the head nuts can be given their final tightening down and the valves re-checked. The actual valve adjustment is carried out on the tappets at the base of the push rods, where three hexagons will be found. The lowest one is formed on the tappet itself, the one next above is the lock nut and the top one is the adjustable tappet head. The last-named should be held with a spanner whilst the lock nut is slacked off. The tappet itself should then be held whilst the head is screwed to the appropriate position; the tappet and head are then held whilst the lock nut is retightened.

The clearance itself should be tested at the valve end, and when the engine is cold should be the nearest approach to nil obtainable; that is to say, there should be no appreciable play, but it should be possible to revolve the valve stem caps with the fingers. (In the case of o.h.v. J.A.P. engines a clearance of .002 in. is recommended.)

The method of dealing with side-valve engines is very similar except that the complication of the overhead-valve gear is absent and that there are seven head nuts.

The best method of removing the valves is by means of a hook-shaped lifter engaging with the head face and the valve-spring collar, although it is possible to carry out the job by slipping a block of wood in the valve chest to act as a fulcrum and levering up the collar and spring by means of a screwdriver. The valve head must, of course, be held down whilst this is done.

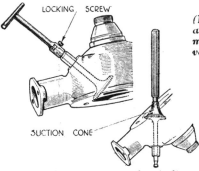

(Below) The valve adjusting arrangements of the side-valve Matchless engines.

LOCKING SCREW

SUCTION CONE

(Above) Two means of grinding in the valves of the o.h.v. twins. The suction cone is also suitable for the four-cylinder engines.

The valves, incidentally, are slotted so that they can be ground in with the aid of a screwdriver. The actual valve adjustment is carried out on the tappets after the manner of the o.h.v. engine, but in this case larger clearances are necessary, the actual recommendations (for both Matchless and J.A.P. engines) being .004 in. for the inlet and .006 in. for the exhaust.

With both engines it is desirable to have a spare set of gaskets available in case the existing ones are defective.

Inspecting Pistons on Twin-cylinder Engines.

Should the owner decide to inspect the pistons on either side or overhead-valve engines, the job can be done fairly readily when the heads are removed for decarbonizing, as the cylinder barrels are detachable, being held by four nuts at the base. The lower water connections will, of course, have to be disconnected, whilst it will also be necessary to undo the two unions between the cylinders where the oil pipes from the pump to the tank are held by a bracket, and to detach this bracket from the crankcase. Incidentally, the oil pipes should be plugged, as otherwise the tank will empty itself over the engine.

Owing to the fact that the cylinder barrel nuts at the back of the engine are very difficult of access, it will be necessary either to take the engine out of the frame or, at any rate, to undo the four bolts on the engine bearers

and slide the engine forward slightly. Before the unit can be moved, however, the ignition control and exhaust valve lifter must be disconnected.

Reverting to the pistons, these are of the three-ring type with the gudgeon pins held by circlips. A ring compressor of the normal clamp type will be needed to enter them into the cylinders on reassembly.

Should end play develop on the rockers of o.h.v. Matchless engines the cure is fairly simple. Actually, the rocker arms are on a serrated shaft and are held in place at the external end by means of a nut and split pin. At the other end the splines are merely tapped over to lock the rockers in position. If end float develops the rockers should be tapped along the shaft until they come against the external end nut, when the splines should be tapped over to lock them in place.

On o.h.v. J.A.P. engines end play in the rocker boxes can be dealt with in the following way after the rocker boxes have been detached from the cylinder heads. Unscrew the four ¼-in. clamping nuts, remove the cover plate by taking off the lever nut and then hold the rocker box face downwards, giving a sharp tap at each end. This will cause the races to slide through their housings slightly and stand proud to the face of the box.

The clamping nuts should then be screwed up finger-tight, the cover plate carefully replaced and the lever nut tightened, which will have the effect of forcing the rockers and races back into their boxes in such a position that there is no end play. The ¼-in. clamping nuts and lever nut should then be finally tightened.

Decarbonizing the Fours.

Decarbonizing the four-cylinder models is quite a straightforward job, although some difficulty arises with regard to tappet clearances if the valves are ground-in; this, however, will be referred to in due course.

The actual dismantling procedure should be carried out

HEAD

LOCK NUT

TAPPET

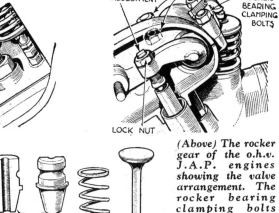

ADJUSTMENT

ROCKER BEARING CLAMPING BOLTS

LOCK NUT

(Above) The rocker gear of the o.h.v. J.A.P. engines showing the valve arrangement. The rocker bearing clamping bolts are also shown.

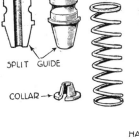

SPLIT GUIDE

COLLAR

(Above) Valve parts of the four-cylinder engines. Owing to the special valve shape, the split guide has to be removed before the valve can be extracted; this is best done by means of a hardwood or brass drift (right).

HARDWOOD DRIFT

in the following order :—Drain the radiator, disconnect the starter motor cable (in case of accidental shorts) and slacken the nut on the taper pin holding the dynamo support to the cylinder head; this releases the support and allows the dynamo to be lowered and the fan belt slipped off the pulley. Then disconnect the lead on the cut-out terminal and lift the dynamo, together with its support, off the cylinder head.

Next detach the leads from the sparking plugs, marking them first for correct replacement, and pull the high-tension lead from the coil out of its spring contact in the centre of the distributor. The lead from the coil to the side of the distributor must also be detached, when the screw holding the distributor body clamp to the cylinder head can be taken out and the distributor lifted out of its socket in the cylinder head. The nut on the distributor clamp holding the distributor body should not be disturbed or the timing will be upset. Also remove the plugs.

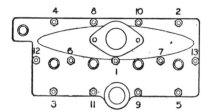

It is important to tighten the nuts on the four-cylinder model gradually and in their correct sequence — given here by numbers.

The two screws holding the water outlet to the cylinder head should next be removed, thus freeing the water connection without the necessity of disturbing the hose joints.

As it will be necessary to remove the manifolds to deal with the valves and ports, the wire to the self-starting carburetter device should be disconnected and also the accelerator pedal rod (by means of the spring joint which may be pulled off at the throttle end) and the petrol pipe; it is then necessary only to undo the nuts holding the manifolds on to the cylinder block and the clip attaching the exhaust manifold to the pipe, when the manifold may be removed. The two manifolds, incidentally, are bolted together to give a hot spot, but there is no need to separate them or to remove the carburetter from the induction pipe.

Removal of the cylinder head is then a perfectly straightforward job entailing only the undoing of the various head nuts. The actual scraping away of the carbon from the head and piston crowns calls for no comment other than to stress the need for keeping carbon chippings out of the cylinder bores by stuffing rag into them.

Grinding-in the Valves.

The question of dealing with the valves, as already mentioned, is rather complicated from an amateur's point of view, as no adjustment is provided on the tappets and if the valves are ground-in, reducing the clearance to less than the recommended .013 in.-.015 in. it is necessary to grind the end of the stems to restore the status quo. This, of course, is a job which cannot be undertaken by the average amateur, as very accurate grinding is needed. Any Ford agent is equipped for the work, however.

To take out the valves, the cover plate enclosing the tappets on the near side of the engine should be detached, the valve springs lifted with one of the special tools obtainable for the purpose from any accessory dealer, and the collar holding the spring on to the valve stem removed. The spring itself should also be taken out. The valve should then be pushed upwards as high as possible and a piece of wood slipped under the head into the valve port, so that it engages with the top of the valve guide; by tapping the wood the split valve guide will be pushed into the valve chamber, whence it can be withdrawn.

As it is important that the guides are replaced in their initial positions, it is a good plan to have a series of small numbered boxes into which the respective valves, together with their springs, collars and guides can be placed.

Before the actual grinding-in process is commenced some clean rag should be inserted in the valve chamber to pre-vent any carbon chippings entering the sump via the passages leading from the chamber, and any carbon that has accumulated in the ports should be scraped away. Grinding-in can then proceed, but it is to be noted that the valves have no screwdriver slots or pinholes in their heads so that a suction-type valve grinder will be needed.

Reassembly of the engine is a fairly straightforward reversal of the dismantling procedure, but one or two points call for note.

As already explained, any valves which lack the necessary clearance must be removed and taken to a Ford dealer for the stems to be ground. A further check be made after reassembly, and should the clearance exceed .015 in. it will be necessary to carry out further grinding-in of the seatings to obtain the correct clearance.

Distributor Replacement.

The order of tightening the cylinder head nuts is, of course, important, and is shown in one of the accompanying illustrations. Owners, incidentally, need not be concerned with regard to the replacing of the distributor, as it is necessary merely to slip the shaft into its hole in the cylinder head and rotate it until the tongue on the spindle engages with the slot in the drive shaft. The tongue, incidentally, is offset so that it cannot be replaced incorrectly.

With regard to ignition and carburation, for all normal purposes there should be no need to disturb the manufacturers' standard setting, and all that need be done is

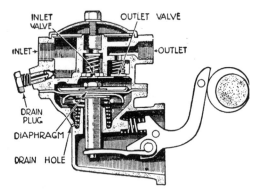

A sectioned view of the camshaft-driven petrol pump used on the four-cylinder engines.

occasional dismantling and cleaning in the case of the carburetter and maintenance of the correct contact breaker gap (.012-.015 in. for all two-cylinder models with coil ignition and .018 in. for the four-cylinder engines).

The sparking plugs should also be taken to pieces and cleaned from time to time, and their points set to the correct gap of approximately .020 in. in the case of magneto ignition models and .025 in. for coil ignition models.

Four-cylinder engines have a camshaft-driven petrol pump, but the only maintenance normally required for this is occasional removal of the sediment chamber drain plug. Should there be any traces of starvation in spite of this, the central screw in the top cover plate should be removed, giving access to the filter, which may be taken out and cleaned. There is, incidentally, a vent hole in the lower half of the pump body, and if petrol should at any time be observed coming out of this hole it is an indication that the diaphragm is faulty and needs renewal.

The only other engine adjustment likely to concern owners is the exhaust valve lifter or decompressor on the two-cylinder models. This is provided to facilitate easy starting, and should it ever fail to open the valves sufficiently, the Bowden cable controlling it should be adjusted at the point where it enters the stop on the timing case. This adjustment is of the normal Bowden cable type, the procedure being to slacken off the lock nut, screw out the adjusting sleeve to increase the effective length of the outer cable as necessary and then retighten the lock nut.

79

The MORGAN THREE-WHEELER

Dealing in Detail with Brakes, Wheel Bearings and Front Suspension

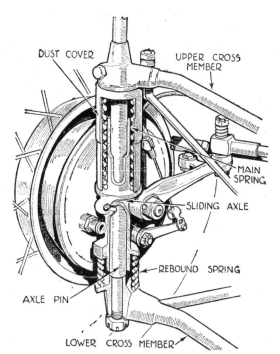

A broken open view of the independent front suspension of current models. Earlier types differed slightly in detail. How to replace a worn sliding axle on both models is explained in the text.

IN previous articles in this series lubrication and engine adjustments have been dealt with in some detail. This week it is proposed to consider the various adjustments that become necessary from time to time on the chassis.

Braking, being a matter of considerable importance, may well be dealt with first. The braking is carried out by means of a normal internal expanding system, the pedal taking effect on the back and the hand control on the front wheels. In each case Bowden cables are employed, and an adjustment is provided at the cable stop adjacent to the brake drum. The screwed sleeve into which the outer casing fits should be screwed out from the stop to take up play or farther into the stop to provide more play, the lock nut, of course, being loosened before this is done and carefully retightened afterwards.

If, after considerable wear, all the adjustment is taken up at these points, a further adjustment can be made at the camshaft spindle arms. It will be observed that each inner cable end is sweated into a fork end secured to the cam spindle arm by means of a clevis pin retained by a split pin. The forked cable ends have two sets of holes, and it is a simple matter to remove the pins and replace them in the inner holes of the yoke ends. This, of course, makes a very large difference to the adjustment, so that after it has been done it will be necessary to slack off the cable adjustment at the stops.

To Avoid Brake Re-lining.

It occasionally happens that both these adjustments are fully taken up, or the cam levers go over centre when the brakes are applied hard, although the linings themselves are not completely worn out. To avoid renewing the linings it is sometimes worth while to sweat 1-32 in. sheet metal pads on to the heel pieces of the cams, thus avoiding immediate renewal of the lining.

It is worth noting that a single cable is used, this starting from one front brake, passing round a pulley attached to the hand-brake lever and so on to the other front brake. The advantage of this continuous cable is that it provides compensation for the two front brakes, so avoiding the need for equalization when adjusting.

To gain access to the front brake shoes on either side the wheel should be removed, and the nut which holds the steering arm on to the sliding axle assembly unscrewed. This nut is locked by a star washer, and a new washer should be used for replacement. The steering arm can then be removed. This enables the hub spindle to be tapped out of the sliding axle after disconnecting the brake cable and, on the off side, the speedometer cable.

It is a good plan to rub the spindle with emery cloth before tapping out, as occasionally traces of rust may be present on the portion on which the steering arm fits, and this rust, naturally, tends to make the spindle bind in the sliding axle.

Another sound precaution is to replace the nut before tapping out the spindle to prevent the thread being

damaged; the nut, of course, has to be removed before the spindle can be withdrawn completely. With the spindle tapped out, the hub, brake drum and back plate come away together. There is a distance piece adjacent to the back plate, and this should next be removed when the back plate and drum will come apart. The distance piece is a sliding fit on the hub spindle, and should it prove obstinate it should be tapped round with a punch until free.

The brake shoes, of course, remain held to the back plate by means of their pull-off springs, and they can be detached by levering their ends away from the pivot pin. This should be done before any attempt is made to unhook the springs, which is a very difficult job with the shoes in position, but quite easy when they have been unhooked as a pair from the back plate. As it is important that the shoes should be replaced in the same position and the same way round, they should be punch-marked before they are detached.

Should it be desired to separate the drums from the hubs, the six nuts holding them should be undone. On the off side it will be necessary to remove the speedometer ring, and a special tool (made out of a sheet of steel plate cut so that the two tongues are provided to engage with the teeth) will be required to unscrew it.

Replacing Hub Bearings.

If it is desired to reach the hub bearings for replacement—they are non-adjustable—the hub cap must be removed and the hub spindle should be gripped in a vice so that the castle nut can be unscrewed. The hub spindle can then be tapped out, leaving the two ball races in the hub. The outer race is a push fit, and can easily be removed complete, but the inner race is retained by a ring screwed into the shell. This ring in turn is prevented from working loose by a spring circlip. The procedure, therefore, is to remove the circlip, unscrew the ring (it has three holes with which a punch may be engaged to tap it round), when the race can be withdrawn.

Replacing is a straightforward reversal of dismantling, but care should be taken to make sure that the felt washer which fits between the inner race and the brake drum is in good condition. So far as refitting the brake shoes is concerned, these should be assembled together as a pair with their springs; one shoe should be placed in position and the other one pulled away from it and slipped over the pivot pin and cam. Take care when doing this not to bend or break the forked end of the shoe that fits into the recess on the pivot pin. Needless to say, a little grease should be applied to both the pivot pin and the cam.

If occasion ever arises to remove the speedometer pinion, this can be done simply by withdrawing the split pin which holds it to its shaft. The speedometer drive bracket is screwed into the brake back plate, and can be removed after taking off the lock nut. An important point here is to make sure on replacement that the pinion does not foul the brake drum nuts when everything is re-assembled. If it does, the lock nut should be loosened and the drive bracket unscrewed a turn or so in the back plate.

Reverting to the front hub bearings, older model Morgans had ball bearings of the cup and cone type in place of the journal ball bearings at present employed. Play can be taken up on these models by removing the split pin, castellated nut and tongued lock washer on the hub spindle and screwing in the cone.

It is essential with a bearing of this type that a little play is left or the bearing will rapidly wear. Screw up the cone, therefore, until all appreciable play has disappeared, but there is no suggestion of tightness.

Rear wheel removal is quite simple on the three-speed models. The first job is to disconnect the tail lamp lead, which has an easily detachable screw connection, take off the spare wheel and then undo the four nuts and withdraw the rear panel. This gives easy access to the wheel,

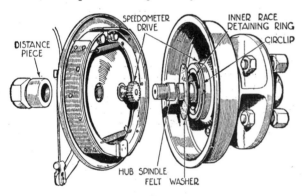

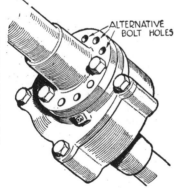

(Above) An "exploded" view of a front hub and brake assembly showing various points mentioned in the text. (Right) The steering box showing the three alternative holes provided for each bolt to allow the eccentrically mounted pinion to be brought into deeper mesh to take up wear.

which should be jacked up by placing the jack under the frame cross-member, just at the rear of the gearbox.

The nut on the knock-out spindle should then be removed, the brake cable slipped out of the slot in the brake cam lever, and the knock-out spindle pulled or tapped out, thus allowing the wheel to drop. The driving chain can then be lifted off the sprocket and the wheel will come away as one unit. It is retained on the hub assembly by means of four nuts.

When the wheel is removed the brake back plate, complete with shoes, pulls straight out, as it is merely spigoted on to the main hollow spindle. The brake shoes themselves can be levered off by inserting a screwdriver between the ends of the shoes.

So far as the bearings are concerned, there is a roller race on the driving side and a ball race on the near side. To remove the bearings, the spindle should be driven out by tapping through from the sprocket side. The roller race can be removed by taking off the six nuts which hold the brake drum to the hub, removing the drum and taking out the ball race housing cover and leather seal, which, incidentally, is held by a spring. The race can then be tapped out from the opposite side.

The ball race on the opposite side can be removed by taking off the plate behind the wheel hub flange (which is free when the wheel nuts have been removed) and tapping out the race from the opposite side.

Independent front suspension has always been a special feature of the Morgan, and provided that lubrication is carried out at regular intervals the system is very trouble-free. As an accompanying illustration shows, the weight of the car is taken by helical springs bearing on the upper of the two front cross-members, whilst below the phosphor bronze sliding axles carrying the wheels are smaller helical springs which act as rebound dampers.

Renewing Sliding Axles.

After a considerable mileage, wear may develop in the sliding axles, a fault which is conducive to wheel wobble. Renewal of a sliding axle is not a very difficult matter. The wing should first be removed and the wheel, together with the hub spindle, should be detached from the sliding axle, as explained in connection with removal of the hubs; the castellated nut under the lower cross-member should also be taken off.

The next job is to slack off the split clamp which forms the end of the upper cross-member, when the axle pin that passes through the whole assembly and forms the wing stay at its upper end can be pulled right out. The whole spring assembly should then be pushed sideways, free of the upper cross-member, but care should be taken to hold the casing tight so that the spring does not fly so soon as it is relieved of compression.

The dust casing and two springs can then be detached, fitted over the new sliding axle and the whole assembly replaced between the cross-members. It is quite possible to compress the springs sufficiently by hand to do this.

On older models the construction differs slightly in that the sliding axles work on a steel tube fitted between the upper and lower cross-members, the wing stay passing through the centre of this tube and serving merely to hold the assembly together. The tube fits into recesses in the lugs at the ends of the frame cross-members, and it is necessary to spring the two cross-members apart slightly to allow the tube, complete with spring and sliding axle, to be withdrawn. The caution regarding the spring flying applies with this design as well as to the current type.

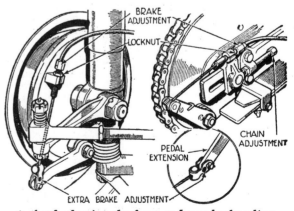

A sketch showing the front and rear brake adjustments; when the limit of the Bowden cable adjustment is reached, further play may be taken up at the yoke ends of the cables. The sketch also shows the rear chain adjusters.

THE MORGAN THREE-WHEELER

This Concluding Instalment Deals with Steering, Rear Wheel and Clutch Adjustments

THE steering connections are straightforward, so far as the drag link is concerned, normal ball joints with the usual cup and spring adjustment are provided. The track rod joints, on the other hand, are unusual in that the track rod is connected to the steering arms by means of spring-loaded taper pins so designed that the track rod is forced tightly on the taper. This sets up sufficient friction to act as a steering damper and overcome any tendency towards wheel wobble. Should it be necessary to adjust the track of the front wheels (which should toe in ⅛ in. when the car is stationary), the length of the track rod can be altered by disconnecting the near-side pin and screwing the end of the track rod in or out, as desired, after slackening the lock nut.

The steering box is of the epicyclic type and the planet wheel is eccentrically mounted so that play may be taken up. If the steering box is examined it will be noticed that the top tube surrounding the column has a series of holes round its flange and is held in place by three bolts. To take up play these bolts should be removed, the tube turned until excessive play disappears and the bolts then replaced in new holes.

After the job has been done, incidentally, the front wheels should be jacked up and the steering turned to make quite sure that it is free on full lock, as the majority of wear obviously takes place when the wheels are in the approximately straight ahead position, and it may be that in taking up this play completely the gears become too tightly meshed on full lock.

So far as rear wheel suspension is concerned, there is nothing calling for comment other than the need for keeping the wheel in proper alignment and for the rear forks to be free from side play.

Alignment can be altered by means of the chain adjusters on each side of the rear fork after slacking off the spindle nut; these adjusters are of the conventional motorcycle type and serve to slide the whole wheel assembly

that there is no side play on the fork arms. If there is, the nuts holding the tie-bar should be removed, the necessary number of shims taken out and the tie-bar replaced and tightened.

Apart from the chain, the only part of the transmission likely to require adjustment is the clutch, which is liable to judder if the toggles are unevenly adjusted. If this is suspected, the thrust block should be pulled against the thrust pad with the fingers, when it will readily be seen which of the toggles needs adjustment, as the thrust pad and block will not make contact all the way round. The actual adjustment is by means of the thrust pins near the outer extremities of the toggle arms; these can be screwed in or out as desired after slackening their lock nuts.

Fierceness in the case of the old cone clutches can be caused in a variety of ways, but as our contributor " Triangle " is dealing with this very matter in his next page of three-wheeler notes, the subject can be omitted here.

One other matter likely to concern ordinary owners is the adjustment of the dynamo drive pinions. As has been stated already, the driving pinion is of fibre to ensure quiet running, and it is not only essential that the pinion should be adequately lubricated, but, also, that it is correctly meshed. Occasionally owners experience trouble due to the teeth being stripped on the fibre pinion, and these difficulties are almost invariably due to incorrect meshing, the common mistake being to allow too much play between the opposing teeth.

The dynamo bracket is held to the gearbox by means of three bolts, and to adjust the mesh all three should be slackened. The bracket can then be swung round on the pivot bolt until the two pinions are fully meshed without any actual tightness being present. The dynamo should be held in this position whilst the nuts are tightened.

Another point to watch is that the pinions are correctly lined up and mesh over the full width of their teeth. Mis-

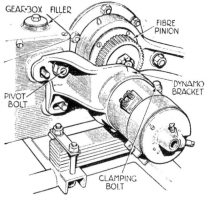

GEAR-BOX FILLER
FIBRE PINION
DYNAMO BRACKET
PIVOT BOLT
CLAMPING BOLT

(Left) Details of the dynamo mounting, showing the provision that is made for the adjustment of the pinions. (Right) This sketch of the clutch shows the withdrawal gear and toggle-arm adjusters. To test for correct adjustment the fork arm should be pulled in the direction shown by the arrow, to bring the thrust and withdrawal blocks together. Any misalignment will be obvious from underneath as shown in the inset sketch.

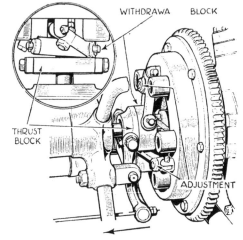

WITHDRAWA BLOCK
THRUST BLOCK
ADJUSTMENT

backwards or forwards in the fork ends. Correct alignment is obtained when the distance between the wheel rim and the fork arm is the same on each side.

While this is being done, an eye should, of course, be kept on chain adjustment, which should be such that there is about 1 in. of up-and-down movement on the bottom run of the chain midway between the sprockets. When the correct adjustment is obtained, the lock nuts on the adjusters and the spindle nut should be firmly tightened and the rear brake adjustment checked as, naturally, it is upset when the wheel is moved in the forks.

So far as the forks themselves are concerned, an important point is to make sure that the tie-bar is tight and

alignment can be cured by slacking off the dynamo clamping bolt and sliding the instrument in or out of its bracket.

This concludes all the maintenance work that the average owner is likely to undertake. Some enthusiasts, of course, may carry out more ambitious jobs, but they are few in number, and in any case their skill and knowledge are usually a sufficient guide for the work they do.

MORGAN THREE-WHEELERS for 1937

Three Main Types Retained Without Alteration in Price or Design

The Morgan models shown on this page are representative of the three main types—sports, super-sports and four-cylinder.

EXCEPT for the fact that Family models no longer figure in the list, the Morgan range of three-wheelers is being retained without modification for the coming season; that is to say, the super-sports, the four-cylinder and the sports models are all continued for 1937 without any alteration either to price or to specification.

The super-sports model is, of course driven by an o.h.v. twin-cylinder Morgan-Matchless engine, which can be either of the air-cooled or water-cooled variety. Much the same applies to the sports two-seater, which, however, can also be obtained with a side-valve engine. The four-cylinder three-wheeler is offered with either a two-seater body or as a four-seater.

The full list of models and prices is as follows:—

	£	s.
Sports 2-str., s.v., water-cooled	101	17
Sports 2-str., o.h.v., air-cooled	107	2
Sports 2-str., o.h.v., water-cooled	115	10
Super Sports, o.h.v., air-cooled ...	126	0
Super Sports, o.h.v., water-cooled ...	136	10
Four-cylinder, 4-str., 8 h.p. ...	115	10
Four-cylinder, 2-str., 8 h.p. ...	120	15

Extra for 10 h.p. engine in four-cylinder models £7 7s.
Extra for two-door body on Sports 2-str., £5.

Although all these models have much in common, apart from the engine, there is a considerable difference between the chassis of the four-cylinder types and that of the twin-cylinder models, the difference mainly lying in the fact that the former have two deep channel-sectioned frame members, one on each side of the central propeller shaft tube, whereas the two-cylinder types have a tubular chassis.

The suspension, transmission and braking systems are similar on all types. The suspension includes the well-known independent Morgan system employing helical springs at the front and two quarter elliptics, one on each side of the rear wheel, at the back. So far as the transmission is concerned, the drive is taken through a dry-plate clutch fitted with a Borg and Beck flexible centre and thence by a propeller shaft to a three-speed and reverse gearbox fitted just forward of the rear wheel, the final drive being by a roller chain on the off side. Internal expanding cable-operated brakes are used, the pedal taking effect on the rear wheel and the central brake lever on the two front wheels.

Representative examples of the three types are shown on this page. The four-seater, four-cylinder model, it will be observed, provides generous accommodation in the rear for two children, but there is room, when occasion demands, to carry adults in the back seats. The sports two-seater on the four-cylinder chassis is similar in frontal appearance, but has a tail somewhat after the lines of the two-cylinder sports model. This type, it will be recalled, was introduced just before the Motor Cycle Show last year. For those who want extra lively performance a 10 h.p. engine can be fitted to either of the four-cylinder types at an extra charge.

It will be noticed in each case that a spare wheel and tyre is provided, and this feature nowadays is standard on all Morgan models. Other items of equipment common to all types are a windscreen wiper, speedometer, hood and electric starter.

Morgan three-wheelers have, of course, always been famous for their acceleration, hill-climbing and lively turn of speed, and the satisfaction they have given in the hands of their owners is proved by their long period of popularity, which dates back to well before the war. An announcement regarding the four-wheeled Morgan, introduced some time ago, will be made next week.

---IN BRIEF---

Sports and Super Sports

ENGINE: Two cylinders; overhead or side valves and air-cooled or water-cooled (see price list); 85.5 mm. by 85.5 mm. (990 c.c.). Tax, £4.

TRANSMISSION: Single dry-plate clutch; enclosed propeller shaft to three-speed gearbox; ratios, 4.58, 7.5 and 12.4 to 1; reverse, 16.5 to 1. Final drive by worm gear and roller chain.

DIMENSIONS: Wheelbase, 7 ft. 3 ins.; track, 4 ft. 2 ins.; overall length (sports), 10 ft. 6 ins.; (super sports), 10 ft. 4 ins.; overall width, 4 ft. 11 ins.

Four-cylinder Models

ENGINE: Four cylinders; side valves; 56.6 mm. by 92.5 mm. (933 c.c.) or (see price list) 63.5 mm. by 92.5 mm. (1,172 c.c.). Tax, £4.

TRANSMISSION: As sports above.

DIMENSIONS: Wheelbase, 8 ft. 3 ins.; track, 4 ft. 2 ins.; overall length, 11 ft. 6 ins.; overall width, 4 ft. 11 ins.

MORGAN MOTOR CO., LTD.
Malvern Link,
Worcestershire

A TWIN-ENGINED MORGAN

" Triangle " Describes an Interesting Conversion Featuring Two Scott Motorcycle Engines

The pair of two-cylinder two-stroke engines fits neatly in the usual place and, as this photograph shows, they do not look unwieldy.

IMAGINE a super-sports Morgan in which the cylinders have somehow become spread out into a much wider Vee than usual and have been individually distorted into oval section. Imagine also the machine travelling along with an unusual degree of silence and a very multi-cylinder purr about its exhaust.

If you can do that you have an excellent first impression of the machine described on this page; but, perhaps, if you live down Weybridge way, you have no need to imagine these things but have actually caught a glimpse of this strange three-wheeler and wondered at its odd-looking " engine " and the unfamiliarity of its exhaust note.

If you have, here is the explanation. The " engine " is not one engine at all, but two, and its exhaust is explained by the fact that they are Scott two-stroke motorcycle engines combining the power of their 596 c.c. two-cylinder units into one harmonious 1,192 c.c. whole. Each delivers something like 30 b.h.p., so there is no need to explain why they are to be found where they are. Smooth torque and unbounded power (for all practical purposes) have ever been the aim of enthusiasts.

The enthusiasts in this case are Mr. J. Granville Grenfell, M.I.B.E., the well-known racing engineer and tuner, of Brooklands Aerodrome, and Mr. K. S. Alderton, of Harpenden, Herts, who conceived the idea of fitting two reconditioned Scott engines into a 1934 super-sports Morgan.

It did not quite prove a case of " no sooner said than done," for although the two engines sat nice and comfortably on the front of the Morgan frame with their crankcases back to back, the problem of how to combine the power of those 1,192 c.c. into the harmonious whole just mentioned was not quite so straightforward.

How it was eventually done can be seen in the sketch at the foot of this page.

The engines, it should be explained, run in opposite directions—which enables their respective torque reactions and vibrations to wage a nice little civil war, leaving the rest of the chassis in a pleasant state of non-intervention.

The near-side engine drives direct by means of a roller chain on to a central shaft coupled to the clutch. Power from the off-side engine takes a rather more complicated course and four sprockets are concerned in sending it the way it should go.

If you follow a link of the chain round, on its journey from the engine sprocket, you will find that it first passes downwards round an idler sprocket, then upwards round a sprocket on a countershaft (from which another chain drives the magneto), downwards again and round the underside of the clutch shaft sprocket and then back again to the engine once more. The whole drive is enclosed and runs in an oil bath.

The rest of the transmission—in fact the rest of the car, apart from the engine, is of normal Morgan type and the whole job cost something in the region of £200 to build.

On the road, the machine possesses the attraction of remarkable flexibility and smooth running (four two-stroke cylinders, remember), terrific acceleration (bear in mind the 60 b.h.p. and the light weight of the Morgan) and a reserve of maximum speed under all but the most exceptional conditions (*second* gear suffices for a mere 70 m.p.h.). In short, a " special " of more than usual interest and attraction.

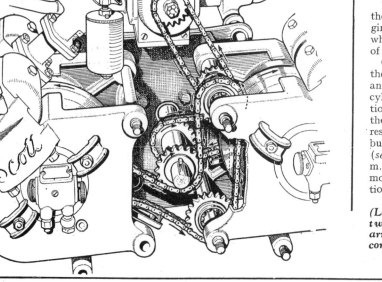

(Left) A sketch showing how the two engines are ingeniously arranged to drive a common shaft connected to the clutch. Normally, the drive is totally enclosed.

The MORGAN 4-CYLINDER THREE-WHEELER

A Machine for Those Who Like Open-air Motoring and a "Car with a Kick in It"

These two pictures give an excellent idea of the trim lines and low build of the four-cylinder version of the famous three-wheeler which forms the subject of this test report.

ALTHOUGH the subject of this test report was a two-seater Morgan of the four-cylinder variety, much of what is said applies equally to the four-seater model. Both cars differ from other Morgans not only in the type of engine employed, but also, of course, with regard to various features of construction. The chassis frame, for instance, is entirely different.

Since the arrangement of the various controls must be known before a car can be driven and because they have much to do with the pleasure of driving, let us discuss them first. On the facia board is an oval panel carrying the ammeter on one side and the ignition and lighting switch on the other. In between is a trip speedo-meter of which the "30" mark can be seen without difficulty from the driving seat.

Just below the steering wheel and operable by the right hand is a dipping switch. Above the steering column on the facia board is a pull-out control for the starter motor and in the corresponding position on the near side is a similar knob which brings into action the easy starting device on the carburetter.

Three pedals, arranged as usual, operate the clutch, brake and accelerator, but there is also a Bowden lever attached to one spoke of the steering wheel and connected to the throttle so that the engine can be accelerated by hand. The horn button, by the way, is placed near the bottom of the instrument panel, within easy reach of the left hand.

The gear lever is mounted centrally above the prop.

shaft tube and operates in a neat gate. First gear is engaged by pressing the lever towards the off side and pulling it back towards the seat. For second ratio the lever is moved forward and over towards the near side, while to engage "top" it is pulled straight back from that position. For reverse, the lever is moved into a position directly forward of the bottom gear location.

A point of difference from twin-cylinder Morgans is that the brake pedal is connected to all three wheels. The lever, however, operates the rear brake only and is intended for parking. It is placed a little to the left and slightly forward of the gear lever and its ratchet is controlled by a sliding trigger mounted on its front edge and easily moved by the fingers.

In spite of the low seat, there is no difficulty in judging the width of the vehicle, because the headlamps are mounted on the wings and both can be seen easily by the driver. On the score of visibility, the Morgan should be particularly good in fog because its screen can be folded down on to the scuttle.

Each seat consists of a padded cushion resting on thin three-ply, which gives a resilient effect. At the back is a one-piece squab which can be hinged forward to disclose a large space in which tools and small parcels can be carried. Underneath each seat also there is a shallow compartment which can be used for this purpose.

On the particular car tested there was no door, but one can be fitted on the near side at no extra cost. A folding hood stows neatly away behind the seats and is enclosed in an envelope when not in use. It can be erected very quickly simply by removing the envelope and pulling the hood fabric forward so that its front edge can be attached to the windscreen by means of Lift-a-dot fasteners.

As to accessibility, the engine oil filler and dipstick are both conveniently placed on the near side. The plugs, distributor and carburetter also can be reached without difficulty. A neat mounting for the spare wheel is obtained by recessing it into the back panel of the tail, where an aluminium disc keeps its spokes free from dust or mud and acts as a rear number plate.

Although the rear wheel may seem to be not too accessible, actually it can be reached with very little trouble. When the spare has been removed, the panel on which it is mounted can also be taken away by undoing four nuts and the driving wheel can then be detached.

Wheel removal at the rear is not quite so easy as

Important features of the model F two-seater Morgan shown in these pictures are the four-cylinder side-valve engine, the snug all-weather equipment and the accessible controls.

on a normal car owing to the fact that the wheel is carried in a fork and has chain drive, but the provision of a knock-out spindle which enables the wheel to be detached, complete with the chain sprocket, reduces the work to fairly simple terms.

A high power-weight ratio makes the Morgan a very lively little vehicle. As our test figures show, it accelerates rapidly and the time taken for the standing start quarter-mile is appreciably better than would be recorded by any four-wheeler short of an expensive sports car. Part of the credit for this result is undoubtedly due to the easy gear-change. The latter incorporates no synchromesh or other special device,

but appears to follow motorcycle practice, in which any ratio can be "crashed" into engagement without let or hindrance.

The brakes are good. It is true that they require a fair pressure on the pedal, but when this is applied the

IN BRIEF

ENGINE: Four cylinders; side valves; 56.6 mm. by 92.5 mm.=933 c.c. Tax, £4; power output, 24 b.h.p. at 3,500 r.p.m.

TRANSMISSION: Single dry-plate clutch; three-speed gearbox. Ratios, 4.85, 8 and 13.1 to 1; reverse, 17.5 to 1. Final drive by enclosed propeller shaft and single roller chain.

GENERAL: Cable-operated brakes; independent helical springs front and quarter-elliptic rear; 5-gallon petrol tank under bonnet.

DIMENSIONS: Wheelbase, 8 ft. 3 ins.; track, 4 ft. 2 ins.; overall length, 11 ft. 6 ins.; overall width, 4 ft. 11 ins.

PERFORMANCE: Flying ¼-mile, fastest one way, 66.2 m.p.h.; mean speed, 64.8 m.p.h.; standing ¼-mile, 24⅘ secs.; petrol consumption, 40 m.p.g.

PRICE: £120 15s.

MORGAN MOTOR CO., LTD.
MALVERN LINK,
WORCS

car stops promptly and without any trace of misbehaviour. Also commendable is the steering. It is highly geared so that only a small movement of the wheel is necessary for all ordinary purposes.

Its self-centring action is sufficient to straighten the car after a corner, but not so pronounced as to make the steering unduly heavy. Cornering is, in fact, a pleasure, and contrary to the idea (which should have died years ago) that a three wheeler is liable to overturn, we found that this Morgan can be turned as quickly as most cars of any build and that its limit is imposed by tyre grip only. In short, it will slide before it dreams of capsizing.

To judge by the growth in popularity of the closed car, there may be fewer people to-day than there used to be who enjoy the masculine style of motoring. For those, however, who do like plenty of fresh air and a car with a kick in it, a Morgan such as this four-cylinder model should certainly fill the bill. If still more verve is desired, a 10 h.p. engine is available at an extra cost of £7 7s.

NEW MORGAN THREE-WHEELER

Super Sports Four-cylinder Model with Girling Brakes

CHIEF interest in the Morgan three-wheeler programme for the coming season is centred in the new four-cylinder super-sports two-seater. Basically similar to the other four-cylinder models, it is mounted on a somewhat shorter chassis, whilst the body, as can be seen in an accompanying photograph, is very like that of the super-sports twin-cylinder model.

(Right) The "old faithful" Morgan with a twin-cylinder Matchless engine is continued unchanged.

More important, however, than the new body is the fact that Girling brakes are fitted. There is no need

(Left) The new model has attractive lines and its performance should be in keeping. (Below, centre) A "close-up" of the near-side front wheel, showing (A) the connection of the operating cable and (B) the adjusting nut of the Girling brakes.

here for us to describe this system at length, as readers should already be familiar with it. In the case of the Morgan, however, the conventional rods connecting brake pedal and wheel units are replaced by Bowden cables—an eminently satisfactory substitution since, by the design of the brakes, all the cables will be in tension. Moreover, cables are somewhat lighter than rods, and this is important when one considers the 8 cwt. legal limit.

The power unit is actually a four-cylinder side-valve affair with a Treasury rating of 10 h.p. Other features are the downdraught carburetter, three-bearing crankshaft and the single-plate clutch. Where, however, in a four-wheeled car the gearbox would be mounted with the engine, it is, in the case of the Morgan, mounted at the rear of the chassis, whence it drives the single rear wheel by means of a chain. A three-speed and reverse gearbox is incorporated in the transmission.

Suspension, both front and rear, is of the type already well tested on Morgan three-wheelers. At the front it consists of vertical helical springs encased in telescopic tubes, whilst the rear wheel is carried on swinging arms controlled by quarter-elliptic laminated springs.

As for the other three-wheeler

models, they are all unchanged from the 1937 designs. It should be noted, however, that the water-cooled sports two-seater has been dropped. There remain, therefore, the super-sports two-seater fitted with an o.h.v. 990 c.c. air-cooled Matchless twin engine and the two four-cylinder models (two-seater and four-seater), which are available with either 8 h.p. or 10 h.p. power units. It should be emphasized at this point that the new super-sports in no way replaces the twin engine super-sports; this latter model will continue to hold its popularity.

IN BRIEF

FOUR-CYLINDER MODELS

ENGINE : (10 h.p. model) four cylinders, side valves, 63.5 mm. by 92.5 mm.= 1,172 c.c. Tax, £4. (8 h.p. model) four cylinders, side valves, 56.6 mm. by 92.5 mm.=933 c.c. Tax, £4.

TRANSMISSION : Single dry-plate clutch; three-speed and reverse gearbox. Ratios, 4.85, 8 and 13.1 to 1; reverse, 17.5 to 1. Final drive by chain.

GENERAL : Mechanical brakes ; helical front springs, ¼-elliptic rear ; 4-gallon petrol tank.

DIMENSIONS : Wheelbase, 7 ft. 3 ins. ; track, 4 ft. 2 ins. ; overall length, 10 ft. 8 ins. ; overall width, 4 ft. 11 ins.

PRICES : Two-seater, £120 15s. ; four-seater, £115 10s. (both are available with either 8 h.p. or 10 h.p. engines).

SUPER-SPORTS FOUR-CYLINDER

ENGINE : As 10 h.p. above.

TRANSMISSION : As above.

GENERAL : As above, except that Girling brakes are fitted.

DIMENSIONS : Not yet available.

PRICE : 10 h.p. two-seater, £136 10s.

TWO-CYLINDER MODEL

ENGINE : Two cylinders (50-degree V-twin) ; overhead valves ; 85.5 mm. by 85.5 mm. = 990 c.c. Tax, £4.

TRANSMISSION : As above, except that gear ratios are—4.58, 7.5, and 12.4 to 1 ; reverse, 16.5 to 1.

GENERAL : As four-cylinder models.

DIMENSIONS : Wheelbase, 7 ft. 3 ins.; track, 4 ft. 2 ins. ; overall length, 10 ft. 4 ins. ; overall width, 4 ft. 11 ins.

PRICE : Super-sports two-seater, £126.

THE MORGAN MOTOR CO., LTD., Malvern Link, Worcs.

MORGAN FEATURES

3 SPEEDS & REVERSE

SINGLE CHAIN

REDESIGNED ENGINES

LUCAS ELECTRIC LIGHTING

ELECTRIC STARTER

SPEEDOM.ETER

SCREEN WIPER

PRICES FROM £95

The great arterial road flies arrowing northward . . .

The way winds echoing beneath the grandeur of the mountains . . .

On every side a myriad winter colours glow . . .

Out west a fading sun bids us good afternoon . . . and far ahead twinkling lights invite us on toward bright scenes of crackling fires and pleasant talks, and things to eat and drink !

So let her go ! . . . and end our symphony accellerato !

The thrill of Winter Morganing !

M O R G A N

MORGAN 1932 LITERATURE

Please send me the 1932 Catalogue

Name...

Address.....................................

....

CUT OUT AND POST

ISSUED BY MORGAN MOTORS, LTD., MALVERN LINK, WORCESTERSHIRE.

MORGAN THREE-WHEELERS

A "No-change" Policy Adopted for 1939.
Three Distinct Types Available

SO far as prices and specifications are concerned, the Morgan three-wheelers of 1939 will not differ from the current models. The model F.2 tourer, however, is to be discontinued, thus leaving the 8 h.p. four-cylinder four-seater, a 10 h.p. two-seater sports model and the ever-popular V-twin two-seater sports model.

We will deal with the last-named example first. It has a high performance twin-cylinder Matchless engine with the cylinders set at an angle of 50 degrees. Air cooling is normally used, but, at an extra cost of £10 10s., the model can be had in water-cooled form. In either case the engine is of the "square" type, in that the bore and stroke are both 85.5 mm. The capacity is 990 c.c. Push-rod operated overhead valves are used; the rocker gear is fully enclosed and positively lubricated, but valve stems and the springs, which, by the way, are of the hairpin type, are exposed in order that they may be adequately cooled.

On this model the standard, well-tried tubular chassis construction is continued; it has, naturally, the advantages of lightness and strength. Front suspension is, of course, by means of independent helical springs controlling sliding axles and, as hitherto, the rear wheel is carried in swinging arms which, at their front ends, are pivoted on large bosses on the worm-drive box. The radius of the arms is equal to that of the chain sprocket centres, so that the tension of the driving chain remains constant under all conditions. Movement of the wheel is controlled by a pair of quarter-elliptic springs.

An economical car for the family man, the four-seater model has an 8 h.p. four-cylinder engine and adequate weather protection.

No change has been made in the three-speed and reverse gearbox, which is operated by a centrally mounted lever, at the side of which is another lever controlling the brakes on the front wheels, the rear-wheel brake being operated by the pedal.

Equipment includes electric lighting and starting, the dynamo being driven from the off side of the countershaft, pneumatic seat cushions, luggage grid, spare wheel, windscreen wiper and hood.

Turning now to the other models in the Morgan range we have the Model F Super and the Model F four-seater. On both of these the chassis frames are built up of deep-section channel steel, but there is a tubular backbone enclosing the propeller shaft, and tubular front cross-members are retained as part of the standard Morgan independent suspension system. Girling brakes are used on both models and are coupled for simultaneous operation.

The body of the four-seater model is designed for the comfortable accommodation of two adults and two children. In this connection, however, it may be mentioned that the rear compartment is of sufficient size for occupation by two adults in an emergency. In this model a four-cylinder side-valve water-cooled engine

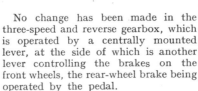

Capable of a high performance, the V-twin sports model is based upon the original Morgan design. A spare wheel is housed in the tail.

IN BRIEF

TWIN-CYLINDER MODEL

ENGINE : 9.9 h.p.; two cylinders, 85.5 mm. by 85.5 mm.= 990 c.c.; overhead valves. Tax, £4.

TRANSMISSION : Single dry-plate clutch; three-speed gearbox; ratios, 4.58, 7.5 and 12.4 to 1. Final drive by roller chain.

GENERAL : Cable-operated brakes. Suspension : front, independent helical ; rear, quarter-elliptic.

DIMENSIONS : Wheelbase, 7 ft. 3 ins.; track, 4 ft. 2 ins.; overall length, 10 ft. 4 ins.; overall width, 4 ft. 11 ins.

PRICE : Super-sports two-seater, £126.

FOUR-CYLINDER MODELS

ENGINE : 7.98 h.p.; four cylinders, 56.6 mm. by 92.5 mm.=933 c.c.; side valves. Tax, £4.

TRANSMISSION : Single dry-plate clutch; three-speed gearbox; ratios, 4.85, 8 and 13.1 to 1. Final drive by roller chain.

GENERAL : Girling brakes. Suspension : front, independent helical ; rear, quarter-elliptic.

DIMENSIONS : Wheelbase, 8 ft. 3 ins.; overall length, 11 ft. 6 ins. Otherwise as twin-cylinder model.

PRICE : £120 15s.

The 10 h.p. model is similar to the foregoing except as follows :—

ENGINE : 10 h.p.; 63.5 mm. by 92.5 mm. =1,172 c.c.

DIMENSIONS : Overall length, 11 ft.; wheelbase, 7 ft. 11 ins.

PRICE : £136 10s.

THE MORGAN MOTOR Co., LTD., Malvern Link, Worcs.

(Left) Arrangement of the engine, fuel tank and tool box on the four-cylinder models. (Below) The 10 h.p. two-seater, which has a high cruising speed.

model. The windscreen is of the fold-flat type and one door on the near side is provided. This model has a maximum speed in excess of 70 m.p.h. and will cruise at 60 to 65 m.p.h.

An interesting point in connection with the four-cylinder model Morgans is the use of the combined gravity and pressure feed of the carburetter. The fuel tank is mounted beneath the bonnet, but, as the carburetter is of the down-draught type, a sufficient head of petrol cannot be ensured under all running conditions and, of course, it would be a pity to risk spoiling the performance of the engine by the use of a horizontal carburetter with which the

is used. It transmits the drive through an enclosed single-plate clutch to a standard Morgan gearbox. Both dynamo and distributors are carried above the cylinder head and, of course, an electric starter is part of the specification. The dynamo is belt-driven in the ordinary way from the crankshaft, but no fan is fitted.

We mentioned at the beginning of these remarks that there was no change in Morgan models for next season. This is perhaps not entirely correct, as the F-type Super model, which is available to anyone wishing to couple refinement with performance, differs somewhat, apart from coachwork, from the four-seater model. The chassis has been shortened to accommodate the two-

seater body and to improve cornering; in addition, a 10 h.p. engine is fitted instead of one of 8 h.p. The design of the body combines, in effect, the front end of the normal four-cylinder model and the rear end of the V-twin Super

necessary head of fuel could no doubt be obtained. The manufacturers have overcome this difficulty by the simple expedient of feeding the petrol by gravity to a mechanically operated fuel pump, whence it is passed under pressure to the carburetter.

Six Hundred Miles in

"... with my arm over the side of the body and my fingers touching the ground to show how remarkably low - built the Morgan is"

R ORTY, naughty and delightful—that sums up the 990 c.c. Super-Sports Morgan I have been driving for the last 600 miles. I cannot imagine a vehicle that fills its appointed niche better than this lively, racy-looking three-wheeler. If you want sport—*super*-sport —you have it to a degree just about impossible to obtain with anything else. It is not that you have colossal speed, but you have acceleration greater than that of many five-hundred solos, and you have a vehicle which seems to be made from nose to tail *for* sport.

Years had passed since I had previously driven a Morgan. The last time had been when I had a flip in the pet bus of the Morgan general manager, Mr. Goodall, and the thrill of it stuck—so much so that some little time ago Mr. Goodall received a letter saying that I wanted one of the latest Super-Sports models, not for a road test but my own use. Eventually that water-cooled, Girling-braked, streamlined beastie you see in the pictures arrived at Dorset House. Would I get the same thrill afresh? I did!

Being introduced to an out-of-the-ordinary vehicle in the heart of London at a time of the day when the roads are choked with people hurrying homeward is calculated to be neither pleasant nor too safe. That hand throttle on the wheel did not always seem to be exactly where I wanted it ; the steering seemed very, very heavy ; traffic appeared to loom high above me. No, I was not very happy on the ten miles that led to my first stretch of "derestricted." But I was learning. Already I had found that the steering was not heavy if only one used the throttle correctly, and that the throttle control on the steering wheel is, in fact, a boon.

You may query this last point if you have driven a car and, therefore, had an accelerator. With this arrange-ment, however, you have a blessing you get with no

"Torrens" Tries the Latest Super=Sports Morgan=Matchless — and Recaptures the Thrills of Driving a Lively Three=wheeler

normal car—the ability to keep one foot poised over the brake pedal and the other over the clutch pedal. There is no changing your right foot from the accelerator to the brake, and vice versa. There is thus no wasted time if the brakes have to be used in a hurry, and this can mean a lot under all manner of conditions, not least in traffic.

Almost mile by mile I seemed to get more at home with this joyous, peppy "eight hundredweight." On bends the Morgan feels more like the one racing car I've ever handled than any other three- or four-wheeler I have driven. Place it right on a bend, use the throttle to accelerate round it, and you swing round with an effortlessness that is a delight. It is only at very slow speeds, and especially if you have the tyre pressures lower than the makers recommend, that the steering is at all heavy. Those 100 degrees, or thereabouts, that the steering wheel moves through from full right lock to full lock to the left, suit the machine perfectly. The lock struck me as being on the small side, but, of course, one has in these days a reverse gear.

What is sheer joy is the beefy power of the overhead-valve, vee-twin Matchless engine. On an ethylised fuel, which was in the tank when I took over, and was there-fore adhered to, the engine is exceptionally flexible. With the ignition retarded, the engine will tick-tock along at some 15 m.p.h. in top gear ; at 20 m.p.h. it is perfectly

a SUPER-SPORTS MORGAN

Motor-cycle type carburettor and ignition controls are employed. Note the spring-spoked steering wheel, the aero-type windscreens and the position of the gear and hand-brake controls

"clacking," which emanated either from the valve gear or from a slightly blowing exhaust flange—the engine is, of course, bang in front of you. At a steady 48 to 50 m.p.h. the engine was merely on about a quarter throttle and just "rustling."

Gentle Starting

Starting from cold with the throttle barely open, the air full open, and the carburettor flooded, was merely a question of a gentle pull-up on the starting handle. The coil ignition needed to be fully retarded or there might be a kick-back. From hot I generally started with a similar setting and no flooding. Usually this was quite all right, and the engine would immediately turn over lazily. Sometimes with this self-same setting nothing would happen, and, finally, I started up with the throttle well open. The self-starter was rather liable to jerk into engagement with the gear ring on the flywheel and come to a halt.

The brakes are very good indeed, the seating comfortable if a little narrow as to the air cushion on which my large bulk sat, and the springing hard super-sports. The degree of comfort proved appreciably greater than I expected. Those little screens you see in the photographs are really efficient. The breeze is diverted above your face rather after the style of a correctly set handlebar screen on a motor cycle, and, being set at an angle, keep very reasonably clear in rain. A suction-type windscreen wiper is fitted, though I never found occasion to use it even in wet weather encountered after dark, and I never found it necessary to use the hood, for on the open road the rain seemed to swish harmlessly past. The hood was, however, used for parking in the rain.

Unless you are sylph-like it is a bit of a slither to get into the cockpit, and there was not a lot of room for my legs. The gear change is handy, just alongside the propeller-shaft. A car-type of box is fitted, and the change is thus normal "car," though quick. On the far side of the gear lever is the hand control for the brakes. This gives me my one criticism of any merit: the ratchet did not mate in with the brakes that are now standard; a ratchet with finer teeth seemed needed.

Oil consumption proved minute, while as for fuel I carefully checked what distance I covered on the first nine gallons—it was just over 390 miles, which gives a consumption of nearly 44 m.p.g., obtained under mixed conditions that included traffic-work and a fair amount of batting.

I said a couple of paragraphs ago that the brake lever

happy with the ignition fully advanced. Open the throttle and away you shoot in a manner that is enthralling. I checked the acceleration roughly with a stopwatch. From 20 to 50 m.p.h. in top gear took only a fraction over 13 seconds, which compares well with almost any five-hundred solo you like, and many of them it beats! Moreover, you get an impression of super-acceleration to a degree that a solo seldom gives you, unless it be of 1,000 c.c. And the Morgan will dart away if you unleash the power on a hill. Main-road climbs are gobbled up in top. For instance, on one long main-road climb which brings the majority of cars down a gear I was baulked to approximately 20 m.p.h. From this the Morgan darted to 55 m.p.h., and would have gone higher if the road conditions had permitted. The sheer maximum proved just over 70 m.p.h.—you can make it more, of course, if you do a little swooping. Cruising speed depends upon yourself. I did quite a lot of driving around 55 m.p.h. Above this there is a certain amount of vibration, and at this speed there is some

"At a steady 48 to 50 m.p.h. the engine was merely on about a quarter throttle and just 'rustling'"

constituted my one criticism. You may say that I have raised a number of points, and I have, but not as criticisms—alter almost anything in or on this Morgan and you would start to strike at the root of its appeal, which I tried to convey in that opening sentence, "Rorty, naughty and delightful." I would perhaps tone the exhaust down a trifle more, because I hate running any risk of keeping people awake at night and I know what it is like to be ill and hear loud exhausts.

No, this Morgan gives you sheer unadulterated sport, and every single feature of it conspires towards this end. You leap and hop if it's not a billiards table surface you are on when doing seventy, but doesn't she give you a marvellous feeling of sheer speed? And isn't this latest job delightfully safe? I've purposely had a photo taken with my arm over the side of the body and my fingers touching the ground to show how remarkably low-built the Morgan is. With so low a centre of gravity

there is, of course, stability, and I believe that if you go really wild (and silly) on a bend all that can happen is that the model slides—which reminds me that tramlines included I had no fun and games of any sort on wet roads.

The "looks" I need not dwell upon, for the photographs give an idea of the lines of the black-and-chromium bus. I must, however, mention that I left the Morgan in the garage of a Bentley owner for a few days—the days when I went to the Isle of Man—and on my return found that the lady of the house had had all she could do to stop herself borrowing it and going for a joy-ride. The looks alone had captivated her; she would have been more thrilled still after an hour or two at the wheel.

At £136 10s. one has a sports car on three wheels that provides sport unlimited, and acceleration and general liveliness you just can't get except with a really hot motor cycle or something much more expensive—some super four-wheeler. I wish I could run a "stable." . . .

INTO BATTLE 1929-1938

Below: EXETER TRIAL, 1929: J. S. Thulby's 1,100c.c. JAP-engined Aero Morgan climbs Little Minterne hill.

Above, right: LEEDS £200 TRIAL, 1930: Druids Altar Lane made up for its lack of gradient with an appalling, waterlogged surface—which failed to stop F. W. James's 1,100c.c. Aero.

Below, right: LANDS END TRIAL, 1938: R. C. C. Palmer's 1934 Super Sports—which retained, as an option, the beetle-back tail as distinct from the barrel-tail introduced in 1934—makes a clean climb of Doverhay, watched by hundreds of spectators.

The SUPER-SPORTS MORGAN

High Performance and Comfort are Features of the Latest Model of a Famous Series

Built for speed and comfort, the Morgan has an attractive streamlined body. In the picture below is shown the spare wheel mounting; luggage may be carried on the grid on the tail.

UNDOUBTEDLY, one of the most exhilarating vehicles we have tested in recent months is the Super-sports Morgan, naïvely described on its licence as a "tricycle." The writer had not experienced three-wheeled motion for some time past, and during the long week-end in which he had the car it was a constant source of pleasant surprise.

It is generally acknowledged that a three-wheeled sports car is not everyone's ideal of perfect transport. It has been pointed out that it is a vehicle with definite limitations. This is true. It is a car in which white tie and tails might be out of place; on the other hand, the Morgan fulfils a very definite function.

Here is a conveyance for the enthusiast, the man who enjoys developing "urge" in a big twin. It is a car which offers high speed and really rapid, safe cornering. It gives performance the equal of many four-wheeled sports cars, but with a new thrill. Its acceleration is astonishing, its braking powerful and its road-holding superb.

In appearance, this latest product of the Morgan works follows the well-tried lines of its very successful predecessors. The body is carefully streamlined, and is beaten from a single sheet of metal. The spare wheel is housed in a recess in the tapered tail, on which is a luggage-grid, capable of carrying one or two suitcases. A broad, vee-shaped screen gives the occupants complete shelter from wind and rain. A further measure of protection for the passenger is provided by the extension of the scuttle.

Both seats are comfortable. The squab is deep and well sprung, and the cushions are pneumatic. There is ample legroom on the passenger's side, but, although there are only two pedals, the driver's footroom is rather restricted. The driving position is eminently satisfactory, at once imparting a feeling of confidence. Admirably raked to come into the lap, the steering wheel, of flexible type, carries manual controls for ignition, air and throttle. The dipswitch is mounted on the steering column. Visibility is excellent: the near-side wing can be seen without effort, but a rear view mirror would be appreciated.

The remote control gear-lever is placed very conveniently where the left hand drops on to it. Alongside is the brake lever. Beneath the driver's legs, and protruding through the floor is the electric starter button, which is operated in conjunction with an exhaust lifter.

Power, in large quantities, is derived from an o.h.v. water-cooled vee-twin Matchless engine of 990 c.c. Transmission is by shaft to a sliding-pinion type of gearbox, thence to worm and wheel. Final drive is taken by a short chain of ¾-in. pitch.

To start the engine from cold requires careful adjustment of the ignition and mixing controls and a few moments' work with the crank. Practice reveals that little difficulty is experienced when the Amal carburetter has been flooded, the ignition fully retarded and the air lever moved to the "closed" position. The compression ratio is in the region of 6 to 1; some care should be exercised in using the starting handle.

When the engine is once firing, the ignition may be advanced, and the air control opened. Here it may be remarked that the exhaust note, whilst pleasing to some, can be regarded somewhat gravely by officers of the law and anti-motorists. It is possible, however, to proceed comparatively quietly in town traffic when the revs. are kept down to "tick-over" speed.

Suspension at low speeds has all the firmness of the four-wheeled sports car. Steering is high-geared and, therefore, apparently heavy at low speeds, but it is exactly right on the open road, when it is immediately responsive. The certainty of control at high speeds is one of the most attractive features of the car; coupled with the front-end stability provided by the famous Morgan helical springing, fast cornering becomes almost a matter of course.

The Girling mechanical brakes fitted on all three wheels are powerful and smooth in action. All wheels are interchangeable, and little more than 10 mins. is required to remove the spare wheel and replace the driving wheel.

In traffic the Morgan is perfectly tractable, and showed no tendency to oil plugs. Tramlines present no particular difficulty, and the three-wheeler is surprisingly steady, even on such surfaces as wet wood blocks.

It is on the open road, however, that the Super Sports model shows its true colours. This is a car which really does thrust the driver in the back as it gets away from traffic hold-ups. With such widely spaced gear ratios as 12.4, 7.5 and 4.58 to 1, a quick change is almost impossible, but the fraction of time lost in closing the hand throttle and snicking into another gear is amply compensated for by the heartiness of the acceleration.

Best results were obtained when second gear was selected at about 15 m.p.h. and top at 40 m.p.h. It is possible to reach 50 m.p.h. in second, but at this speed the engine goes through a noisy period. Once in top gear, one has the gratifying impression that the car is impatient of restraint.

Cruising speed is in the region of 55 m.p.h. This can be maintained indefinitely with a very small throttle opening. Acceleration at this speed is as rapid as in the lower speed range, and the car reaches its maximum in a very short time. Over a timed flying

Removal of the floorboards reveals the gearbox, dynamo and battery. Rear suspension is by quarter-elliptic springs.

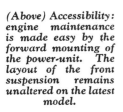

(Above) Accessibility: engine maintenance is made easy by the forward mounting of the power-unit. The layout of the front suspension remains unaltered on the latest model.

IN BRIEF

ENGINE: 50-degree watercooled V twin; pushrod overhead valves; 85.5 mm. by 85.5 mm. = 990 c.c. Tax, £4.

TRANSMISSION: Single dry-plate clutch; three-speed gearbox. Ratios, 4.58, 7.5 and 12.4 to 1; reverse, 16.5 to 1. Shaft drive, with centre bearing, to gearbox, worm and countershaft to final drive chain.

GENERAL: Tubular frame; independent front wheel suspension (helical springs); quarter-elliptic rear; 4-gallon forward petrol tank, 1-gallon oil; 6-volt electrical equipment.

DIMENSIONS, Etc.: Overall length, 10 ft. 4 ins.; overall width, 4 ft. 11 ins.; track, 4 ft. 2 ins.; weight, 8 cwt. 58 lb.

PERFORMANCE: Flying ¼-mile (best), 73 m.p.h.; mean, 70.87 m.p.h.; standing ¼-mile, 21.0 secs. Petrol consumption (average), 40 m.p.g. Braking, by Ferodo-Tapley meter, 88 per cent.

PRICE: £136 10s.

THE MORGAN MOTOR CO., LTD.
MALVERN LINK
WORCS.

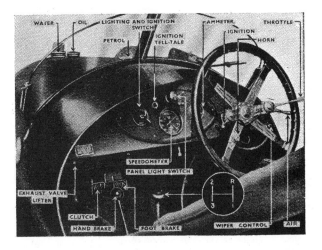

quarter-mile, the Morgan averaged 73 m.p.h., but the zest in driving the car lies more in the manner in which it reaches its maximum than in merely motoring with the taps wide open.

The stability of the three-wheeler at high speeds deserves more than a perfunctory word of praise. On fast bends (and to a Morgan most bends are fast) the car is rock-steady. There is no tendency to slide, nor for the tail to swing, and the steering is such that a flick of the wheel is sufficient to maintain a straight course over the roughest of surfaces.

Mounted on the wings are head lights which are well up to their job. For wet weather driving, a suction-operated windscreen wiper is fitted, but the low hood restricts visibility. It was found, however, that rain tended to be deflected over the heads of the occupants, and the enthusiast will probably dispense with the hood except when parked.

At £136 10s., the Super Sports Morgan represents a form of motoring which is rare enough in these days of small car luxury. It is a real sports car, combining high performance with economy.

MORGAN MUSINGS

[Many enthusiasts are interested in the Morgan three-wheeler, and especially so now that we have to contend with the heavy h.p. tax and strict rationing of fuel. The Morgan can be taxed for £5 per annum, against £10–£15 for a small sports-car, while possessing extreme performance and a fuel consumption around 40 m.p.g. Consequently, these remarks, by that well-known motoring sportsman, Martin Soames, will be of considerable value to prospective owners, as well as of great satisfaction to present Morgan " fans." M. S. Soames is better known as a skilful trials and rally competitor with special Ford V8 and Allard-Special cars, and for his Brooklands successes with Harmer's old Type 37 Bugatti. However, he has owned three Morgans, and while apprenticed to Leyland Motors Ltd., where he was closely in touch with the Arab car as well as with Leyland vehicles, he modified his 1931 8/55 J.A.P.-engined Morgan for racing. In this article he contributes his experiences of this Morgan in particular and comments on this fascinating animal in general.—Ed.]

A WISH to learn about the ways of fast motor cars and insufficient money to gratify it provided my introduction to Morgans. My regard for them increased with ownership and, although in part the appeal was to the pioneer spirit, which rejoices in difficulties overcome *en route*, one could not but respect their businesslike appearance, lively performance and original, accessible design.

The 1931 Morgan to which the following remarks chiefly apply was my third of this make and one of the few which left the works with an 8/55 J.A.P. engine. The only one, I think, with this motor and the then new " M " chassis. The engine was air-cooled, of 996 c.c. (80 × 99 mm.), and basically similar to those in the late E. C. Fernihough's World's Record Brough-Superior [incidentally, Fernihough started his career with a one-cylinder racing Morgan—Ed.] and Mrs. Stewart's Morgan which did 115.6 m.p.h. over the mile and 101.5 miles in the hour in 1929. These engines are generally considered to be the best racing twins ever made by J. A. Prestwich & Co. The " M " chassis had an entirely new " rear end " with an improved bevel box, forged girder-section forks, underslung springs, an 8 inch internal expanding brake (instead of a contracting band), and a knock-out spindle which permitted the back wheel to be removed in five minutes. The wheelbase was 6 ft. and the front track about 4 ft. 4 ins. Power was transmitted by cone clutch and two-speed gear (chains, countershaft and dogs) as always on the " works " racing machines.

I bought it from the original owner early in 1933. He had used it a little on the road and had competed at some B.M.C.R.C. meetings. When seeking first-hand racing knowledge from this gentleman, I remember being awestruck by his lurid account of the difficulties and dangers of speed on the Brooklands outer circuit. His contention that the

chains became red-hot in a few laps particularly appalled me.

For two years this vehicle gave me many miles of most enjoyable road motoring. Speeds were around eighty in top, and forty-five in bottom. The acceleration excelled that of the average sports 500 c.c. motor-cycle. Performance figures were never taken, as the speedometer was unreliable. Petrol consumption was over 30 m.p.g. although the engine was not in good tune at this time. The brakes, or rather lack of them, were an exciting feature and acute or bumpy corners merited respect. When the limit was reached on the former a front wheel would leave the ground. This source of embarrassment was later removed by lowering the back of the chassis by 1½ ins. I did feel, however, that the poor brakes and lack of margin for errors in cornering were helpful in developing judgment. Road-holding on straights was good considering the short wheelbase, and the three-track layout with which the back wheel encounters its own set of road inequalities.

An ambition was to cover in six hours the 260 miles between the Lancashire works where I was apprenticed and my home on the South Coast. This was never realised for, although successful in reaching the half-way mark from each end in under three hours, the necessity of stopping for an adjustment or to tie something on would invariably intervene. Those who have driven through Wigan and Warrington will sympathise with me in these efforts. During this period, I had no major mechanical troubles, but certain small parts needed frequent renewal and attention. Once the cockpit had to be hurriedly evacuated in deference to a rush of flames round the pedals and petrol tank, when a ride on the tail at 60 m.p.h. with the hand brake on followed. On another occasion, when push-starting in the middle of Portsmouth, I was unable to knock the gear lever into neutral when the engine fired, and I held on (because of a third party insurance policy), with the throttle wide open in bottom gear. A brace of cyclists were unhorsed and a brick wall demolished, but fortunately, as in the incident above, no blood was spilt.

By the end of 1934 I was able to contemplate a very limited racing programme. I had been watching the achievements, at Lewes, of G. E. W. Oliver's Super-Sports Morgan with 10/40 watercooled J.A.P. engine. At one meeting in 1934 it won the 1,100 c.c. and 1,500 c.c. Super Sports classes in 25.8 secs.—a very good performance at that time. The Lewes speed trials were one of the few remaining events open to both cars and three-wheelers. They were held on an interesting course, invariably attracting an excellent entry. My Morgan seemed to stand a chance here, so I decided to run in all the 1935 events and started to prepare for the opening meeting.

I knew enough about vee twin engines to leave this part to an expert, and decided

on E. C. E. Baragwanath. One of the greatest authorities and holder of the Brooklands sidecar lap record, he was always very helpful and encouraging. His work included the fitting of a big end bearing of his own design (the Achilles heel of all J.A.P. twins), special connecting rods, and Martlet pistons with larger gudgeon pins. The compression ratio was thus raised to just under 12 to 1, that of the wet, or off side cylinder being the higher. A double Best & Lloyd oil pump was added to an improved oiling system. He used his own cams, with special followers, push rods, rockers and valve timing. The inside flywheels were lightened by four pounds and the balance weights modified. I machined a new outside flywheel in nickel-chrome steel. This tapered in all directions and weighed eight pounds as against sixteen of the original cast iron component. We " bumped up " the 11 in. diameter blank for this from a 5 in. bar, the biggest available, on a gigantic steam hammer. The bronze clutch cone which engaged with the flywheel was balanced statically, several ounces being removed in the process.

Continuing with the transmission system (the machine by now being reduced to its component parts), the propeller shaft was the next problem. This had a bad vibration period at about 4,000 r.p.m. I had a special one designed and made for me by R. R. Jackson. He has forgotten more about Morgans than I ever knew, and used to race them successfully [including a 500 c.c. vee-twin job.—Ed.]. It was the Blackburne engine developed by him for his machine which was afterwards used in the Freikaiserwagen (and subsequently blown) with such terrific effect. Even this new shaft did not quite cure the trouble—an indication of the need for a central steady-bearing as used on the " works " racing chassis. The bronze bevel box was hand scraped and the top cover, filler cap, inspection plate and new drain plate underneath made in Electron. The box was originally intended for grease lubrication, but the seals were improved and a vegetable engine oil used. I machined a new countershaft of very tough steel, leaving large radii at changes of section. This overcame the twisting tendencies of the standard type. The selector-forks had been a source of rapid wear so some were cast in phosphor-bronze and proved far more durable.

The rear wheel spindle and adjacent highly stressed parts were replaced in alloy steel. Bronze bushes were fitted to shackles and spring eyes and the sprockets were drilled with d'oyley-like designs. The arm of a specially-adapted double Hartford shock-absorber was attached to a " hoop " over the back wheel, which it satisfactorily damped and stabilised in the vertical plane. This wheel was rebuilt and fitted with a fat 140/40 Michelin " Real Low Pressure " tyre.

Dunlops built me some light front wheels to take their 3.25″ × 19″ ribbed tyres. These were dished severely inwards, bringing the centre point of tyre contact with the ground some 1½ ins. nearer the steering pivot line, or about 1 in. from it. This materially reduced wheel-flap and loads on the front suspension and steering arrangements generally. The front hubs were machined to take Timken taper roller bearings (in place of the unsatisfactory cup and cone type), and new stub axles were made to suit, with Electron distance pieces and hub caps. Special telescopic Newton shock-absorbers controlled the front springs. A point to which Morgans are sensitive on corners is the angle of the steering arms. I got the best results when the lines through the steering pivots and track rod ends, if produced backwards, met in the rear wheel spindle (with the wheels straight). For this purpose the steering arms should be bent at red heat. The strip steel drag-link with yoke and pin ends was replaced by a rod with spring-loaded ball joints and an adjustable track rod was made up. The above ministrations, and attention to a number of smaller points, resulted in general handling comparable with that of an average sports-car, and the Morgan would then slide round dry corners in normal style.

I used the latest type of Morgan front brake drums, which were now flanged at the open end and as rigid as, though much lighter than, some home-made cast iron, aluminium finned versions which I had tried. The shoes were re-lined with the correct grade of Duron. All three brake cables were connected to a cross shaft mounted, on cast aluminium bearings, across the lower chassis tubes. On the end of this was a long outside lever. The foot pedal operated the back cable through a slotted link. The leverages of the system were carefully worked out and the brakes proved to be surprisingly good from all speeds.

Nearly all the standard nuts and bolts had Whitworth threads and these were replaced by the lighter and stronger B.S.F. type. Assisted by first-class machining facilities and a wide selection of high duty materials, I was able to lighten practically every part of the machine. The dry weight in road trim was 7 cwt. 2 qrs., and 5 cwt. 1 qr. 14 lbs. when ready for Lewes. This saving of 2 cwt. 14 lbs., or just over 28 per cent., seemed satisfactory in a machine already built down to a taxation "formula" of 8 cwt. maximum. Of this saving nearly 40 lbs. was unsprung weight.

The blow fell when I applied for an entry form. I was told that, because three-wheelers were controlled by the A.C.U. they could not, in future, compete in events run with an R.A.C. Permit. This was crushing news as much fairly honest sweat had gone into the preparation. I had even (funny though it now seems) obtained a contour plan of Race Hill, Lewes, from the local surveyor. With this and b.h.p. and torque curves a slide-rule-pushing friend deduced the "optimum" gear ratio values. Oliver's Morgan weighed just under 8 cwt. and gave not more than 45 b.h.p. at 4,500 r.p.m. Figures for mine were 5¼ cwt. and 60 b.h.p. at 5,500 r.p.m. with better rear wheel adhesion, and greatly reduced

flywheel and road wheel inertia. Although data of this kind is usually deceptive, it was sufficiently encouraging to make us curse the fate which denied us the consummation of months of toil.

On recovery it was decided to convert the Morgan into a token four-wheeler with rear track of 19¾ ins., which would bring it under R.A.C. jurisdiction. I got out some drawings, proposing to use the existing springs, forks, and two-speed gear, with some extra top linkage for rigidity. (This system was only intended for Lewes and had to be readily re-convertible. The easier "standard" method of conversion, with G.N.—or Frazer-Nash—countershaft, radius rods, springs and axle, as exemplified by Woodall's "Chatterbox," Lones's "Tiger Cat," and Breyer's "Salome," appears to provide good all round controllability.) The axle forgings for this had just been machined when I ran into J. H. T. Smith, who suggested that we make up a team for the forthcoming L.C.C. Relay Race, then in its prime. Smith had just bought the K3 M.G. in which Gardner and Benjafield had finished third in the previous "500"; his warmish road Aston-Martin was to complete the trio. Here was a chance to compete in a more important event on level terms with cars. I decided in favour of it and started to replace the back wheel, increase the tankage, alter gear ratios and tyres, improve the streamlining and make various other necessary changes, with none too much time to spare. Meanwhile friends prophesied, with gloomy relish, that suspension parts which I had lightened for Lewes would fail me on the outer circuit.

The week-end before the race, which was on a Saturday, I worked two nights without sleep and left Lancashire for London on Monday morning. The Morgan

was on a sort of trailer, hired from a farm and previously used for manure, behind a 10/23 Talbot. This had ignition trouble on the way down which I was too tired to deal with and left to a garage while I fed. They failed to cure it but replaced an ignition control rod in such a way that it fell into the clutch and knocked off all but two of the clutch springs. On these and about two cylinders I pressed on, finally to acknowledge defeat near Coventry in the small hours of Tuesday morning. I awoke at about 6.30 a.m. from some sleep on the grass beside the Talbot, and, after stopping a number of lorries, found an angel (disguised as the driver of an old Leyland with an overload of boiler plate) who towed the whole outfit right to Marble Arch.

The days before the race passed quickly in the usual rush and excitement which was heightened when we saw the programme and found that we were expected to be the fifth fastest team. The Morgan lapped at 90 m.p.h. quite easily though we never timed a flat-out lap. The speed seemed prodigious at the time, and the bumps unbelievable, but the only thing to give way was my air cushion. I soon learned how to avoid the worst bumps, but was unable occasionally to prevent my foot being jolted off the throttle pedal. Owing to the sensitivity of a twin to lubrication and mixture adjustments this occurrence always oiled or wetted up one of the plugs, which could never be induced to clear itself. This trouble, which was later partially rectified, was apparently not peculiar to my machine. Lones was rumoured to drive on his hand throttle, which he opened flat-out and retained in that position by a rubber-band! I used a 3.9 to 1 top, with 4.50″ × 19″ back tyre. My engine had one carburetter

Continued on page **165**

Martin Soames's 8/55 h.p. J.A.P.-engined Morgan stripped for action

On Buying

The First of a Sh
wheeler Enthusiast w
Perfect Solution of

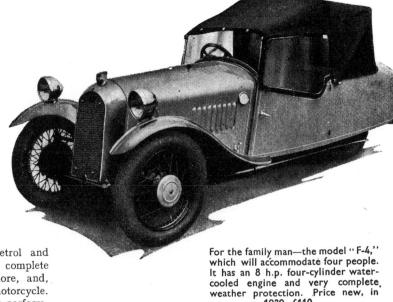

A typical super-sports Morgan powered by an air-cooled 990 c.c. o.h.v. engine. The 1939 purchase price was £120.

For the family man—the model "F-4," which will accommodate four people. It has an 8 h.p. four-cylinder water-cooled engine and very complete weather protection. Price new, in 1939, £110.

THIS article is intended largely for those who, for one reason or another, contemplate the purchase of a s/h. "Moggie," and there are many who could do much worse. Those whose car is proving too expensive; those car owners who must cut down the amount of petrol they use; the solo rider whose newly acquired wife is a non-motorcyclist; those whose solo or sidecar no longer provides sufficient or suitable transport or accommodation for the family—for each and any of these a Morgan might well provide the perfect solution. It is cheap to run and service, economical on petrol and oil, provides reliable, sociable transport with complete protection from the elements for two or more, and, besides this, has the performance of a good motorcycle. It provides almost car comfort with motorcycle performance at motorcycle expense.

The Time To Buy

There are one or two things to remember. As the war goes on prices will rise, and probably they will not go any lower than they are now until long after the war is over. Meantime, the supply of s/h. Morgans is decreasing. The other point is that those who buy now will have the long, dark winter nights for any overhauling that needs doing; when lighter evenings come the garden will demand that time!

If you have decided to purchase a Morgan, first read all the literature you can about them and make up your mind just which model will suit your needs and purse best, e.g., do you want a four-cylinder or a twin-cylinder; a four-seater or a two-seater; a water-cooled or air-cooled s.v. or o.h.v. engine? The twin-cylinder models are more economical on petrol and oil and easier to service, the s.v. being mechanically the quieter; they all have, however, the typical motorcycle exhaust note. The four-cylinder models are quieter on the exhaust and are, I think, a little more comfortable. The two-seater models are snug little jobs for two, but the four-seaters provide room for the family or for luggage, where it will be protected from the elements.

Having made your choice, it is as well to have a second string in mind in case the first proves unobtainable. Now go through all the advertisements in "The Motor" and "Motor Cycling" and see what is being advertised. This procedure should also give you some idea of the price likely to be asked. Before actually going to inspect the vehicle, have a talk with an experienced "Moggie" owner; better still, persuade him to come with you and help you choose your bus and run the rule over it.

Now for the actual vehicle. Stand back and get a general idea of it; note whether it has been taken care of or scratched and dented, showing rough usage. Don't take much notice of mud and oil splashes, as many people and firms have little time for cleaning these days. Look for a vehicle that has been kept neat and tidy and in correct adjustment. If it has been knocked about it is probably best left alone.

The Chassis

Having decided that the machine is worth closer examination, next scrutinize it carefully. Pay particular attention to the chassis. Stand beside one of the front wheels and run your eye along the cross-members; these, as seen from above and to one side, should be straight and lie vertically one above the other. If they are bent or do not lie above each other the job has been crashed, and while the model may still handle well in this condition and the damage is comparatively simple to correct, given time, etc., the alignment of the rest of the chassis may have been upset. These cross-members should also be examined carefully for cracks close to the lugs, especially on the four-cylinder models.

While examining the cross-members see that the stays joining the lower ends of the sliding axle pins to the chassis are not damaged. The next chassis point to check is the alignment of the back wheel. The only way to check this satisfactorily is to have the model

Second-hand Morgan

...ies of Articles Written by a Three-
...ieves that the Type Provides the
...nomical Passenger Transport Problem

By "TREPENPOL"

on a level surface and then to die down some way to the rear, so that you can sight along the wheel. If the wheel is much out of the vertical, then that particular "Moggie" has been ill used and the chassis or rear forks are twisted and the bus is best left alone. While checking this, get someone to rock the machine sideways, as any slackness in the rear fork-arm bearings will then show itself; this play is easily corrected, given the necessary time. Very slack rear fork-arm bearings may allow the wheel to lay over and give the impression of a twisted chassis, but don't be misled by give in the tyre.

Another popular member of the Morgan family—this time a water-cooled side valve, twin-engined model.

The last chassis point to check is the lug in front of the gearbox. See that there are no cracks at the joint between this lug and the propeller shaft tube. While I have dealt very thoroughly with the chassis, this should not be construed as meaning it is a weak point. It is not, but most people seem to ignore it in preference for the inside of the body and the engine.

The Suspension

The springing and steering are next in importance and are, to some extent, interdependent. The rear springs can easily be examined by looking under the rear of the body and their action tested by bouncing the "tail." In any case, trouble here is most unlikely. The front springs rarely break; it is sufficient to see that the telescopic spring covers have been working an inch or so and that both sides are of equal strength.

A very important item in the front suspension and the steering are the bronze "sliding axles," into which the stub axles are bolted, and the pins on which these "axles" slide. To test these, place a foot against the lower edge of the wheel, then alternately pull and push hard on the top of the wheel. Much rock means that a new "sliding axle" and pin are needed, an expense of approximately 27s. 6d. for the two. These are easily

fitted, even by a novice. The rest of the steering is likely to be sound, but it might be as well to see that the ball joints are not unduly worn and have some adjustment left; also that the lower end of the steering column is securely fastened to the body and the moving portion tight in the drop arm.

Chains, sprockets, lights and brake linings might be examined next. Hooked sprockets mean replacements, as do worn chains. The condition of the brake linings will be evident by the position of the cam levers when the brakes are on; levers that have come well round indicate worn linings.

The Power Unit

Now for the power unit. A filthy, oily job is probably much worn, as the engines usually keep oil-tight if in reasonably good condition. With the twin-cylinder types, see that the light-alloy rockers are tight on their shafts and that the valves cannot be rocked sideways in their guides. Fit the starting handle and pull the engine over slowly, noting if the resistance of each cylinder is the same. Ask to have the engine started up and see that it idles smoothly, accelerates briskly when the throttle is opened and is free from rattles or knocks. The exhaust smoke should not be more than faintly blue after the initial accumulation of oil in the crankcase has been blown out; more than this indicates worn pistons, piston rings or cylinders.

Finally, get the owner or dealer to take you for a short run. This should give you some idea of the handling and performance, besides providing an opportunity to see that the dynamo charges and the brakes work. Note if the engine is smooth and picks up well, that the clutch takes up the drive smoothly and doesn't slip on sudden acceleration. Ask the demonstrator to do some little distance in each gear, preferably on an up grade. Top gear should be dead silent, but second and, to a lesser extent, bottom gear may be rather noisy. Check also that the gears change well and do not slip out of engagement. Whilst the engine is running it is also possible to test the windscreen wiper and to examine the exhaust pipes for leaks and rattles due to looseness.

When you return, try the starter. On the four-cylinder models this should be capable of starting the engine at all times—hot or cold. On the twin-cylinder models it is always necessary to use the exhaust-valve lifter when employing the starter, and it may not be capable of turning the engine over sufficiently fast when the latter is cold and gummed up with oil, but should be perfectly efficient when the engine is hot. Tyres, hood, upholstery, windscreen, wings, and so forth, can also be thoroughly checked over after the run.

During the examination and testing you are certain to have found some defects. In peace-time dealers would often agree to correct at least the lesser ones or those that are vital, but in these war days this will probably be impossible owing to shortage of staff and you will have to set about the job yourself. Don't jib at that for most of the work on a Morgan can well be done by the veriest novice, and you will find that any Morgan owners in your district will probably be only too willing to help. There is a camaraderie amongst "Moggie" owners, which must be almost unique.

A three-wheeler, the Model F Super.

The Morgan

"THE LIGHT CAR" gives you first details of the post-war version of—

TWO four-wheelers and two three-wheeled models are already in production in Malvern. So far as the latter pair is concerned, there are no alterations from the 1939 specification. The four-wheelers, however, have one or two small changes as well as a new engine which, although delivered before a few of these cars just before the war, has not been described hitherto.

Manufactured specially for the Morgan Motor Co., Ltd., by one of the largest Coventry car makers, this new power unit has all its valves overhead and operated by push rods. Dimensional details will be found in a separate data panel. With a larger capacity at 11½ per cent. more power (40 b.h.p.) at 4,300 r.p.m. instead of 4,500 r.p.m., the new engine is also appreciably lighter than its predecessor.

This unit is mounted, it may be recalled, in a remarkably low chassis. (The floor boards are only 7½ ins. above ground level.) A short enclosed shaft drives a four-speed synchromesh gearbox located amidships, where its stubby lever is very conveniently placed.

Suspension at the rear is conventional except that there are no shackles for the semi-elliptic springs; instead, the master leaves slide in trunnions. At the front there is independent suspension of the type which has been used in Morgans for some 35 years, each wheel being arranged to slide vertically under the control of a helical spring to carry the load and a smaller spring as a necessary check on rebound.

Here some modifications are to be found. As a result of alterations to the springs themselves and particularly to the rebound springs, shock absorbers are no longer necessary and are not fitted at the front.

Another change is the incorporation of very simple steering dampers which have eliminated wheel wobble. A flat strip of saw steel, suitably tempered, is attached at one end to the chassis frame. At the other, bronze washers are riveted to it and these are placed between the main spring and the sliding axle where they provide enough friction to prevent oscillation but do not tend to make the steering heavy. A third change is the radiator mounting. This unit now rests on a pair of brackets attached to the front of the chassis frame.

Two body types are available on this chassis—an open two-seater with large luggage space, which also houses a concealed hood, and a drop-head coupé. Both have two spare wheels carried in a special trough.

The three-wheelers are unchanged. The four-seater has an 8 h.p. engine and the Model F Super a 10 h.p. unit, both being water-cooled. The single rear wheel is carried in a robust swinging fork, with a pair of quarter-elliptic springs.

The Super is a two-seater with a high performance, and the four-seater is more of a family vehicle designed to provide a fair measure of liveliness with highly economical transport for four.

These, incidentally, appear to be the only three-wheelers likely to be available on the British market at present, and they should be of very considerable interest, particularly in these days of high taxation. There will, indeed, be a warm welcome for the Morgan both in three- and four-wheeled form.

The 4/4 Two-seater

Engine.—O.h.v., 4-cyl., 63.5 mm. by 100 mm. (1,267 c.c.). Tax, £12 10s. Thermo-siphon cooling. Solex carburetter. A.C. mechanical fuel pump from 9-gallon tank. **Transmission, Etc.**—Dry-plate clutch, gears 5.0, 7.1, 12.1 and 17.1 to 1. Steering, Burman-Douglas. Suspension, independent at front with helical springs; semi-elliptic at rear with Hartford shock absorbers. Girling brakes. Tyres, 4.50-17. **General.**—12-v. electrical equipment; wheelbase, 7 ft. 8 ins.; track, 3 ft. 9 ins.; length, 11 ft. 4 ins.; width, 4 ft. 6 ins. Unladen weight, 14½ cwt. Price, £355, plus £99 15s. 1d.

The 4/4 Coupé

Same as Two-seater except length, 11 ft. 7¼ ins.; height, 4 ft. 1¾ ins., 15½ cwt. Tyres, 5.50-16. Price, £110 18s. 3d.

Three-wheeler. Model F (4-seater)

Engine.—S.v., 4-cyl., 56.64 mm. by 92.56 mm. (933 c.c.). Zenith carburetter; 4-gallon gravity tank. **Transmission.**—Dry-plate clutch; enclosed propeller shaft to gearbox; gears 4.85, 7.9 and 15.3 to 1; reverse, 18.8 to 1. Worm gear and ¾-in. pitch roller chain to rear wheel. Steering, independent at front, with helical springs: quarter-elliptic at rear. Brakes, Girling. Tyres, 4.00-18. **General.**—6-v. electrical equipment, wheelbase, 8 ft. 3 ins.; track, 4 ft. 2 ins.; length, 11 ft. 6 ins.; width, 4 ft.; Unladen weight, under 8 cwt. Price, £205 plus £57 13s. 10d.

Three-wheeler. Model F Super.

Same as Model F Four-seater except 62.5 mm. by 92.5 mm. (1,172 c.c.). Gears, 4.58, 7.45 and 14.4 to 1; reverse, 17.8 to 1. Wheelbase, 7 ft. 11 ins.; length, 11 ft. 1 in. Price, £245 plus £68 16s. 1d.

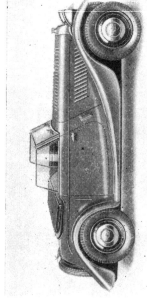

(Right) Four seats, three wheels. This is the Model F— very popular before the war. (Below) The attractive 4/4 drop-head coupé. Another illustration appears on page 28.

Outline for speed and sport: the 4/4 two-seater.

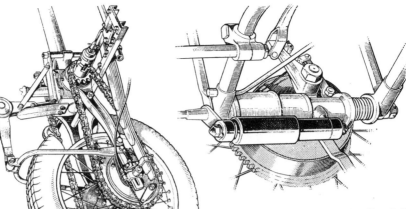

Three-wheeler Fans may find this article—No. 2 in the Series—of some assistance to them if they have come by one of the—

Older-type Morgans

ALTHOUGH second-hand Morgans are pretty scarce these days, many machines were acquired only just before the war, and their owners are now managing to get them on the road for the first time. It is astonishing how many of the older-type two speeders one sees around. The following hints, based on the writer's experiences when he, too, was an ardent "Morganite," may prove helpful to owners.

Steering wobble at low speeds can be quite as alarming as at high speed. That awful feeling of having oval shaped wheels has been experienced by most Morgan owners, especially with cars which have been recently thoroughly lubricated. Whether through forgetfulness or not I do not know, but people will insist on greasing the conical steering-arm pins. These pins must be kept dry; their purpose is to set up friction in the tapered holes in the track rod in order to damp out any tendency to wobble.

Badly worn sliding axles will almost certainly cause erratic behaviour of the front wheels and these should be renewed so soon as wear is apparent. Always fit a new sliding-axle tube as well as a replacement sliding axle. Incidentally, when reassembling the front suspension, on no account overlook the large star washer which locks the wheel spindle nut. Should this work loose, the entire front wheel and spindle may part company from the car.

Steering wobble can, of course, be due to a variety of other causes, as on every make of car. For instance, the steering

A 1931 Aero Morgan with 10/40 h.p. o.h.v. J.A.P. engine.

column may be loose where it is attached to the body, or the steering wheel itself may not be tight. The nuts securing the column to the body, if allowed to slacken off, will almost certainly cause the bolts to enlarge the holes in the woodwork. The steering drop-arm may be slack where it is fitted on to the square end of the column; also, it is possible that the square end itself may have worked loose on the column. The only cure for this is to remove the column and fit new rivets; it may be necessary, in bad cases, to reamer out the holes and fit oversize rivets.

The rivets securing the steel blocks in the steering universal have also been known to work loose. Removing the universal and riveting the pins should cure this. Another cause of wheel wobble is that the bolts and set-bolts on the track-rod and universal may have worn threads. Slack wheel bearings are also suspect, or the wheel spindle nut may require tightening. Don't overlook the possibility of a bent rear-wheel spindle. It is surprising how often a violent front-wheel wobble has been traced to this source.

On many older o.h.v. J.A.P. engines excessive clatter of the valve gear can

Older-type Morgans

be caused by dryness of the ball joints between the top of the push-rods and the rockers. This is nearly always traceable to blocking up of the hollow push-rod tubes by grease exuded from the rocker bearings. The grease finds its way down the tubes, and, as they are wider at the top than at the bottom, it effectively seals them. It is not always realized that the ball joints depend solely for their lubrication on oil mist blown up from the timing-box.

Leather-faced cone clutches are always prone to judder unless steps are taken to overcome it. The most effective cure is fairly regular "doping" with

An effective method of mounting a friction-type rear shock absorber on sports models fitted with the M-type chassis.

Collan oil. A large grease gun, to which was attached a piece of flexible tube, was part of my stock-in-trade so long as I owned a cone-clutch Morgan. I recommend that the best time to apply the oil is the night before you want to use the car; this gives the lubricant a chance to work itself into the leather and thoroughly soften it. Other people, of course, prefer to ensure adequate lubrication of the clutch by the time-old method of flinging large quantities of grease into it. This always strikes me as a particularly messy business. I can vindicate the Collan oil tip in so far that I never once suffered clutch judder from the time I started using it.

Morgans, as is the case on all cars fitted with exposed brake cables, may suffer from the cables rusting up. To overcome this, I found that the best thing to do was to paint them with a solution of linseed oil which had been boiled. When this dries, it forms a hard, varnish-like protective coat, which lasts for many thousands of miles.

Finally, I would like to draw your attention to an ingenious method of fitting a friction-type damper to the rear of your Morgan. As the illustration shows, this is fairly simple and inexpensive. Many of the chaps in the late twenties and early thirties fitted rear shockers; they certainly help to smooth out the ride when travelling at speed over indifferent roads.
G.

Newton shock absorbers were first fitted on certain models in 1928. This drawing clearly shows the steering connections and hub spindle nut referred to in the text.

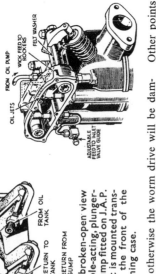

OIL TOGGLE PINS

(Below) The arrangement and lubrication points of the o.h. valve gear on Matchless engines.

(Above) A broken-open view of the double-acting, plunger-type, oil pump fitted on J.A.P. engines. It is mounted transversely on the front of the timing case.

The Morgan Three-wheeler

THE articles to which we refer in our heading were subsequently reprinted, but, we regret, the supply of reprints—for which there has been a steady demand—is now exhausted. In due course, we hope to summarize the second and third articles, which covered top overhaul, and brakes and suspension. Below, we devote our attention to lubrication.

Engine, 8 h.p. and 10 h.p. Ford-engined models.—Sump capacity is 4 pints on the early 8 h.p. engine, 5¼ pints on later types, and 4½ pints on the 10 h.p. unit. The submerged gear-type pump is driven by camshaft. Oil is drawn through a gauze filter which completely surrounds the pump and is passed upwards through a passage in the pump body to the main distribution gallery, thence into four oilways leading to the pressure relief valve and the three camshaft bearings respectively.

From each of these bearings the oil continues to the main bearings, where drilled passages in the crankshaft lead it to the big-ends. Cylinder walls, pistons, and little ends are splash-lubricated. The surplus from the relief valve oils the timing wheels. Drain and refill sump every 1,000 miles. Remove and clean sump and filter every 5,000 miles.

(Left) How the oil filter element is removed on the four-cylinder models and (below) on the Matchless-engined cars.

Matchless and J.A.P. Two-cylinder-engined Models.—Dry-sump lubrication. From the one-gallon oil tank under the bonnet two copper pipes connect to the supply and return side of the oil pump—of double-acting plunger type—operated by worm drive and mounted transversely on the front of the timing case.

As with the four-cylinder engines, there is no pressure gauge fitted. A test of the return pipe in the tank will indicate if the system is functioning properly. The oil tank should be drained and cleaned out every 5,000 miles. Matchless-engined models have a cartridge-type filter mounted on the tank; this should be cleaned in petrol every 2,000 miles. It is very important to note that, when dismantling a Matchless engine and splitting the crankcase, the oil-pump plunger must be removed first,

(Right) The two types of oil pressure relief valve on the four-cylinder engines. The adjustable type figures only on early 8 h.p. models. (Below) Cut-away view of the Matchless oil pump. Correct replacement of the paper washer is important to avoid blanking off the supply to the engine.

otherwise the worm drive will be damaged. Similarly, the crankcase should be reassembled before the plunger is refitted. The rockers of the Matchless o.h.v. engine are supplied with oil direct from the pump and the surplus drains to the sump via the push-rod tubes. These are telescopic; the lower portions are arranged to slide up to facilitate valve adjustment. In the bases of the tubes are round, spring-loaded rubber washers, which form an oil seal when the tubes are in place. Leaks will occur if these are not seating correctly, and if, for any purpose, they have to be removed, they should be replaced by new ones, as they are inclined to swell and cannot be satisfactorily refitted.

Transmission.—The plate clutches fitted to the later models require little in the way of attention; however, should juddering during engagement become noticeable, a little thin oil (preferably graphited) should be brushed on the splines along which the driven plate assembly slides. Apply sparingly; any excess of oil either through overfilling of the gearbox may find its way to the clutch lining.

Early 1932 and previous models have cone clutches, which must be lubricated if smooth action is to be maintained. Engine oil is suitable for this purpose; it can be applied with an oil gun. The withdrawal and inner thrust races can also be lubricated in this manner, and if these are generously oiled, sufficient oil will find its way to the spigot race.

Other points for oiling are the squared end of the propeller shaft, on which the cone slides, and the pins carrying the springs. The centre bearing of the propeller shaft can be dealt with by a grease gun.

A gear oil should be used for the three-speed type gearbox.

A heavy grease is recommended for pre-1932 cars with the two-speed gearbox, not oil. The sliding dogs which engage the gears should be kept well oiled, also the joints in the control lever.

The final-drive chains should be lubricated frequently and allowed occasionally to soak in a bath of warmed graphited grease. This grease should also be smeared liberally on the fibre pinion which drives the dynamo on the two-speed models.

Chassis.—Grease-gun nipples will be found on each sliding axle, shackle slipper and rear-fork arm bearing, also on the steering reduction box and rear hub. For the front hubs a little grease should be inserted inside the hexagonal cap, exposed by removing the Magna caps. An excessive quantity should be avoided; it may be forced through the bearings to the brake linings.

Points requiring attention with the oil-can are the front-brake camshafts (each has a hole covered by a clip), the various steering joints, the clutch toggle arms, the gear-change lever, the distributor, and various other small joints, such as the ends of Bowden cables, small control joints, door hinges, and so on.

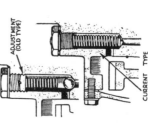

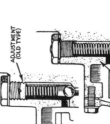

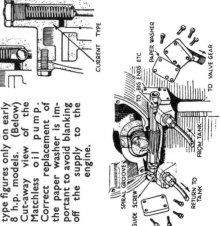

The Morgan Three-wheeler

THE procedure for decarbonizing twin-cylinder engines is described in connection with the Matchless, but owners of J.A.P. models should have no difficulty in allowing for slight differences in design.

In the case of water-cooled engines, first drain the radiator and disconnect the water-outlet joints from the cylinder heads. With o.h.v. engines, the next job is to disconnect the oil and petrol pipes. Slacken off the two union nuts holding the manifold to the cylinders, so that the carburetter can be lifted out of the way.

Before detaching the rocker-boxes, the small pipes carrying lubricant to the inlet valve stems should be disconnected. Four bolts secure each rocker-box. The two exhaust pipes must be detached at their flanges before the cylinder heads are taken off.

The heads should be placed on the bench, and the valves removed with the aid of a suitable valve-spring compressor. The heads and piston crowns should be scraped free of carbon, and the exhaust and inlet ports cleaned out. For grinding-in purposes, a special tool will be needed (see accompanying sketches).

Reassembly of the engine is merely a reversal of the dismantling procedure. Tighten the cylinder-head (and rocker-box) bolts half a turn at a time, in the correct sequence.

When all is reassembled, the valve clearances should be checked on the tappets at the base of the push-rods. The tappet head should be held with a spanner whilst the lock nut is slacked off; next the tappet itself should be

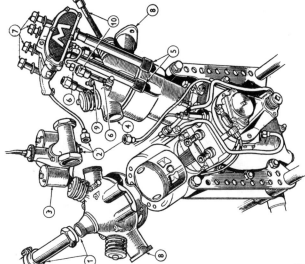

Procedure for the four-cylinder models is as follows:—Drain the radiator, disconnect the main battery lead, and slacken the nut holding the dynamo support to the cylinder head; this releases the support and allows the fan belt to be slipped off. Disconnect the lead on the cut-out terminal and remove the dynamo together with its support.

Detach the leads from the sparking plugs, marking them first for correct replacement; pull out the main high-tension lead from the distributor. The lead from the coil to the side of the distributor must also be disconnected, when the screw holding the distributor body clamp to the cylinder head can be taken out and the distributor withdrawn. The nut on the distributor clamp should not be disturbed or the timing will be upset.

The two bolts holding the water outlet to the cylinder head should next be removed. The choke and accelerator controls and the petrol pipe should be detached from the carburetter. Undo the manifold securing nuts, and the manifold will come away complete with carburetter.

To take out the valves, the tappet cover plate on the near side of the engine should be detached, the valve springs lifted with a suitable tool, and the collars and springs taken out.

The valve should be pushed upwards and a piece of wood slipped under the head into the valve port, so that it engages with the top of the valve guide; by tapping the wood, the split valve guide will be pushed into the valve chamber, whence it can be withdrawn.

Some clean rag should be inserted in the valve chamber to prevent any carbon chippings entering the sump, and any carbon that has accumulated in the ports should be scraped away.

Reassembly is straightforward. All valve parts must be replaced in their initial position. Refitting the distributor need cause no anxiety, as the drive fitting is off-set so that there is only one possible engagement. Finally, clean and adjust the plugs and contact-breaker points.

Removal of the cylinder head is quite straightforward, and the actual scraping away of the carbon calls for no comment.

Dealing with the valves, however, is rather complicated as no tappet adjustment is provided, and if the valves are ground-in, reducing the clearance to less than the recommended .013 to 0.15 in., it is necessary to grind the ends of the stems to restore the status quo. Accurate grinding is essential, and it is far better to entrust the work to a Ford repair agent.

gripped whilst the head is set; the tappet and head are then held whilst the lock nut is retightened.

The clearance, tested at the valve end when the engine is cold, should be nil; but it should be possible to revolve the valve stem caps with the fingers. With J.A.P. o.h.v. engines a clearance of .002 in. is recommended.

The method of dealing with side-valve engines is very similar, except that the complication of the o.h.v. gear is absent. The J.A.P. s.v. unit has fixed cylinder heads, making it necessary to remove the cylinder barrel. Incidentally, the valves on s.v. engines are slotted to take a screwdriver for grinding-in purposes. For Matchless and J.A.P. s.v. engines a clearance of .004-in. inlet and .006-in. exhaust is recommended.

(Above) Valve parts of the four-cylinder engine. See text for method of removal.

SPLIT VALVE GUIDE. COLLAR.

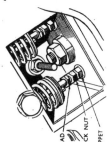

(Below) The valve-adjusting arrangements of the Matchless s.v. engine. Three spanners are needed for the job.

HEAD. LOCK NUT. TAPPET.

ROCKER BEARING CLAMPING BOLTS. The rocker gear of the o.h.v. J.A.P. engine. ADJUSTMENT. LOCK NUT.

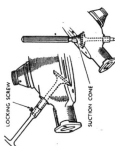

Two methods of valve grinding on o.h.v. engines.

LOCKING SCREW. SUCTION CONE.

A spring compressor for dealing with o.h. valves.

SPLIT COTTER. SPRING COMPRESSOR.

CUT-AWAY drawing of the o.h.v. Matchless engine. Parts are numbered in order of removal. (1) water outlet joints, (2) petrol and oil pipe unions, (3) carburetter, (4) induction pipe unions, (5) push rod tubes: raise telescopic lower portion, (6) inlet valve oil supply union, (7) rocker box head nuts, (8) exhaust pipe joints, (9) sparking plug, (10) cylinder head nuts.

The Morgan Three-wheeler

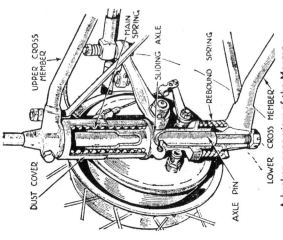

DUST COVER · UPPER CROSS MEMBER · MAIN SPRING · SLIDING AXLE · REBOUND SPRING · LOWER CROSS MEMBER · AXLE PIN

A broken-open view of the Morgan independent front suspension.

To gain access to the front brake shoes, the wheel should be removed and the nut which holds the steering arm on to the sliding axle assembly unscrewed. The steering arm can then be removed. This enables the hub spindle to be tapped out of the sliding axle after disconnecting the brake cable and, on the off side, the speedometer cable. With the spindle tapped out, the hub, brake drum and back plate come away together. There is a distance-piece adjacent to the back plate, and this should be removed, when the back plate and drum will come apart.

The brake shoes are held to the back plate by means of their pull-off springs; they can be detached by levering their ends away from the pivot pin. The springs themselves can then be unhooked. As it is important that the shoes be replaced in the same position and the same way round, they should be punch-marked before removal.

To separate the drums from the hubs, the six nuts holding them should be undone. On the off side it will be necessary to remove the speedometer ring. A special tool is required for this purpose.

If it is desired to reach the hub bearings for replacement—they are non-adjustable—the hub cap must be taken off and the hub spindle gripped in a vice so that the castle nut can be unscrewed. The hub spindle can then be tapped out, leaving the two ball races in the hub. The outer race is a push fit, but the inner race is retained by a ring screwed into the shell. This ring is prevented from working loose by a spring circlip. Replacement is straightforward, but make sure that the felt washer which fits between the inner race and the brake drum is in good condition.

To refit the brake shoes, assemble them together as a pair with their springs; place one shoe in position, pull on the other and slip it over the pivot pin and cam.

Reverting to the front hub bearings, older model Morgans had ball bearings of the cup and cone type. Play can be taken up on these bearings by removing the split pin, castellated nut and tongued lock washer on the hub spindle and screwing in the cone. It is essential that a little play is left or the bearing will rapidly wear. Screw up the cone therefore until all appreciable play has disappeared, without leaving any suggestion of tightness.

Rear wheel removal is quite simple on the three-speed models. Disconnect the tail lamp lead, take off the spare wheel and the rear panel and jack up. The nut on the knock-out spindle should then be removed, the brake cable slipped out and the knock-out spindle pulled or tapped out, thus allowing the wheel to drop. The driving chain having been lifted off the sprocket the wheel will come away as one unit. It is retained on the hub assembly by four nuts. The back plate complete with shoes will then pull straight out.

So far as the bearings are concerned, there is a roller race on the driving side and a ball race on the near side. To dismantle the bearings, the spindle should be driven out by tapping through from the sprocket side. The roller race can be removed by taking off the six nuts which hold the brake drum to the hub, detaching the drum and taking out the ball-race housing cover and leather seal which, incidentally, is held by a spring. The race can then be tapped out from the opposite side.

The ball race on the other side can be extracted by taking off the plate behind the wheel hub flange and tapping out the race from the opposite side.

After a considerable mileage, the sliding axles may wear; renewal is not a very difficult matter. The wing should first be taken off and the wheel, together with the hub spindle, detached from the sliding axle; the castellated nut under the lower cross-member should also be taken off. The next job is to slack off the split clamp which forms the end of the upper cross-member, when the axle pin can be pulled right out.

The whole spring assembly should then be pushed sideways free of the upper cross-member, but care should be taken to hold the casing tight so that the spring does not fly off so soon as it is relieved of compression. The dust cover and two springs can then be detached, fitted over the new sliding axle and the whole assembly replaced between the cross-members.

On older model Morgans, construction differs slightly in that the sliding axle works on a steel tube fitted between the upper and lower cross-members, the wing stay passing through the centre of this tube and serving merely to hold the assembly together. The tube fits into recesses in the lugs at the ends of the frame cross-members and it is necessary to spring the two cross-members apart slightly to allow the tube, complete with spring and sliding axle, to be withdrawn.

ALTERNATIVE BOLT HOLES

The steering box; showing the three alternative holes provided for each bolt to allow the eccentrically mounted pinion to be brought into deeper mesh to take up wear.

INNER RACE RETAINING RING · CIRCLIP · SPEEDOMETER DRIVE · HUB SPINDLE · FELT WASHER · DISTANCE PIECE

CHAIN ADJUSTMENT · PEDAL EXTENSION · BRAKE ADJUSTMENT · LOCKNUT · EXTRA BRAKE ADJUSTMENT

(Above) An "exploded" view of a front hub and brake assembly. (Right) The front and rear brake adjustments; when the limit of the Bowden cable adjustment is reached, further play may be taken up at the yoke ends of the cables.

1949 MORGAN THREE-WHEELERS

Two-model Four-cylinder Range Unaltered

The 1949 F. Super Morgan listed at £260 plus £72 19s. 5d. P.T.

THE sole manufacturers of passenger three-wheelers now in production in this country, the Morgan Motor Co., Ltd., of Malvern Link, Worcs., are continuing unaltered their programme of four-cylinder water-cooled models. There are two types, the Model F-4, occasional four-seater, and the Model F-Super, a plus-70 m.p.h. two-seater.

Morgan "four" details are almost too well known to necessitate reiteration, but for the benefit of those who may not be familiar with the construction of these two machines it may be briefly stated that both are generally similar, with "Z" section steel chassis incorporating a central tube between engine and gearbox and a side-valve engine of 1,172 c.c. The latter incorporates thermo-siphon cooling, dynamically balanced crankshaft, automatic control to the coil ignition system, turbulent cylinder head, and down-draught carburetter. The compression ratio is 6.2 to 1. Transmission is from a single dry-plate clutch with a flexible centre, by shaft to the three-speed-and-reverse gearbox. the ratios being 4.58, 7.5 and 12.4 to 1; reverse is 16.5 to 1. Final drive is by worm and wheel built into the rear of the gearbox and thence by a ¾-in.-pitch, slow-speed chain to the single rear wheel.

Independent wheel suspension is on the well-known Morgan system. coil springs being used at the front and long, leaf springs at the rear. Wheels are of Dunlop Magna type. detachable and interchangeable with a spare carried at the rear of the body. Tyres are 18-in. by 4-in. Dunlops. Girling brakes are fitted on all wheels. Lucas 6v. electrical equipment, including starter and horn, is employed and car-type steering, very light in operation, is featured. The fuel tank holds four gallons and the oil capacity of the sump is one gallon. A pneumatic windscreen wiper is fitted.

The single-door body of the four-seater is fitted with all-weather equipment and adjustable front seats. Lamps, radiator shell and fittings are chromium plated, and the standard colour is Saxe blue with black wings and wheels. The short-wheelbase sports model has two doors, folding windscreen, and hood, while finish is red, black or British Racing Green.

Both touring and sports models are equipped with Moseley Float-on-Air cushions.

Morgan prices for 1949 remain at £246 15s. (plus £69 5s. 10d. purchase tax) for the Model F-4, and £260 (plus £72 19s. 5d. P.T.) for the Model F-Super. Deviation from standard finish costs an additional £3 10s. in each case. Tax is £5 per annum.

Two Morgan Three-wheelers

Two-Seater and Four-seater Models With Water-cooled, Four-cylinder Engines for 1951

MORGANS, the extremely lively three-wheelers, famed for 40 years for their combination of snappy motor cycle performance with sports-car comfort, remain unchanged for 1951. The programme comprises two models, the "F" Super, a two-seater sports machine, and the "F4", which has a four-seater body.

Independent suspension of the front wheels is provided by means of coil springs

In each case the power unit is a Ford Ten car engine, especially adapted for Morgans. The engine is a side-valve, water-cooled four in-line of 1,172 c.c., with a compression ratio of 6.2 to 1. Power output is claimed as being 32.5 b.h.p. at 3,500 r.p.m.,

and when it is realized that the total weight of the Morgans is in the 8-cwt region it is not difficult to see the "wherefore" behind the high performance! Good power-to-weight ratio pays dividends all along the line—especially so in terms of acceleration and economy. The two-seater is said to have a cruising speed of about 65 m.p.h.

Transmission is via a single-plate dry clutch with a flexible centre and a shaft to the gear box, and thence by worm wheel and a ⅜in-pitch roller chain to the single rear wheel. The gear box has three forward speeds and reverse. In the case of each model the ratios are 4.58, 7.5, and 12.4 to 1, with 16.5 to 1 reverse.

Light, and possessing immense strength, the chassis has side members of deep Z-section steel and retains the all-important tubular member between the engine and gear box. Independent suspension of the front wheels is provided by means of coil springs. Suspension of the rear wheel is by quarter-elliptic leaf springs. Brakes are Girlings, the front pair being coupled to the pedal; the rear brake is connected to the hand lever and is intended for parking purposes only.

The body is coach-built from seasoned wood and sheet metal. It is entirely separate from the chassis and, indeed, is easily detachable. Standard finish of the four-seater is a saxe-blue body with black wheels and wings. The two-seater is available in black, red or British racing green. Deviations from the standard finishes are available at extra cost. Morgans, incidentally, come under the £5-a-year Road Tax ruling.

Makers are The Morgan Motor Co., Ltd., Malvern Link, Worcs. Prices are as follows:—

	Basic Price £	Total Price £ s d	
Model "F" 4	270	345 15 0	
Model "F" Super	285	364 18 4	

Both Morgan models have a four-cylinder engine; this is the "F 4" four-seater

The 122 c.c. Bond Minicar.

Three-wheelers Have a Future

A brief résumé of the advantages and potentialities of the three-wheeled light car with some details of current models.

WHEN this journal originally appeared in 1912 it was, as it is to-day, the champion of the cause of true economy motoring. It is only natural, therefore, that we should still hold the three-wheeler in high regard. In our view, it is a most attractive type of vehicle for both seekers after performance, and for those mainly concerned with very low upkeep costs.

In the commercial sphere, vehicle users are not unmindful of the advantages of petrol-engined, as well as electrically propelled three-wheelers for light transport and delivery work. At the recent Cycle and Motor Cycle Show at Earls Court, five manufacturers exhibited three-wheeled commercial vehicles (disregarding sidecar outfits) and provided a wide variety of body designs.

At the same Show, potential buyers thronged the Morgan and Bond stands.

The former attracts sportsmen and family men, who see in the Morgan a machine with the upkeep and performance of a powerful sidecar outfit, with none of its disadvantages. The Bond, on the other hand, breaks comparatively new ground in so far as this country is concerned; it is the sole representative in the U.K. of a popular Continental type of machine, the ultra-lightweight runabout.

Undoubtedly economy is the major attraction of the three-wheeler. In comparison with a four-wheeled machine having an engine of similar capacity, the three-wheeler scores heavily. It offers a much better power-weight ratio, and, in consequence, the power-unit is able to work well within its limits, with resultant much-improved fuel consumption, better acceleration and, in general, a livelier all-round performance. In these circumstances, an engine of comparatively low power can be employed in a three-wheeled chassis, to do the same work that would require a much larger engine in a four-wheeler.

The very simplicity of three-wheeler design is another point in its favour, for it enables maintenance costs to be kept to a minimum. Again, the annual tax of £5 is reasonable, even in comparison with the £10 flat rate charged for present-day new cars. In short, the type meets a strong need which exists in this country, for reliable, inexpensive and economical personal transport.

Both the 1950 Morgan models have a similar chassis. The "F-4" has a four-seater coachwork with an 8-ft. 3-in. wheelbase, whilst the "F-Super" is a sporting two-seater with a wheelbase four inches shorter. A modified version of the well-known 1,172 side-valve Ford Ten engine is used in both cases. It develops 32.5 b.h.p. at 3,500 r.p.m., with a resultant power-weight ratio in the case of the "F-Super," of rather more than 81 b.h.p. per ton.

The i.f.s. is substantially the identical vertical sliding axle and helical spring design which appeared on the original Morgan of 1910. Quarter-elliptics take care of the single rear wheel, and Girling brakes are fitted. The modern Morgan is, of course, completely equipped with starter, dynamo, car-type controls, spare wheel, all-weather equipment and three-speed gearbox.

Only one model of the 122 c.c. Bond is at present marketed, but it is possible that the range may eventually be extended. The well-tried Villiers, air-cooled, two-stroke engine drives the single front wheel by chain. Light alloys are used extensively in the design, with the result that the 5 b.h.p. produced at peak r.p.m. by the power unit, has only 310 lb. of vehicle to propel. Rear suspension is dependent entirely on the resilient properties of the "balloon-type" tyres.

Despite its miniature appearance, there is more than ample room for two adults with reasonable luggage accommodation behind the bench-type seat. Full weather protection and other features of a normal-sized car are provided. Average fuel consumption is stated to be over 100 m.p.g., and maximum speed is around 40 m.p.h.

In view of the unsettled conditions of post-war motoring, and the genuine market for machines of absolute economy, it is rather surprising that other makers have not entered this field.

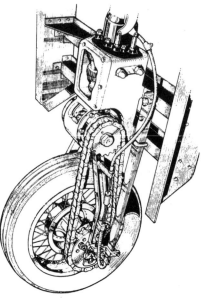

MORGAN: Drive from the rear-located gearbox is transmitted, via a worm and wheel, by chain to the single rear wheel. Suspension is by two quarter-elliptic leaf springs, the fork which carries the wheel being pivoted at the worm and wheel housing. The sketch on the right shows the sliding axle i.f.s. arrangement.

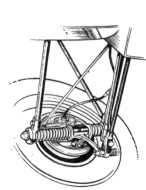

(Above) The Morgan "F-4" and (left) the "F-Super."

BOND: Mounting of the front wheel and engine and gearbox unit. A single helical spring and a Hartford friction damper take care of the suspension.

The Light Car
FOUNDED 1912
THE MOTORIST'S MAGAZINE

Proprietors - - - - TEMPLE PRESS LIMITED
Chairman and Managing Director - ROLAND E. DANGERFIELD
Editor - - - - F. J. FINDON, A.M.I.Struct.E.

No. 1547.   Vol. LXV

Three-wheelers

IN an age when the most austere critics of automobile design are talking in appreciative—even laudatory—terms of the simplest and most inexpensive forms of motorcar, there is surely a place for the low-taxed Three-wheeler. Yet, at the Motor Cycle Show only two makes were on view—Morgan, the pioneer, and Bond. The latter is a modern conception of an old principle exemplified in its time by the Harper and the Raleigh—names which instantly recall the A.C. Sociable, Scott, Castle Three, L.S.D., M.B., Coventry Victor, Omega, Stanhope, T.B., and, of course, the redoubtable Morgan and B.S.A.

Of all these only the Morgan has survived. Why has it not gone the way of the rest? The obvious answer is that the design was what the public wanted—and still wants; the pity of it is that to-day, owing to the ramifications which control output, that need cannot be fully met. It will be interesting to see whether the interest which the public is showing in the Bond is genuinely deep rooted. Basically it has little in common with the Morgan—except its three wheels. What it really does is to offer motoring on three wheels at the lowest possible running cost. While that is the main attraction it will undoubtedly prosper; but when (for example) petrol ceases to be so important will the Bond grow up? At the moment the question, we admit, would appear to be superfluous.

We are as certain now as we were nearly 40 years ago that there is a very definite place for three-wheelers, and we find ourselves speculating what kind of vehicle it would be if one of the "big six" decided to build one. Imagine a three-wheeler bearing, shall we say, the magic word Ford on the front (with its guarantee of service all over the world); but perhaps that is stretching imagination too far: let us keep our minds on Morgan and Bond.

Still going strong after 40 years — that sums up the history of a famous three-wheeler which is outlined below and which explains—

How the Morgan Began

H. F. S. Morgan, who contributes the accompanying story of the three-wheeler which he designed, at the controls of the first model. It was built in 1909 and had a 7 h.p. Peugeot engine.

BORN in 1881, H. F. S. Morgan, founder of the Morgan Motor Co., Ltd., was educated at Stone House, Broadstairs, Marlborough and the Crystal Palace Engineering College. In 1900 he became a pupil of Mr. W. Dean, chief G.W.R. engineer at Swindon Works, and, after the usual course, he got a job in the works drawing office. How did this erstwhile railway engineer become mixed up in the motor business? Invited by "The Light Car" to answer the question, this is the story that Mr. Morgan unfolded; the story of the famous Morgan.

My first motoring experience (said "H.F.S.") was in 1899, when I rode a Minerva motorcycle; a little later a 3½ h.p. Benz ran away with me down a steep hill and cost my father £28 for repairs. Both machines had been hired from Mr. Marriot, the first motor trader in Hereford.

After this experience I waited until I was 21, when, having collected a little cash, I purchased an Eagle Tandem—a three-wheeler fitted with a water-cooled 8 h.p. De Dion engine. It was fast, but not too reliable, and gave me considerable experience during the 18 months I owned it. I then bought a 7 h.p. two-cylinder car called "The Little Star," which, with modifications, gave good service for many years.

On leaving Swindon in 1906, I opened a garage and motor works in Malvern Link. I was district agent for Wolseleys and Darracqs, and I also started one of the first bus services in the country, running special 10 h.p. Wolseley 15-seaters from Malvern Link to Malvern Wells and, later, from Malvern to Gloucester.

Now, during this period, I had purchased a 7 h.p. twin Peugeot engine, intending to build up a motorcycle. Although I had been a keen cyclist, I never cared for motorcycles. I, therefore, decided to fit this engine into a light three-wheeled chassis I had designed, and as I had little facilities for machine work, this was mostly done for me. The chassis was, in fact, assembled in the Malvern College workshop, through the kindness of my old friend, the late Mr. Stephenson Peach, then engineering master at Malvern and Repton.

I drove the machine, which I called the Morgan Runabout, in 1909. It was most successful, due to its rigid frame, independent front-wheel suspension and light weight; the power weight ratio was

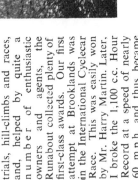

The prototype two-seater Morgan of 1911, with "H.F.S." at the controls. It had an 8-h.p. a.c. J.A.P. engine and tiller steering.

How the Morgan Began—Contd.

about 90 h.p. per ton, and it was, therefore, more than capable of holding its own with any car on the road at that time.

Although I had made the Runabout for my own use, and had no intention in the first place of marketing it, the car caused such favourable comment wherever it was seen that I decided to make a few, and with the enthusiastic support of my father, the Rev. Prebendary H. G. Morgan, who risked some capital in the venture, I bought a few machine tools, enlarged the garage and started to manufacture.

I obtained my first patent for the design in 1910, my patent agents being Stanley, Popplewell and Co., of Chancery Lane. It is interesting to recall that the patent drawings were produced by a bright youth (then articled to Mr. Stanley) who is now the famous Sir John Black, of Standards.

Two Runabouts were shown at Olympia in 1911; they were single-seaters fitted respectively with J.A.P. 8 h.p. twin and 4 h.p. single-cylinder engines, and they created quite a stir! They were too novel to attract many orders (about 30 materialized), but I found there would be a very much larger demand for a two-seater model. Meantime, just after the Show, I entered my first, important trial, the "London-Exeter," and won a gold medal.

During 1912 I tested a few chassis fitted with two-seater bodies and wheel steering. They were satisfactory, and one of the first was lent to W. G. McMinnies for a long week-end. I must say I was surprised at the very enthusiastic report he gave it in "Motor Cycling." It was the first Press road-test report of my product ever published.

Later McMinnies was closely associated with "The Light Car and Cyclecar," which had been founded in 1912 with the idea of catering for the owners of machines like the Morgan. I recall that F. J. Findon, the present editor of "The Light Car," collected his first Morgan on a day when there was much rejoicing on the birth of a son! How time flies. To-day, son Peter is a director of the company I founded.

In 1912 I showed several two-seaters at Olympia. They attracted a good deal of attention and with trade support, I obtained far more orders than I thought I could meet. I approached several large manufacturers and (luckily) they turned the proposition down, so, partly with the aid of deposits on orders, I bought machine tools, built some new workshops and, giving up my garage business, did my best to satisfy the demand.

The Morgan Motor Company was turned into a limited company in 1912, with two directors, my father being chairman—a position which he held until he died in 1937—and myself, managing director.

During 1912, 1913 and 1914, I entered for many trials, hill-climbs and races, and, helped by quite a number of enthusiastic owners and agents, the Runabout collected plenty of first-class awards. Our first attempt at Brooklands was in the International Cyclecar Race. This was easily won by Mr. Harry Martin. Later, I broke the 1,100 c.c. Hour Record at a speed of nearly 60 m.p.h. and thus became the first holder of "The Light Car and Cyclecar" Challenge Trophy.

In 1913 I produced some racing cars with a longer chassis, low seats and o.h.v. J.A.P. engines. One of these was bought by Mr. McMinnies, who ran it in the Cyclecar Grand Prix at Amiens and won the race. It was a wonderful performance, as he had to change an inner tube of one of the front tyres during the race. After the race this model was called the Grand Prix, and was popular for many years.

During the Kaiser war I was able to maintain a small production, but the works were chiefly concerned with munitions. In 1915 I built a four-seater model for myself and family to get about in. Again it was a stepping-stone, for it was later marketed as the Family Runabout: it filled a long-felt want and sold in large numbers.

For some years little alteration had to be made to the chassis, but all sorts of engines were fitted and various modifications made to the bodywork. Electric lamps and starters were added and, as a result of trials experience, front-wheel brakes were soon installed.

In 1931 I brought out a model with three speeds and reverse, one chain and detachable wheels. Previously, all models had had a simple two-chain drive giving two speeds. On the sporting side the Runabout continued to uphold its reputation, winning race after race, for example, at Brooklands. In 1930, driving a 1,100 c.c. J.A.P. racer, Mrs. Gwenda Stewart (now Mrs. Douglas Hawkes) broke the Hour Record at a speed of over 100 m.p.h. As the attempt was made at Montlhéry, Mrs. Stewart could not claim "The Light Car and Cyclecar" Cup.

The year 1935 marked the advent of a new model fitted with Ford four-cylinder 8 h.p. and 10 h.p. engines. This was the best all-round three-wheeler we had turned out and, with slight modifications, it is in production to-day.

For some years, competition from light cars had been getting very severe, owing to the improved performances and low cost of these four-wheelers. Our output dropped, and to keep the works busy I decided to produce a small four-wheeler, light in weight and with plenty of power. I had already experimented with various types. One of the first (in 1914) was fitted with a Dorman four-cylinder engine. Taking the successful four-cylinder, three-wheeler as the basis of the design, I produced the four-wheeled models first shown in 1936 at the Paris and Olympia Shows. It was called the 4/4.

Looking back through the years, seeing both errors and triumphs in their correct perspective, I feel I have enjoyed it all; the motor trade has been—so far as I am concerned—a most interesting business.

For many years Mrs Morgan always accompanied her husband when he took part in trials. Here they are, in a 1913 Sports Runabout, setting out for the A.-C.U. "Six Days."

The Morgan Three-Wheeler

THIS pioneer pre-war three-wheeler is of simple construction, and the later models with their detachable and interchangeable wheels, three-speeds-and-reverse gearbox, single-chain drive, etc., make maintenance easier than ever.

Lubrication

One of the first essentials to good motoring is to pay strict attention to lubrication, and to use only those lubricants known to be specially suitable, according to maker's instructions.

The reader is referred to the chassis plan (Fig. 1) which gives a clear indication which parts should receive attention. (Fig. 2 depicts the chassis.) Figures in the circles represent periods at which attention is required in 100's of miles, i.e., 5 denotes 500 miles, 10 denotes 1,000 miles, etc. In addition, every 1,000 miles apply the grease-gun to the nipple on the steering box, and every 500 miles apply a graphited grease to the dynamo drive. Periodically apply a few drops of oil to all

Lubrication : Keeping the Engine in Tune : The Carburetter : Clutch : Steering : Gearbox and Rear Forks : Electrical Equipment

By A. THOMAS

mum engine efficiency is dependent on correct tuning of the various associate components (carburetter, ignition system, etc.) so that they operate in perfect harmony. A dirty engine cannot give its maximum power output, so it is important to decarbonise at least every 4-5,000 miles. During this process do not forget the piston rings and valves. Remove all

renewed. Check the valve springs for strength, and when replacing cylinder heads do not forget the extra tightening of the bolts after the engine has been warmed up. See that all water passages are clear, and allow sufficient water circulation. Tappet clearances should receive frequent attention. Excessive clearances promote valve-gear noises, and in no way improve the running. In the case of the side-valve engine, inlet tappets should have .004in., and exhaust .006in. clearance. Clearance in the case of the overhead-valve engine should be negligible, obtainable with the engine cold. The end caps on the valve stems should be just free to be rotated by the fingers, while no perceptible up-and-down movement of the rockers is possible. Regular attention to sparking plugs will help towards maximum efficiency, and the spark gaps should be kept to .018in.

The Carburetter

Carburation plays an important part in the behaviour of the engine, and should receive occasional attention. It is advisable to remove the carburetter now and again and clean out carefully. Heavy, "thumpy" running can result from too rich a mixture, and this usually indicates the need to lower the needle in the throttle valve. Where strict economy is aimed at, adjustment sometimes results in too weak a mixture, which makes starting difficult, and the engine has a tendency to fire back through the carburetter. In such cases the needle should be raised a notch. Needle positions are counted from the top of the needle, the top groove being No. 1. The normal setting of the needle is notch No. 3.

The ignition should be kept in correct adjustment, as nothing has so pronounced an effect on the running of the engine as incorrect adjustment. The distributor should be kept clean; also the contact-breaker points. Do not file the contact-breaker points; they should be dressed smooth with an oilstone if they become worn, pitted or burned, and should be set to .018in.

Brakes

With the engine in good tune the Morgan three-wheeler possesses considerable acceleration and speed, and it is imperative that all brakes should be in efficient working order. See that these are adjusted periodically in the

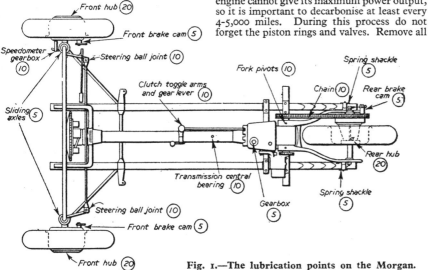

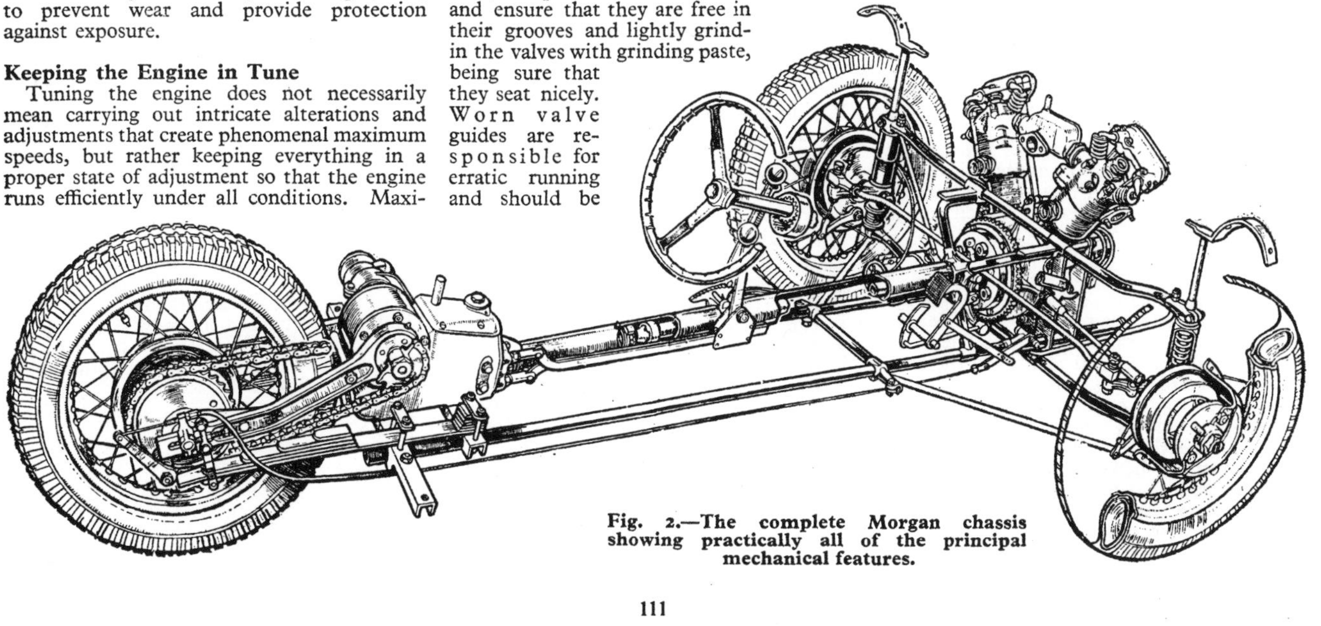

Front hub (20)
Front brake cam (5)
Speedometer gearbox (10)
Steering ball joint (10)
Fork pivots (10)
Spring shackle (5)
Clutch toggle arms and gear lever (10)
Chain (10)
Rear brake cam (5)
Sliding axles (5)
Rear hub (20)
Transmission central bearing (10)
Steering ball joint (10)
Gearbox (5)
Spring shackle (5)
Front brake cam (5)
Front hub (20)

Fig. 1.—The lubrication points on the Morgan.

brake and engine controls, door hinges, etc., to prevent wear and provide protection against exposure.

Keeping the Engine in Tune

Tuning the engine does not necessarily mean carrying out intricate alterations and adjustments that create phenomenal maximum speeds, but rather keeping everything in a proper state of adjustment so that the engine runs efficiently under all conditions. Maxi-

carbon deposit from the former and ensure that they are free in their grooves and lightly grind-in the valves with grinding paste, being sure that they seat nicely. Worn valve guides are responsible for erratic running and should be

Fig. 2.—The complete Morgan chassis showing practically all of the principal mechanical features.

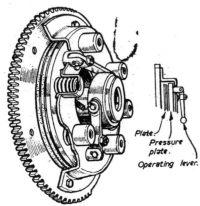

Fig. 3.—Showing the clutch, partly broken away for clarity. Inset is shown a section through the plates.

usual way, and ensure that cables are free in their outer casings. Brake efficiency can be impaired by cables rusting and interfering with ease in operation. Remove the cables occasionally, clean and well oil, and if in correct adjustment the brake will be found to be powerful and efficient at all speeds. After adjusting, it is sometimes found that the brakes do not pull the machine up as quickly as might be desired. The cause may be traced to the linings possibly—contaminated by a smear of grease from the hubs. Constant application of the brakes generates heat and allows grease to escape past the felt retainers. Remove the wheels in such cases and swill with petrol or burn off the lubricant from the linings.

Clutch

Do not apply oil to the plate clutch. The only points that need a spot of oil are the toggles indicated in Fig. 1. Should at any

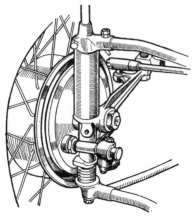

Fig. 4.—The helical front-wheel suspension and steering arm.

time the engine be taken out of the chassis, damp the splined end of the transmission shaft with an oily rag—avoid excessive oiling with the oilcan. Fig. 3 shows the clutch and a section through the plates.

Steering

The Morgan steering should be steady at all speeds. Any tendency to pull to one side can be traced to uneven tyre pressures. The front wheels should be inflated to 19, and the rear to 25 lb. per sq. in. Occasionally check the front wheel track, as the front wheels may receive severe shocks sufficient to upset alignment. The helical front-wheel suspension and steering arm are shown in Fig. 4. Wheels are correctly tracked when " toeing in " at the front not more than ⅛in. This means that the distance from rim to rim is ⅛in. narrower in the front than at the back of the wheels.

The track rod (the adjustable ends of which allow the wheels to be tracked) has a tapered pin at both ends, which act as dampers. If too freely oiled these are inclined to lose their damping properties and wheel wobble is likely; so instead of applying oil with the oilcan, remove them at intervals and damp with an oily rag, just sufficient to prevent rusting and stiffness in the steering.

Gearbox and Rear Forks

The rear end of the vehicle calls for little attention, except lubrication and brake adjustment as before mentioned. The gearbox, which is shown with the rear-wheel drive in Fig. 5, requires no adjustment or other attention beyond " topping up " to the level indicated on the dipstick. Keep the tie bar holding the rear fork arms together tight at all times, so that no side movement can occur, and also the rear wheel spindle nut. The single driving chain must be kept at the correct tension—1in. up and down movement in the bottom run is sufficient. The rear-wheel

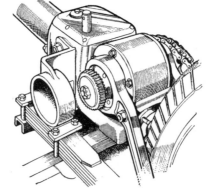

Fig. 5.—The gearbox and rear wheel of the Morgan.

hub is shown in Fig. 6. Adjust with the machine standing on the level. Lubricate as already directed and occasionally remove and immerse in warm oil to ensure ample lubrication of the rollers and rivets. Never allow the dynamo gears to develop excessive backlash;

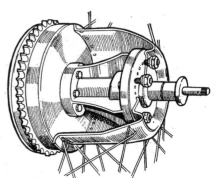

Fig. 6.—A view of the rear-wheel hub partly broken away.

keep them well meshed and maintain a constant charging rate.

Electrical Equipment

Night driving, of course, calls for reliability from the lighting equipment. In the summer months the factor is often neglected and it is found that when wanted the lamps do not give the illumination necessary. Examine them occasionally during the daytime and make sure that bright and dim filaments are sound and the dimming gear in order. The battery should receive periodical attention. At least once a month the vent plugs should be removed and the acid level checked. This should be kept level with the separators and only distilled water added when " topping-up." The battery should never be left in a discharged condition and connections should be tight and smeared with Vaseline. The dynamo should require little attention, and only very occasionally should it be necessary to examine the brushes and commutator. Ensure that the brushes press firmly on to the commutator and that the spring arms securing them move freely on their pivots. Range of visibility depends on the correctness or otherwise of the alignment and focusing of the lamps. Alignment and focusing are best carried out at night with the car on a straight, level road. Metal polish should not be used on the reflectors.

Tyre Pressure Maintenance
An Extension for an Existing Foot Pump

By S. STEEN

THE situation of the spare wheel in the luggage boot often causes difficulty in maintaining the inflation pressure owing to insufficient length of foot pump connection.

To obviate removal of the spare wheel from the boot in such cases the following

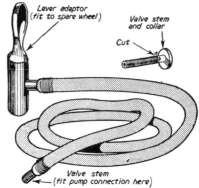

Details of the extension.

method was utilised to provide an extension of the existing pump connection.

Two feet of rubber tubing with an internal bore of 3/16in. was obtained, and into one end was inserted a thumb-lever pump adaptor.

A valve stem, from which the valve " insides " had been extracted from an old inner tube and the metal collar cut away at the base.

This stem was then fitted inside the other end of the rubber tube and to ensure that both fittings were air-tight the tubing was bound tightly with thin wire or twine at each end.

To use this extension the foot pump adaptor was fitted to the valve stem on the extension tube, and the lever adaptor of the latter connected to the valve on the spare wheel as shown in the sketch.

1939 MORGAN SUPER SPORTS

Three wheels

were enough . . . for **40** *years*

THE MORGAN TRIKE might be called the forerunner of the present day sports car except that for over forty years Morgans did the job with three wheels while today's sports cars require four. The front wheels travel on sliding stub axles and the rear wheel is supported by a pivoted fork and quarter elliptic springs. Three wheel independent suspension!

Eliminating a wheel was done more for tax purposes than for weight saving, three-wheelers being licensed as motorcycles at quite a saving. Today's auto builders couldn't hold a candle to Morgan ingenuity when it came to weight paring. In the model described in this article, the following were not to be found: radiator, water pump, fan, fuel pump, accelerator pedal, universal joints, differential and bumpers. There is also just a bare minimum of weather protection.

With the exception of two steel main chassis rails, the frame members and body supports are wood. Boat type construction is used in the body with light wood bulkheads and stringers covered with 24 gauge sheet steel. A combination oil and fuel tank is mounted under the scuttle. This tank is also of 24 gauge steel with a partition soldered in to separate a three quart oil tank from the four-and-a-half gallon fuel tank. This is fine for the sake of weight saving, but a leak in the partition suddenly causes the oil to get very thin and the gas to get very greasy.

The few pounds saved by the elimination of universal joints causes quite a bit of work when replacing the engine. The engine must be shoved home on its mounts on top of washers cut from .002 inch shim stock repeatedly until the engine shaft is in perfect alignment with the spline on the clutch.

Much has been said concerning the poor stopping ability of Morgan brakes. The original brakes on HJO-401 have been converted to Girling mechanical, which can, if properly adjusted, stop the machine in a very short distance.

Morgan three-wheelers were built with very few changes for over forty years. They used sliding stub axles from 1911 until 1952. "V" twin motorcycle engines such as Blackburne, Anzani, J.A.P., and Matchless were used through 1939. From 1946 till 1952, the last year of the three-wheelers, the Ford 8 and Ford 10 engines were used. Approximately nine-hundred machines were produced each year.

HJO-401 is a 1939 Super Sports, model MX2, the last of the hairy two-lungers. It is powered by a "V" twin Matchless engine of 990 cc, overhead valves, and air-cooled. The eighteen-year-old engine is "square" with a bore and stroke of 3.366 inches. It also features inclined valves, hemispherical combustion chambers, and a dry sump oiling system. Compression ratio is 7.5 to 1. The engine develops 39 bhp at 4200 rpm. This with a total weight of 896 pounds equals a power to weight ratio of 1 to 23, which makes for very lively performance. Top speed is around 85 mph. Gas mileage at a cruising speed of 50 mph is 35 to 40 miles per gallon.

The power is taken from the engine by a single dry plate clutch, then through a shaft to the gearbox behind the seat. A steel worm on the gearbox mainshaft engages a bronze worm wheel and takes the power out of the gearbox at 90 degrees to the drive shaft, delivering it to the rear wheel through a sprocket and ¾ pitch roller chain.

The steering is ¾ turn from lock to lock. Handling is very precise and a quick tug at the wheel causes the car not to swerve but literally to jump from one side of the road to the other. This violent maneuverability makes it necessary to carry a passenger or ballast when in any type of competition from hill climbing to a Gymkhana. If this precaution is not followed, the inside wheel will lift in a hard left turn.

"Two pedal" control is achieved with clutch and brake pedals projecting from the firewall. Hand brake and gear selector lever are fastened to the torque tube just forward of the seats. Throttle and mixture control levers are mounted on the right side of the steering wheel hub and the spark control is on the left side. The compression release lever is under the dash panel directly behind the steering wheel.

An electric starter is furnished to be used in conjunction with a manual exhaust valve lifter. However, the power required to turn over the two big cylinders is too much for the small starter and battery; so the engine is usually attacked with a bent piece of iron to bring it roaring to life. The owner of HJO-401 advises that the spark be fully retarded before cranking a Morgan and he has a sprained wrist and a "written-off" shock proof watch to prove his point.

Another thing to watch out for when operating a "Moggie" is too much oil being pumped to the exposed overhead valve gear. This results in automatic windshield, hair, and elbow lubrication.

The Morgan Three-Wheeler is very rare in America, there being only six in the country at this time, two of which are 1939 Super-Sports.

HJO-401 is the proud possession of Dan Dreeben of San Antonio, Texas, and is the only Morgan Trike in the Lone Star State. Because of close quarters, the throttle lever on the steering wheel is easily caught in the shirt front while making a turn. Turning left then slows the engine, while a right turn causes the engine to speed up. Since shirtless driving is, therefore, safer and easier on the nerves, the Texas climate is very suitable for Morganeering. ●

Logically, the body tapers back to a conic section, ending with the spare wheel.

Close up above shows 39 brute horses, fully exposed except for the owner's bumper-badge bar.

The seating position is so low that the occupants can readily reach out and touch the ground.

An electric starter is supplied but it obviously develops less than one man-power.

1939 MORGAN SS

July 1939. H.F.S. Morgan has been building and selling his amazing three-wheeled vehicles for nearly two-score years, and the latest 1939 model, though improved, is basically the same design as the earliest machines.

In super-tuned form and running on fuel (alcohol) some of these machines have lapped the Brooklands track in England at over 100 mph. However, our test car was the more docile, more practical version powered by the big Matchless Twin, a V-type motorcycle engine. Behind this powerplant is a conventional clutch and a Ford "10" 3-speed and reverse transmission. The output shaft of the transmission drives a worm gear box which provides the necessary right-angle turn for a final drive by sprockets and chain to the single rear wheel. Ratio changes are easily and quickly effected, and the accompanying data is based on an overall high gear ratio of 3.70, a ratio which proved to be near-ideal for best possible top speed.

The cockpit of the Morgan is crowded for two adults but offers (as compared to a motorcycle) the advantages of weather "protection." At first it seems very difficult to drive, with no foot accelerator and very heavy and ultra-fast steering (¾ turns, lock to lock). However, the hand throttle has advantages including the ability to keep the right foot poised for instant braking. Also, one soon learns that proper use of the throttle on bends can almost steer the car, reducing steering effort considerably.

By passenger car standards the engine is not very docile, but with ignition retarded it will tick-tock along at as low as 15 mph in high gear. Above 20 mph it accelerates fairly easily without downshifting, and the normal comfortable cruising speed is about 55 mph. Above that speed there is some vibration and at over 70 mph the suspension feels too solid to be described as "firm." In truth the car leaps and hops, and 70 mph feels more like a 100. The gear ratios are rather wide-spaced, but when used properly (see acceleration curve) the performance is very good—approximately the same as a typical "500" solo motorcycle.

Evaluated in terms of its purpose, a motorcycle which can be used the year 'round, the Morgan is truly a fun machine and one wonders why Harley-Davidson in Milwaukee have never seen fit to market a product such as this. ●

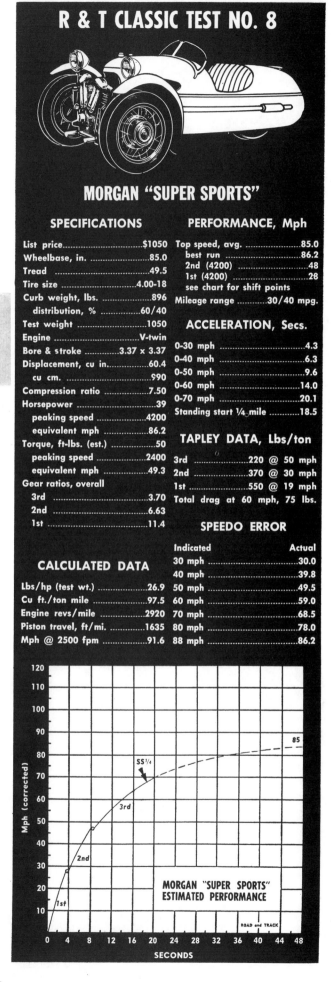

R & T CLASSIC TEST NO. 8

MORGAN "SUPER SPORTS"

SPECIFICATIONS

List price	$1050
Wheelbase, in.	85.0
Tread	49.5
Tire size	4.00-18
Curb weight, lbs.	896
distribution, %	60/40
Test weight	1050
Engine	V-twin
Bore & stroke	3.37 x 3.37
Displacement, cu in.	60.4
cu cm.	990
Compression ratio	7.50
Horsepower	39
peaking speed	4200
equivalent mph	86.2
Torque, ft-lbs. (est.)	50
peaking speed	2400
equivalent mph	49.3
Gear ratios, overall	
3rd	3.70
2nd	6.63
1st	11.4

CALCULATED DATA

Lbs/hp (test wt.)	26.9
Cu ft./ton mile	97.5
Engine revs/mile	2920
Piston travel, ft/mi.	1635
Mph @ 2500 fpm	91.6

PERFORMANCE, Mph

Top speed, avg.	85.0
best run	86.2
2nd (4200)	48
1st (4200)	28
see chart for shift points	
Mileage range	30/40 mpg.

ACCELERATION, Secs.

0-30 mph	4.3
0-40 mph	6.3
0-50 mph	9.6
0-60 mph	14.0
0-70 mph	20.1
Standing start ¼ mile	18.5

TAPLEY DATA, Lbs/ton

3rd	220 @ 50 mph
2nd	370 @ 30 mph
1st	550 @ 19 mph
Total drag at 60 mph, 75 lbs.	

SPEEDO ERROR

Indicated	Actual
30 mph	30.0
40 mph	39.8
50 mph	49.5
60 mph	59.0
70 mph	68.5
80 mph	78.0
88 mph	86.2

MORGAN "SUPER SPORTS"
ESTIMATED PERFORMANCE

ROAD and TRACK

CULT OF THE MOGGIE

Familiar scene at Brooklands track about 30 years ago. This picture shows R. T. Horton leading round the turn at Chronograph Villa during the Light Car Club's meeting in July 1930

UNLIKE the Dodo or Queen Anne, the Morgan three-wheeler is far from dead although the last of them left the Malvern works about 10 years ago. You might wonder why. Why, indeed, true enthusiasm for the breed is probably as high as ever it was.

Is it because the Moggie is the only three-wheeler to see 40 years of production ? Or the fastest-ever of its type (116 m.p.h. by Gwenda Stewart in 1930)? No one can pinpoint the answer in a few words. But there are plenty of reasons which might add up to the explanation.

Morgans set the standard in the early days of the cyclecar, from 1910 to 1914, giving the comfort, sociability and performance of an expensive sporting car for the cost of a sidecar outfit. When most cyclecars were either excessively crude or excessively heavy, the Morgan weighed 3¾ cwt fully equipped, with hood and screen; it combined a top speed of about 60 m.p.h. with excellent acceleration and hill-climbing powers. Of the 72 makes of cyclecar on the market in 1914, only the Morgan continued in production through the vintage era. Its very simplicity was its saving grace.

Take a look at a Morgan two-speed chassis. Nothing surplus is carried, many parts serve a dual role. The two lower frame tubes are also the exhaust pipes; the prop-shaft runs through the main tube. The bevel box supports the rear suspension, and the sliding-dog, two-speed chain drive is robust and reliable. The sliding pillar, front springing was the first independent suspension to be standardized on any British vehicle and is still in use today on four-wheel Morgans.

How many people know that H. F. Morgan designed his first four-wheeler back in 1914 ? A weird machine based substantially on the three-wheeler, it was built in 1915 with a Dorman four-cylinder side-valve engine. It cannot have been much of a success, for it does not seem to have survived the war. In any case, the G.N. light car suddenly sprouted a four-speed chain drive much on the lines of the Morgan gear, which probably dissuaded Mr. Morgan from further experiments in this direction.

The three-wheel Morgan, at any rate, was supreme in its field during the vintage period 1920 to 1930. Unfortunately, the three-speed jobs with Matchless and Ford engines did not carry on the vintage

Famous Morgan exponent G. N. Norris at the start of an acceleration test at Brooklands in 1924. His Aero model is fitted with a Blackburne engine

WHAT MAINTAINS ENTHUSIASM FOR THE FAMOUS THREE WHEELER?

By David Wise

. N. Taylor with a Blackburne-quipped Super Aero about to ake best time of the day in a ambridge University Club hill-imb near Newmarket in 1929

tradition. In the original design, H. F. S. Morgan showed his belief in "simplicating and adding lightness." The heavier three-speed-and-reverse gear box was added, not in the interest of better acceleration, but because many fringe Morganists had been lured away to Austin Sevens. This was understandable, since those who bought Morgans merely as a means of cheap transport were not enamoured of having to get out and push every time reverse was called for.

The Super Sports Morgan, admirable car though it was, never was the equal of the Super-Aero Morgan, which, with engines such as the J.A.P. 8/55, 8/80 or 10/40, was good for almost 100 m.p.h., with top gear usable from 12 m.p.h.

The finest years of Morganing were between 1919 and 1931—that is, the years in which the two-speed Aero and Super Aero were available. The Aero had a character all its own and made an indelible mark on the memories of its countless drivers. Handsomest of all the Aeros was the Brooklands model Super-Aero, with its polished copper exhaust pipes and lowered chassis. Later Morgans never had quite the lines of the Aeros; slight alterations to the contours of the bonnet and tail resulted in an unbalanced, tail-heavy look.

Many are the tales about Aeros. In the early thirties, two brothers in the West Country bought one for £2 10s. They tuned the engine and removed the body-work, leaving only two bucket seats. Then they waited on the Bath Road, the engine of this fearsome contrivance ticking over, until an M.G. hove into view. They thumbed their noses at it as it passed, and then gave chase. . . .

Then there was the noisy Aero, whose silencers the owner had filled with chicken wire in an attempt to deaden the sound. However, the engine would habitually backfire on the over-run, scattering wire

This lethal-looking Meggie was raced by the famous W. D. Hawkes in the early 1920s. The engine is an eight-valve, 1,100 c.c. M.A.G.

to the four winds. The same car suffered a bent chassis when the owner, turning round to wave to some friends, collided with a gatepost. He proceeded to straighten out the chassis using a hockey post as a lever. Ever after, the front wheels of that Mog wobbled alarmingly. . . .

Obviously, not everyone can understand the attitude of mind of a person who is prepared, not only to ride in, but actually to *own* such a Moggie. For these doubters, of course, there are the weird bubble cars, with their scooter engines hidden under hygenic plastic and chrome, and which appear to offer the refinement of a roller skate powered by an outboard engine. There is none of that desirable "long stride" possessed by the big-twin engine of the old Morgan.

Incidentally, the number of different makes of engine fitted to the Morgan must constitute something of a record—Peugeot, J.A.P., Blackburne, Anzani, M.A.G., Precision, Blumfield, British Vulpine,

Matchless, Green-Precision, Ruby, Clerget, Ford 8 and 10 h.p.—all but the last three makes lusty vee-twins of around 1,000 or 1,100 c.c.

The beauty of the Morgan for competitive record-breaking events was the ease with which various sizes and makes of engine could be exchanged. Thus the Morgan was the first three-wheeler to beat 100 m.p.h. in the 1,100, 1,000 and 750 c.c. classes; in 1929 Morgans held 84 per cent of all world's three-wheeler records in classes from 350 to 1,100 c.c. and in 1930 they became the fastest three-wheeler in all capacity classes. Most of the credit for these remarkable achievements must go to a woman—Gwenda Stewart who, as well as being the fastest-ever three-wheeler pilot, broke 71 world's records in 1929 alone.

The machine in which she covered the flying kilometre at 116 m.p.h. is worthy of examination. To a chassis six inches longer than standard was fitted a tailor-made *monoposto* body. Two 2½-gallon fuel tanks

formed the basis of the bucket seat. A battery of hand-pumps was fitted to transfer the fuel to a header tank in the dummy radiator. The engine, specially built by J.A.P.s, was Mrs. Stewart's old 996 c.c. record-breaking engine enlarged to 1,100 c.c.

However, the firm sporting tradition of the 'twenties was replaced by the more touring outlook of the thirties. The introduction of the Austin Seven had been a cruel blow to the entire cyclecar industry. The three-speed Morgan was an attempt to win back those who preferred a reverse gear, albeit coupled to an exceedingly pedestrian performance.

True believers needed no such incentive. It came as a bitter blow to them when lack of suitable engines caused the production of Morgan three-wheelers to cease in 1951. If one is so minded, though, it is still a feasible proposition to build a vintage model from second hand parts.

Probably 40,000 Morgans were built, and about 1,000 are believed to have survived. About 500 of these are owned by members of the Morgan Three-wheeler Club. Among them are such rarities as a 1913 Runabout with only six months' usage in its entire life and the ex-Clive Lones Brooklands job which at one time held 36 world's records.

Promising augury for the future—one member has in hand a special with a Vincent engine. . . .

H. F. S. Morgan with one of the racing models built for the never-to-be-held Cyclecar T.T. in the Isle of Man in 1914. It is basically the same three-wheeler as that shown above

DAF 488

MORGAN

My name is...
MORGAN
...but it ain't J.P.!

BY WARREN WEITH

**ILLUSTRATIONS BY
KEN DALLISON**

Why am I driving to the ice-coated North Shore of Long Island? It's Saturday morning, I don't have to get up, and besides, I have a slightly distended head from the night before. Why continue further along narrow roads becoming whiter and whiter under the malignant touch of freezing rain, looking in vain for a country retreat that houses two Morgan three-wheelers, an unmet English artist, and a car collector? Conceit. ("You can write a great story on Morgans for us, Warren.") Yeah, that's part of it. But conceited as I am about my ability on the Olivetti, it is as nothing compared to my sloth. It has to be more than conceit. After all, a man who has been awarded the black pajama belt for artistic—and at times frightening—ability to handle early morning, late morning, and afternoon sleeping doesn't thrust himself lightly into a winter-besotted dawn.

Disgustedly, I admitted to myself that it was the same damn thing that's never failed to move me since I became a mobile being: a car. Or two cars to be exact. I had never seen a Morgan trike close up; all the logic of my so-called mature mind was stumped by this simple off-the-wall fact. I was angry—thinking of my wasted youth spent genuflecting before some greasy hunk of metal or other—hung over, and lost. A roadside phone booth clutched me to its cold glass and aluminum embrace. I searched for the wrinkled envelope that contained the magic number that would let me reach out along ice-draped wire to artist Ken Dallison's home. With any luck at all he would already have gone, sketched the three-wheelers and returned home. I could then, with good grace, apologize for missing the show and go back to my still-warm sack. The first number gave me a second number that would get right through to the Morgan's hideout. A London voice came clinking through the tube like bright English pennies dropping on marble. "Warren, where *are* you? I've been here for *days* . . ." A picture of London docks spattered with bright points of fire floated by. "Warren, where *are* you?" Where the hell was I? Why was I thinking about docks, for God's sake? "I'm in a phone booth." "What phone booth?" I knew he'd ask. Quick people are always doing things like that. Quick, wild answer! "On Old Westbury Road." "Good, that means you're right close by, now do all the things I tell you. . . ."

There was a gate house and a long winding road that led past smaller houses now sharing what must have been a huge pre-income-tax estate. A

A Super Sport

In 1912, H. F. S. Morgan averaged nearly 60 mph in his V-twin runabout. The man in the top hat is his father.

at Brooklands during a 1933 Race.

man in blue coveralls and gum boots wig-wagged me to a parking space in back of a Jaguar 3.8 sedan. He introduced himself as my host and led the way into his weekend house. Artist Dallison came bustling into the hallway with his light-blue eyes gleaming in the white light reflected from the snow outside. We drifted into a large living room on a wave of apologies for my being late.

Ken Dallison, sitting composed on a small French sofa, was a combination of Tom Jones (suede pullover, long-skirted sports jacket) and an angry young man (beatle haircut, and dedicated to the job at hand) as he minutely questioned Mr. Morganowner on the best possible arrangements for sketching the cars. Mr. Morganowner was looking at Ken and me with a vaguely puzzled expression. Like who were we, and what did we really want to do to his treasures? And they were treasures, safe and dry in

The latest Morgans; Peter and the 4 plus 4.

a series of connected cedar-shingled garages forming a wide spread "U" at the side of the house. There was a two-seater Rolls-Royce Ghost convertible, Delage, Ford 'T' station wagon, two different 1930's Mercedes Benz', a late model Bentley Continental, 3-liter Blower Bentley and the two Morgan three-wheelers, one just arrived from England.

They reminded me of British bulldogs. All chest and no hind quarters. The chest was composed of a big V-twin engine of about 1.1-liter capacity. Mounted so far forward, the crankcase cover just about made it behind the leading edge of the two front wheels. The lean-haunched look came from slim, tapering bodywork jutting back to cover the skinny, single rear wheel. One car had a JAP engine with a twin chain-drive—one chain and sprocket for each speed—and no reverse. The other was a later, more civilized model with proper clutch, three-speed-with-reverse gearbox and everything. The engine on this car was a water-cooled Matchless with hoses veeing back to a tiny radiator mounted behind the two thrusting cylinders. Fresh off the boat, it gleamed with those wonderful shades of silver and bronze that can only come from 30 or so years of tender polishing and massage.

Both cars had independent front suspension on a system substantially unchanged since 1910. This consisted of two bronze slides working on guide pillars. The stub axles were attached to the slides, and the whole works restrained by upper and lower coil springs.

Crude, but effective. Throttle control was by a lever mounted on one of the steering wheel spokes. Up was go, down was no go—unless you had the steering locked over. Then the operation was reversed. On the other horizontal wheel spoke was a spark lever. Silent contemplation of this system—keeping in mind the 40-hp and under 800-pound weight, which is about 20 lbs. per hp as the engineer flies—brought forth certain unspoken conclusions. Being a soft American, I'm not up to driving a vintage Morgan, and those among us who are had better remember which lever is which. Not only that, they'd better remember the right way to push the correct lever or they're going on their heads. And American heads are unprotected by nature's crash helmet, the English haircut.

Mr. Morganowner gazed fondly at the red and cream Morgan. He was a collector. This was the newest addition, always the best of the lot—the best, until the next one. It was waiting its turn to go into the small shop situated in the last building at the end of one leg of the "U". The Bentley Continental was in there at the moment having some work done on a right rear brake drum. Never will the place of so much motor car be taken by one that's so little!

We thanked our host and let him return to his quiet, snow-filled country weekend. Following Ken towards Rothman's for a pint and a chop, I ruminated on car collectors and Morgans.

Why would a man who had all of those magnificent big cars acquire not one, but *two* trikes? Admittedly they had a visual appeal—all the dash and derring-do exuded by a World War I fighter plane. But, like those stuttering bumble bees, the Morgans were crude. Mr. Morganowner had owned up to the fact that the first one was a handful to drive. He had bought the second example apparently because he hoped it would be a little gentler, more befitting a part-time Morgan driver. Could be people were tougher in the Twenties. Hundreds of three-wheelers struck gold (or silver plate, to be exact) in all sorts of motoring competitions. The Morgan must have been the bee's knees in its day. And its day was 1927, when 1700 were run up from bits of wood and tin and God knows what. It was a sports car for Labour party voters. A Cloth Cap Chap could—for £80 or £90—out-accelerate diamond-mogul Woolf Barnato in

his 3-liter Bentley, providing they found themselves together on the same stretch of public road, which is a doubtful assumption in the England of the Twenties.

No doubt about it, the three-wheelers had a definite appeal. An appeal that was strong enough to sell 40,000 replicas (I don't think you could call them production cars) between 1911 and 1952. Even today there is a strong Morgan Three-Wheeler Club with, naturally, a triangular club badge. It was all rather casual. H.F.S. Morgan built these funny little cars which he ran in races and hill climbs. If you wanted one like his he'd build it for you . . . or try and sell you one that had already been languidly hammered together at Malvern Link. "And please, don't be a bore with a lot of correspondence to the factory about tie rods falling off. They fall off *my* car, so I know all about it."

H.F.S. was not only a letter-writer without peer, he was a man with a definite style on the circuit. One day during a hill climb he managed to get a trike up on two wheels in a corner. He repealed that particular law of physics by pushing with a gauntleted hand against the asphalt, and then calmly continued his furious assault on the gradient. Now, that's class! It's on record that he built and sold his self-propelled devices with the same sort of *brio*.

All of this might explain why Morgans—both the three- and four-wheel variety—stop auto nuts in their tracks. Cars built by a man like H.F.S. seem to sing a siren song to that addicted band.

The car they buy is substantially the same as the one the factory decided to build in 1936. H.F.S. kept on with the *real* Morgan, possibly thinking that the four-wheeler was merely an answer to eccentrics that flower in England's damp climate. Having gone to the extra wheel he added two spares on the tail—six wheels should really silence the critics. The car had the same front suspension as the three-wheeler with semi-elliptics at the rear. The result was something that would blur your vision on any but the smoothest surfaces. It was powered by a romping, stomping, 34-horsepower Coventry-Climax of some 1122cc. There was also a 45-hp Le Mans model. This one used a smaller 1098cc Climax, and was patterned after the ones that had done well in France. Shortly before the war a switch was made to a 40-horsepower Standard engine. This remained the 4/4 Morgan until 1950 when the

Standard Vanguard was used, along with a centrally-mounted Moss gearbox driven by a short shaft from the powerplant. This became the Plus 4 model. At the same time the chassis was strengthened and lengthened by four inches. In 1953, the flat grille was replaced by a curved one, and the headlights faired into the fenders. In 1954—God, things were happening *fast* around Malvern—the Triumph TR-series of engines went into the Plus 4s. In '55 the 4/4 came back into the line and continues to be produced to this day. Three different English Ford four-cylinder engines have been used in the new 4/4. In 1960, 11-inch Girling discs became the standard front wheel brakes on the Plus 4 and the 4/4.

And that, by God, is the complete engineering history of the Morgan four-wheelers. I don't know of any other sports car that's been produced in such basically-similar form for so many years. What's really astounding is the fact that the same chassis and suspension setup has been able to more or less cope with power ranging from the original 34 hp to the 140 hp that Morgan maniacs are now extracting from tuned versions in England.

The stock (if you can use the word when talking about a Morgan) machine is an interesting tool all by itself. You have to approach it in the right frame of mind though. It senses rejection, and tends to sunfish and buck if ridden by the unsympathetic. Firstly, either you fit in or you don't. There is no seat adjustment as we have come to know it in this Mach-3 age. You can move the squab ahead about two inches if you happen to be under the ideal Morgan height of 5'10". This lets us guys who are substandard get our little paddy-wackers on the pedals. Those of you who are substandard in the other direction could—if desire had made you take leave of all sense—buy a four-seat Morgan tourer and drive from the rear seat.

Once in, with your seat cushion puffed up to the proper pressure (what's the matter, haven't you ever been in a car that uses pneumatic seat cushions? Check almost any of Jules Verne's books—he used them all the time), it's quite comfortable. You sit well down in the car, and high side-rails add to this feeling of security. Post-war drivers, or at least those who never saw Hans Stuck conducting a Merc up a mountain, will consider the proximity of the steering wheel to one's chest as a completely hopeless driving position. Vintage steering lock—2⅔ turns from stop to stop—and little side lights on front fenders marking where tire and wheel start, make it all very simple. The younger set will also learn how easy it is to see through a windshield that's close to your nose. Even in rain or snow the focal length of the Morgan glasswork is such that you just look around drops and splatters . . . except when they sneak under the edge and catch you right in the eye. You definitely know what's going on out there in front of that narrow, louvered hood. It's like sitting in the first row of a Cinemascope movie. And if you're awkward, you're the first—or, at the very least, the second —person to know all about it.

A lot can be going on too. When a 100-horsepower leans on 1800 pounds, something usually gives. And in this case it gives, if the road is smooth and dry, 60 mph in 11.8 seconds. A tight grip on that four-spoked wheel makes you hunch over and get your elbows up. In top, and going as hard as the marks on your license allow, you notice little things: the side screens tend to flop open at exactly 50 per, the top of the long hood dances over ripples (and you can count them right through the wheel rim), there's more room around the pedals than you thought, and shifting by ear is no trick when your right foot is connected directly to a noisy engine.

Judging the Morgan's handling takes a little more time—and, let's face it—really more talent than we had in the car at the time. At first it seemed a little short on sticktion, but then it dawned on us. In motoring's Golden Age it was no crime to skid, it helped you around corners. So the Morgan was *meant* to skid. It tells you it's going to skid, and then it skids—gently—and, after an easy correction, continues right on down the road pointing the same way as before it told you it was going to skid. As soon as you lose your 1965 notions (cars shouldn't get out of shape, everything has to look smooth) you and Morgan have come to a meeting of the minds. You find yourself sliding it everywhere. Suddenly there's a young Jack Brabham fresh from the midget dirt tracks of Australia loose on the quiet, night-scene streets of lower Manhattan. As long as the road is smooth the Morgan is as predictable as a bulldozer, and almost as agile. You can make it hang out at will and, with a flick of steel-like wrists, get it right back into contemporary shape. If I owned one I'd probably broadside it up to the car-wash wait-

ing line—that's the kind of show-off I am. For those among us who never cut their eye teeth (and other parts of the anatomy) on '32 Ford coupes, the Morgan will prove to be a safer, and better-looking modern replacement. It unlocks the door to an area of motoring that's closed to anyone who drives modern, softly-suspended cars. It is, essentially, a piece of sporting equipment that rewards conscious effort and lots of practice. What it ain't is dual-purpose transportation. You just don't do the Saturday shopping chores in a Morgan. It would be like hammering tacks with a custom-made putter; the tacks would be in to stay, but your right arm might fall off.

The Morgan in charge of the factory at present is Peter, son of H.F.S. He is tall, painfully English, and given to statements like, "My father built a unique sports car in 1910. It is my aim to build the type of car he would be proud to offer for sale today." And Peter Morgan is a man of his word. Pop wouldn't have a quibble with either the Plus 4 or the 4/4. Or the way they're put together. The Morgan Motor Co., Ltd. lives in seven or eight long narrow brick buildings that sort of all lean together the way mellow structures have a habit of doing. At the head of this veteran column is a small square office building about the size of two living-rooms in a modern apartment. The first long building shelters the stock of spare parts, and the man who sorts out the leather hides. The next building echoes to the hammers and electric drills of several muscular chaps bolting together chassis consisting of Z-section side rails and a few cross members. The main connection, however, is the long-lived Morgan independent front suspension. The lower leg of the Z rail turns in, to serve as a foundation for the wooden flooring.

The next building is a little quieter because this is where serious-looking blokes, in round, National Health Service eyeglasses, fashion the wooden body-frame. With a shave here, and a rasp there, and many a dip into a giant glue pot that's always bubbling on the bench, a spectral version of the flat Morgan stern and flowing front fenders takes shape. This furniture gets slapped with a coat of paint—any color that's left over from the body shop—to protect it from the foggy, foggy dew. It then gets levered onto a chassis that's complete with running gear, engine, etc. It then goes to the panel beaters. They hide its

nakedness in sheet metal that's been more or less pre-formed to shape. With a tug here, a tug there, and a hell of a big hard-rubber hammer, the body work is screwed and tacked (yes, I said *tacked*) to the wood framing. On to the paint shop! Here two men with modern spray guns give it what-for, sand it down and give it what-for all over again. They fiddle around with it until it looks nice, then push it into the upholstery shop. Here they do appropriate things with the leather hides the guy picked out in the first building, and then push it next door.

In the next shop-and-a-half (half is taken up by a blacksmith and his forge making front-end parts needed in the chassis shop, but he has a window and likes to look out at the English countryside while flailing the hell out of a piece of iron) they make it run. It's then given over to the test-driver for a blast around the roads of Worcestershire. I can hear him talking to his wife now: "I'll just take supper here at the mantle, luv, tough day at the works."

And that's the way it has gone for 54-odd years. Peter Morgan and his 90 helpers turn out from seven to nine of his namesakes every week. About 75% of them are sold in the United States. The money value of a year's worth of Morgans could be around $200,000. Considering the payroll, and the fact that the machinery must have been amortized sometime during the First World War, a good portion of this must be profit. I'm not against all this mind you—I think it's great. Where else can a Cloth Cap Chap of the Sixties get a beautifully-restored vintage sports car like Lord Montague drives around for under £1000? No place else but Malvern. The same holds true for us CCCs here in the States.

What must be understood is that the Morgan is the biggest automotive put-on in the post-war history of the automobile. As long as you're in on the gag, it's good fun. (I'd like one of the Vanguard-powered cars with the flat grille myself.) I don't care if old Peter chuckles all the way to the bank in his Ferrari 2+2, he and his old man have given thousands of people a lot of healthy exercise out in the fresh air. There can't be anything wrong with that. And if after a long hard ride you feel like you've been caned, that's part of the camp: all upper-class Englishmen have gone to public schools where they still cane a recalcitrant pupil. Some of them get to like it—it's very English. **C/D**

THE MORGAN THREE-WHEELER

Half automobile, half motorcycle, the bizarre solution to a loophole . . .

STORY & PHOTOS BY TONY HOGG

THE world of motor enthusiasts is a strange one: some people prefer two wheels and others prefer four, but for those who were unable to make up their minds there used to be the Morgan Three-Wheeler, which combined all the virtues of both methods of transportation.

The "Moggie" was the result of a loophole in the English road tax laws which used to be very severe on automobiles, but classified all vehicles with three wheels as motorcycles under a very much lower rate. In consequence, H. F. Morgan's particular breed of sporting machinery enjoyed a steady popularity among a select group in England who revelled in fast driving but couldn't see their way to paying the tax on it. Although these machines, with the exception of a few units, have not been made since 1939, a small number have found their way to America and a 1934 model is owned by Earl Strout of San Francisco, California.

Strout's car is typical of a long line of these cars. Its chassis consists of two steel tubes running the length of the body, and the rest of the frame members and supports are of wood. The V-twin engine is mounted in front of the radiator on the ends of the two frame tubes, and power is transmitted by a single plate clutch to a propeller shaft which passes through a tunnel in the cockpit to a three-speed transmission behind the seat, and from there by a chain to the rear wheel. This general layout, combined with 40 bhp and a weight of 900 pounds, is sufficient to keep the driver from falling asleep under all circumstances.

A number of different engines were used by Morgan including Anzani, Blackburne, J.A.P., Matchless and Ford and these were variously air or water cooled. However, they were all big V-twins with the exception of the Ford which was an in-line four and, instead of being hung on the front, this unit mounted under the hood in the conventional automobile manner and was always considered most unsporting.

During the late 20's and early 30's, the products of J. A. Prestwich were the most common and it is a water-cooled "JAP" that powers Strout's car. Unfortunately, JAPs were built to an incredibly large number of different detail specifications and data about them is extremely vague and confusing, with the result that it is impossible to give accurate technical information about this particular unit. However, it is a water-cooled twin of 1,100cc giving 40 bhp. The valves are operated by long pushrods and the combustion chambers are hemispherical in the normal motorcycle manner.

Engine lubrication is by a dry sump system from an oil tank situated under the hood, but Strout's car has been modified so that a cycle oil tank is slung from one of the front suspension supports to the right of the engine. The valve springs and rockers are open to the atmosphere, which reminded me of a 300 mile trip I once took in England in a "Moggie" which was admitting too much oil to its valve guides. This, in conjunction with a broken windshield, resulted in me arriving at my destination almost entirely black from the chest up.

Carburetion is by a single Amal fitted with two float chambers to ensure an even level of gas during cornering, because otherwise this instrument will dry up due to centrifugal force, and the fuel is supplied by gravity from a tank under the hood. Contrary to normal cycle practice, ignition is by coil and distributor.

Fitted to the engine shaft is a flywheel which accepts an automobile type single plate clutch. The flywheel carries a ring gear for the electric starter but, despite an exhaust valve lifter control, the only way to start a Morgan is with the crank, because it seems that 60 degree V-twins and starter motors just aren't in sympathy.

The drive is taken from the clutch by a propeller shaft to the transmission situated just behind the seat. For some strange reason, there are no universal joints in this shaft and in consequence the engine has to be very carefully aligned with shims when replacing, and periodic realignment is necessary because the frame has a tendency to sag after a period of time. The transmission is a three-speed unit with a worm on the end of the mainshaft which engages with a worm wheel to take the drive through 90 degrees, and a sprocket on the worm wheel delivers the drive by chain to the rear wheel. On the opposite side of the transmission to the chain sprocket is a pulley which drives the generator, so the battery is not being charged unless the car is actually in motion.

After it has become worn, the transmission has a tendency to engage two gears at once, which happen to be first and reverse, with the result that all forward motion ceases instantly. However, an advantage of the Morgan is that one can then lift up the rear end of the car, wheel it to the side of the road, and effect the necessary repairs with the minimum amount of delay and embarrassment.

In 1911, H.F.S. Morgan designed a system of independent front suspension which incorporated sliding stub axles and it is the same basic design which is used in Morgan cars today. At the rear, the wheel is carried on two arms pivoted at the transmission and supported by two quarter elliptic springs and, in general, the suspension is extremely hard indeed. Furthermore, it is not softened very much by the 4.00 x 18 tires all·round.

The braking system is peculiar because the foot pedal operates a brake on the rear wheel which has to be applied with considerable discretion or the wheel will lock, and the front brakes are applied by the emergency brake lever. This, of course, is pure cycle practice and does not present much of a problem once one has experienced the effect of each individual system and can tailor one's braking to the needs of the moment. Both systems are cable operated and require much stronger pressures than are normal today.

The cockpit of the car is comfortable, but cramped when a passenger is carried, and one has to be careful

Throttle is controlled by the long lever on the right of the steering wheel.

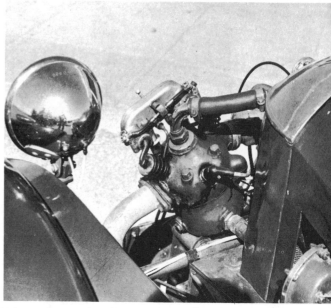

Valve springs and rockers are exposed to the atmosphere.

The Morgan sliding stub axle front suspension.

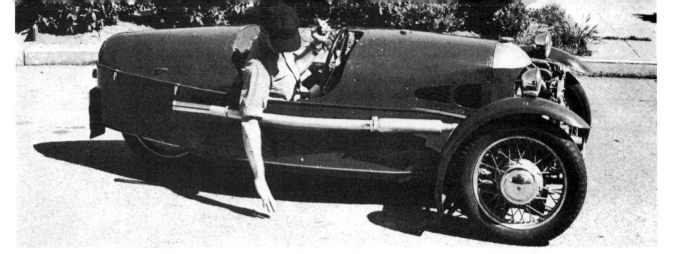

1934 Morgan three-wheeler. The car is powered by a V-twin J.A.P. engine.

The end of the tail.

to avoid the hot exhaust pipes which run along each side of the body. The controls are laid out in the conventional manner except that the throttle, air and ignition controls are situated on the steering wheel and, in consequence, a well-educated thumb is required to accurately control the engine speed when shifting, although this becomes surprisingly easy after a short spell at the wheel. The steering is extremely quick with 3/4 turn from lock to lock and is also very heavy, but the heaviness disappears as soon as the car is in motion.

To start the engine is quite easy provided one knows the correct setting for the controls for a particular car. The throttle must be opened a little and it is essential to retard the ignition because these big twins have a kick like a mule. In cold weather, it is necessary to choke the engine and flood the carburetor, but after making these preliminary settings, the motor will usually fire after two or three sharp pulls on the crank. The idle is very steady and slow and each beat of the engine can be felt through the car. This slow idle is due in part to the fact that the normal flywheels inside the crankcase are assisted by the outside flywheel and automobile type clutch, all of which contribute to the flywheel effect. This arrangement also has a bearing on the low speed torque of the car, which is surprisingly good.

First gear engages quite easily although, if the alignment of the engine is not true, considerable clutch drag will be experienced. The car moves away without fuss provided the throttle opening is increased slightly as the clutch is engaged, and the road speed can be taken up to 25 mph before shifting into second. Second is good for between 40 and 45 mph and after making the shift into high, a pleasant cruising speed will be found in the 60-65 mph range and a maximum of 80 mph is attainable.

As far as road holding is concerned, the car is greatly affected by the road surface and, while it is quite comfortable and steady on freeways, it tends to jump around all over the road on an uneven surface. This is due in part to a tendency for the rear wheel to bounce, causing the car to steer with both ends at the same time. However, the extremely quick steering is useful in correcting these deviationist tendencies once one has become used to it, and the machine as a whole presents quite a challenge to one's driving skill if the best performance is to be gotten out of it.

A family automobile business, which has existed on a minor and specialist scale for over fifty years, is a rarity. H.F.S. Morgan died in 1959 and left it to his son Peter who is well equipped to carry on the traditions of the Morgan company. The current Morgans still have an independent front suspension based on the old man's design and a considerable amount of timber is included with every car. Totally unconcerned with mergers, takeover bids and other financial wizardry, Peter Morgan calmly goes about his business of building limited production sports cars and enjoys a fair degree of prosperity from his labors.

During a recent conversation with him, I asked if he planned a return to the Three-Wheeler and he pointed out that it was no longer necessary to make them because of a relaxation of the English road tax. However, after renewing my acquaintance with one of these vehicles, the possibility of a four-wheeled sports car using a big V-twin cycle engine slung on the front is an intriguing one, particularly to those people who are cycle enthusiasts at heart. For sheer simplicity, accessibility and low manufacturing costs it seems to be a natural for any manufacturer who has some big V-twins to spare, so how about it up there in Milwaukee?   •

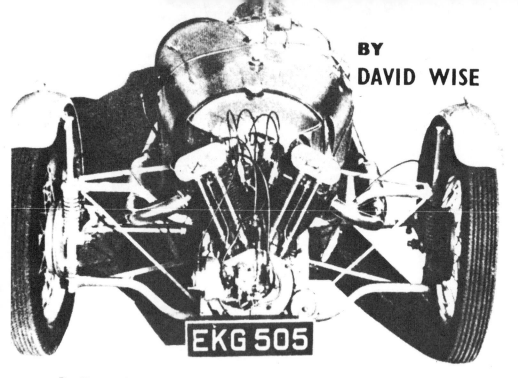

BY DAVID WISE

EKG 505

This Moggie is built even nearer the ground than most in order to hold the road better

I COULD hardly believe it; here I was at last, looking at probably the most famous Morgan in existence, the ex-Clive Lones Brooklands job. Although familiar with vintage machinery, I experienced a feeling almost of awe when the sleek red-and-grey Moggie was wheeled from its garage.

This car was built to the order of Clive Lones, a noted Morgan pilot of the twenties, and was designed expressly for use on the Brooklands circuit. The original engine was an o.h.v. 750 c.c. J.A.P. tuned by the great Bert le Vack; the Moggie lapped Brooklands at over 100 m.p.h. —the only 750 c.c. car ever to accomplish this feat.

A very special

The model as it was—Clive Lones (in cap) at Brooklands in 1932

With a 1,100 c.c. J.A.P. it had been the first three-wheeler to lap the Outer circuit at over the ton. Driving procedure was to hold the throttle wide open with an elastic band and hang on tight! And this Moggie could touch 114 m.p.h. along the straights. . . .

In 1955 John Lindop of Chester found this historic Moggie in a dilapidated state in Derby. The irreplaceable 750 c.c. engine had been scrapped in favour of a tired 996 c.c. J.A.P. from a Brough Superior.

The car was completely

The 996 hungry c.c. of the J.A.P. are fed by twin Amal T.T. carburettors and a duplex Pilgrim oil pump

Moggie

stripped and rebuilt and, by a stroke of luck, the engine from another works Morgan was located in Liverpool.

This was an o.h.v. 996 c.c. J.A.P., formerly fitted to the T. A. Rhode Morgan, and tuned by the late E. C. "Barry" Baragwanath. With a 10 to 1 compression ratio the increased urge proved too much for the original clutch and counter-shaft, which had to be replaced with special components.

It was when the Moggie recently passed into the hands of Mr. E. A. Goldsmith that I had the chance of a ride in this old warrior.

As the mighty J.A.P. was swung into life a deliciously deep boom came from the twin Brooklands cans. Like most Moggies, this one was difficult to get into, but the staggered seating proved most comfortable.

Mr. Goldsmith showed me the hand-pump which, as passenger, I had to operate to keep the pressurized fuel tank at about 1 lb per square inch, then, putting the car into gear, moved away.

Even the most pedestrian Moggie has the sort of acceleration usually referred to as 'breath-taking': the all-too-brief ride was an experience of a lifetime.

Lower-built and wider-tracked than usual, this Moggie really clings to the road; the purposeful boom of the exhausts echoes behind, and the road hurtles up towards you—it is the nearest thing on earth to the old-time stick-and-string biplanes. For one short minute you live with the gods.

The cockpit. Built for speed, not comfort; there is just room for driver and mechanic

Salon

MORGAN Super Sport

BY TONY HOGG

PHOTOS BY WILLIAM A. MOTTA

ANY NATION that perpetuates a currency system which has as its units farthings, halfpennies, pennies, three-penny bits, sixpences, shillings, florins, half-crowns, pounds and a non-existent guinea, and bases its measurement of the proof spirit of alcoholic beverages on the amount required to burn a quantity of gunpowder with a steady flame, can reasonably be expected to be equally illogical in its motoring habits. This is evident from the popularity enjoyed in England by the Morgan Three-Wheeler almost from its inception in 1909 until the beginning of World War II.

Actually, there is more logic to the "Moggie" than meets the eye because it was the result of a loophole in the English tax laws which, at one time, were very severe on automobiles, but classified all vehicles with 3 wheels as motorcycles under a very much lower rate, provided, of course, that they had a total weight of under eight hundredweight (896 lb).

In consequence, H. F. S. Morgan's particular breed of sporting machinery found favor among a select group in England who reveled in fast driving but couldn't see their way to paying the tax on it. Sanity prevailed in America at that time, so that it is doubtful if any cars crossed the Atlantic during the period they were being manufactured. However, since the war a number of cars have been brought over, and an excellent example is owned by Robin King of Costa Mesa, Calif.

The Morgan Motor Co.'s records indicate that King's car has been bastardized at some time or another, although all its components, with the exception of the headlights, are perfectly authentic. In fact, without checking the frame and engine numbers, it is impossible to tell that the car's ancestry is not completely legitimate. It appears that the chassis was built in 1932, but the engine and body are of 1935 vintage, and

*With three wheels, a big V-twin and chain drive,
what more could the sporting motorist ask?*

one can only assume that they were brought together at a later date, possibly as the result of a wreck.

This car is one of the Super Sports Models, which were the most exciting cars in the Morgan range and, because the company has always pursued its familiar policy of not changing anything unless it is absolutely necessary, this particular car can be taken as a typical example of the Three-Wheeler conceived by H. F. S. Morgan.

Surprisingly enough, the Anglican Church plays a major part in the activities of the Morgan company, because it was the Reverend H. G. Morgan who encouraged his son H. F. S. in the venture, and H. F. S. later married the daughter of another neighboring churchman.

When not ministering to his flock, the Reverend Morgan was something of a pioneer motorist, and he served as chairman of the company from its formation in 1912 until his death in 1937. Apart from his official company duties, he found time to put together a large number of scrap books which detail all Morgan activities, and he also seems to have been present frequently at Brooklands and other circuits, always suitably dressed for the occasion in a top hat.

At 18, H. F. S. was apprenticed to the chief engineer of the Great Western Railway so, in common with many of the founders of the industry, he served his apprenticeship in steam before moving on to the internal combustion engine. After seven years at the GWR, he settled in the small English town of Malvern, noted for its spa waters and its school for the sons of the nobility and gentry. There he opened a workshop and started a bus service.

A year later, in 1909, he built the first 3-wheeler, using a V-twin Peugeot engine and incorporating his own patented form of independent front suspension of the sliding pillar type, which is still a feature of Morgan cars today. With his father's encouragement he exibited two cars at the London Show of 1910, which resulted in 30 orders being placed. Using the deposits on the orders as capital, he was able to acquire more machinery, and the result was the founding of the Morgan Motor Co. in 1912.

Although competition was very keen during the 20s and many companies fell by the wayside, Morgan prospered and the Super Sports Model of the 30s was the culmination of his

life's work. When he died in 1959 at the age of 77, the 3-wheeler had been discontinued for 20 years because there was no longer any tax advantage, but undoubtedly he lamented its passing and looked on the 4-wheeled models as a spurious substitute.

Robin King's car is typical of the line. Its chassis consists of two steel tubes running the length of the body, and the rest of the frame members and supports are of wood. The V-twin engine is mounted on the ends of the 2 frame tubes, and power is transmitted by a single plate clutch to a propeller shaft which passes through a tunnel to a 3-speed transmission behind the seat, and from there by a chain to the rear wheel. This general layout, combined with a weight of 850 lb, is sufficient to keep the driver from falling asleep under any circumstances.

A number of different engines was used by Morgan including Anzani, Blackburne, J.A.P., Matchless and Ford, and these were variously air or water cooled. They were all big twins, with the exception of the Ford, which was an in-line four. Instead of being hung on the front, the Ford was mounted under the hood and was always considered rather unsporting by the Morgan *aficionados*.

Although King's machine is powered by a Matchless engine, J.A.P.s were most commonly used, and J. A. Prestwich cooperated closely with Morgan in developing suitable engines for the cars. Little known in the automobile world, old J.A.P. was a great inventive engineer whose "JAP" engines still dominate certain forms of motorcycle racing.

Slightly eccentric, he always wore a frock coat and winged collar even in the late 30s and, apart from engines, he developed such diverse equipment as pencil-making machinery and movie projectors. He was also something of a sport and liked to frequent the dance halls, presumably attired in his frock coat and winged collar. Perhaps it is significant that so many of the founders of the automobile industry were men of great character, but the second and third generations seem much more inclined to the security and obscurity of the godly, righteous, and sober life.

JAP engines were built to an incredibly large number of different specifications, and data about them is extremely confusing, with the result that it is difficult to obtain accu-

Morgan Super Sport

rate technical information about any particular unit. Fortunately, the Matchless engines were confined to three basic types, so they present less of a problem.

The Matchless unit in King's Morgan is an air-cooled V-twin of 990 cc with a bore and stroke of 85.5 x 85.5 mm. The crankshaft is built up in the conventional motorcycle manner, and supported by a bronze bush on the timing side and by 0.25 in. x 0.25 in. roller bearings on the driving side. The connecting rods are of the forked type running on three rows of roller bearings and the compression ratio is 6.2:1, but a few were built with domed pistons, giving a ratio of 7.5:1. This ratio was too high for the gasoline of the day and required a mixture of 50/50 gasoline/benzole. The power output from the standard ratio is 39 bhp.

The valves are inclined in the heads, which have hemispherical combustion chambers, and are operated by long pushrods from the timing case. The rockers and springs are exposed to the atmosphere and one can observe their operation from the cockpit. Lubrication is by a dry sump system from an oil tank located under the hood, and the Amal carburetor, fed by a fuel tank under the hood, is a conventional motorcycle unit except for twin float chambers to avoid fuel starvation due to centrifugal force when cornering fast. Contrary to normal motorcycle practice of the day, ignition is by coil and distributor with the distributor driven off the cam gears through the timing cover.

Big twins of this type have an appeal all their own. They look extremely fierce, but actually are very docile indeed. Starting is not a problem provided one has the knack, but they can break your arm if you don't. They have a strange rhythmic beat which is unique, and the whole car has a perceptible rocking motion at idle, and one can feel each power stroke of the engine through the seat of the pants when accelerating hard.

Fitted to the engine shaft is a flywheel which accepts an automobile-type single-plate clutch. The flywheel carries a ring gear for the electric starter but, despite an exhaust valve lifter control to eliminate the compression when the engine is turned over, the only way to start a Morgan is by the crank, because it seems that big V-twins and starter motors just aren't in sympathy.

The drive is taken from the clutch by a propeller shaft to the transmission situated just behind the seat. For some strange reason, there are no universal joints in this shaft and, in consequence, the engine has to be very carefully aligned with shims, and periodic realignment is necessary because the frame has a tendency to sag after a period of time.

The transmission is a 3-speed unit with a worm on the end of the mainshaft which engages with a worm wheel to take the drive through 90°, and a sprocket on the worm wheel delivers the drive by chain to the rear wheel. On the opposite side of the transmission to the chain sprocket is a pulley which drives the generator, so the battery is not being charged unless the car is actually in motion. King's car has been modified at some time by the addition of a pulley between the crankcase and flywheel to drive the generator, but this modification is quite acceptable to purists because it was offered in kit form during the 30s.

After it has become worn, the transmission has a tendency to engage two gears at once, with the result that all forward motion instantly ceases. However, an advantage of the Morgan is that one can then lift up the rear end of the car, wheel it to the side of the road, and effect the necessary repairs with the minimum amount of delay and embarrassment.

The front suspension is of course by the Morgan system. At the rear, the wheel is carried on two arms pivoted at the transmission and supported by two quarter elliptic springs and, in general, the suspension is extremely hard indeed. Furthermore, it is not softened very much by the 400 x 18 tires all round.

The braking system is peculiar: The foot pedal operates a brake on the rear wheel, which has to be applied with some

discretion or the wheel will lock, and the front brakes are applied by the emergency brake lever. This, of course, is pure motorcycle practice and does not present much of a problem once one has experienced the effect of each individual system and can tailor one's braking to the needs of the moment. Both systems are cable operated and require much stronger pressures than are normal today. Furthermore, they are hardly adequate if one uses the car's full potential.

The cockpit is reasonably comfortable for one person, although it is somewhat difficult to put yourself in the driver's seat. When a passenger is carried, it is necessary for the driver to get in first, and one has to remember to avoid the hot exhaust pipes which run along each side of the car.

The controls are laid out in the conventional manner, except that the throttle, choke, and ignition advance and retard are situated on the steering wheel, so a well educated thumb is needed to accurately control the engine speed when shifting. The steering is extremely quick, with ¾ turn from lock to lock, and it is also very heavy, but the heaviness disappears as the car gains momentum.

It is necessary to know the correct control settings for a particular car in order to start the engine without trouble. The throttle must be opened a little, and it is essential to retard the ignition because big twins have a kick like a mule. In cold weather, it is necessary to choke the engine and flood the carburetor, but after making these preliminary settings, the engine will usually fire after two or three pulls on the crank.

The idle is very steady and slow, due in part to the fact that the normal flywheels inside the crankcase are supplemented by the outside flywheel and automobile-type clutch, all of which contribute to the flywheel effect. This arrangement also has a bearing on the low speed torque of the car, which is surprisingly good.

First gear engages easily, although if the alignment of the engine is not true, considerable clutch drag will be experienced. The car will move off at remarkably low engine revs and can be taken up to about 30 mph in 1st gear. 2nd is good for between 45 and 50 mph and, after making the shift into high, a pleasant cruising speed will be found in the 60-65 mph range. The maximum speed with a well tuned engine is over 90 mph, but the car becomes pretty lethal at that speed.

As far as roadholding is concerned, it is greatly affected by the road surface and, while the car is comfortable and steady on freeways, it tends to jump about like a young gazelle if the surface is uneven. However, the quick steering is useful in correcting these deviationist tendencies once one has be-

come accustomed to it, and the machine as a whole presents quite a challenge to one's driving skill if optimum performance is to be gotten out of it.

From the point of view of appearance, the car looks even meaner in the flesh than it does in pictures. Like other sports cars of its era, there is nothing on it that doesn't help to make it go faster—which is the acid test of the true sports car—and as far as popsy-collecting qualities are concerned, it has built up an envious reputation for being the greatest thing since diamonds.

A family automobile business which has existed on a minor and specialist scale for over 50 years is a rarity. H.F.S. died in 1959 and left the company to his son Peter who is well equipped to carry on its traditions. Totally unconcerned with mergers, take-over bids and other financial wizardry, Peter Morgan calmly goes about his business of building limited-production sports cars, and enjoys a fair degree of prosperity from his labors. In 1964 the company built 434 cars with a labor force of 95 people and 374 were sold overseas, with the majority going to America.

Strangely enough, it was the export market that finally killed the 3-wheeler, because it was apparently unacceptable to anyone but the English who, of course, went out in it in all weathers and even in the midday sun. As far as the future is concerned, there is absolutely no chance of it being re-introduced, and the English are even talking about changing their currency to the decimal system, which proves that they are losing their grip on the more vital aspects of life.

Three-Wheeled Romance

BY MRS. KEN MILES

I WAS ABOUT 16 years old when the events of this particular evening took place. In fact, things being what they are, or were, in England, it was one of my first dates, and my parents only consented to my going with reluctance. It all started with an invitation to dinner at a delightful little restaurant in Henley in Arden, which is a small country town about 30 miles from where my family lived.

My date arrived looking very smooth and well turned out, his appearance only slightly marred by the fresh streaks of oil on his hands and face, a condition which should have rung a loud warning bell to me. My confidence was only mildly disturbed by the sight of the car which he had borrowed for the evening—a Morgan 3-wheeler of about 1925 vintage, which I quickly discovered was driven by chains and had no reverse gear and no starter, not even a hand crank. There was only one way to get the engine running; however, the man was out to impress me, and I was allowed to sit within the conveyance while he did the pushing (a situation which, I have since noted, is frequently reversed after the exchange of the marriage vows).

After several false starts, we were finally on our way and it did not take me long to discover that there was no windshield on the passenger side. I also began to feel some misgivings about the engine, which lay open and exposed to the common gaze in front of the car—somehow it seemed rather indecent to watch it working as we drove along. My uneasiness increased as it grew dark and the flames from the exhaust were clearly visible through the cracks in the exhaust pipe, and I began to doubt the wisdom of the whole expedition.

Entering the historic old town of Kenilworth, we rounded a corner with considerable verve, and there was not time enough to see that the river ford, usually a mere damp patch across the road, had gained some eight or ten inches of water. This was very quickly brought to our attention, however, when a load of muddy water was dumped over the side of the car and into my lap, bearing with it a few small pebbles and three bewildered tadpoles. Oh well, *toujours gai,* as Mehitabel would say, and I tried to be a good sport about the whole thing, but it was getting harder by the minute. However, nothing else untoward occurred before we reached our

threshing engine, valve gear, and sheets of flame, I didn't feel too bad. Suddenly, out of the night, a pair of massive stone gate posts appeared in front of us, and the road turned sharply to the right. Unable to make the turn with the road, we careened straight on, headed directly for what appeared to be a large and impressive wrought-iron gate of beautifully intricate tracery. Fortunately for us, this proved to be an optical illusion, merely the shadow of a large tree with bare branches, and the gate itself was open. In the excitement of the moment, however, the driver had succeeded in breaking the top gear chain.

Always full of resource, he got to work, unshipped the bottom gear chain and fitted it to the high gear sprockets, so that all we had now was high gear. The work completed, he began to push vigorously, tripped over his own foot and fell to his knees, while the car bounded away into the night with the hand throttle wide open. The now-hysterical passenger, unable to drive, was only able to bleat feebly while making totally ineffectual grabs for the wheel as the car headed for the bank at the side of the lane, crashed and came to a quivering standstill on its side with the contents of the gas tank running out onto the road.

It took some time to get me calmed down after this one, but finally the false tranquility of despair set in; after all, it was too far to walk home. Providence just had to do something, and after she had regarded our misfortunes for a sufficient length of time, she acted. She sent a solitary motorist along the road and, like the Good Samaritan, he took pity on our plight, stopped, and offered a lift to the nearest gas station. This being in the depths of the English countryside, and around midnight, the nearest gas station proved to be nineteen miles away, consisted of one pump and a small general store, and was closed. Much hammering and shouting ensued, and eventually a bleary white head was thrust out of a small window above the store, inquiring petulantly, "Wassermatter?"

With increasingly frenzied shrieks and gesticulations the situation was eventually made clear, and the head was withdrawn, reappearing reluctantly a few minutes later atop a body draped in a striped nightshirt, and adjusting an upper set of dentures en route. Muttering to himself, this apparition unlocked the pump, filled up a gallon can of gas, and we were soon on our way back to the Morgan. We only got lost once, and I shall always recall that Samaritan with so very much gratitude.

Once again we started on our way toward home, but by this time there was a sort of pall hanging over the evening, and conversation, when unavoidable, was brief and rather chilly. After the earlier events of the evening, it came as no shock to me when it became apparent that more mechanical trouble had developed (the thing had dropped a valve, but at this point I wouldn't have cared if it had dropped a golden egg). I knew where we were and, extricating myself without a word, I set off at a brisk trot in the direction of home, followed sheepishly by my date.

Five miles or so later, when we finally arrived home, we found an excited knot of people milling about; the police and fire departments had been alerted and the whole scene for some reason reminded me irresistibly of the Thurber story about The Night The Bed Fell. It was all a very traumatic experience and I have never quite trusted automobiles since. As far as I know, the Morgan 3-wheeler is still sitting in the country lane where we abandoned it so long ago.

destination, and once there, everything was very enjoyable, except that I could not shake a slight feeling of self-consciousness with regard to the large mud stain on the front of my dress, and my eyes were still watering from the rush of wind on my face.

The dinner really was excellent, but eventually it became impossible to delay our departure any longer, and I climbed reluctantly back into the monster for the return trip. The first thing I noticed was that as soon as we got the engine running the clutch caught fire, which I thought was a bit alarming, but the man in charge seemed to think nothing of it. Shortly afterward the generator gave up the ghost and we were without lights. The chauffeur at this point decided that it might be more prudent to take a back route through the country lanes, rather than the more direct route by which we had come. I could see the logic of the argument, but, nevertheless, I had many qualms as we turned off the main road into the starlit night, and the sight and sounds of other human beings died away into the distance.

It was a beautiful night, if you liked fresh air. For a short while all went well, and as long as I avoided looking at the

Sixty Years of Sliding Pillars

A brief history of Morgans

IT all began with a fright in a 3½ h.p. Benz that ran away with its driver, the young H. F. S. Morgan, on a 1-in-6 hill between Bromyard and Hereford in 1899, when "H.F.S." was 18. The son of a parson like a lot of other enterprising men, he started his engineering career in steam (like W. O. Bentley), at the G.W.R. works at Swindon, eventually working there as a draughtsman. It is interesting that, like Mr Bentley, Morgan had the right idea about power-to-weight ratios, though his thoughts were obviously on the small-capacity end of the scale.

An Eagle Tandem—a three-wheeler with an 8 hp De Dion engine—was bought, and set off the train of thought that became the first three-wheeler. He opened a garage and motor works in Malvern Link in 1906. Like many at that time (and like many people up till only the last 15 or so years) he was a keen cyclist, but acquired a dislike for motor-cycles. So a 7-hp Peugeot twin-cylinder engine intended for his first attempt at building a bike went instead into a light three-wheeled tubular chassis designed earlier. Morgan had little in the way of machine tools in his garage, so most of

the machining needed was done in Malvern College's workshop under the eye of the engineering master.

There was then no intention of trying to sell the device (1909). It worked well however, and attracted much attention, provoking a decision to build a few. The Rev. Prebendary H. G. Morgan provided capital to extend his son's garage and buy a little machinery and manufacture of the first car, a single-seater, began. A patent was prepared and granted, covering the sliding pillar independent front suspension which has only changed in detail up to the present day. A young man called John Black made the patent drawings, and he was later to become Sir John Black of the Standard Motor Co; he was also to help Morgan greatly 29 years afterwards. Two three-wheelers made their bow at the 1910 Olympia Motor Show, both single seaters with 8 hp twin and 4 hp single cylinder J.A.P. engines. Though about 30 orders were taken, the demand was for two seaters, which first appeared in the following year.

The demand now became so great that Morgan felt obliged to ask various large

manufacturers if they would build the cars for him. No one did so, and with the help of deposits on orders he bought more machinery and further extended the garage. The firm was formed as a private limited company in 1912 as the Morgan Motor Company Ltd. That is what it is still called today, the name bearing no scars of the financially calamitous 1920s—dates of reforming in brackets etc—and is still in the hands of the Morgan family of course. Its survival during those dangerous years is probably partly owed to the fact that unlike many of its cyclecar competitors it was a very well-designed vehicle, and also to its excellent value for money.

This was already becoming obvious before the Great War. By the end of 1913, the Morgan Runabout (as it was called) had won more awards for speed and reliability than any of its competitors. 1913 saw the first Morgans made specially for racing, with longer chassis, lower seating and ohv J.A.P. engines. Such a car driven by McMinnies won a Grand Prix at Amiens that year against strong competition, and from this came the well known Grand Prix Morgan. But in 1914 three wheels meant exclusion from the RAC Light Car and Cyclecar trial, and prompted the design of a four-wheeler, though full four-wheeler production didn't begin till 1936. A four-seater three-wheeler designed three years earlier was made for Mr Morgan's family in 1915; as the Family Runabout it was successfully marketed later.

After the War the works had to be enlarged again to meet demand, the remarkable number of 50 cars being turned out per week. For the time the Morgan was an advanced design, with all-independent

Top left: H. F. S. Morgan in the original single seater three-wheeler Morgan Runabout with tiller steering in 1910. Above: "H.F.S." in the driving seat of the first two-seater of 1911

SIXTY YEARS OF SLIDING PILLARS . . .

springing and its praiseworthy simplicity, great power for its weight, and also by three-wheeler standards ideal weight distribution. Little had to be done to keep up with the times, apart from the addition of electric lighting, an electric starter and front-wheel-brakes, in which last point Morgan were early exponents. It was as a competition car that the make made motoring headlines. In 1925 a beautifully streamlined Blackburne-engined example in which as in all racing Morgans the driver sat almost *under* the line of the scuttle was driven by H. Beart at 104.68 mph over a

kilometre, making it the fastest unsupercharged car in the world. Race after race went to Morgans at Brooklands. In 1930 Mrs Gwenda Stewart took the Hour Record at Monthlèry at over 100 mph in an 1,100 c.c. racing model. More records were gained in the early thirties.

Even in the ordinary cars sold to the public the performance was extremely good for the period. A report in *The Light Car and Cyclecar,* a contemporary of *The Autocar,* of the three-wheeler's ability to climb the famous Cotswold hill Sunrising in top gear made a strong impression; that was good going for a decent motorbike and better than many cars could manage. The majority of early Morgans were two-speeders; in 1931 there came a three-speed-and-reverse gearbox and detachable wheels. 1933 saw the first Ford 4-cyl

engines in the three-wheelers, commercially very successful and in 1936 the Ford-engined four-wheeler was introduced. Here began the familiar 4/4 name, indicating four cylinders and four wheels. In 1937, the Rev. Morgan died and H.F.S. Morgan became Chairman and Governing Director; the first four-wheeled four-seater appeared then and, the following year, a drophead coupé. The sporting side was by no means in the background however; one of the special 1,100 c.c. Coventry Climax-engined cars qualified for the Biennial Cup at Le Mans in 1938.

That young draughtsman who did the patent drawings made his second entry in the Morgan story in 1938. Sir John Black said he would be interested in building a suitable engine for Morgan, and thus came about the pushrod ohv 1,267 c.c. Standard engine developed from the 9 hp side-valve Standard unit; it was not fitted to any Standard. This was the appearance too of the Moss gearbox located separately from the engine in the centre of the chassis. Such an arrangement persists today, so that the Morgan is one of the few cars around where the gearlever is mounted not at the end of a remote control mechanism, but directly on top of the gearbox, which gives a characteristically precise "mechanical" feel to the change.

Just before the 1939–45 War the Plus 8 was foreshadowed by the experimental installation of a 22hp Ford Vee-8, which to quote Morgan's own history "gave a most vivid performance". Also to quote the company "due to difficulties with braking" and a regrettable increase in taxation, this project was abandoned.

After the war many Morgan employees returned to the company, and are still with it; Morgan is a family firm more than simply in its owners. Afer demobilisation, H. F. S. Morgan's son Peter Morgan joined the firm as development engineer and draughtsman; since H.F.S. died in 1959, Peter is now of course Managing Director. Three-wheeler production continued alongside that of the 4/4 until 1950 when concentration on export—where it was the four-wheeler that was the star—killed the F 4 and F Super models. 1950 saw the Plus 4, the 2-litre Vanguard-engined car, with stronger Moss four-speed box and a Salisbury back axle, and this was a great success both in sales and competition. Then came the TR2-engined cars in 1955, in which year the 4/4 Series 2 began, the very tuneable (for a side-valve) Ford 10 engine. An aluminium-alloy bodied lightweight car, helped by the 100 bhp TR3 engine began anew a long run of successes in production sports-car races from 1956, culminating eventually in the Plus Four Super Sports model of Chris Lawrence and Richard Sheppard-Baron taking the 2-litre class award at Le Mans in 1962.

The Plus Four Plus, an all-enveloped Morgan with glass-fibre body appeared in 1963. Forty-nine of these were built but the idea did not really appeal to the traditionally minded people who were now buying Morgans in increasing quantities, and so it was dropped. Latest and most enjoyable of all Morgans is the somewhat controversial 124-mph Rover-3½-litre engined Plus 8. About 200 of these have been made since the car's inception two years ago, and having been modified in the light of American safety and pollution regulations, Morgan hope to start exporting it to the many "Morganeers" in the States at the end of this year.

Left: A famous Morgan customer—Capt. Ball, V.C., the First World War flying ace, in his M.A.G.-engined Grand Prix Morgan (1916). Below left: The original factory in Worcester Road, Malvern Link (now Bowman and Acocks garage) with the ACU Stock Car Trial team in 1921

Below: The Goodalls father and son hillclimbing

Above: H. Beart in the famous Blackburne-engined car of 1925. Below: 1962; the Chris Lawrence-Richard Sheppard-Baron Morgan Plus Four Super Sports crosses the line at Le Mans winning the 2-litre class

out of the past
1935 MORGAN SUPER SPORTS

THE hardy individualism so characteristic of Englishmen is nowhere more evident than in the long career of Morgan cars.

Here is a car that even today clings to the traditions of the twenties and thirties with its wooden construction, ladder frame and Z-section chassis members.

The Morgan first made a name for itself as a three-wheeled "cycle-car", which provided the sort of honest performance and economy dear to the hearts of English enthusiasts.

They weren't particular about comfort — just so long as their mount went quickly and didn't use too much petrol.

Builder H.F.S. Morgan saw to that. He built his first car — sorry, cycle-car — in 1910, and from that time until the three-wheeler Morgan went out of production in 1951 the concept varied hardly at all.

The "Mog" as it became known affectionately, was powered by a violent motor-cycle engine with two cylinders, and a volume of about one litre.

The engine lay naked and unashamed at the front of the machine, on a tube that formed the front of the chassis.

During their 40 years in production, engine types changed. from time to time, but Morgan always ensured that he had the best available, and by keeping weight — and creature comforts — to an absolute minimum he was able to ensure pretty startling performance.

A stripped-to-the-bone (not that there was too much to take off) Morgan could be guaranteed to reach 115 mph!

So determined was Morgan to keep the car simple, and light that he used the lower chassis tubes as exhaust pipes, while the engine was braced precariously by a slender rod situated beneath the chassis.

One owner is reported to have said that when his clutch throw-out bearing shed all its balls, it continued to work every bit as well as before.

SUPERB Sydney-based Morgan is 1935 Super Sports with "barrel-body". It was bought in England, fully restored in Sydney.

It seems that the Morgan was built in the Model-T Ford tradition. If there was some chewing gum or wire handy, the Morgan could be kept running.

Morgan the man, loved motor sport and competed in his own cars whenever the opportunity arose.

After World War I, he began marketing his car in Grand Prix sports car guise, with a tubular steel frame, independent front suspension by coil springs and sliding axles (retained in modified form even today). Rear suspension for the single wheel was by quarter-elliptic leaf springs. Transmission was by means of a leather-faced cone clutch, and drive — to the rear wheel — was by means of two chains, driving a sprocket on each side of the hub.

The wheelbase was seven ft. and ground clearance a modest — for those days — six in.

Steering ratio was, believe-it-or-not, one-to-one — guaranteed to produce very strong wrists on the average Morgan driver. By today's standards the car was seriously lacking in many features, not the least being very modest braking arrangements.

An external contracting band on the rear wheel was the sole brake.

Despite this, the car was warmly greeted by vintage hotshoes who used its galvanising performance at every possible opportunity.

The car had no reverse gear, and an electric starter that seldom worked. A 180 deg. change in direction usually involved wide swoops which embraced gutters, sidewalkes, and grassed banks beside the road.

The GP series went out of production in 1924, replaced by the Aero, which was a bascially similar car but had a different range of engines — J.A.P., Anzani, or Blackburne. The fastest of the lot was the overhead-valve Aero-Blackburne, an example of which set a new record for the flying kilometre — 96 mph — at Brooklands.

It was around this time that Morgan gave in to pressure and started refining the car. Three wheel brakes were incorporated, together with reduction tyre steering. In a 1927 the Super Aero was guaranteed to do 80 mph in showroom form.

All this refining added inexorably to the car's weight, until it reached about 900lb. Despite that, the most-used water-cooled J.A.P. engine was still able to propel the car at a very reasonable rate.

At the turn of the Thirties, Morgan produced a revised chassis that was a notable improvement in terms of stability and road-holding, as well as having a three-speed-forward and one-reverse gearbox. Power unit was mostly either air or water-cooled Matchless.

Not long after this, Morgan produced his first four-wheeler, powered by an overhead-inlet Coventry Climax engine. This was changed just prior to the outbreak of war to a overhead valve Standard engine of 1267cc. This 4-4 was the forerunner of today's conventional Morgan sports cars.

The three-wheeler continued in production until 1951, when Morgan Cars finally realised that it was indeed, a car which belonged to a bygone era. THE superbly restored example which appears in the accompanying photographs is a 1935 Super Sports with "barrel body". It was imported in original state from England by its present owner, Mr. John Maxwell of Sydney, and restored for him by Brookvale specialists Rodney Hoffman and Kevin Delbridge. ∎

Ye Olde Yuletide Roade Çest

John Bolster relives the old days in Peter Agg's magnificent Morgan at Effingham Park. Note the external gear lever and neat exhaust system.

Morgan Super Sports Aero

At Effingham Park in the wilds of Sussex, Peter Agg has a magnificent automobile museum. There, delectable vintage cars rest on thick pile carpet, but this is no mere static display, for they are all in full running order and ready to go. They really are the *crème de la crème*, from luxury cars such as the Rolls-Royce Phantom III, adorned with the creations of the great coachbuilders, to competition machinery ranging from an Indianapolis "Offy" to a D-Type Jaguar.

Yet, when David Watson, Peter's right-hand man, offered me a drive in any one of these beauties, I did not hesitate for an instant. To me, the apogee of tough, he-man motoring is represented by the really hot versions of the Morgan 3-wheeler, and Peter Agg has the

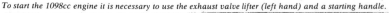

To start the 1098cc engine it is necessary to use the exhaust valve lifter (left hand) and a starting handle.

ultimate in road-going "Moggies", This, the Super Sports Aero of circa 1929, has the specially tuned version of the 1100cc JAP V-twin engine, two speeds and no reverse, selected by a right-hand lever outside the body, and non-detachable wire wheels.

We dyed-in-the-wool Mog enthusiasts look down our noses at the later models. There's something effeminate about 3-speeds and reverse, and who wants the extra weight of a spare wheel, when any real motorist carries tyre levers and an inner tube in the pockets of his oil-stained leather coat? Good heavens, its almost as bad as putting up the hood, and only cissies do that!

The appointed day was blessed with brilliant sunshine and there she stood, incredibly low

and wicked. Surely no car could be smaller, and yet carry two people! The V-twin engine looks enormous, standing naked and unashamed ahead of the radiator. The "cooking" Morgans had air-cooled engines of 980cc but this one has water-cooling by thermo-syphon, needing no water pump. The big 10/40 hp JAP is 10mm longer in the stroke than the air-cooled jobs and Peter's car has the magic letters CS stamped on the aluminium crank-case. This means such things as polished ports and saucy cams, the roller-bearing engine having a total-loss lubrication system, with visible drip-feed from a gravity tank. The petrol tank is also scuttle-mounted and feeds a twin-float Amal carburettor.

Such a hand-built engine was naturally expensive and while the basic Morgan cost £85 this speed model had a ticket of no less than £145. A light cone clutch takes the power to the crown wheel and pinion, via a propeller shaft that is sensibly enclosed in the main frame tube, thus avoiding the embarrassment of having one's trousers whipped off by the revolving rod. Two smaller tubes, running down either side, support the body, and everybody knows that the chassis floats on the traditional Morgan sliding stub axles and coil springs in front. Behind, the single wheel is located by a fork and rides between a pair of quarter-elliptic springs, the drive from the bevel gears to the hub being by two chains and their appropriate sprockets, selected by dogs.

I nearly forgot the brakes, and perhaps HFS Morgan did too. For years, his trikes had only band brakes on the rear hub, but later he would fit, tiny, cable-operated front brakes for £6 extra. The Super Sports Aero, being an 80 mph car, had front brakes as standard, operated by

Morgan Aero

the left hand, the right foot applying the rear brake, without any inter-connection. The left foot controls the clutch and there is no foot accelerator, the throttle lever being on the steering wheel, along with those for the air and ignition. Another little lever, on the side of the body, lifts the exhaust valves to reduce compression when starting, which is achieved after inserting a handle in the side, to engage the bevel shaft.

There's some knack in starting the big motor, but it soon idles impossibly slowly, with a deep mutter from the two huge exhaust fishtails. It's easy to get into a Moggie, assuming you're an acrobat, and with great courage David Watson jumped into the staggered passenger's seat. The sensation of travelling in this tiny projectile is a complete contrast to anything else, and entirely different from what one would imagine.

For a start, the ride is incredibly comfortable, which is contrary to most of the literature on the subject. Other three-wheelers, with their high, heavy bodies, pitch and roll sickeningly, but in a Moggie you sit almost on the road, which you can touch with your hand. The test car had no shock absorbers and the supple springs simply ironed out the bumps. The very high-geared steering—three-quarters of a turn from lock to lock—lies steady in the hands and the car runs straight, without any conscious correction. Cornering is typical of a low-built sports car, with a neutral response but with power-oversteer available at will. When racing, Mogsters used to carry passengers to balance the ship, but the little thing seemed quite stable when driven one-up. Like the early Bugattis, Moggies were made for going rather than stopping, but there's so little weight that one can soon scrub off the speed.

I didn't time the machine as the setting of the carburettor was on the weak side, and obviously it would have been inadvisable to hold peak revs for the necessary distances. However, with 42 bhp and lots of mid-range torque applied to a 7 cwt car of an excellent aerodynamic shape, it can be calculated that the acceleration must be something like that of quite a good 2-litre car. The light weight renders the very high bottom gear (or should I say chain) ratio entirely practicable and I can state definitely that two speeds are ample.

Fully equipped, a Super Sports should be capable of something in the region of 80 mph. With the mudguards and lamps removed, and using the racing JAP engine, many Morgans have lapped Brooklands at well over 100 mph, which means a good deal more than that down the Railway Straight. Having watched them racing there, I can bear witness to their extraordinary stability over the famous bumps. The fastest Moggie ever was Gwenda Hawkes's, and she averaged 115.66 mph both ways over the kilometre at Arpajon in 1930, brave girl!

The popularity of 3-wheeled cyclecars rested on their tax of only £4 *per annum*, their petrol economy, and their better weather protection than any motorcycle could offer. Most owners graduated from two wheels, hence the hand-throttle, but above all the Morgan was so much more attractive than that unsociable device, the sidecar. As a sports car, its enormous fun to drive, much of the attraction coming from the type of engine employed. To watch the big valves opening and closing as one drives, plus that deep throb from the exhausts, makes one feel absolutely a part of one's mount.

As for picking up a bargain, Peter Garnier has pointed out that the Mog he once bought for thirty bob—£1.50 to you, young man—would now fetch £2500 plus. Nevertheless, if somebody would make a few copies at a sensible price, I for one would be greatly tempted to join the queue. ∎

Above: The rear wheel is enclosed in the tapered tail. Below: The cockpit—the long lever on the steering wheel is the throttle, mounted with the air regulator while the ignition advance/retard is on the left.

Specification and performance data

Car Tested: Morgan Super Sports Aero 2-seater, price £145.
Engine: V-twin JAP, water-cooled, 85.7 x 95mm (1098cc). Compression ratio 7.5 to 1. 42bp at 4000rpm. Pushrod-operated inclined valves. Amal twin-float carburettor.
Transmission: Cone clutch. Enclosed shaft drive to bevel gear, plus chains and sprockets to rear wheel, engaged by dogs with outside RH lever. Overall ratios 4.5 and 8.0 to 1.
Chassis: Steel tubular frame. Independent front suspension by sliding stub axles on vertical pillars with coil springs. Direct steering with epicyclic reduction gear in column, threequarter turn lock to lock. Rear wheel in pivoted fork with quarter elliptic leaf springs. Cable-operated drum brakes on front hubs, with central hand lever. Band brake on rear hub, with foot pedal. Non-detachable wire wheels, fitted 27 x 4in tyres.
Equipment: Electric lights and hooter. Speedometer. Adjustable oil drip feed. Starting handle.
Dimensions: Wheelbase 6ft 11in. Track 4ft 3in/zero. Weight 7cwt.
Performance: Maximum speed 80mph. Speeds in gears: first 45mph.
Fuel consumption: 45 to 50mpg.

BIBLIOGRAPHY
MORGAN SPORTS. An Autocar and Motor Cycle Special. £1.50
THE THREE WHEELER. By Brian Watts. The Morgan Three-Wheeler Club. £2.20.
MORGAN. By Gregory Houston Bowden. Gentry Books. £3.95.
MORGAN THREE-WHEELER CLUB
Hon Sec: N. H. Lear, Flat 2, The Grange, Cannington, Bridgwater, Somerset.

The purposeful JAP V-twin is the special, water-cooled, engine producing 42bhp and endows the Aero with a top speed of 80mph.

Above: The man himself. HFS Morgan and passenger during a trials event in the Blackburne-engined Grand Prix Morgan of the early 1920s. The model celebrated a Morgan win at the 1913 Cyclecar Grand Prix at Amiens.

HFS and the…

TRIMOGS

Three-wheeler Morgans dominated British trials and class speed records virtually from their inception. They went like hell and didn't have a third and reverse gears until 1931, when the first major changes were made since 1910. Simple it may have been, but HFS Morgan's idea was also a bright one and the car lasted 43 years to become a unique and enduring legend, as Terry Wright explains.

OLD MEN tell you they had one. Little boys laugh at the three wheels and the valves going up and down. It's the engine that stirs them — V-twin, usually water cooled JAP or Matchless, bared to the elements and perched crosswise on a tubular frame between the two front wheels.

Starting it up soon sorts out the little boys. If the luxury of a starter motor isn't available, you poke the handle into either the crankcase at the front, or the gearbox at the back, depending on the model. It's not the best way to start a big V-twin, as it's bad for the wrist if it backfires and for the knuckles if the ground clearance is poor. But it's good for the arm muscles

and if the weather hasn't got to the most exposed ignition system ever made, the effort is well worthwhile.

Once the motor has settled down to the classic thump, thump, thump of the big twin, the next hurdle for the out-of-training is getting in. You step over the skirt onto the seat squab, let your hands take your weight on the sides, and slide your legs down the narrow gap between the wheel and the seat. On the wheel are throttle, choke and ignition advance/retard levers. The rest is rudimentary motor car — clutch and footbrake pedals, gear shift and handbrake.

Driving off isn't quite so conventional. Steering wheels and V-twins don't very

often come together and the result in this case is one of the few successful examples of a compromise between a motorcycle and a motor car. But this is no skinny cyclecar or plastic bubblecar. The Morgan takes off with all the excitement you'd expect of 30 kW of torquey V-twin pulling a mere 400 kg plus crew.

Two forward gears only were the rule until 1931, and first takes you straight up to around 65 km/h, and then second is good for anything up to 130 km/h. Cornering is therefore rarely interrupted by gearchanging, which is probably just as well as the handbrake lever controls the two front wheels and the modestly geared steering calls for more hard work. Having most of the weight at the front is responsible for pretty fierce understeer, at least in the dry. But that's something you just accept, especially as there is the compensation of independent suspension all round, firm and precise, in the best vintage tradition.

It was Harry or "HFS" Morgan who started it all. He was the son of a country vicar, public schoolboy, Great Western Railway apprentice, garage owner, and like many of his time, a dabbler in the new art of motor car design. Early in 1909 he and a couple of friends wheeled out of the workshops of Malvern College a three-wheeler which was a triumph of simple and effective engineering. Its essential features were to remain largely unchanged and be a resounding success for the best part of the next 40 years.

The two front stub-axles were fixed to sprung pillars which moved up and down, and pivoted on vertical pins. Connecting these was a simple tubular frame on the front of which was bolted a motorcycle engine with a cone clutch. Joining this assembly to the back wheel were a big tube and two small ones. The propshaft was housed in the big one and the exhaust went down the little ones.

At the back was a simple cast bronze bevel box which converted the drive to a countershaft on which either of two sprockets and chains could be engaged by sliding dogs to drive the back wheel. This was suspended from forks and quarter elliptic springs which pivoted from the bevel box. And apart from a body, that was more or less it. The

cheapest 67 kW per tonne available which with 72 km/h, put it straight into the sports car class. HFS' friends were enthusiastic. The vicar, the Rev. George Morgan, put up the capital and HFS went into production.

There was nothing new about three-wheelers, of course. The first Benz of 1885 had one wheel at the front and two at the back and had been followed by a succession of three-wheelers which ranged in sophistication from the motorised tricycles of de Dion-Bouton through a variety of "tri-cars" and "forecars" by Leon Bollee, AC, Singer, Rover and many others.

Morgan appeared relatively late on the scene, with motoring well established and growing rapidly. There were 8465 cars in use in Great Britain in 1904, 53,196 in 1910, and by 1913 the figure had shot up to 132,015, with even more motorcycles. Henry Ford had started production of the Model T in 1908 and in 1909 Herbert Austin produced a very presentable 5 kW two-seater for £150. By 1913, no less than 198 models of British cars had been marketed — but less than half them were still in production.

Having patented his design, but not the sliding pillar suspension which was preceded by several French cars with transverse leaf rather than coil springs, and followed by Lancia in a more sophisticated form, Morgan launched his three-wheeler at the 1910 Olympia Cycle and Motorcycle Show. There were two models, one with a single-cylinder 3 kW JAP and the other with a V-twin 6 kW JAP. Both had tiller steering, which was already rather old hat, and the major disadvantage of being single seaters with negligible bodywork. They weighed only about 150 kg.

Although the prototype had been a bit tatty, the first production model had a lean and hungry look about it that went well with the sporty image it was soon to acquire. Being well conceived in its technical simplicity, without any frills whatsoever, it had none of the Edwardian grotesqueness of some of its much more

TRIMOGS

Right: The Trimog technique: letting it all hang out of Rex Turner's 1935 JAP-engined Super Sports at Winton's 1978 Historic meeting.

Below: A 1939 F2 holds a 1938 F Super at bay.

Above: 1935 Matchless-engined Super Sports.

expensive contemporaries in the car field. It was neither over-endowed with expensive coachwork nor handicapped by the clumsy styling of its sportiest competitors which were probably the English GN and the French Bedelia, both of which also first appeared in 1910.

So it looked right, went well, was cheap at 85 guineas, but one seat wasn't a big selling point and it was untried. You can take your pick of four or 30 as the number reported sold at the show. But Harrod's took up an agency and orders began to come in, helped no doubt, by the development of a two-seater during 1911 and the string of successes which HFS began to record in the long distance trials which were important proving grounds in those days.

The works at Malvern Link were established with a capital of $7000, and by 1912 had made a profit of $3000. This was the year of the cyclecar boom, as scores of hopeful manufacturers sought the magic compromise between the cheapness and simplicity of the motorcycle, and the capacity and comfort of the motor car. At the show of that year, the new magazine The Cyclecar is reported to have sold the enormous number of 100,000 copies, and HFS was ready for the new enthusiasts with Standard and Sports Runabout models.

Motor Cycle's comments in its show editorial were prophetic. "The greatest interest is displayed in the miniature motor cars and the cyclecars of both three and four wheeled types. While there are tried and tested designs on view, many of them have hardly smelt the road, let alone been tested as they should have been, for a few thousands of miles before being offered to the public. Like the motor bicycle, the fittest will survive, but we think some are born to disappointment". The names of the models displayed include a formidable roll call of lost causes: AC, Alldays, Arden, Autotrix, Bedelia, Chater-Lea, Day-Leeds, Duo, Eric, Girling, GN, Gordon, GWK, Humberette, LM, Media, Matchless, Morgan, PMC Motorette, Premier, Perry, Rollo, Rudge, Singer, Surridge, Swift, Tinycar, TMC, Tyseley, Wall Tri-carriage, and Wilton.

Morgan's persistent success in trials was to be of major importance, not only for publicity purposes (which was exploited to the full), but also for developing mechanical reliability. Starting with the 1911 London-Exeter-London Trial HFS won a gold medal and started what is frankly a rather monotonous string of successes in this and other major events such as the ACU Six Days. By 1914 the company was able to advertise its three-wheelers as being the only cars to have won gold medals in every Exeter Trial since production started in 1910. The total of Golds was 10.

Splashing across Scottish rivers, and struggling over Lakeland passes (still hard work even today) was one kind of test, speed at Brooklands was naturally another. Morgans were soon out on the banking and winning the first cyclecar race in March 1912, when Harry Martin won at 92 km/h, and there was fierce competition for the coveted one hour record. During the first part of 1912, Bedelia had struggled to raise it from 70 kilometres to 77 kilometres. Morgan then stepped in and in his first attempt lifted it to 88 kilometres, only to have Wood's GWK manage nearly 90 kilometres a few days later.

In November, Morgan just missed the magic 96.5 km (60 miles) with 95.95 km (59 miles 1120 yards), and so too the Cyclecar Trophy for the year. "Nearly 60 miles in one hour" proclaimed the front cover advertisement in The Cyclecar.

The big event of 1913 was the Cyclecar Grand Prix at Amiens, which the French had been running in various forms since 1905. In addition to a number of sidecar outfits, there were French entries by Violet Bogey, Bedelia, Mathis, Ronteix, Noel, du Guesclin, Automobilette and Super, while the English sent over two GNs, two Duos, one Bolton-Precision, one Marlborough, one Spinx-Globe and four Morgans.

HFS, McMinnies (editor of The Cyclecar), Mundy and Holders were all driving a new model of Morgan, later sold as the Grand Prix, fitted with a variety of exposed engines with brass-domed radiators behind and a lengthened chassis so that the driver and passenger sat in front of, rather than on top of, the bevel box. It was the beginning of the style since firmly associated with Morgans and everybody thought they looked magnificent in green paint and polished brass. In the race, which was over the substantial distance of 262 kilometres, Holder was a non-starter, Morgan broke a piston, Mun-

TRIMOGS

dy's front wheel collapsed and McMinnies survived a puncture and plug trouble to come home first at an average speed of 67.4 km/h (41.9 mph). As everyone was crazy about cyclecars at the time and the British had beaten the French, it was regarded as quite a victory back home. However the French decided that the Morgans should really have been in the sidecar class as they only had three wheels, and gave the outright victory to the Bedelia which came second. Morgan and the British public ignored this nonsense and the company wasted no time taking another front cover advert in The Cyclecar. The Cycle and Motorcycle Trader enthused, "It was a near thing but the Old Country did it; we said the Morgan was hot stuff".

At the 1913 show, when the Grand Prix was added to the range, the whole of the 1914 output was taken up. Then came World War One, and production continued but eventually slowed to a trickle. There were a few changes taking place, though. The Standard had become the De Luxe, a four-seat model called the Family made a preliminary appearance, and the Grand Prix benefited from a few refinements. After the war there were Grand Prix, De Luxe, Sporting, Family and Standard Popular models, with the gem of them all being the Aero which evolved out of, and eventually superseded, the Grand Prix. Early engines had been Precision, Green and MAG, with JAP predominating. Later there were to be Anzani and Blackburne (1922) and Matchless (1933).

The works expanded to a production rate of about 40 to 50 cars a week in the post war boom, and prices soared in line with demand. But the bubble soon burst for the cyclecar business, and many manufacturers gave up the unequal struggle, especially in the face of the competition from the Austin Seven. Morgan had already started to cut back its production and prices but it continued to prosper. When the Austin went into full production in 1923 the cheapest Chummy was 165 pounds and Morgan's range was

now down to 128-163 pounds with internal expanding front brakes now available for an extra six pounds. Dynamos, electric lighting and self starters were other fairly inevitable refinements.

Despite paying only half the road tax of the Austin and being driveable on a motorcycle licence, there wasn't much hope of the more sober Standard and Family models competing against the highly successful Austin and its followers. As the twenties progressed, press attention tended to concentrate on the sportier models, especially the Aero and its boy racer derivative, the Super Sports Aero. But HFS's design was still proving itself adaptable to the varying demands of police patrol work, delivering bread, breaking world speed records, carrying families of four, and most importantly, to satisfying what one reviewer called the vast crowd of young, moderately well-off people who had become tired of motorcycles yet required the reserve of power which only higher priced cars could give them. Or, as Motor Cycle put it when reviewing the Aero in 1928: "There are many young men and maidens whose wishes are centred in a high speed two seater of sporting appearance, who have no use for the estimable but rather dull performance of the modern low-price car, which is, nevertheless, far more in keeping with their means. To such as these the Aero should make a very strong appeal, for its appearance is distinctly racy and its road capabilities are astounding. The particular machine under review has completed a lap of Brooklands at well over 70 mph and will exceed the mile a minute mark on the road with ridiculous ease and without the need for full throttle."

But later that year, when the Motor-Cycle Show opened at Olympia, only two makes of cyclecar were represented, Morgan and Coventry-Victor. BSA later produced a front-wheel-drive three-wheeler of advanced design but it only lasted until 1936 when the Coventry Victor and the Raleigh, which was introduced in 1931, were still going, after a fashion. The Raleigh car division was later sold and production of commercial vehicles continued under the name of

Reliant. None of these competitors, however, could match Morgans in competition, despite efforts by BSA.

Maintaining the sporty image was no problem for Morgans. Brooklands was the scene of the more dramatic achievements and not a little controversy when in 1924 three-wheelers were banned from competition against cars on the grounds that they were dangerous — but more probably because they usually won.

A number of specials had been built for competition at Brooklands and one of the most notable was built by Harold Beart (no relation to Francis) in 1925 with the intention of being the first to break the 160 km/h "barrier". The chassis and steering were strengthened to resist the notorious bumps, steel sliding axles replaced the usual phosphor-bronze, Hartford friction dampers were fitted all round, the rear brake was dispensed with, 64 litres of fuel were carried, and the whole car was streamlined, with the engine enclosed. In low gear it would do 97 km/h, with more than 160 km/h in top at about 4300 rpm using a water-cooled Blackburne engine.

In July he set new class K2 (two seater up to 1100 cm³) records for five and 10 kilometres and miles. In August he lifted the flying start kilometre and mile records to 103.37 and 102.56 mph respectively, and a month later took out the 50 and 100 kilometre and one hour records. The latter was 91.48 mph and his mile speed still stands as a British National Record in the 1300 cm³ cyclecar class. Morgan lost no time in advertising Beart's car as the fastest unsupercharged car of its size in the world.

Another successful Morgan driver of this period whose name also still appears in the British record book is Eric Fernihough who later held the world motorcycle solo record. His specialty was a 500 cm³ JAP which first appeared in 1926 and took a whole series of class One records from the flying kilometre to six hours. His flying mile at 71.94 mph (115.75 km/h) also still stands as a British record. However it must be pointed out that as the 350 cm³ record is now 105.30 mph (169.4 km/h), and the 1000 cm³ record is 120.84 mph (194.4 km/h), the

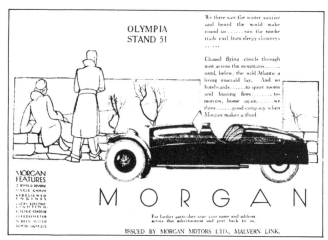

A 1930s advertisement for Morgan: ". . . good company when Morgan makes a third". The price was from 95 pounds.

A three-wheeler lets go at an uphill hairpin in one of the early Scottish trials. The three-wheeler's numerous trials wins were one of its strongest selling points.

survival of Beart's and Fernihough's records for 40 years must be something of a fluke.

In 1928, three-wheelers were allowed back into competition against four-wheelers and celebrated the occasion by trouncing a large field which included Amilcars, Salmsons, Rileys and Austins. The next year, Beart's records were eclipsed by Gwenda Stewart, who took her car to the French Monthlery track and amongst many other records, pushed the hour distance over 160 kilometres for the first time. In 1930, she broke dozens more, and at Arapajon, set what is almost certainly an all-time Morgan record with a mean speed over the flying kilometre of 115.66 mph (186 km/h), which compares favorably with Owen Greenwood's British National Record at 123.65 mph (198.95 km/h) in his Mini Cooper powered device.

Mrs Stewart's record breaking of 1930 in a standard looking car, but with an expertly-tuned, unsupercharged 998 cm³ JAP probably represents the marque's highpoint. At the time that she set the hour record of more than 160 km/h, the motorcycle record stood at 143.8 km/h, and the car record was held by a *supercharged* Cozette at 166.1 km/h. The Morgan she used was the Super Sports Aero, which was about as practical as a Lotus Seven, and had first appeared in 1927. Its ohv 1096 cm³ LTOW JAP (with Blackburne as an option) produced about 30 kW, which was good for well over 113 km/h in standard trim and they still do about well under 20 seconds for the standing 400 metres. There was just enough room for a suitcase balanced on the tail but the performance could match cars of at least four or five times its price. There had been many improvements during the twenties but none had really made much difference to the original design, and the two-speed transmission had remained unchallenged, despite various proprietary attachments designed to give a reverse gear.

It was light, strong, efficient and adaptable. Transmission losses were low, and ratios were simple to change, an important asset when the same machine might be called upon to do duty at Brooklands, Southport Sands or the Scottish Six Days. But the competition from Fords, Austins, Morrises and the rest was beginning to make more fundamental changes essential.

In 1931, Motor Cycling reviewed the latest Super Sports Aero, which had improved transmission, particularly with a split prop shaft and central bearing, which prevented the previously annoying tendency for the shaft to vibrate alarmingly at high speeds. As usual, the magazine was impressed: "The outstanding feature of the Super Sports Morgan is, of course, that its 1096 cm³ ohv water cooled engine, developing some 30 kW, gives it a performance streets ahead of the bulk of combinations, and all the small four-wheelers. On almost any kind of going, practically nothing on four wheels can hold the Super Sports Morgan and it is seldom indeed that one comes across a sidecar driver who can keep its tail in sight for long. And it is not only on short fast runs that the Morgan shines, for it has few equals for runs which involve really big mileages at very high speeds. Two days stand out in this connection. One Sunday, Gloucester was left at about 10 am, lunch was taken in Cardiff and dinner in London, 225 miles having been covered in six hours' running time. The other notable day's work followed the London-Land's End Trial, when the 280 miles from Penzance to London were written off in seven hours."

At and soon after the 1931 show came about the first really major changes since 1910. The two-speed bevel box was replaced by a three-speed and reverse gearbox, with a worm gear drive to the countershaft which now only needed one pair of sprockets and chain. The 50-degree JAP engine became 60 degrees with dry sump fully-automatic lubrication intead of the previous arrangement which involved sight feed regulators on the dashboard. The motor was now started at the front, instead of via the bevel box, but JAP's solution to this was the not very satisfactory one of turning the crankshaft via the timing gears! Detachable wheels and high level exhausts followed for 1933 and more refined Matchless motors began to replace JAP which had become a bit expensive.

The Model Y Ford Eight had started production in 1932 at the new Dagenham factory, and its 933 cm³ sv four-cylinder engine, which with the E93A 1172 cm³ version was to power many a special and production sports car for the next 25 years, was the starting point for a new Morgan. This was the F (for Ford) type. It retained the general principles of the front and rear suspension and the transmission but used a conventional pressed steel chassis with a new body. The engine was now enclosed, of course, and was much smoother than the twin, but something of the old style was maintained by mounting it rigidly which meant that when pushing hard in second gear, an almighty vibration would appear at about 3500 rpm. The brave just drove through it!

On the whole there wasn't much to choose between the three speeders. Both came in Super Sports, Sports and Family, with various other combinations available if required. Both had much the same accommodation and performance and it really came down to a choice between the unmistakable characteristics of the V-twin and the (relative) smoothness of the four.

Only about 1500 of the Ford and Matchless engined models were built. Not only were the days of the three-wheeler numbered but Morgans had a new success in production — a four-wheeler which had quite a lot in common with the F type. Like the first car of 1910 it was a stylish, cheap, relatively fast and uncomplicated sports car. It also proved itself successful in competitions and easily adaptable to technical progress, as it is still in production today, in the same factory, with the Rover-Buick 3.5-litre V8 powering the fastest models.

Production of three-wheelers was down to 29 in 1939 and ceased during the war. In 1946 the factory's stock of parts was assembled into 12 Matchless-engined Super Sports models of which nine were shipped to Brylaws of Melbourne. The twin had now ceased production, and the F type followed it in 1952. The good idea of 1909 had lasted for 43 years — a record the four-wheeler has only just broken. □

Who says Ford Australia invented the ute! This adaption of a standard Morgan was an option offered by the factory before World War One.

Morgan's first four-seater was made in 1912, but production didn't proceed for the company decided to concentrate on sports models.

COAST-TO-COAST IN A 3-WHEELER

A fitting tribute to Morgan's 70th anniversary

BY THOS L. BRYANT
PHOTOS BY JOHN H. SHEALLY II

DRIVING ACROSS AMERICA 45 years ago was an adventure, marked by poor roads, irregularly placed refueling points, chancy eateries and automobiles that were not fitted with super-cushion seats, air conditioning, power-assist options of every description and AM/FM-multiplex-stereo-cassette-tape-recorders with quadrophonic speakers, doo da doo da. Today, of course, driving the breadth of the U.S. is less taxing, although the food is still risky. But adventure is where you find it, or perhaps seek it, and for John Sheally II and Tim Hund, the search led to the cramped confines of a 1935 MX-4 Super Sports Barrelback Morgan 3-wheeler, to be driven from the shores of Virginia's Atlantic coast to California for the West Coast Morgan Club's 25th anniversary meet, Morgans on the Lawn—Sheally's

idea of a "U.S.A. salute to the 70th anniversary of the Morgan Motor Co." If the cross-country driving conditions are no longer the challenge of yesteryear, the obvious answer is to do it in a car that is 45 years old and thus recapture some of the adventure.

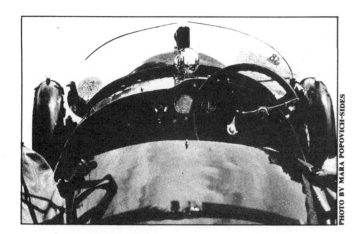

PHOTO BY MARA POPOVICH-SIDES

It's clear that John Sheally II is a Morgan nut; in fact, he may well be the leading Morgan proponent in America. He owns five Morgans (including a 1933 Beetleback 3-wheeler he bought the day he was leaving California to fly home), he races Morgans, is writing his third book on the marque, sponsors the John H. Sheally II Award for Best Morgan of the Year at the annual conclave, and simply is totally immersed in Morgan romance, history and technical data. But unlike many people who carry on automotive love affairs, Sheally believes his cars are meant to be driven and enjoyed—no up-on-a-pedestal lover is John. And that's one of the major reasons why he set out on his madcap cross-country jaunt: "I did it to show that 3-wheelers are not fragile little things; they're sturdy cars that can be used. Most of the Morgan people at the Fullerton meet didn't really expect us to make it all the way across the U.S." Sheally adds that he knew it could be done, and his riding mechanic, Tim Hund, while not a Morgan man, was reasonably confident they would succeed.

Such confidence may have seemed entirely misplaced on the first day of the 3328-mile journey, as Sheally hit a 100-lb sack of

across the desert, like with a sailboat, while the blowing sand was scouring most of the paint off the car."

Eight days from the start, near-disaster struck as they were leaving Tucson, Arizona following a fuel stop. An oil line ruptured, having been badly chafed by the leaping and landing in Georgia, and Sheally and Hund found themselves facing 2–3 ft flames from the engine. Sheally recalls that his first inclination was to scoop up dirt from alongside the highway to quell the blaze, only to discover that sunbaked Arizona soil doesn't scoop, whereupon he started beating at the fire with various articles of clothing. Hund remembers that the fire was burning directly beneath the gravity-feed fuel tank, and when it began to whistle like a teapot, he had visions of the promised land.

Unfortunately, among all the people who stopped to gawk, no one had a fire extinguisher, but just prior to what Hund is sure was the moment when the whole thing would blow and Morgan 3-wheeler pieces would shower the desert, a trucker showed up with an extinguisher and the fire was smothered as the local firefighters were arriving on the scene. The singed trike was

cement in the dark of night on the interstate near Charlotte, North Carolina. One doesn't make sudden darting maneuvers in a 3-wheeler, so Sheally and Hund held on tightly while the trike was airborne for about 30 yards, making a 2-wheel landing but staying upright. There was little apparent damage, but the effects of the flight were enough to stress the Morgan's parts and systems. The most immediate problem was that the engine had jumped its timing, which led to overheating, glowing exhaust pipes that burned both men's jackets, a broken valve, scored piston and damaged valve guide. This was all put right the next day in Atlanta at the Harley-Davidson dealership by a man named Ray Lyttle, one of those mechanics you always hope you'll meet on just such an occasion. The valve was replaced by one from a Harley 74, the guide was trimmed, and the piston was practically remade through the heliarc welding talents of a local shop teacher.

A variety of niggling mechanical problems plagued the cross-country effort as Sheally and Hund pushed on through the southern states, fighting a soaking rain (no top, of course, on the 3-wheeler) from Atlanta to Birmingham, Alabama; the generator threw a pulley between Birmingham and Shreveport, Louisiana, an 18-hour day fraught with minor repairs and adjustments. The crossing of Texas was uneventful until they were west of Dallas, headed for Abilene, where they encountered 30–40 mph crosswinds. The ever-smiling Sheally, who seems to thrive on misadventure, recounts, "I was tacking and jibing

pushed two miles up the road to a service station, and a passerby invited Sheally and Hund to use his shop for repairs.

"All the way across the country, the camaraderie and help from people were simply terrific," Sheally says. "The television station in Virginia had filmed our departure and sent tapes to various other stations along our route, and it was amazing how many people we met who told us they had seen us on the news."

The two Virginians spent the next day rewiring and repairing the Morgan, and then set off for Phoenix, where they took a day off to relax and recuperate. The last leg of the trip took them across the desert to Palm Springs, fighting crosswinds up to 70 mph this time, and as the end of the adventure was almost in sight, the demon of things mechanical got in one parting shot as the engine threw a valve spacer and bent a pushrod. Once more into the breach, lads, and all that. So Hund and Sheally pulled the pushrod and straightened it by beating it with a rock against the freeway guardrail, but they had no replacement spacer. Would the whole adventure come to an ignominious conclusion on the Riverside Freeway just a few miles from their destination? Not a chance! Sheally eyeballed the size of the pushrod end and guessed that the 7/16 socket in their repair kit would fill the gap, which it did. With a flashlight taped on the front of the car (the headlights had not worked since the Tucson fire), Sheally and Hund motored on to their destination. And Sheally, in his boyishly enthusiastic way, sums it all up: "My only regret is that we don't have time to drive it back home to Virginia."

WHEN THEY WERE NEW...
No 15

Harold Hastings looks back on two very different cars that had one thing in common — performance

IN CASE YOU wonder why I am dealing with two cars this month, a word about this series might help. 'When They Were New' arose out of a casual remark to the Editor. Would he be Interested, I asked, in impressions and experiences of some historical cars as I remembered them when they were in their first flush of youth?

His agreement was so immediate that I went ahead for the next issue without any detailed consideration of how long the series might last or even just what cars would be included.

All I had decided was that they would have to have some special memories for me over and above the more transcient impressions one obtains from carrying out a Press road test, meticulous as one may have been in assessing every aspect of a test car's behaviour at the time.

Thinking of a suitable subject for this month, I found myself dithering over two cars, both of which *nearly* qualified for inclusion but did not quite justify the full treatment by my criteria. As both were outstanding for performance in their respective eras — although totally different in every other way — it suddenly struck me that they might well be grouped up as a notable twosome which could show a clean pair of heels to most of their contemporaries. So this month, you have two for the price of one!

And the two cars? The Aero Morgan three-wheeler of the mid-'twenties and the 1935, 1½-litre Singer Le Mans Special Speed model. We'll take the Morgan first — as befits a marque that is celebrating seventy years of manufacture this year.

If there is a name in the motor industry for which I have a whole-hearted respect it is Morgan — Morgan père et Morgan fils. The former started in the business of making three-wheelers of his own design in 1910 and continued to take an active part in the business up to his death in 1959 at the age of 77. His son, Peter, runs the business today. And both have always known just where they intended to go.

For them, none of the grandoise biggest-is-best ideas that have brought most of the remaining British motor makers into a single seeker of tax-payers' money! In spite of pressures to expand and overtures for amalgamations, the business has remained a

family concern steadily and modestly developing a sound engineering theme.

It all started in 1910 when H. F. S. Morgan — he was always known simply as 'H.F.S.' — went into production with a simple three-wheeler, the prototype of which he had completed the previous year. In the form shown at Olympia in 1910, it had a single-seater body with neither windscreen nor any other weather protection, and the chassis was a simple backbone affair of longitudinal tubes. At the front, an arrangement of cross-tubes carried vertical spindles on which the steering swivels were free to move between two helical springs — the top one carrying the weight of the machine and the lower and, smaller, spring looking after the rebound. The result, of course, was independent suspension on exactly the same principle as used on the Morgan four-wheeler today.

Ahead of all this was a V-twin, air-cooled JAP engine rated at a nominal 8hp. It drove the single rear wheel via a clutch and enclosed propeller shaft to a countershaft, whence the final drive was by chain. The rear wheel was carried in a fork-shaped member pivoted to the rear of the backbone frame and a pair of quarter-elliptic springs provided the suspension.

Performance, even in those days, must have been phenomenal for the whole outfit turned the scale at only three hundredweight.

ENTHUSIAST'S DELIGHT — The author at the wheel of the 1935, 1½-litre Singer Le Mans Special Speed model which he drove in the London to Land's End trial of that year and subsequently took to Brooklands for performance tests. The recorded mean maximum speed of 86.54mph was one that few 1½-litre cars could better in those days.

MORGAN STABILITY is, oddly enough, demonstrated by this picture taken at the hairpin on Bluehills Mine in the London to Land's End Trial of 1932. Had the Morgan been unstable, it would have overturned in the opposite direction even before it bounced off the wall. The author, on this occasion, can be seen at work, just to the right of the Policeman, complete with enormous cap, cigarette and notebook.

This gave a bhp per ton figure of 90! Unfortunately, no performance figures as we know them today are available for comparison, but Brooklands Track was already in existence and the practice of taking cars there for officially timed records had already begun; and it is a matter of history that, within two years of showing his 'Runabout' — as he first called it — at Olympia, 'H.F.S'. took one down to the Track and broke the 1,100cc Hour Record.

If he'd only managed to cover another 640 yards before the hour was up, he'd have taken the record at the magic mile a minute. As it was he had to be content with 59 miles 1,120 yards. A. V. Ebblewhite — the famous 'Ebby' whose name will always be associated with Brooklands — was the timekeeper and his father, the Rev. Prebendary H. G. Morgan, who had put up the money to start manufacture, was there to see fair play — complete with long black coat and top hat!

This was the beginning of many years of competition driving by 'H.F.S.' — often with his wife as passenger — in which he was never afraid to pin his faith in his own product. And he was still at it in 1939, by which time his son, Peter, was doing the same thing!

My own first experience of the marque was early in 1925, a few months after I had joined 'The Light Car and Cyclecar' as 'junior

Editorial assistant', to use the Management's euphemistic phrase for Editorial office boy. At the time, the Technical Editor, one Bernard M. Jones, had just finished running-in an Aero Morgan fitted with the 1,098cc, V-twin, water-cooled, ohv, Blackburne engine and he offered me a lift to some sporting event or other.

I was only 18 at the time and my experience was limited to the family Rover Eight, a friend's GN and one or two very staid small cars. In consequence, a lift in an Aero Morgan had something of the quality of a flight in Concorde today — only more so.

I climbed into the cramped cockpit — cramped, that is, in all but leg room — and off we went. Progress through Town was sober enough and as we emerged into the country, we were baulked by a chap who evidently didn't want to be passed — they existed then as today — and we had to wait our chance. When it came, Bernard Jones gave the hand throttle a quick tweak and we were away and out of sight in what seemed to me a fantastic burst of acceleration.

"Once you do that to 'em, they don't bother you again!" he said.

And that phrase has lingered in my memory for 55 years because it so typifies the dominance of the Aero and Super Sports

Morgans in the 'twenties.

There were, of course, a few super-sports cars that could beat the Aero's 70-75mph maximum — but not many and by not much — but I doubt whether any could have beaten the Morgan from the traffic lights . . . if we'd had any then.

What made the whole performance seem even more impressive was the fussless way it all happened. A big V-twin has a leisurely beat in any case and when it has to be accelerated through only two gears from rest to maximum, progress seems surprisingly relaxed, apart from the accompanying kick in the back! And to add to the effect, what mechanical noise there was, could not be heard because the small aero screens served to keep the sting of the wind out of one's eyes but not its roar out of one's ears. There's nothing like a spot of wind to carry the noise away.

Power-weight ratio was, of course, the secret of the Aero Morgan's phenomenal performance. Various proprietary engines were offered, all of around the one-litre mark, and the type fitted to the model in question knocked out 45bhp at 4,500rpm. With a weight of only 7cwt 1qr 21lb to cope with, it couldn't help being a phenomenon.

On the principle that the more power you have, the fewer gears you need, the Morgan did splendidly on its two ratios of 4 to 1 and 8½ to 1, although the latter meant that, if you found yourself tackling a freak hill, you couldn't afford to hang about; there was plenty of power there if you went fast enough for the engine to develop it, but hairpin bends could be a bit fraught.

The two gears were provided on the same principle as on the original model with a bevel-driven countershaft at the rear end of the propeller shaft, and sprockets for two chains, one on each side of the rear wheel. These were arranged to give different ratios and were engaged by dog clutches.

All round brakes were an extra and a very worthwhile one at that, but had no connection with the standard braking system. The latter took effect on the rear wheel and was controlled by a pedal and a very awkwardly placed external lever which had a crude friction arrangement to serve instead of a ratchet for parking. The front brakes were controlled by an entirely separate hand lever bolted to the propeller shaft housing — making *three* brake controls in all.

Another unusual aspect of the controls was the use of Bowden-type hand-throttle and ignition-control levers clamped to one of the spokes of the steering wheel. Owners of modern cars with twirly-wirly steering may wonder how this was possible without the cable tieing itself in knots on full lock. The answer was that the steering was what was known as direct; that is to say there was no form of reduction gear. Instead, the steering column terminated in a drop arm connected directly to the steering linkage. As a result, the wheel had to be turned through only a small angle to go from the straight-ahead position to full lock in either direction and there was no question of the now-familiar 'turns from lock-to-lock'.

Needless to say, the steering was extremely heavy and it was also very sensitive. To ensure that there was no lost motion and to give some damping effect, the track-rod connections were of the spring-loaded taper-pin-

MALVERN MANAGEMENT was always to the fore in sporting events. In this case, George Goodall, for many years the right-hand man of "HFS" at the Malvern works, is toying with the double bend on Summer Lodge hill in a London to Edinburgh trial — leaving the farm horses in the foreground without a job to do.

and-socket type — whereby hangs one of my most vivid memories motoring a Moggy.

As those readers of 'Collector's Car' who remember 'The Light Car and Cyclecar' in pre-war days may recall, a special feature of the magazine was its pictorial front cover. Most of the photographs used were staged by the Editorial staff and taken by staff photographers. One day, somebody suggested that a shot in London's Chinatown might make a change and Hastings and another member of the staff were detailed to produce a suitable picture, together with one or two other East End pictures whilst we were in the area.

We took two cars, one a road-test Aero Morgan which I drove. Having got a selection of Chinatown pictures (one of which is

reproduced here) my colleague went off with the photographer to get some other photographs and I waited for him. To pass the time, I got out an oil can and lubricated everything I could see that I thought might benefit, including all the steering joints.

When the other car returned, we set off back to the office. All was normal for a hundred yards or so until one front wheel hit a bump. Then all hell broke loose. With no gearing or any form of damping to restrain it, the steering went violently from full lock to full lock, taking my arms with it. No effort of mine could restrain it. I tried slowing down but that didn't seem to help either. Only a dead stop ended the agony. So a dead stop it was — with pedestrians eyeing me curiously. I climbed out and went over the entire linkage, but everything seemed disconcertinly in order. So I restarted and this time managed to cover quite half a mile before my arms disappeared in a blur and I had to stop again — this time alongside a man on the pavement who looked at me and roared with laughter. I could have hit him!

When, after a wearying succession of long and short hops, I finally did reach the office, I borrowed a petrol squirt and washed off every trace of oil I could see — and all was bliss on my way home!

I never experienced the trouble again — but then I never, never went anywhere near a Morgan steering with an oil can again. I wonder if any other Morgan owners ever experienced the same trouble, or whether my spot of bother was just a fluke. I'd like to think so because the Aero Morgan, despite a few crudities which weren't so crude in 1925 as they would be today, was really a splendid performance wagon.

Many years later, long after the three-wheeler had finally gone out of production in 1950 — a victim of its lack of overseas appeal

OTHER DRIVERS' USUAL VIEW of the 1½-litre Singer Le Mans Special Speed model — from the rear! As the picture shows, the six-cylinder engine dropped surprisingly well into the Nine chassis, without creating any appreciable overhang. Note the competition tyres — "knobblies" in the jargon of the day — on the two spare wheels and the other various items of sporting equipment.

at a time when the Ministry of Supply limited steel supplies to makers without a sufficient export performance — I asked Peter Morgan if he'd ever thought of reviving the Aero for those who wanted maximum performance at minimum cost.

"Yes," he said, "But it wouldn't work. To have the advantage over the rest that the Aero had before the war, it would have to do a hundred and twenty — and that wouldn't be safe." Sad, but time does march on.

And that brings me forward ten years to the second subject this month — the 1½-litre Singer Le Mans Special Speed Model, to give it its full title. As with the Aero Morgan, I never owned one, but I do have rather special memories of it.

This model was announced in October 1933 and is not to be confused with the much larger 1½-litre Singer Sports which had been introduced the previous May and was a full four-seater on a much longer and wider chassis.

The Le Mans 1½-litre, by contrast, was an example of that highly desirable formula — when it works out right — of a large engine in a small motor car. It consisted of the new overhead camshaft, six-cylinder engine of 1,493cc dropped into the chassis of the already-popular Nine Le Mans sports. Room for the extra two cylinders was obtained by moving the seats back a few inches in the chassis. This, however, created no undesirable overhang, but merely called for the second spare wheel being mounted behind the rear cross member instead of in front of it, so that handling was unaffected and wheel-grip for muddy trial hills markedly improved.

The whole thing was done out very much to the liking of the sports enthusiasts of the period — Hastings amongst them — and the equipment included oversize headlamps, a central Lucas road light, stoneguards for the

IN LONDON'S CHINATOWN — One of the potential front-cover pictures for "The Light Car and Cyclecar" referred to in the text. When the Morgan stopped, a curious little crowd gathered — but the moment the photographer got out his camera, every adult disappeared!

radiator and the sides of the slab-shaped 15-gallon rear tank with its quick-release filler-cap, a sump thermometer in addition to the normal comprehensive array of instruments, knock-on wheels, Hartford shock absorbers and, in case anybody wanted to drive it at Brooklands, regulation bonnet straps.

Add to these desirable items the facts that the engine developed 64bhp at a modest 4,800rpm, that large wheels and tyres (4.75 by 18in) were fitted, that the axle ratio was a

leisurely 4.44 to 1, and you have all the ingredients of effortless high performance.

My particular affection for this model arose from its behaviour in and after the Motor Cycling Club's classic London-Land's End trial of 1935. As readers may recall, I had driven a Singer Nine Sports in the same event the previous year and this seemed a good follow-up; and as in the previous event, I was invited by J. A. ('Jackie') Masters who presided over the fortunes of the MCC for so many years, to act as last Travelling Marshal — a job in which one combined the activities of competitor, club official in the event of something unusual happening and official 'whipper-in' to keep track of stragglers and bring the welcome news to officials at the various controls and observed sections that they could go home.

The word 'welcome' was certainly the operative one since I was No. 430 and they would have been at their jobs for seven hours or more by the time I arrived.

This is not the place for a hill-by-hill description of the trial. Highlights were shooting up the dreaded Beggar's Roost on about three-quarters throttle, having to take my foot off to get round the top hairpin of a very wet Darracott because we were going far too fast, and arriving at the steep and rocky Hustyn near Wadebridge to find that the 429 competitors ahead had carried water up the hill from the watersplash at the foot to wash away much of the surface and leave the rock outcrop bare, bumpy and incredibly slippery; there was only one thing to do — go flat and hope momentum would make up for grip in the worst places. It did — but only at the expense of being catapulted off the seat and completely losing the pedals at one spot. But we didn't stop!

I have one other memory that I'd rather forget. Up to Bluehills Mine, the last hill, we had a clean sheet in what had turned out to be one of the most difficult 'Land's Ends' for years — which meant that a first-class award would have been especially worth winning. But at Bluehills, I let myself be influenced by a spectator instead of using my loaf. He told me an awful tale of mud on the inside of the famous hairpin which was stopping car after car. The only way to get round, he said, was to take it wide. So I did — and found myself facing the well-known rock wall. The Singer could have clawed its way through the mud — but it couldn't turn more sharply than its lock — which was one of its few faults.

After that, I chuntered away to myself all the way to Land's End!

Back in London after the trial, I took it down to Brooklands to get the usual road-test performance figures. Although it had not been touched in any way, it clocked 10.4 seconds for a quarter-mile down the Railway Straight and exactly the same time for another quarter-mile coming off the Byfleet banking on the opposite side of the track, which the Brooklands Speed Tables said was a speed of 86.54mph. It also clocked a 'standing quarter' of 23.4 seconds without resorting to snatch changes which we felt were cheating in those days.

Other performance details included a maximum of just on 70mph in third and a petrol consumption of 23mpg including the trial and Track tests. And all for £375. □

KNOCKING-OFF TIME for marshals and officials at the Barton Steep re-starting test in the 1935 "Land's End" — the arrival of the author in the 1½-litre Singer which was running last of the entry of 430. With him out of the way, they were free to go after more than seven hours on the job.

THREE WHEELER

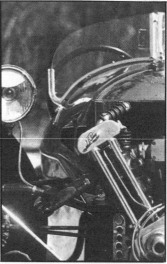

Super Sport with 1096cm³ JAP twin is regarded as the best of the Morgan three-wheelers; detailing to the exposed engine—you can actually see the valves flickering from the driver's seat—and beautifully shaped body is superb. Cockpit is on the narrow side

EARLY ON in the motor age designers decided a car went best with four wheels, one at each corner, like legs on a horse. The Cugnot steam tractor of 1769 and the Benz car of 1885 were three-wheelers, but that plan generally failed to catch on. After the basics of car layout were fixed in the early '90s, the only three-wheelers were motorised tricycles.

But a few years before World War One the cycle-cars appeared. They were a first ranging shot at providing cheap motoring for the masses. They were fragile, spidery machines with painfully simple chassis and bodies, with two-cylinder motorcycle pattern engines and belt or chain drive. Most had four wheels like regular cars, but a few got away with three.

Cyclecars became a craze. It's said a new magazine, The Cyclecar, sold 100,000 copies at the London Cycle and Three-wheeler Show in 1912. Any young man with basic mechanical knowledge and an armful of tools could build a cycle-car prototype in a garden shed, and a good few young men did. One was Henry Frederick Stanley Morgan.

H. F. S. Morgan was born in 1881 and educated at Marlborough and the Crystal Palace Engineering College. For a few years he worked in the drawing office of the Great Western Railway. In 1906 he opened his own garage and motor works at Malvern Link, Worcestershire, and started a local bus service.

He was the local agent for Wolseley and Darracq, but he decided to build himself a light runabout in his own works. He put a seven hp Twin Peugeot engine in a light tubular steel chassis with two front wheels and a single rear wheel driven by a shaft and short chains. It was a single-seater with tiller steering. Its most advanced feature was its independent front suspension. This was in 1909.

Morgan meant it for a one-off, but he was talked into making a few more. He took out a patent on the coil spring in sliding pillar front suspension, and his father helped pay for extensions to the garage. (John Black, the young man who did the patent drawings, ended up as head of Standard-Triumph.) Two Morgan three-wheelers appeared at the 1910 Olympia Motor Show.

People liked the cars but Morgan realised they'd have to be two-seaters to sell in numbers. While the first two-seaters were building he scored the marque's first success in competition, winning a gold medal in the London-Exeter-London trial in a single-seater. At the 1911 Olympia Show the Morgan two-seaters with eight hp JAP engines and wheel steering drew more orders than he could cope with. The first ones sold turned out to be as good as they looked. Morgan had designed them to be economical rather than fast, but their combination of high power and light weight gave them 88 km/h. This was as good as most fast tourers of the day and right at the top of the cycle-car class. Morgan's suspension gave them fine road-holding and they needed it.

In 1911 a Morgan won an international cycle-car race at Brooklands and in 1912 Morgan himself broke the 1100 cm³ one-hour record there, covering nearly 100 km. In 1913 a Morgan won the Cycle-car Grand Prix at Amiens, although the French disqualified it so a French Bedelia took the prize.

In the same year another Morgan won the Cycle-car Club's fuel consumption trial with an average of 24.6 km/l (69.4 mpg). By the end of 1913 Morgan had won more prizes for performance and reliability than any other cycle-car or light car make.

In 1914 the Grand Prix model came out. It was a lengthened sports version with a water-cooled 986 cm³, V-twin engine. The Royal Automobile Club ruled it out of their Cycle-car and Light Car Trial because it was a three-wheeler, so H. F. S. Morgan planned a light car with four wheels and a four-cylinder Dorman engine. Then war broke out and the works went over to munitions making. A Morgan four-wheeler wasn't to appear for another 22 years.

Captain Albert Ball, V.C., the air ace, drove a Grand Prix Morgan in England during the war. In 1920 the Aero improved sports model reached the market and the Duke of York, then a junior naval officer, later King George VI, bought one. Meanwhile H. F. S. Morgan had built a four-seater for his own family's use, and this was marketed too as the Family runabout.

There was another cycle-car boom after the war. People were car-minded now and there weren't nearly enough cars to go around. A rush of new makes hit the market, trying to cater to people wanting cheap, simple transport. The Morgan works were expanded again and production approached 50 a week.

The Sandford and the Darmont were French three-wheelers copied from Morgans. In Britain Morgan's closest competitor was the GN of H. R. Godfrey and Archie Frazer-Nash, which also had a fine speed and competition record. In the middle '20s the Austin Seven began to kill off the cycle-cars in the British market and the GN went under, but Morgan had a secret weapon.

As a three-wheeler, the Morgan could be registered as a motorcycle outfit at a lower tax rate, and it could be driven on a motor-cycle licence. This gave it a better hold on the economy end of the market. Nonetheless, sales of the tamer Family and Standard models dropped and Morgan concentrated on sports models.

There were a few design improvements. Until 1926 the hand and foot brakes only worked on the back wheel, but from that year the foot-brake worked on the front wheels and the hand-brake on the back one. Electric lighting and starting came in in 1925. Four forward speeds had been offered as an extra from 1920 and three speeds and a reverse were standard from 1927.

At the 1928 Motor Show the Super Sport appeared. This was the Morgan for serious speed work. Its chassis was 150 mm longer, its frame was 63 mm lower and its track was wider. Weight had gone up to about 400 kg from the 250 kg of the pre-war cars, but its 1096 cm³ JAP engine gave it a top speed of 130 km/h and neck-snapping acceleration.

From 1930 on, Morgan started to lose even its sport-minded customers to cheap light sports cars like the MG Midget. But a hard core of cycle-engine-minded enthusiasts and lovers of sheer speed stuck to the three-wheelers. There was also the Depression, and fuel economy was a sales point.

Record-breaking was always good publicity. In 1925 Harold Beart's 1100 cm³ Blackburne-engined Morgan, streamlined into a fat cigar on three wheels, covered a flying kilometre at 168.53 km/h (104.68 mph). This made it the first three-wheeler to break 160 km/h—the fastest unsuper-charged car in the world.

But the greatest Morgan record-breaker was a woman, Mrs Gwenda Stewart. In 1930 this small, tough lady gathered together an expert Morgan mechanic, Douglas Hawkes, a specially bodied and geared Super Sports and a range of engines to match the international record classes.

Women were banned from racing at Brooklands then, so she crossed to the Montlhery autodrome outside Paris. With Hawkes switching and tuning her engines and S. C. H. Davis of the Autocar and the Bentley team as co-driver on endurance runs, she set 44 records over distances between five and 1500 kilometres. With the 1100 cm³ JAP engine she covered 163.4 km (101.5 miles) in an hour, five kilometres at 182.36 km/h (113.27 mph), and a flying kilometre at 199.07 km/h (123.65 mph), making her the fastest Morgan three-wheeler driver of either sex ever. At the end of the marathon program she celebrated by marrying Hawkes.

The car pictured with this article is a Super Sport with a 1935 1096 cm³ water-cooled 60 degree twin JAP engine, belonging to Rex Turner of Sydney. It's a frequent appearer in historic meetings at Sydney's Amaroo Park and Victoria's Winton. It's a fine, virtually standard example of what's probably the best three-wheeler Morgan.

To start with it's a surprisingly fine-looking car. Three-wheelers have always generally had an unfinished look about them. Early Morgans tended to go a bit short on bodywork aft of the seats, so they looked notably makeshift and when seen from anywhere more or less ahead they also looked about twice as wide as they were long. But the Super Sport's body is elegant and enveloping, with a narrow nose, a rather graceful bulge amidships and the rear wheel well hidden under the fat bob-tail. The fine curve of the lower edge of the body shell down each side can't be praised enough. Cars are made or broken by details like this.

One of the finest features of vintage sports cars is the way you can tell how the engine is going just by listening. The Morgan goes one better, because its engine can be seen as well. What you see hanging out in front of the axle is all there is, and you can watch the valve on your side flickering up and down from behind the steering wheel.

Getting in you have to watch the hot exhaust pipe down each side, remembering how the blameless Sir Henry Birkin was written off after the Tripoli Grand Prix. A thick tweed sports jacket and leather gloves would be the shot.

The cockpit is long enough because all the space under the nose is leg room, but it's on the narrow side. Rex Turner is a big chap but not all that bulky and the writer is on the thin side, but we filled the cabin to overflowing.

There aren't many instruments to distract you, nor is there much room for them. There are a lot of controls, though. Besides the pedals, there's another bunch on the steering wheel, throttle, choke and ignition. Morgan hand throttles are reputed to stick, often at full speed, and this car has been fitted with the foot pedal we're all more used to.

The engine starts off a crank in front. The Super Sport's silencing is pretty vestigial and it makes an amazing racket even when idling, a kind of a whining roar with a steady rattle running through it. The machine whips off the mark with an amazing feeling of lightness.

THREE WHEELER

On the road the engine puts out a high-pitched throbbing howl and talk in the cockpit is restricted to shouts in the ear. You notice the windscreen is fixed at a perfect height, deflecting the wind so passengers can breathe but letting it blast through your hair. The front springs have about two inches of travel, so the ride is good and hard.

In the average strange car there may be one odd feature you have to get used to. But the Morgan has a range of odd features packed in together. There's a heavy crash gearbox, the pedals are so close together you could cover the lot with one foot, and the steering is frightening.

You're coming up to a corner. You know the steering is very direct, geared one to two so lock to lock is only about half turn of the wheel. You slow right down, edge the wheel a fraction just to get a measure of it, and the next you know you're in a different street. It's a handful. Rex Turner says it will outcorner most four-wheelers. You get a bit of lift on the outside wheel if you're pushing it, but if you turn into it it goes down pretty quickly. It handles better with tyres fully inflated so it will drift. Actually after a few more corners you do start to feel better about it.

Rex bought the Super Sport from the man who brought it out from England in 1960. It had been partly reconstructed, and then the owner had lost interest and left it on display in Green's Motor Museum for years.

"I don't know why he brought it here," he says. "If I hadn't got it I think it would have gone to America. It was a mechanical abortion when we got it. It wouldn't go, the rear forks were cracked. But it looked pretty.

"The engine is a pretty rare bird, and that's one of our worries. The barrels are fatiguing, and one day it's going to meet its Waterloo. We're on the watch for a spare engine of that type, so we can let it go at places like Amaroo. Some good friends of mine, the Sunderland brothers, Jim and Hector, know a lot about JAP engines. It's their hobby, and they saw I was struggling and helped out, which is how we were able to get this one into good reliable order.

"It's not perfectly standard. The original wheels were 4.50 by 18, but now it has 16-inch wheels in the interests of safety. For 18-inch wheels you can only get motorcycle tyres with a very rounded profile, which give you a very tiny surface on the track. I've still got original wheels so it could be put back to standard."

The JAP-engined Super Sport was the peak Morgan three-wheeler. In the late '30s Super Sports were given cheaper Matchless engines as public interest in three-wheelers faded more. Meanwhile H. F. S. Morgan had put the 933 cm³ sidevalve engine from the Ford Eight light sedan in a new chassis for a smoother, less sporting three-wheeler This led to the first Morgan four-wheeler which arrived in 1936.

Only 29 three-wheelers were made in 1939. All post-war three-wheelers had Ford engines, except for a batch of 12 Matchless-engined Super Sports run up from spare parts in 1946 and exported to qualify Morgan for a quota of rationed steel. Nine of these cars were shipped to Brylaws, the Morgan agent in Melbourne. Morgan three-wheeler production

finally ended in 1952. About 40,000 of them had been made in just over 40 years. About 20 examples are left in Australia.

A small wave of three-wheelers, Coventry-Victor, BSA and Raleigh, appeared in England in the late '20s and '30s. Morgan outlived them too, although the Raleigh led to the utilitarian Reliant three-wheelers seen in England today. Morgan production even ran on into the bubble-car age of the '50s.

The Morgan three-wheeler was proba-

bly the best cycle-car ever made, and certainly the most successful. The original design was admirable, and H. F. S. Morgan took it through age after age of a changing world, out of fashion and then back in again.

There are no sporting three-wheelers today.. The nearest thing on four wheels is probably the Lotus, now Caterham, Seven. Yet Morgan's first cars were meant to be economical, not fast, and economy is an issue now. Everybody is

The three-wheelers have an illustrious race and record-breaking history; this Greg McBean shot of a Super Sport in flight captures the Morgan three-wheeler spirit perfectly—hang on, chaps!

making smaller cars. Somebody in England has even built a fibreglass three-wheeler looking a whole lot like a Super Sports. Maybe we'll find that H. F. S. Morgan made a rash step in the dark, and abandoned three-wheelers too soon. Time will tell.　　□

1929 Aero Morgan

Michael Brisby finds the Morgan Tricycle from the Twenties Takes Some Taming.

My feet were dancing across the floor in time to the vibration of the engine and the smell of hot vegetable oil filled my nose. My backside was uncomfortably close to the surface of the road and I was peering anxiously through the passenger side of a tiny windscreen as we rushed towards a cluster of modern cars weaving and jockeying for position on the busy three lane main road. I felt the urge to suggest to the driver that slowing down might be a good idea, but his hand still held the hand throttle wide open and as we went faster still the exhaust pipes on either side of the car provided an ever louder impression of being strapped between two very loud bird scarers.

Several times when I felt an accident was certain and that Ivan should be standing on the brake pedal and hauling on that man-sized lever that applies the front brakes to at least reduce the violence of the impact, Ivan flicked the steering wheel a fraction and changed lanes to find a gap as we passed modern car after modern car.

The exhaust kept up its violent bark, the vibration was never ending and we fairly flew. Does this man never shut down I wondered? We approached a junction, the hand and foot brakes went on, and the throttle lever was flicked shut. So this was the maximum braking the machine could summon — terrible! Ivan changed down and fairly threw the car left and as he did so whipped the hand throttle wide

open again and away we went again, bouncing here and there over man-hole covers and poor road surface repairs. Always faster than seemed decent or safe for a little car fifty-two years old, we jumped and banged our way along.

Watching Ivan Dutton at the controls of the 1929 Morgan Aero he obviously loves so much was something to see, but all the time I had to remember that sooner or later I was going to have to take my turn at the wheel, and driving a two-speeder Morgan was not something I was really looking forward to! The worst part of driving someone else's car is worrying about damaging the car and a natural desire not to make a fool of yourself in front of everyone — and the complexity of the Morgan terrified me!

They say that you can get used to most things and gradually it dawned upon me that Ivan Dutton dearly loves his Morgan and drives it with all the skills that made him Production Saloon Car Racing champion in 1972 and 1973. He has absolute faith in a car which he has very thoroughly restored, largely with his own hands to the sort of standards you might expect of a man with an interest in racing which goes back to his father's career as a riding mechanic at Brooklands in the twenties.

In truth the Morgan is not at all complicated in its construction or to drive — just very, very different to modern cars and, indeed, to many cars of its own period.

At the turn of the century, car engines produced very low power outputs per litre — to go fast you either had a large engine in a correspondingly large car or a comparatively small engine in what amounted to a motorised pedal tricycle — the smaller vehicle having the attractions of relative economy and ease of maintenance coupled to the fact that if the car proved temperamental it could often be pushed home by the operator. Unfortunately, the lack of power of early small cars quite often called for pushing on steep climbs too.

For a time very small cars went into eclipse, but around 1910 there was a revival of what

Don't let the quaint appearance of the 1929 Aero Morgan fool you, even by modern standards it is not slow and in its day it offered outstanding performance for only £105.

1929 Aero Morgan

were called "cycle-cars" and typical examples used proprietary V-twin engines of about 1-litre capacity, chain drive and rudimentary steering arrangements. Weight was kept to the minimum and while low price economy motoring was the main consideration in some cases, the power to weight ratio gave both three and four-wheeled cycle cars pretty remarkable performance.

Of the four wheelers the G.N. (initially with belt drive) was one of the best, but it was the Morgan which led the three-wheeler contingent.

H.F.S. Morgan constructed his first three-wheeler in 1909 with an interesting, very simple tubular chassis (the outer tubes served as exhaust pipes on early examples) and independent front suspension by coil springs, and sliding pillars (a system which avoids camber changes and which has been used on all Morgans since then).

Reactions to the little car were very favourable, but no manufacturer wanted to produce the design and H.F.S. Morgan and his father, the Reverend Prebendary H.G. Morgan, formed the Morgan Motor Company

TECHNICAL DATA

Engine: J.A.P. V-twin. Bore 85.7mm, Stroke 85mm. Capacity 980c.c. Cylinders cast with fixed head mounted at 50 degrees on common crankcase. Water cooled. Valves — side. Ignition — magneto. Carburation — single Amal. Power output — approx 15 b.h.p. (Note: Various engines were available producing up to 40 b.h.p.).

Transmission: Fabric lined cone clutch lubricated with grease. Two speeds, no reverse. Two sets of chains and sprockets engaged by sliding dogs provide the ratios and serve as the final drive.

Chassis: Tubular. Two parallel transverse tubes support the front suspension. Three parallel tubes running back to the rear suspension pivot point — larger central tube encloses the prop shaft.

Suspension: Morgan independent front suspension with sliding pillars controlled by coil springs. Rear suspension — trailing link controlled by leaf springs.

Braking: Foot operated external contracting rear brake. Lever operated internal expanding front brakes operated by cables and also serving as the handbrake.

Steering: Geared down steering box providing two thirds of a turn lock to lock.

Wheels: Split rim, non-detachable.

Dimensions: Wheelbase 6 feet. Track 3 feet 9 inches. Weight 4-6 cwt.

Performance: No figures available, but maximum speed approx. 70 m.p.h. (More potent Morgan 3-wheelers had a maximum close to 100 m.p.h. — one covered a flying kilometre at 116 m.p.h.)

The engine is a side-valve, water cooled J.A.P. unit of 980c.c. and its forward position combined with the wide front track and fairly short wheelbase gives the Morgan more stability than one might expect. The cogs on the back of the off-side front wheel, more clearly visible on page 48, are to drive the speedometer.

Limited in 1912 at Malvern. All Morgans built up to 1936 were three-wheelers and the last left the factory in 1952. Up to 1926 the only braking was on the single rear wheel although with an all up-weight of 4-5 cwt that was not the severe handicap it might at first seem, (to be fair, front brakes were an optional extra after 1922). Detachable wheels and a three speed gearbox did not come until the 1934 models — earlier cars had a two speed gearbox and split rim wheels.

Ivan Dutton's Morgan is a 1929 B-type chassis Aero model fitted with a water-cooled side-valve J.A.P. engine of 980c.c. producing about 15 b.h.p. — enough to provide good acceleration and a top speed approaching 70 miles per hour. When talking of the Morgan's performance it should be remembered that this was the "middle" model — the four-seater Family and the van were slower and the Super Sports Aero was the out-and-out performer. In addition, there was a choice of engines for the Aero — it could be had with a side-valve or overhead J.A.P. engine or an overhead valve British Anzani unit. The engine in Ivan's Aero is the "cooking" version of the J.A.P. with fixed heads cast integral with each cylinder and detachable valve covers to allow decarbonisation to be done without a complete strip down.

The carburettor is tiny and sits ahead of the radiator. What hot air from the radiator does not go out through the bonnet louvres wends its way through the bonnet past the fuel tank to warm the occupants' legs — something I noticed later in the afternoon when Ivan demonstrated hood-up motoring to me.

A 1,000 c.c. V-twin is rather a daunting prospect to start by hand, but Morgan ingenuity comes to the rescue. From the crankshaft, drive is taken through a cone clutch to a sleeved shaft running through the cockpit to a counter-shaft just ahead of the rear wheel. To start the car the handle is inserted in the end of the counter-shaft and a lever on the side of the car pulled to lock the exhaust valve open. With no compression the handle can be wound to get the engine turning nicely, then, leaving it to free-wheel, the exhaust valve lifter control is released and the engine should burst into life with a noise like a well amplified cement mixer. Obviously this procedure was

A close up of the engine with its removable cylinder head caps to allow decarbonising without removing the cylinders, priming taps. behind the plugs to assist starting, and tiny carburettor. Note the period hose clips and gilled radiator core.

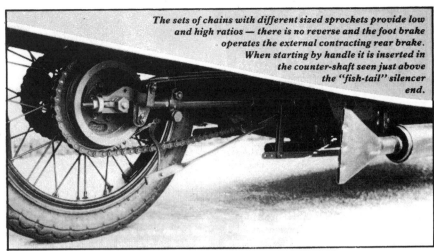

The sets of chains with different sized sprockets provide low and high ratios — there is no reverse and the foot brake operates the external contracting rear brake. When starting by handle it is inserted in the counter-shaft seen just above the "fish-tail" silencer end.

The independent front suspension used on all Morgans from the 1909 three-wheeler prototype to the present day was an unusual sophistication for a cycle car — the track rod ends should not be lubricated or the dreaded speed wobble will set in, by the way. ▼

This lever is the exhaust valve lifter which allows the engine to be turned over briskly before allowing the valve to close and compression to take place. The engine is stopped by lifting the valve again — without compression the engine stops.

Strictly a two seater, the cockpit is neither luxurious or spacious. The instrument panel has the lighting controls on the left, the adjustable oil feed with sight glass in the centre above the horn button, and a rotating drum speedometer on the right. The taller lever applies the front brakes and serves as the handbrake, the short one is the gear-lever — originally mounted on the right of the car. The steering wheel is nice to hold but requires a great deal of effort. The left-hand lever controls the ignition timing, the shorter of the two on the right adjusts the carburettor mixture and the long one is the throttle.

1929 Aero Morgan

not everyone's idea of entertainment and Ivan's car has the £3 optional extra electric starter.

With the exhausts banging away and the sides of what bodywork there is fluttering in time to the trembling front wings, the Morgan looks and sounds fear inducing — and when you first get behind the wheel that fear turns to terror.

The seat is surprisingly comfortable, the all round visibility could not be bettered and the instrument panel is as uncomplicated as any I have seen. The trouble starts with the pedals and ends up at the steering wheel.

Ivan's Morgan has been very carefully restored from a large pile of bits, using a friend's almost totally original Aero as a pattern. Although a foot operated accelerator was optional, Ivan's car never had one, so there are only two pedals — clutch on the left, brake in the centre and a space for the right foot to rattle about in. The engine speed, ignition timing and petrol-air mixture controls are all mounted on the steering wheel and operate through cables so that the wheel can turn the two thirds of a turn from lock to lock without tangling everything up.

I took over the car on a deserted industrial estate with plenty of room to concentrate on this novel control layout without fear of running amok. You need to depress the clutch pedal fully before pushing the gear lever into first. The clutch can judder if you attempt to slip it and first is reasonably high but that V-twin engine seems to pull strongly from about 200 revs. You open the throttle with your thumb and try the steering — then try again. In desperation you heave at the wheel and get some response, there is no play in it is just *terribly* heavy and this is the geared steering — earlier Morgans had direct steering which must have been ideal for Charles Atlas and his buddies.

Acceleration is quite good, devastating by the standards of most cars of the later twenties. When the noise level seems desperate the throttle is closed fully, you engage neutral and tentatively feel in second, top or high, call it what you will. The "gears" are engaged by dogs which select which of the two chains with their different sized sprockets driving the rear wheel is to do its stuff. Ivan explains that you cannot break anything, but it is quite a relief to get the change over without any problems.

The downward changes are not too bad either *if* you remember which way the throttle lever moves to speed up the engine mid-

There is a tradition that Morgans should not be seen with the hood erected and Ivan Dutton had a long search to find a photograph of what the hood should look like.

CLUBS

Morgan Three Wheeler Club. Send SAE to Kay Smith, 1 Que-Sera, Box Hill, Corcham, Wilts for details.
Morgan Sports Car Club, Send SAE to C. Smith, 33 Seymour Avenue, Worcester.
Vintage Sports Car Club, 121 Russell Road, Newbury, Berkshire.

change. The throttle lever does not shut down when you let go and I found it a bit confusing at sharp corners — finding where the lever had got to and then remembering which way to move it to obtain the desired alteration in speed.

Having nothing to do with the right foot is a bit unsettling — on one occasion I found I was trying to speed up the engine using the brake pedal. Of course, this whole fiendish exercise in co-ordination is no trouble to Ivan but he pointed out that even he'd drawn the line somewhere. Originally the gear-lever was on the right — the same side as the hand throttle, and changing gear with that set up was such a struggle for those with only two arms that Ivan re-sited the lever in the middle of the car next to the big lever which works the front brakes.

The brakes are interesting. As I mentioned, the footbrake works the rear brake, a loop of friction material which when applied, closes on the outer surface of its drum. The single brake works not badly by Austin Seven

If you can only just see out the weather probably cannot get in! And neither can anything else — the hood has to be lowered to get in and out.

standards; the lever which puts on the front brakes also serves as a handbrake and to slow the car the lever is pushed away from its ratchet and pulled back.

With so much to think about, the newcomer to Morgan three-wheelers probably collapses from nervous exhaustion after an hour at the wheel, but it *is* fun! If ever a car was a challenge to drive this is it and when you get the thing going it really seems to fly even if it would take a month or two to develop anything like the mastery over the machine that Ivan Dutton displays without apparent effort.

At one point Ivan shouted over the noise of the engine as we took a corner at seemingly impossible speed, "Makes you wonder how they ever sold an Austin Seven, doesn't it?" — well, he's right in some ways because compared to the baby Austin the Morgan really is dynamite, but on the other hand some people prefer the quieter life!

I asked Ivan if he had not been tempted by various offers for the Morgan. "No, not unless I get the chance of a Bugatti or even the parts to build one. That's what I want more than anything else". I left Ivan and his beloved, brutal Morgan with the impression that one day he will get that Bugatti and it will be as beautifully restored as his Morgan, but I think it will have to share a garage — I don't think he will ever part with the Morgan. □

Simple, but very effective, the Aero Morgan is one of those cars that once tried will not be forgotten in a hurry.

RICHARD SEAMAN TROPHIES MEETING, Oulton Park 1970 Special Morgan Diamond Jubilee 4-lap Race.

Right: M. A. H. Duncan's 1934 990 c.c. air-cooled Matchless-engined three-wheeler, with a J.A.P.-engined car astern.

Right : E. A. Bayley's sadly non-standard 1172 c.c. Ford-engined 1936 F-Super (?) waits on the starting grid.

Below: K. M. Poulton's well-preserved and standard-looking 1933 1,200 c.c. J.A.P.-engined Super Sports in the paddock.

MORGAN MUSINGS—continued from page 99

and magneto. With two of each the lap speed would certainly have been over the 100 m.p.h. mark. Fuel was R.D. 1 at 6/- a gallon, for which I had to pay. The M.G. Magnette was lapping at about 110 m.p.h., although Smith was a stranger to the " C " and the Aston was making a creditable 88 m.p.h.

On the afternoon before the race we all qualified early and prospects seemed bright. Then appeared that bane of amateur motor racing, the superfluous spare driver. Where he came in I never could discover, but he expressed a desire to " qualify " and proceeded to lap flat out on the Aston-Martin until a timing wheel broke. This was (but shouldn't have been) of fibre, which permeated the oiling system and made it impossible

to put it right in the time. As this was our " C " car, which had to cross the finishing line, team No. 5 was out of the race. We were the only non-starters, and were thus not able to avail ourselves of the rule whereby depleted teams could make up their number from others similarly placed. Next day, with a whole machine and mixed feelings, I watched the new 1,100 c.c. Singers pull off a well-deserved win.

And so ends this pathetic tale of frustration. I was too late with my Morgan. Prejudice, or some other factor, had gradually ousted them from all forms of racing. Their racing heyday was from about 1924 (when they even competed in the J.C.C. 200 Mile Race) to 1931 or '32. In this period the owner of a fast

Morgan could, and did, enjoy a full season of varied events with large fields of three and four-wheeled competitors. At that time Morgans were, generally speaking, faster than cars of equivalent capacity. (In connection with this, I believe that Lones did a Brooklands lap at over 100 m.p.h. with an unblown 750 c.c. two-seater Morgan. I cannot recollect any unblown 750 c.c. car having done this.)

I hope that the Morgan Motor Co. will excuse such criticisms as have been made about an obsolete model. Mr. H. F. S. Morgan's feat in producing a tubular " backbone " chassis with Lancia-type front suspension in 1910 (well before the great Commendatore himself) has never received sufficient appreciation.

Owner polishes radiator before photographer moves to front of car!

Winged 'Aero' radiator badge proclaims aircraft similarity.

The controls look deceptively simple, but can confuse a newcomer.

Three-wheeler Morgans

Jeremy Jones explains their enormous appeal

The economy and sheer performance of the Morgan gave it a very special appeal.

As a marque always synonymous with sporting but affordable motoring, Morgans of all types arouse the most extreme kind of enthusiasm, but the three-wheeler cars — made in various guises between 1910 and 1952 — often seem to produce in their owners a single-mindedness which those unfamiliar with the cars may find difficult to understand. 1984 brings the seventy-fifth anniversary of the building of H.F.S. Morgan's prototype, and will also mark my ownership of my 1929 Morgan Aero — for over twenty years. It seems an excellent opportunity to try to explain the fascination of these vehicles.

The basic design of the first Morgan was incorporated in all cars until 1932 with a light tubular frame using a sliding pillar system to provide independent front suspension. Mounted across the front of this frame, a motorcycle type V-twin engine driving through a cone clutch and propshaft to a pair of bevels housed just behind the seats. From here two sprockets at opposite ends of a cross shaft drive through ¾" chains to corresponding sprockets on either side of the rear wheel to give two forward speeds, engaged by means of substantial dog clutches.

H.F.S. Morgan's original intention was probably to produce an easily managed vehicle that was cheap both to buy and to run. Throughout the production span of the three-wheeler, a large proportion of the cars made were 'Family' and 'Standard' models with the emphasis on economy. However, the basic design, with its light weight and simplicity of construction, offered a favourable power to weight ratio and correspondingly lively performance, and it was inevitable that sporting versions were soon in demand.

In 1912 H.F.S. himself covered sixty miles in one hour at Brooklands; two years later the Cyclecar Grand Prix at Amiens was won by F.G. McMinnies' Morgan. Following these achievements and countless others in the trials and speed events of the day, the Grand Prix model became popular with enthusiasts. The Grand Prix evolved into the Aero and Aero Super Sports models, all featuring handsome radiators mounted behind their exposed engines. This layout perhaps looks odd to modern eyes, and is no doubt what prompts young onlookers to ask the Morgan driver whether he has made his car himself. In the twenties, however, the Morgan was reminiscent of the latest aircraft — biplanes with visible rotary or radial engines — and this resemblance is particularly strong in the case of the Aero, with its straight crosshead tubes, flared wings and upswept tail.

By the late twenties output had reached some fifty Morgans a week. Using the latest overhead-valve JAP and Blackburne engines, based on motorcycle practice but with watercooling, the sporting Morgan was by this time a very potent vehicle easily able to outperform almost everything encountered on the roads of the period. In racing and record-breaking too these were golden years for the Morgan, Gwenda Hawkes covering the flying kilometre in 1930 with her JAP powered car at an amazing 115 mph.

Though fundamentally unchanged in basic layout since 1910, the two-speeder had undergone development over the years when refinements such as front wheel brakes, detachable bevel boxes, underslung rear springs and bearings to support the propshaft were added. It remained an esoteric machine, however, having no reverse gear and employing a starting handle inserted into the side of the car behind the seats. The Morgan's rivals for sales were no longer sidecar outfits or crude cyclecars, but miniature conventional cars like the Austin 7. This is the explanation usually given for the abandonment of the two-speeder in 1932 and for its replacement by the three-speed Morgan, using a conventional gearbox with

The 1929 Aero Morgan, then owned by Ivan Dutton, which the Editor tried in 1981. In the owner's hands it exhibited exciting performance, but one's first drive in a Morgan is a daunting experience. (Photo: John Williams, Practical Classics).

Characteristic shape of the cast rocker standards explains 'dog-ear' nickname for this type of JAP engine.

Front view of the Morgan emphasises its biplane-like appearance.

The appeal of the Morgan's performance, looks and sound has never faded — they breed addicts.

three forward speeds and reverse, electric starting (or at least a handle on the front of the engine) and — a year later — interchangeable Magna wheels with a spare included.

The JAP and Matchless V-twin motors were still exposed on the sporting three-speed models which, in Super Sport form at least, continued to use uncompromising doorless bodywork. In 1934 the 'F-type' Morgan appeared, with a Ford engine enclosed in a conventional bonnet and behind a conventional radiator like that used on early four-wheel Morgans. Today all these models have an enthusiastic following, though my own favourite is the two-speeder

of the late twenties: these cars retain the vision of the H.F.S. Morgan's original design, are light (about 7 cwt) and powerful (40 bhp or so), and have reasonable lighting and braking systems so that they are quite usable in modern conditions.

Attitudes towards Morgan three-wheelers have changed a good deal over the last twenty years or so. When, in 1962, I placed a 'wanted' ad in the Vintage Motorcycle Club's magazine I was offered no less than twenty-three cars — all pre-1930 and none priced at over £100! I bought TE 6857 in Chorley, Lancashire, from an enthusiast whose girlfriend did not care to ride in the Morgan as this tended to destroy her 'bee-

hive' hairstyle; he was therefore concentrating on his vintage saloon car. I considered myself fortunate, even in 1963, to have found a Morgan which had been spared the usual bodged modifications, as the three-wheelers generally were particularly easy to modify, with many parts interchangeable between models and years. They have also tended to appeal to practical types who, in the days before originality became the fetish it is today, stuck on all kinds of gadgets to keep their Morgans mobile, in misguided efforts to improve performance or to bring a car's appearance up to date.

In daily use over several years my Morgan suffered only one breakdown, when a chain

A drive in a two-speed Morgan is naturally quite an experience. Having started the engine (remember that the starting handle fits into the side of the car and works through the bevels, so the assistance of a valve lifter is necessary and its lever is screwed to the bodywork) you lower yourself into the driving seat to the accompaniment of the peculiar booming rhythm of the V-twin. To the uninitiated the control layout is utterly puzzling; in fact it combines standard car controls with the contemporary motorcycle's lever throttle and hand gear change. There are clutch and brake pedals in the conventional positions, the footbrake in this case operating an external contracting band brake on the rear wheel. A large lever to the driver's left operates the front brakes, while to the right is the gear lever. On the steering wheel are several controls: a long throttle lever, an air control (only needed when starting), and a single lever to control the magneto advance and retard.

Morgan bodywork is very narrow and worn, so to speak, tight under the arms. Nevertheless there is a surprising amount of legroom in the Aero, which also has more space around the pedals than the slimmer Super Aero and Super Sports machines. The clutch has little travel and can be rather fierce — appropriate applications of oil,

broke and damaged the gearchange mechanism. The Morgan's spindly appearance is deceptive: the three-wheelers are surprisingly robust and reliable provided they receive conscientious maintenance. In the sixties Morgans like mine were relatively inexpensive and not difficult to find; spares were plentiful as cars were still being broken up. Today the prices paid for Morgans have increased, so that you may have to give as much for a good example as you would for a mediocre new family saloon. Some might argue that these are excessive prices, but I can think of few old cars that are as much fun to own and use as a Morgan. Moreover higher values have had some beneficial effects: the supply of high quality new spares is constantly increasing, and the standard of rebuilding and maintenance of most Morgans today would not have been believed twenty years ago. It is now a worthwhile and practicable proposition to rebuild a wreck or to build up a Morgan starting with a very incomplete car, and this must surely increase the number of three-wheelers in use.

A 1927 Standard model from Chris Booth's collection of Morgans. Even at this date this model was supplied without front wheel brakes, and used its main chassis tubes as exhaust pipes. Morgan's cheapest and simplest car, the Standard sold in large numbers, but very few examples have survived.

Another of Chris Booth's cars, this 1928 Super Sports Aero was modified for racing and appeared at Brooklands driven by G.C. Harris. The handsome tail conceals the rear wheel, unlike the earlier Aero model. Production examples did not have the additional hump above the back wheel, which clears the shock absorber on this lowered racer.

grease, Fuller's Earth and similar substances to the fabric lining being one of the subtler points of maintenance. Once under way, the torquey engine allows an early change into high gear, the car pulling strongly from low speeds. The steering appears very heavy to the unaccustomed driver; there is a reduction box in the column but the steering wheel moves less than a turn from lock to lock, and you adapt to using the wheel like

Harris, who drove the Morgan works trials cars, used this beautiful 1924 Blackburne engine on his racing car. Dismantled in 1930, this car did not run again until Chris Booth rebuilt it some fifty years later.

a motorcycle's handlebars. Fortunately, perhaps, there are few distractions on the dashboard, but the oil drip-feed indicator has to be watched to ensure that the engine is getting a supply of lubricant for its total-loss system, and adjusted to match the car's speed from time to time. Three-speed cars have automatic dry-sump oiling so this particular complication is avoided.

The level of performance often surprises newcomers to Morgans, and the sensation of speed is heightened because the car is so small, makes a variety of delightful noises

For all its apparent frailty the tubular frame is remarkably durable.

ten sections.

The three-wheelers. of which over a thousand are believed to survive, are supported by the quite excellent Morgan Three-wheeler Club and its associated Mogspares scheme which supplies an increasing range of mechanical and other spares. There are several firms making parts and offering specialist services for owners who do not want to tackle them for themselves. Few machines today need to be off the road for the want of some elusive spare part.

Morgans have always been active in

The sliding pillar independent front suspension which is still a Morgan "trademark".

The Morgan's rear forks and springs, the band brake and the secrets of the two speed transmission.

The Ford engined Morgan three-wheeler, in this case Chris Booth's 1935 four seater (F4) version, has a more orthodox appearance.

and carries its occupants so close to the road. In fact an overhead-valve Aero's maximum speed is about 75 mph. It is, above all, the effortlessness of its cruising and hill-climbing that makes the Morgan so attractive. The standard ratios leave the two-speeder rather undergeared in top; substitution of a 30-tooth rear wheel sprocket gives a longer-legged top gear at the expence of inter-changeability of the drive chains — an aid to maintenance. The ride is firm and the Morgan's three tracks seem to find every pothole; this is accentuated on cars like mine which, unlike some later models, have no shock absorbers fitted. Cornering, however, is outstanding, as anyone who has watched Morgans racing — some cars nowadays developing over 100 bhp — will realise. Braking is not the Morgan's strong point but, as with all early cars and motorcycles, one's driving technique evolves to compensate for this.

The Morgan three-wheeler offers a unique kind of motoring — a car with something of the character of a motorcycle or aircraft. There are other attractions for the enthusiast. The ingenious simplicity of the design makes these fascinating machines to work on: the owner can repair or even completely retube his own chassis fairly simply. Body panels have few double curvatures, the Aero style being about the most complicated in this respect, and the supporting woodwork is predominantly cut from flat sheets, facilitating replacement of damaged or rot-

almost every branch of motorsport — trials, road racing, racing at Brooklands and on sand courses, sprints — competing against both cars and motorcycles or sidecar outfits under RAC and ACU regulations. The tradition continues today, and a vast array of events is open to the Morgan; all the three-wheelers qualify for membership of the Vintage Motorcycle Club, while pre-1930 Morgans are now accepted as eligible vehicles by the VSCC.

Like any other old cars the Morgan has its disadvantages. This is a fairly stark vehicle without unnecessary frills such as luggage space or luxurious upholstery. Prices have become rather high over recent years and this may deter the potential owner. As with other cars, though, sleuthing may unearth an incomplete or partly restored example available for much less than the cost of the complete and immaculate runner. The restorer can count on the assistance of other Morgan enthusiasts, as well as on the parts suppliers for help in completing even the most derelict basket-based Morgan.

In one sense the Morgan remained very much an Edwardian car with chain drive and many visible working parts, but Morgans were still being sold and raced long after their early cyclecar rivals had been forgotten. Today — seventy five years after the Mor-

Jeremy Jones' 1929 Morgan Aero as it was when he bought it except for re-painting. Apart from the lamps and silencers the car is remarkably original. The dents on the radiator were put there by "helpers" making up for the Morgan's lack of a reverse gear.

The photographs in this article are by Zoe Jones except where otherwise stated. The Aero registered TE 6857 is Jeremy Jones' car and we are indebted to Chris Booth for making cars from his comprehensive collection of Morgans available to illustrate this article.

gan's first appearance — this extraordinary vehicle continues to attract a band of dedicated followers for its individualistic design, ingenious construction and, above all, its unique manner of going. There cannot be many other cars about which one can say so decisively, as with the Morgan, that there is nothing quite like it. ●

The Club

The Morgan Three-Wheeler Club Ltd., Secretary: Lawrence Weeks, 43 Greenhill Road, Moseley, Birmingham.

INTO EUROPE

HORSE GUARDS' PARADE, 1973: Chris Booth's 1927, Anzani-engined Aero sets off, on a cold January day, for Brussels on the "Run into Europe". This 1,078 c.c. two-speeder was acquired by its owner in 1968 and restored, making its first outing in April 1969. Since then it has rallied as far afield as Ireland, the Isle of Man, and Belgium. It cost £127 new, and now . . . . £2,500-plus?

Three-wheel Racer

It's noisy, bumpy and smelly, but driving a vintage Morgan three-wheeler is an unforgettable experience. Lawrence Pearce reports from the cockpit. Photographs by Maurice Rowe

MORGANS COULD hardly be described as sophisticated cars even today, so just imagine what a 60-year-old one is like. If you can remember your first pedal car as a child, this will give some idea of the seating arrangement. Six inches off the ground and with no padding; there are certainly more comfortable ways to travel and cars which are easier to get in and out of.

The driver has to clamber into the passenger's side and wriggle beneath the steering wheel; the passenger does likewise, thus trapping the driver in place.

It has no ignition key, starter motor or even a starting handle: it has to be push started. But before this, a few "pre-flight" checks are needed, like operating the grease plungers which lubricate the valve-gear, pressurising the fuel system which feeds the twin Amal carburetters and adjusting the flow rate of the drip-fed, total loss oil supply which lubricates the engine. And some of the Morgan's controls look distinctly unfamiliar: where is the handbrake and gear lever; what is that control on the steering wheel boss? No, this three-wheeler is not what you would call "user friendly".

In 1925, motoring was a different experience, Morgan three-wheeler "triking" even more so. This Super Aero Brooklands owned by Lawrence Weeks is an ex-works racer, devoid of such luxuries as lights, mudguards, windscreen and number plates.

Surprisingly, it has a conventional foot-operated throttle, having been converted from the more usual-at-the-time hand control, and a footbrake working on the single rear wheel. An external handbrake provides retardation for the two front wheels — earlier versions did not bother with this "luxury". The gear lever is also outside the body; it engages either of two chainwheel sprockets by means of dog clutches, giving a choice of two forward ratios. Vainly, I search for a pair of L plates.

The start-up procedure is eventful. Having primed the fuel system and retarded the magneto timing, my passenger — and doubtless a very apprehensive owner — starts pushing.

Weighing only about six hundredweights, it rolls easily — at least it seems to from inside!

Disengaging the clutch, with the gear lever back in low ratio, the Morgan slows almost to a halt, then suddenly the rare 1098cc Blackburn water-cooled Vee twin erupts into life.

Immediately, you can feel the vibration, smell the Castrol 'R' vegetable oil and hear the unmistakable off-beat sound that only an unsilenced Vee twin can produce. And so can the entire neighbourhood — the twin fishtail exhaust pipes doing more to amplify than attenuate the glorious sound. I blip the throttle to keep the engine alive and the magneto timing is now advanced to its normal running setting — it really barks, raring to go, but not before my instructor has climbed aboard. Lawrence's job is to regulate the engine's oil feed and maintain pressure inside the fuel tank, using a dashboard mounted pump which resembles that of a primus stove.

Cautiously I edge home the clutch, half expecting it to stall,

Dashboard shot (upper left), shows large steering wheel dominating cockpit. Note manual fuel pump and drip-feed lubrication system on left of dash, advance and retard lever on steering wheel. It helps to have friends (left), showing start up while below, owner seems apprehensive. Inset (far right), handbrake works surprisingly well on front wheels

or go kangarooing down the road. There's no drama though: the clutch plate bites as smoothly and progressively as many a modern car — and we're away amid clouds of blue smoke . . . from the engine. I hasten to add!

Gathering speed, which it does with frightening rapidity, it does not take long to find out that maintaining any semblance of directional control is an acquired art. The Super Aero is fitted with a steering box reduction drive, very similar to that used on the Model T Ford. It lowers the gearing to something approaching half a turn lock to lock, and is supposed to reduce steering effort. However, in spite of this,' and the advantage of a large steering wheel, it still feels immovably heavy, with the slightest twitch sending the car scurrying across the road.

This is unnerving. Obviously it would not do to have a mishap in such a prized possession (especially with the owner on board) — though it would not be the Morgan's first accident in its near 60-year history: it was completely rebuilt in 1928 with the first of what was to become the distinctive "beetle-back" bodies.

Curiosity dictates a brisker pace and a change into second gear. I'm half expecting the transmission to make expensive graunching noises,' or worse, to seize solid — but, depressing the clutch, edging the lever into neutral and pausing, it slips into second smoothly and silently. With only two ratios, they are inevitably wide apart, so there is a considerable drop in revs accompanying the change up. To its credit, the Blackburn engine (of the type that was used in a successful 104 miles in an hour record attempt) is astonishingly flexible, pulling strongly despite revving so slowly that the individual firing pulsations can be felt.

Now, wind in the hair motoring can really be appreciated, but this Morgan does have minor failings. Along with the wind, one's body gets assaulted with oil, water, petrol and grease from every source imaginable, not to mention heat soak from the radiator. And worse, without mudguards, you have to be particularly careful what you run over with the front tyres, lest it ends up in your face!

There's no speedometer fitted, so it is impossible to tell how fast it is going, and the tachometer (reading to 6,000 rpm, though usual maximum is 4,000 rpm) does not work on this occasion.

In any case, the Morgan's performance would depend greatly on what gearing was used — this being easily varied by fitting alternative chainwheel sprockets, just like a bicycle.

Some indication of its performance potential can be gleaned from the Blackburn engine's 45-50 bhp allied to a total weight of around six hundredweight, giving a power-to-weight ratio in the region of 160 bhp/ton. That is better than the Porsche 944 . . .

Unlike most three-wheelers, the Morgan feels immensely stable, with no sign of body roll around corners. This is because all the weight is low down, and contained within a triangle formed by the three wheels. (In concept, the gearbox mounted between the driver and rear wheel and drive to it via a torque tube enclosed propshaft, is similar to that of a Porsche 944.) It is also because the three wheel independent suspension is unyieldingly firm, and the Morgan has a particularly wide front track. Interestingly, the sliding pillar front suspension, which gives zero camber change, continues to be used on modern Morgans.

Every movement of the front suspension (not that there is much) and front wheels can be seen from the cockpit, every ripple in the road, felt. But despite this jarring ride, and nearly 60 years use on the road and track (it was first road-registered in 1928), the lightweight structure still feels incredibly solid and free of the scuttle-shake which plagues too many modern open cars.

Regrettably there was no opportunity to experience the Morgan's capabilities at high speed, but I'm told that over anything less than a perfect surface, most of the time is spent airborne — with the occupants rattling around like peas in a pod. Normal racing practice is to huddle down inside the cockpit, out of the airstream, so improving maximum speed. I preferred a more conventional seating position, allowing me to see ahead.

The dual braking systems work surprisingly effectively — though obviously it is not possible to use the handbrake and charge down simultaneously. With only two gears, it is not a problem which occurs often.

My thanks to Lawrence Weeks for trusting me with his Super Aero (which incidentally cost him just £125, "a few years ago"). It was a challenge to drive and as thrilling as any modern Italian exotic.

BETWEEN 1910 and 1952 you could buy a Morgan three-wheeler — from the debut of H F S Morgan's 8hp, twin-cylinder and more down-market 4hp, single-cylinder Morgan Runabouts (both tiller-steered, single-seater, JAP-engined) at the Olympia Motor Cycle Show, until the last of the post-war, Ford-engined cars left the Malvern Link works. It was through no lack of popularity that production ended in 1952 — simply because, in those drab days, steel supply permits were granted virtually in proportion to export potential: in foreign parts, the three-wheeler did not enjoy the same road fund tax advantages that it did in the UK, and its export potential was minimal. Before the Second World War came along, the home demand for three-wheelers had been as much as the little factory could cope with, as with the world-wide demand for four-wheelers today, and there had been no need for an export drive. For a spell, though, from 1919 until around 1927, Morgan 'trikes' had been built under licence by the Paris firm, Darmont and Badelogue, under the name Darmont. They sold well, and did well in competition against the indigenous French, Ruby-engined three-wheeler, the D'Yrsan.

The little three-wheelers were all things to all men. For a great many families they provided marginal, and extremely economical, motoring, especially the four-seater versions with their adequate (if not too efficient) weather protection; they supplied the solution to parents' concern about their young sons riding "those horrid, dangerous motor cycles"; right from the start, when H F S Morgan (like so many after him) sought to prove his products and to publicise them in competition, they took part in a completely bewildering number of events — racing, record-breaking, trials, hill-climbs and the rest — proving amazingly successful, especially when power outputs were coaxed up to around 100bhp for a vehicle weight of a minimum 7cwt. Many people, destined to become — or already having become – 'names' in motor sport, were

seen at the wheel of a Morgan. These included Dick Caesar, of *Freikeiserwagen* fame, Sidney Allard, 'Sammy' Davis (successful 24-Hour record runs with Gwenda Stewart in 1930), Clive Lones of 'Tiger Kitten' fame in early Formula Three events; Stirling Moss, no less, with his Matchless MX4-engined Super Sports — and many, *many* more. As 'HFS' had shown, when he won a 'Gold' in the first-ever London-Exeter (of 1910) with a tiller-steered, 8hp JAP-engined single-seater, you could enter even the most mundane model in the 'Land's End', 'Exeter' or 'Edinburgh' trials, and a host of other such events, with every hope of success.

One of the cars' special attributes was their amazing accessibility, and the ease with which you could work on them. With the engine out in front — beneath a sort of coal-scuttle lid on the 'family' models, but completely exposed on the more sporting versions — it was as accessible as though on a bench. And, with a bit of practice, you could un-ship the engine complete in ten minutes or so. A great many young men, including myself, learned a lot about car maintenance from Morgans, and the use of tools. We had to. Morgans also formed the basis of a host of specials — they seemed somehow to invite such treatment — including Granville Grenfell's, with two twin-cylinder, water-cooled, two-stroke Scott engines, on which the weight-

Three three-wheelers

By Peter Garnier

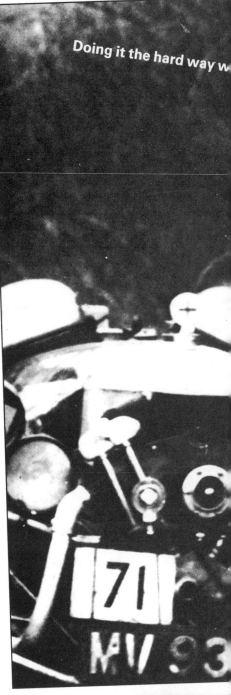

Left, the author at the wheel of the one-time 1926 Family two-seater rebodied in a style which — within the limitations of cash and facilities — was proudly rergarded as rather sporting. Today, it makes its creators blush with shame! Above, Land's End Trial 1938: the 1932 Super Sports tops Barton Steep — the passenger, spanner in hand at the ready, waving to a spectator. Right, BLK 806, the Matchless Super Sports now owned by Warren D Sights MD, of Sturgeon, Missouri, pictured 44 years after being sold by the author

Morgans. By Peter Garnier

distribution must have been a bit intimidating. I believe somebody managed also to squeeze two three-in-line Scott engines into a Morgan. And the sliding-axle independent front suspension (why is it called *sliding pillar* nowadays? — it's the stub-axles that do the sliding, not the pillars) found its way on to many four-wheeled specials.

Since Morgan never built its own engines, these were always bought-in, and included MAG with its overhead inlet and side exhaust valves; Blackburne; Anzani, built specially for Morgan in very small numbers; JAP in many forms, air and water-cooled, and fitted in greater numbers than any others; and the beautifully finished Matchless MX2 and water-cooled MX4 — all, except the very early JAPs, being vee-twins of around 1000cc though a few single-cylinder specials appeared, built for smaller capacity classes. At the Motor Cycle Show in 1933 the first Ford-engined, four-seater F-Type cars appeared, using the 933cc, four-cylinder Model Y engine, developing 22bhp at 4000rpm — distinctly less than the newly-introduced Matchless MX4, used on the Super Sports models, with its 40-plus bhp.

My own introduction to these fascinating vehicles came in 1935, when I was still at school. In a nearby garden we discovered, rotting away, a 1926 'Family' two-seater with sidevalve, air-cooled vee-twin JAP engine of, I think, around 850cc. We quickly came to an agreement with the owner, and bought it for 30 shillings, or £1.50 as it would be today. It was probably a rip-off at that but little did the owner (or we) know that, some 45 years later and properly restored, its value would have risen to a shattering £4000-odd. At the dead of night we climbed out of a window, took possession, and pushed it up the hill to the school, hiding it in the fire-engine shed, inboard of the fire-engine where authority would not discover it, save in the event of a fire.

We had no trouble removing the body, with its timber frame and simple, single-curvature panels — a good heave, and it was away, leaving odd bits of rotten wood bolted to the frame. What this bit of butchery revealed was simple enough. A substantial tube, running from front to back and containing the driveshaft, formed the apex of a triangle with two much smaller-section tubes — maybe one inch bore — running parallel to and below it; they also served as the exhaust pipes, and must have had a somewhat choking effect upon the engine, with ten years' build up of oily carbon inside. At their foremost ends they were brazed across the lower of two parallel, straight front-axle tubes — beyond which they continued forwards to form the lower engine-mounting points — drilled here and there to allow the exhaust gases to find their way out.

At the front, a cruciform of similar tubing located the three frame members, attached at its front ends to the lower members, and at its centre to the main, large-bore tube — whence the upper ends continued upwards and outwards to bend forwards and attach to the uppermost of the two front-axle tubes; they, too, continued forwards six inches or so to form the upper engine bearers. At the back, a simple bevel box converted the drive from fore-and-aft to athwartships, mounted on two cross-members between the lower frame tubes and bolted to a flange at the back of the central, large-bore tube. The rear wheel was carried in a fork, pivoted concentrically with the drive cross-shaft, and driven by two chains from sprockets on either side — one 'top' and the other 'bottom', each engaged by simple sliding dogs. Reverse did not figure in the specification — you dismounted and lifted the tail round until the Morgan pointed in the required direction. In order to prevent the front-axle tubes from sagging beneath the engine's weight, they were braced by a length of rod between the outboard ends of the upper tube and running beneath the lower engine mountings. It was not unknown for this rod to break — in which case you found yourself possessed of a special, low ground-clearance model.

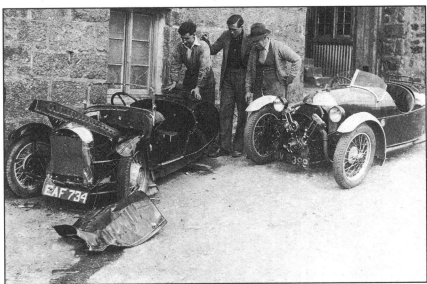

Above, Land's end Trial: the author's 1932 JAP-engined Super Sports and R D Harris' 1172cc Ford-engined F-Super which, within three miles of the finish, had rammed a wall with the driver asleep. Right, winter 1936: the 1932 Super Sports flies the Union Jack (just above the radiator) in celebration of the ascent to the throne of the Duke of York, upon the abdication of Edward VIII

Three three-wheelers

The engine, with its four mounting plates, two each side of the crankcase, simply slid on to its four bearers, the two exhausts running straight down from the ports into small expansion boxes secured to the lower two — by the same nuts that secured the engine. As for the brakes — the less said, the better. They were external-contracting, the handbrake (which you pushed forward for 'on') on one side of the rear wheel, the footbrake on the other. In the dry they slowed the car fractionally (from its terminal velocity of around 35mph); in the wet — not at all.

We were lucky in having the school's engineering and carpentry workshops adjacent to the fire-engine shed, in which our pride and joy lay hidden; and during the long summer term we went to work. I shall never forget the moment when the engine first burst into life, with its flame-throwing glob-glob-glob from the open exhaust ports. We clad its scaffolding with a body — of sorts — made of plywood on a timber frame, the whole lot costing no more than a couple of pounds, which went down on the school bill. We covered it with light canvas, secured by Jeffrey's marine glue, to disguise our hamfisted joinery. We could not improve on its coal-scuttle bonnet which we retained, the combination of mid-Twenties and mid-Thirties 'amateur' looking like an *art deco* flowerpot glued to a Ming vase. We bought it two beautiful aeroscreens from Cooley and Atkinson at Kingston, where such things as brand new Liberty engines, destined for WW1 MLs, could be obtained. And when we sat in it, we protruded like a couple of fence posts, protected only from our navels down.

Towards the end of the term we climbed out once more at the dead of night and pushed it a mile or more towards the newly-opened Guildford by-pass, before starting-up — and off we went. Up and down the by-pass we sped, spellbound at our success, until the magneto fell off and we had to replace — and re-time — it in the dark. Eventually we decided it was capable of the long drive down to Cornwall and, having abandoned it in the forecourt of a local garage, returned to bed undetected. When the end of term at last arrived, it completed the 250-odd miles without any trouble at all.

During the summer holidays it covered many miles on our Cornish lanes. It made several practice ascents of Bluehill's Mine, in anticipation of an entry in the Land's End Trial — but it was the brakes that put paid to that idea. As I descended the — then — muddy, slippery approach to the foot of the valley the rear wheel locked. Instinctively, I pushed the handbrake forward, which had no effect except to make even more certain the wheel didn't revolve, and I slithered towards the edge of a precipice. At the last moment I let-go everything and steered round — but it decided me against using the 'runabout' for my competition debut. I even tried a little elementary courting in it, but it was short-lived. Our plywood front mudguards had been designed with an eye more to their sporting appearance than protection; and when we followed a herd of cows along a narrow lane, their leavings flew up in fair quantities over my light-of-love's left arm and shoulder, which she didn't enjoy much.

I sold it at the end of the summer holidays to a farmer for £4 — which pretty well covered the cost. A year or two later I again discovered it, rotting away in a field this time, and bought it back out of compassion. Bits of it still lie around the garage.

Matchless MX4-engined Super Sports as portrayed by the author in a drawing that originally appeared in Motor Cycle *magazine*

Its replacement was a vast stride forward — a 1932 Super Sports with 60 degree vee-twin, 1096cc, water-cooled JAP LTOWZ engine (L being the type; T for twin; O for ohv; W for water-cooled; and Z for dry sump). What's more, it had the three-speed-and-reverse transmission first announced at the Motor Cycle Show in 1931. A rear-mounted gearbox replaced the bevel box, its output shaft driving a worm gear that engaged with a phosphor-bronze worm wheel on the cross-shaft. At the right-hand end of the cross-shaft was a sprocket driving the single chain, and on the left a fibre gear driving the generator. You started the engine from the front, a starting dog engaging with one of the camshafts, instead of at the side, via the cross-shaft, as with our 'special'. Above all, it had brakes on all three wheels, the handbrake (inboard now, and with a ratchet to keep it on) on the fronts, the footbrake on the rear.

In retrospect, it seems to have been a bit of an oddity for in 1932 Morgan had introduced interchangeable wheels, using 18in Dunlop Magna bolt-ons with re-designed rear forks — which meant that, at least, a Morgan could carry a spare wheel. Yet mine had none of this; if you had a rear wheel puncture, you took the wheel off and mended it. The car was four years old when I bought it, and it cost £37 10s. What with the glorious smell of Castrol R, which the previous owner had used, and the new-found joys of going backwards in a Morgan, there was a strong temptation to go everywhere in reverse!

It brought all manner of adventures. Soon after buying it I was driving up to London when the right-hand cylinder cut out. As I couldn't discover the cause, I continued slowly on one — the left. After a while I noticed a funny smell, and looked down into the cockpit to see a merry glow to the left of the passenger seat — the long silencer mounted below the woodwork, having split, had set the woodwork on fire. When I reached London I decided to have the engine rebored, which cost £1 10s a cylinder, including the piston.

BLK 806 again in its current American home. Apart from the non-standard wings (which should have a central rib), the Morgan appears standard and still wears its original registration plate, though the hood is missing

On the way back from the 1938 British GP at Donington, during a hurried drive, the rear end began to feel soggy on corners. On lifting the lid I found 11 broken spokes in the back wheel!

In 1939 I did the Land's End with it and, as Dr J D Alderson and D M Rushton record in their comprehensive and diligently researched book *Morgan Sweeps the Board* (Gentry Books, London, 1978), failed the re-start test on Bluehill's Mine. I doubt if that was all I failed. With the MCC ban on 'knobbly' tyres, and being an impoverished student, I had bought the cheapest rear tyre I could find — a Henley Key Pattern, which provided the minimum of grip. Likewise the cone clutch, which we cured by tipping the Morgan on to its side and squirting the Pyrene fire-extinguisher into the flywheel. You *never* had clean hands as a Morgan owner. As we drove back to Newlyn from the Land's End finish, the worm wheel disintegrated into powder.

Ever-faithful after the Land's End I part-exchanged it for a 1937 Super Sports, which had all the goodies and set me back something over £60. This time I got the full interchangeable Magna wheel treatment, with the spare set neatly at an angle in the end of the now barrel-shaped tail. The new rear forks consisted of two forged, tapered blades with large-diameter, wide phosphor-bronze bearings on which to pivot, and a tie-bar at their front end with shims to take up the wear. The MX4 Matchless vee-twin was also ohv and water-cooled — 990cc, and it developed around 42bhp. It had handsome, chrome-plated, high-level exhausts running along the sides at waist level, and was painted British Racing Green; and, of course, it too went backwards when asked (and sometimes when not) and had three-wheel brakes. It had a hood too, which you drew over your head like a sweater, and *Lift-the-Dot* fastened to the top of the vee windscreen; it was utterly impossible, unless you were an eel, to get in with the hood up. It had Moseley 'float-on-air' pump-up seat cushions, resting on pieces of plywood with their forward ends raised an inch or two above the floor — which gave extra springiness. Since the cushions were usually punctured, it was mostly 'float-on-wood'. And, to cap it all, it had an induction pipe-operated windscreen wiper *and* a self-starter. It was quiet too, and invariably idled with a regular *plonk, plonk* of both cylinders; and it did around 80mph. What more could one possibly want?

Unfortunately, before I'd had it long, war came and, apart from the leaves, I used it very little. Just before the end of the war a customer with money to burn approached my father with an absurdly handsome offer which he decided on my behalf to accept. The car — BLK 806 — then went to America, and I heard recently from its owner that it is still giving good service. Possibly, distance lends enchantment, but despite driving countless fascinating road test cars during my 25 years on *Autocar*, I still look back on those Morgan years as the greatest fun of all.

THREE WHEELIN'

Mark Hales takes a trip back to the 1930s – before even he was born – to drive a three-wheel Morgan. He even reckons the trike would give a Sierra RS a run for its money. Well, it would. Wouldn't it...?

HOW WOULD you like to make some money? Of course you would. OK, walk to your nearest pub, and strike a conversation with the nearest friendly XR3/GTi owner. Casually drop in to the conversation, that actually you think Morgans are the business. Chances are he will say, sneeringly: "All right if you like that sort of thing but they don't go round corners I know they're supposed to be alright in a straight line anyway I can't see why people want to join the three-year waiting list you wouldn't catch me in one anyway don't they ride like a roller skate?" He *will* say that, I guarantee. Now comes a bit of hustle. Say airily: "Well of course they are a *driver's* car. You do need to be fairly *skilful*

to get the best out of one." Then, before he can reply, say, "Anyway, it's not the four-wheelers I'm talking about. I mean the *real* Morgans. The three-wheelers. The type that held the first 100mph lap of Brooklands. . ." Go on a bit, drop in a bit of history, like the fact that they were banned because they used to beat the Bugattis. But the knowledge that 100mph happened on three wheels in 1934 should have started the mental juices flowing. He will probably decide though that Brooklands was just a speedbowl like Millbrook proving ground, and needed no cornering capability.

Then, when his interest starts to wane because he's sure you're some kind of loony, just drop in to the conversation: "Things haven't come on much since the '30s though, have they? I mean the same Morgan three-wheeler can probably lap Mallory Park faster than a Sierra Cosworth."

Pause for effect. Assess extent of disbelief, number of expletives, shakes of head, size of wad. Assess the right moment for The Sting, and suggest a little wager on the matter. The amount I can leave to your discretion and good tastes I'm sure. . .

Fact One. The Mallory Park circuit lap record for Morgan three-wheelers was set by one William Tuer as long ago as August 26 1979, in a time of 51.8 seconds, an average speed for the one-mile circuit of 93.8mph.

Fact Two. The lap record

years now has been the very Morgan trike that lapped Brooklands at 100mph in the late '30s. In those days it was powered by an 880cc 50 degree vee twin air-cooled JAP engine, developing about 70bhp. Now consider that the tiny, knee-high projectile weighed only five hundredweight, so even then the power-to-weight ratio was similar to that of a large modern touring motorcycle, or more to the point, a modern 250cc racing kart with a very fat driver. The 100mph capability starts to be more believable.

The trike's engine has grown a little since then – original owner Cyril Hale paid Julian A. Prestwich & Co of Tottenham (hence JAP) to develop their engine through the '40s and '50s to an eventual 1,000cc, and Phil has improved the engine a little further still, more for reliability than power. The JAP now gives a useful 100bhp or so from an ultimate 1,300cc capacity and guzzles alcohol rather than petrol, at the rate of three to four miles per gallon. The whole machine still only weighs five hundredweight.

Otherwise, the trike is very much as it would have been 50 years ago, and the only real alterations have been in the interests of safety – some of the steering joints have been replaced by modern rod ends for instance – and the gears have dog engagement to make sure the ratios stay selected when the power is hard on.

The wheels are original-sized 19in diameter spoked cycle items although the tyres, inevitably, are sticky modern motorcycle racing covers. Any advantage given by these though is offset somewhat because they are really designed to be leant with a 'bike rather than kept upright, and a look

for over 2000cc production (road tyred) saloons at Mallory Park is held by Seamus O'Brown's Sierra RS Cosworth in a time of 54.0 seconds, a speed for the lap of 90mph, and was set in August 1987. So, not only is the Morgan faster, it is substantially so. After 25 laps of Mallory the trike would lap the Sierra, and just for the record, it's a similar story at Snetterton (Sierra 1min 16.9sec/Morgan 1min 17.0sec – closer there because the straights are longer. Amazingly it's the *corners* where the tricycle has the advantage).

Now, depending on your hustlee's manners, the imparting of facts one and two either means he pays up, or stalks off in sullen disbelief, determined to prove you wrong. Best keep a copy of *Fast Lane* on hand, for indeed the facts are correct.

The statistics are perhaps more startling than the reality, once you begin to look into it. Recently I underwent a day's education at the very pleasant Mallory Park circuit in the company of Phil Spencer, a cheerful Black Countryman whose pride and joy for some

Morgan Three is more bike than car, middle. Runs on methanol. Left, Hales rounds Mallory hairpin where Morgan laps faster than Sierra Cosworth.

at the scrubbed bit on the tyre surface after action shows a contact strip about two and a half inches wide. In view of that, the available grip defies belief.

The next question: do you need zero imagination in order to be able to conduct the thing at all quickly? Well, not really.

> ## "The brakes aren't very good. Modern lining material just doesn't seem to work in the Morgan's brake drums"

In fact not all, but you do need to suspend any preconceptions before you get in and, just as with a motorcycle, you must dress for the part. Leathers are a must, or at least a leather jacket. If you and Morgan do part company, you need to be able to slide to a stop without leaving most of your epidermis smeared on the track. Thrown out? Ah yes, there are no belts. A simple bench seat lends no restraint either, so any security within the cockpit comes from a wedging process, sitting slightly askew and – provided you have feet which measure less than size nine – bracing yourself by pushing against the bulkhead under the clutch pedal. For company, there's a large aluminium tank on the passenger floor, full of methyl alcohol. Don't think about it.

Starting the engine is straightforward enough, but as with almost everything to do with Morgan three-wheelers, there's a right and wrong way. Three willing helpers push from behind. Let the clutch up and get the engine spinning but keep the throttle closed, otherwise it will flood; now, dip the clutch pedal and imme- diately catch the engine with the throttle before it stops spinning. Trying just to pull away in gear has the JAP spit- ting back and stalling.

Once running, the engine ticks over happily enough. There's a heady taste of meth- anol spraying back from the twin carburettors, and a spicy tang of burning beans as the vegetable-based Castrol R40 oil fries in the cylinders. The big twin's throb sets the whole structure buzzing and zizzing like a cymbal. "*Everything,*" says Spencer, "has to be wired on or split-pinned, else it'll fall off." The exhaust beat's un- even crack, thumping from the twin pipes a couple of feet in front, is already quite addic- tive. It sounds like nothing else I've ever heard and seems to bear no relation to the revs, a sort of half speed *dagga-dagga*, even when spinning well. It gives no hint of strain, or warn- ing that you might be ap- proaching a 30-year-old en- gine's limits. The only instrument in the cockpit is the rev counter so there's no real excuse for driving by ear.

It's as well to be careful too, because the engines are almost irreplaceable, save for remak- ing bits to the original draw- ings. With this in mind no doubt, Phil asks the speed to be kept down to about 5,000rpm – he uses six-five when racing. Reach outside the cockpit again for the gear lever – which also has a brake lever for the rear wheel – and move it left and forward to select first, just like any car.

There's a fair thrust in the back, the tail bobs as the back wheel spins, finds traction and then spins again – 5,000rpm comes up in an instant, so pull the lever quickly back into sec- ond. It clicks straight through, as if the lever isn't connected to anything. Third needs a conscious effort though; guide the lever forward and across the gate in a deliberate dog leg, and it goes straight in. I'm already gaining on the Cater- ham Seven in front. Into fourth. So far it's a doddle. The Morgan rides the bumps easily and goes exactly where you point it. It feels rather like a kart in that it's pure and responsive, hardly any move- ment of the wheel to change direction and no mass of metal taking time to settle on the springs.

The brakes aren't very good. Phil had warned that modern lining material just doesn't seem to work in the Morgan's brake drums, al- though the simple system of cables and levers gave a nice firm pedal even if the hairpin did seem to be approaching at an intimidating rate. A few laps without any dramas breeds a little confidence. Think I'll give it a bootful in first gear at the hairpin and see what happens. *Daggadagga- dagga*. The tail gently but in- sistently slides wide. Instinc- tively I turn the huge string bound four-spoke wheel left to correct. Unrestrained, my up- per body flops left in sympathy as the slide is checked and I find myself hanging on to the wheel now, rather than steer- ing with it. I'm trying to straighten the thing up, but I seem to be pulling the top further to the left and I have now fallen over into the pas- senger space. I want to put out a hand to stop myself disap- pearing below the scuttle, but I need that to hang on to the wheel. Stick out an elbow in- stead – still desperately trying to straighten the wheel. Final- ly, I manage to unravel the steering, and promptly over- correct the other way. Half a turn is full lock and every time I do anything it seems to help the wobble rather than contain it.

Fortunately, we weren't go- ing very fast and, fortunately, I had released the throttle. Oth- erwise we would definitely have charged the wall at some stage, but thankfully the Mor- gan finished its little fishtail with nothing more than the wheel steering me. It felt like trying to keep your balance while walking down a moving

> ## "Any security within the cockpit comes from a wedging process, sitting slightly askew and bracing yourself by pushing against the bulkhead"

bus, only faster.

This is why you have to forget any normal car driving technique. You can't drive the trike with the steering wheel, feeling messages through the rim and adjusting the line to suit. Like a kart or Formula One stock car, the wheel is just there to initiate the turning

Phil Spencer equals lap record most days at Mallory with his JAP vee twin-engined machine.

SPENCER'S TRIKE

process and, in the Morgan, to give you a grab handle. So you can forget the recommended 10-to-two position. Hook the right elbow over the cockpit side and brace it with a hand on the bottom of the wheel rim. Put the left hand on the wheel at about 20 to the hour. Wedge the left foot under the clutch pedal – you won't need that once you get going. You are now ready to trike.

Your corner entry speed needs to be higher than you think possible; so gently ease the wheel with just a squeeze of the rim – don't turn so much as feel, and tramp the throttle earlier than really feels comfortable. Suddenly it's easy. The car is balanced, friendly. There's no fighting, no nervous sawing at the wheel. It's flowing with you. More throttle equals more turn, less lets the nose run wide, but you must steer exclusively with the right foot and relax. The rear wheel needs to be sliding all the time and the faster you go, the less you use the steering wheel. And I couldn't find any real vices. There's no sudden Sierra oversteer on the limit, or Metro Challenge kangaroo hopping, largely I suspect because there aren't any nasty geometry changes from suspension moving outside prescribed limits, and of course the whole lot is very low and light.

This Morgan is no quaint vintage anachronism, wheeled out to remind us youngsters of the good old days. It's a real racing car. The more you take it by the scruff and slide it about, the more it seems to submit and perform. Even without the statistics to support, you can feel how quick it is simply from the forces trying to unhook your elbow from the cockpit rim, and the speed at which it closes the gaps between you and the other cars on the track. Funny how every racing car leaves its own particular legacy of aches the following morning.

The Morgan three-wheeler left some very pleasant memories too. Sitting in that little bathtub cockpit, a mere few inches from the road, looking through the front suspension tubes to pick up the road, and watching the tops of the spindly wheels pattering up and down over the bumps. The clicking sound of the naked rockers, tapping the engine's valves up and down and speckling the visor with a mist of sticky vegetable oil, the thump of two 650cc cylinders and the tingling sensation that stays for ages after the engine has vibro-massaged the body. It's all so different from Kevlar and electronics and, like the uncomplicated enthusiasts who own and race these machines, a welcome breath of fresh air.

PHIL SPENCER'S Morgan is a remarkable slice of motor racing history. In 1937, a Black Country haulier by the name of Cyril 'Charlie' Hale, bought the trike brand new from the Malvern factory, and promptly set about preparing it for racing. He approached JA Prestwich of Tottenham, London, for an 880cc racing version of their air-cooled vee twin to replace the Morgan's standard Matchless engine and, in exchange for the princely sum of £66, the engine was delivered complete with magneto. In those days it was much more common for car and motorcycle builders to use engines made by specialists, and JAP's powerful vee twins were used extensively by the Coventry Eagle motorcycle factory and also powered the Brough Superior, made famous by TE Lawrence. But JAP are perhaps best known for their 500cc speedway engines – actually half of the vee twin – which dominated the shale scene right into the '70s, a long time after they ceased production in 1956. As far as anyone knows, though, Hale was the first person to fit the 880 racing JAP into a Morgan chassis.

Hale carried out a number of other modifications to the car, changing the scuttle and nose, "so he could see the front wheels. . ." and fitting more and more powerful JAPs, ending up with a 1,000cc unit in the '50s. In all, he raced the car continually for 23 years, flying the Morgan flag successfully long after most people had stopped racing them. Hale won a huge number of races with the car, in later years mainly against sidecar outfits until, in 1957, he crashed at Oulton Park, severely injuring his back and legs. The driver thankfully made a complete recovery but the damaged machine lay in a shed for another decade until Spencer, who "did a bit of machining" for Cyril, took over the trike and rebuilt it to its present state. Hale, now 88, still takes a keen interest in the Morgan, and was there to see his baby take yet another win in Phil's hands at last month's vintage races at Oulton Park.

Its very simplicity is actually a major factor in the trike's remarkable performance. A tubular steel ladder forms the basic chassis, and there's a traditional Morgan ash frame to support the boat-like aluminium body. There's a tube sub-frame bolted on at the front which uses the engine's crankcase to lend extra stiffness, and this frame also supports the beam axle sliding pillar suspension. The front springing consists of a steel pillar with a sliding collar upon which the wheel's stub axle is mounted. Above the collar is a large spring, below it is a small one. Hit a bump and the collar is pushed against the large spring, hit a dip and the small spring supports the weight of the wheel and tyre. That is what you call simple, but, it's amazingly effective, not least because the wheel stays perfectly upright all the time and the tyre is always in maximum contact with the road. Wishbones or struts inevitably lean the wheel.

Morgan sliding pillar front suspension is less good at dealing with bumps, and as it's a system to which Morgan have remained faithful to this day, more modern Morgan owners will doubtless agree about the ride. It matters less on the circuit of course – at least you don't have to stiffen up a Morgan in order to race it.

At the rear of the tricycle, a motorcycle-style forked trailing arm supports the wheel and there are metal leaves either side to provide the springing. As there's only one wheel, it can justly claim to be independent, something of an innovation in the '30s. Hydraulic dampers are used at both ends which were a Cyril-inspired '50s addition, but the clutch is more modern; an AP Formula Three item is employed in the interests of reliability.

The Morgan is now worth about £30,000, but Phil's not selling. He reckons that maintaining the tradition should give him at least another 15 years of racing. Besides, more modern machinery isn't as quick.